JAVA™ ME GAME PROGRAMMING

SECOND EDITION

JOHN P. FLYNT, PH.D.
MARTIN WELLS

THOMSON

COURSE TECHNOLOGY

Professional ■ Technical ■ Reference

Important: Thomson Course Technology PTR cannot provide software support. Please contact the appropriate software manufacturer's technical support line or Web site for assistance.

Thomson Course Technology PTR and the author have attempted throughout this book to distinguish proprietary trademarks from descriptive terms by following the capitalization style used by the manufacturer.

Information contained in this book has been obtained by Thomson Course Technology PTR from sources believed to be reliable. However, because of the possibility of human or mechanical error by our sources, Thomson Course Technology PTR, or others, the Publisher does not guarantee the accuracy, adequacy, or completeness of any information and is not responsible for any errors or omissions or the results obtained from use of such information. Readers should be particularly aware of the fact that the Internet is an ever-changing entity. Some facts may have changed since this book went to press.

Educational facilities, companies, and organizations interested in multiple copies or licensing of this book should contact the Publisher for quantity discount information. Training manuals, CD-ROMs, and portions of this book are also available individually or can be tailored for specific needs.

ISBN-10: 1-59863-389-9
ISBN-13: 978-1-59863-389-4
Library of Congress Catalog Card Number: 2007923304
Printed in the United States of America
08 09 10 11 12 TW 10 9 8 7 6 5 4 3 2 1

Publisher and General Manager, Thomson Course Technology PTR:
Stacy L. Hiquet

Associate Director of Marketing:
Sarah O'Donnell

Manager of Editorial Services:
Heather Talbot

Marketing Manager:
Jordan Casey

Senior Acquisitions Editor:
Emi Smith

Marketing Assistant:
Adena Flitt

Project Editor:
Jenny Davidson

Technical Reviewer:
Marcia Flynt

PTR Editorial Services Coordinator:
Erin Johnson

Copy Editor:
Anne Smith

Interior Layout Tech:
ICC Macmillan Inc.

Cover Designer:
Mike Tanamachi

CD-ROM Producer:
Brandon Penticuff

Indexer:
Larry Sweazy

Proofreader:
Heather Urschel

THOMSON
COURSE TECHNOLOGY
Professional ■ Technical ■ Reference

Thomson Course Technology PTR,
a division of Thomson Learning Inc.
25 Thomson Place
Boston, MA 02210
http://www.courseptr.com

This book is dedicated to its readers.

ACKNOWLEDGMENTS

Thanks to Emi Smith and Stacy Hiquet for arranging for the publication. To Jenny Davidson, for watching over the schedule and making it happen. Also, many thanks to Kevin Claver for help and support along the way. As always, thank you Marcia for your faithful hard work, trust, guidance, and support.

ABOUT THE AUTHORS

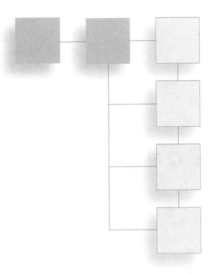

John P. Flynt, Ph.D., has taught at colleges and universities, and has authored courses and curricula for several college-level game development programs. His academic background includes work in information technology, the social sciences, and the humanities. Among his works are *In the Mind of a Game, Perl Power!, Java Programming for the Absolute Beginner, UnrealScript Game Programming All in One* (with Chris Caviness), *Software Engineering for Game Developers, Simulation and Event Modeling for Game Developers* (with Ben Vinson), *Pre-Calculus for Game Developers* (with Boris Meltreger), *Basic Math Concepts for Game Developers* (with Boris Meltreger), and *Unreal Tournament Game Programming for Teens* (with Brandon Booth). John lives in the foothills near Boulder, Colorado.

Martin J. Wells is currently the lead programmer at Tasman Studios Pty, Ltd, located in Sydney, Australia. Throughout his 15-year career he has worked on a wide variety of development projects. He is an expert in multiple computer languages, including Java from its origins, and has extensive experience in the development of high-performance networking and multithreaded systems. His first game programming experience came from writing and selling his own games for the Tandy and Commodore microcomputers at the age of 12.

Contents

PART IV	USING GRAPHICS	259

ABOUT THIS BOOK

This book provides an introduction to programming with Java MIDP classes. It is not intended to fully explore all the potential the MIDP classes offer, nor does it offer a comprehensive view of Java programming. Instead, it provides an introduction to the interfaces provided by the MIDP that allow you to extend your knowledge if you already possess a basic knowledge of how to program with Java.

The first chapters introduce you to the history of the MIDP and its associated technologies. In this respect, it is assumed that you have had no previous exposure to device programming. From there, you move on to set up environments that allow you to get started. You work wholly on a PC, and instructions are provided on how to set up all the tools you need to write programs that make use of the MIDP classes. This book should prove a trusty ally if you have hesitated to explore device programming because it seems to necessitate learning entirely new development techniques or accustoming yourself to new programming environments. Every attempt is made to make the transition into device programming as painless as possible. Among other things, comprehensive instructions are provided concerning how to set up both the appropriate Java packages and the NetBeans IDE on your PC. No other book on the market provides a more comprehensive treatment of the basics of setting yourself up for developing device programs.

Who Should Read This Book

This book addresses people who have a background in Java programming at a beginning or intermediate level. It is not a good idea to turn to this book if you want to learn how to program. For help in that regard, *Java Programming for the Absolute Beginner* (by the same author) provides a suitable foundation for programming at the level required by this book.

This book helps you transition into using Java to program for devices. If you possess a basic understanding of how to program with Java and are seeking a way to extend your knowledge into the realm of cell phones and other mobile devices, then this is the book you want. One of its greatest strengths is that during its early chapters, in addition to helping you understand what mobile devices and mobile device programming involve, it also closely guides you through the somewhat esoteric activities of acquiring (free of charge) the software needed to begin developing programs for mobile devices.

The author enjoys friendships with many professional programmers who have never attempted to program for devices because they have dreaded having to learn about and acquire the equipment necessary to begin doing so. This book attempts to remedy such situations. The equipment needed is freely available and can be readily installed in a very short time. All of the work with JAR and JAD files can be automated. The Java Wireless Toolkit provides an attractive, fun testing environment. The NetBeans IDE provides a free, robust, and increasingly powerful IDE for use in developing using the Java libraries that address mobile devices.

The Chapters

Chapter 1 provides a topical review of the history of Java as related to programming mobile devices. It provides you with a quick summary of the tools you use for developing mobile applications and some of the more promising settings in which to pursue such a line of work.

Chapter 2 furnishes a discussion of the Mobile Information Device Profile (MIDP) and how it forms the foundation of your work using Java to develop programs for phones. It also acquaints you with the notion of a MIDlet (as opposed to an applet). You learn, for example, that at the basis of every Java program you write for a mobile device is an extension of the Java MIDlet class.

Chapter 3 offers a brief overview of some of the devices for which MIDlets can be written. The devices covered constitute an extremely scant survey of the field. Still, references to Internet sites providing comprehensive information on hundreds of possible target devices are provided. No book could possibly hope to provide a comprehensive view of this topic—even the websites are overwhelmed.

With Chapter 4, the work begins. From the first page or two, you are at the keyboard installing and tuning Java, and then using the MIDP to build a MIDlet from scratch. You work at the command line and do everything from scratch. In the end, however, you have the pleasure of seeing a MIDlet compile.

Chapter 5 is all about the Java Wireless Toolkit. It shows you where to acquire it and how to use it. Prior to this chapter, you have been working at the command line only, but now you have a chance to augment your activities by using the Java Wireless Toolkit. Learning to use it is a stepping-stone to more powerful tools.

Since this book's goal is to make you as productive as possible as quickly as possible, in Chapter 6 you learn how to acquire and install the NetBeans IDE and the components associated with it that allow you to develop MIDlet and other Java programs directed toward devices. While it is not by any means suggested that you skip any of the first four chapters, to gain a sense of where the fun begins, Chapter 6 is the place to go.

Chapter 7 works you into some of the most fundamental topics of the MIDP class library. Among other things, you explore the MIDlet class and delve into the `Timer` and `TimerTask` classes. Work with these classes anticipates work with the `Runnable` interface later in the book.

Chapter 8 concerns persistence and the RMS package. The Java MIDP classes provide a set of classes that allow you to store and retrieve data in a complex, robust way. While this is not a database, it does provide a secure way of storing and accessing data placed in a special reserved location in the memory of the device. Chapter 8 also introduces you to some of the classes used for networking.

Chapter 9 provides an introduction to the graphical user interface components offered by the MIDP packages. You can begin seeing the device display different types of applications, at this point textually oriented. In this regard, you concentrate on such classes as `Display`, `TextBox`, and `List`.

Chapter 10 takes you into the world of the `Form` and `Item` classes. This provides interesting contexts in which to work with such classes as `TextField` and

StringItem. As the number of components you work with increases, the MIDlets you work with become more involved.

Chapter 11 provides a transition. You work with the ChoiceGroup, ImageItem, and Image classes. The MIDlet you develop provides pictures of famous comedians and some of their favorite jokes.

Chapter 12 involves you in work on such classes as DateField and Gauge. It also extends work you have done previously with the Image, Form, and Item classes.

In Chapter 13, you work extensively with the Canvas and Graphics class, developing MIDlets that show you the fundamentals of game architecture using the standard GUI classes of the MIDP. What you do in this context provides a solid grounding for working with the Game API.

With Chapter 14, you work exclusively with such classes as Sprite, TiledLayer, and GameCanvas. You explore a MIDlet that allows you to see most of the functionality involved in a basic game. This includes understanding how tiles and frame sets work.

Chapter 15 provides you with a basic game that employs the Sprite, TiledLayer, GameCanvas, and LayerManager classes in the implementation of a game that explores collision detection, scoring, use of Thread, Timer, and TimerTask objects, and other features common in the development of games.

In the appendix, you'll find an extended discussion of how to implement a scrolling background. The information here applies as readily to scrolling in the foreground. Use of the LayerManager allows you to pursue a number of scenarios.

Obtaining the Code for the Book

It is essential to be able to work with the projects the book offers if you are to benefit from reading the book. In this respect, there are two ways to obtain the source code:

- **From the CD.** The CD that accompanies the book provides the most convenient way to acquire the source code. Just install it as directed. The source code for each chapter is in a separate chapter file, and throughout the book, the location of each source file is clearly described. To access the code from the CD, just insert it in your computer's CD drive and access the code folder. The CD should automatically start. If it does not, you can click the start.exe file on the CD.

■ **From the Internet Site.** To obtain the code from the publisher's website, access **www.courseptr.com/downloads** and enter the title of the book. You can access a link to the source code and any resources associated the book that might be made available after the book's publication.

Setting Up Files

Instructions on how to compile files are provided in Chapters 4 through 6. Generally, if you follow the examples in the book, you should find working with the files fairly easy. If you can install and use the NetBeans IDE (instructions are provided), you will get the most out of this book.

How to Use This Book

Start with Chapter 1 and work forward from there. It is suggested that you work through Chapters 4, 5, and 6, and pay close attention to the details they introduce. Unless you establish a comfortable, reliable work setting, there is little hope that you are going to enjoy programming for devices. Take time to set up and familiarize yourself with the tools this book introduces. You can then move on from there.

Conventions

No conventions to speak of have been consciously adopted in the writing of this book. Generally, the coding style is based lightly on the "Java Style" that has been popular for several years now, but formatting the code so that it can be included in the book has often meant that decisions have been made to try to reduce the number of blank lines. Also, a general practice has been followed of removing comments from the code and placing them in the body of the text. In this regard, a system using a pound sign and a number has replaced the practice of referring to code by its line number. In this book, you see numbers placed at certain locations in the programs. Reference is then made to these numbers.

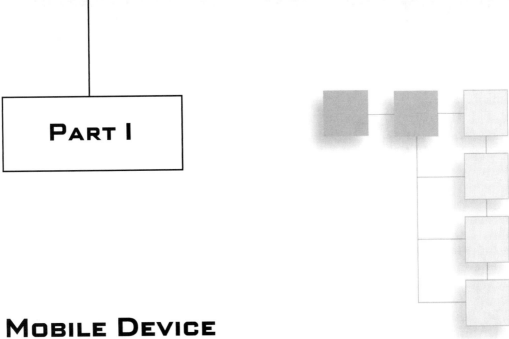

PART I

MOBILE DEVICE FUNDAMENTALS

CHAPTER 1

JAVA ME HISTORY

A mobile information device (MID) is usually understood to be a computer that you can hold in your hand. Such devices are familiar in the world today as cell phones, iPods, iPhones, and BlackBerries. All such devices have their own operating system, but at the same time, they are developed according to standards that international organizations and corporations have established. Java is a popular language for programming such devices because Java runs on a virtual machine. Sun can create a virtual machine for almost any device, and for this reason, Java has become the premier language for mobile information device programming. For those unfamiliar with Java and mobile information device programming, this chapter provides a few introductory notes. It is not intended as a comprehensive introduction to the topic, but it presents a brief outline of the history of the Java programming language and related technologies. It also discusses the capabilities and limitations of mobile phones.

Java's Acorn

In early 1995, Sun Microsystems released an alpha version of a new software environment called Java. During the first six months after Java's release, many people in the software development industry spent their time exchanging bad jokes and puns about coffee beans and Indonesian islands. It didn't take long, however, for the slogan of "Write Once, Run Anywhere" to supplant the jokes and puns. Java was taken up by thousands of developers, and Java began its march to the top.

Figure 1.1
Java had its origins with the *7 device developed by Sun.

The earliest traces of Java go back to the early 1990s, when Sun formed a special technical team (known as the Green Team) tasked with developing the next wave of computing. After an 18-month development effort, the team emerged with the result: a handheld home-entertainment device controller with a touchscreen interface known as the *7 (Star Seven). Figure 1.1 shows *7.

The real action, however, was not with the *7 or the device running it; it was with the backend technology that powered it. One of the requirements of the project was a robust, hardware-independent, embedded software environment that facilitated low-cost development.

At this point, James Gosling entered the picture. Gosling, a Canadian software engineer working with the Green Team, was the primary designer of Java. He began to develop the basics of Java by using some of the best elements of C++, such as its general syntax features and object-orientation. He excluded such things as memory management, pointers, and multiple inheritance. Gosling endeavored to create a simple, elegant language that developers could use to quickly deploy applications.

Gosling's first version of Java, called Oak, ran on the *7 device and featured the familiar Java mascot Duke. Oak's power wasn't only in its language design; there were plenty of other object-oriented languages. Oak blossomed because it encompassed *everything*. Gosling did not create a language and then let other people implement it as they saw fit. The goal of Oak was hardware independence, and with that in mind he created a complete software deployment environment. From virtual computers to functional application programming interfaces (APIs), Oak provided—and, more importantly, *controlled*—everything.

Unfortunately, the *7 did not last long. The notion of running programs on a fixed device (and devices in this respect ranged from toasters to garage door openers) was promising but not what was really needed. What was really needed was something that went worldwide during the mid-1990s: the Internet. With the help of developers such as Bill Joy, Wayne Rosing, John Gage, Eric Schmidt, and Patrick Naughton, Gosling was able to make Java a core programming language for the Internet.

The Internet emerged as the predominant technology of the day. Browsers could be used to transfer and display digital content in the form of pictures, text, and even audio almost universally on a variety of hardware. Servers could link millions of Internet users. Java proved ideal as a programming language that could accommodate the needs of both browsers and servers.

The goals of the web were not dissimilar to that of Oak: provide a system to let you write content once, but view it anywhere (running on a variety of operating systems). Oak was designed to allow programmers to develop on different devices. Programs running on servers or applications running in browsers amounted to the same thing. The Internet became the framework within which Oak software could be distributed and universally deployed.

Java's Growth in the Sun

Given the match between the needs of the Internet and the design of Oak, the mission and description of Java soon emerged from Oak. Gosling and the team at Sun developed a host of technologies around the concept of a universally deployable language and platform. One of their first tasks was to develop the Java-compatible browser known as HotJava. (The early versions were named WebRunner, after the movie *Blade Runner*.) Figure 1.2 shows the original HotJava browser.

If Sun sought to dominate the Internet through HotJava and distribute Java in that way, something even better soon arose. On May 23, 1995, the Netscape Corporation agreed to integrate Java into its popular Navigator web browser, thus creating an unprecedented audience for the Java software.

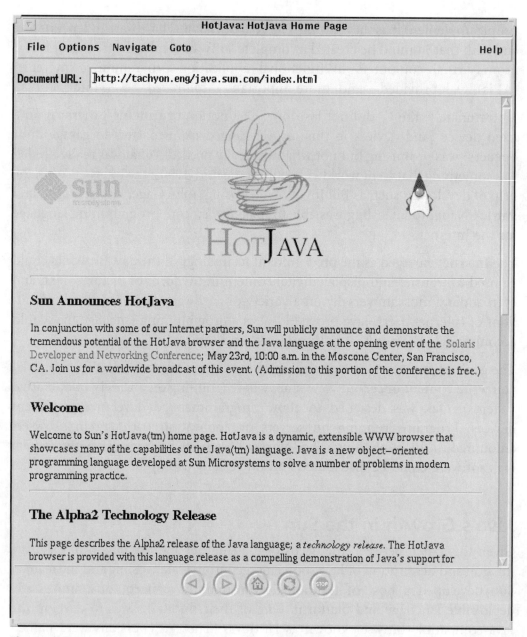

Figure 1.2
Sun developed a browser named HotJava, shown here displaying the original Java home page.

Soon programmers from all over the globe flooded the Java website to download the new platform. Sun completely underestimated the platform's popularity and struggled to increase bandwidth to cope with the rush. Java had arrived.

Development of the Java platform has continued ever since. As the years have passed, it has been expanded to include a number of technologies, such as JSP and XML. Interface components have been rewritten as Swing. The overall platform has been expanded to meet database and security needs. Each new release brings new supporting technology.

Despite Java's complexity, one of its great attractions continues to be Gosling's original design. The syntax remains elegant, the development effort proves much easier than it is in many other languages, and the work of documenting and debugging is much more straightforward.

What Is Java?

Java is an object-oriented programming language that you compile to byte code that runs on a virtual machine. In this respect, it differs from traditional programming languages such as C. The C programming language remains a strong foundation language, but it is also a procedural programming language (based on functions). C++ is the object-oriented precursor of Java, but to develop with C++, programmers compile their code directly to a specific operating system. (Microsoft has changed this picture with managed C++.)

ANSI-compliant C++ makes it possible to port code from one operating system to another with relative ease, but programs still must be recompiled as you move them from operating system to operating system. With Java, programmers can either compile or interpret code. As Figure 1.3 illustrates, the initial compile phase translates your source code (*.java files) into an intermediate language called Java bytecode (*.class files). The resulting bytecode is then ready to be executed (interpreted) within a special virtual computer known as the Java Virtual Machine (JVM).

The JVM is a simulated computer that executes bytecode instructions. It acts as a consistent layer between bytecode and the actual machine instructions. Bytecode instructions are translated into machine-specific instructions by the JVM at runtime. This enables programmers to write one program and run it on different operating systems without having to engage in extensive rewriting (porting) work.

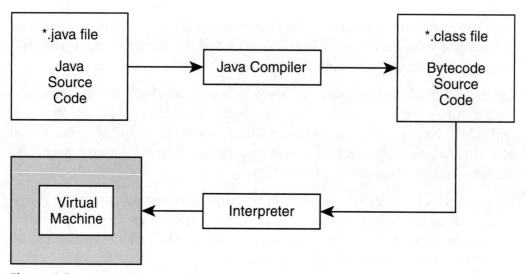

Figure 1.3
Java code goes through two stages: compilation and interpretation.

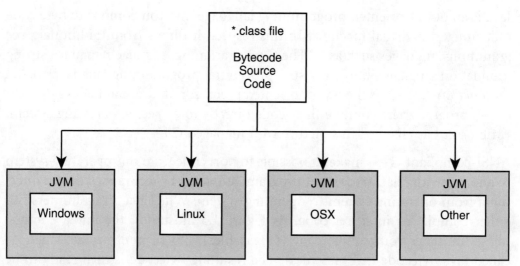

Figure 1.4
Java bytecode becomes a portable program executable on any Java Virtual Machine.

The expression often used to sum up the work of the JVM is "Write once, run anywhere." As Figure 1.4 illustrates, the target platform for a Java program requires only a JVM. Sun provides a JVM specific to each platform (or operating system), and after the JVM is installed, the Java program can run in it regardless of which environment it was developed in.

Running a Java program remains elementary. Developing a Java program involves a bit more activity. You need more than just a programming language; you need a programming platform. The Java platform is made up of three significant components:

- The Java Development Kit

- The Java Virtual Machine

- The Java Application Programming Interface

The Java Development Kit (JDK) is the general name for the entire suite of tools that allows you to develop with Java. Central to this are the compiler and its associated tools. As mentioned previously, the role of the JVM is to provide an interface to the operating system of the underlying device. The Java API provides a limited view of the operating system to the Java program. This makes the JVM the judge, jury, and executor of program code.

The Java API is a collection of Java classes covering a vast range of functionality including containers, data management, communications, IO, and security. There are close to a thousand basic classes available as part of the Java API. Secondary developers provide thousands more that extend and specialize the API.

Java versus C++

An important bond exists between C/C++ and Java. C is the parent language of both C++ and Java. James Gosling implemented the initial versions of Java using C++, but he also took the opportunity presented by Java's unique language model to modify its structure and make it more programmer-friendly than C++.

One major innovation relates to memory management. In practical terms, Java prevents you from going into an operating system and telling it to reserve or in other ways use the memory of a specific machine. Java was designed to do this because memory management is one of the activities that most tends to anchor a program to specific operating systems. Java provides an additional advantage with respect to Internet applications: executables created with Java preserve the integrity of the operating system on which they run. To put it differently, when you develop a program for a browser, for example, with Java you can be confident that if a given Internet user opens a Java applet, the applet is not going to violate the security of the user's system.

One major activity of memory management involves setting aside (allocating) memory used by the program. An object-oriented program often performs this memory-management task by creating a program component known as an object (an instance of a class). In Java, for example, the `JDialog` or `JFrame` classes allow you to create dialogs and windows. When such objects are created, they can bog down the performance of a computer if they are not also destroyed when they are no longer in use. Java takes care of such activity through what is generally known as automated cleanup or garbage collecting. When an object falls into disuse, Java cleans it up for you. You do not have to count and manage objects, as you do with C++.

Java also differs from C++ along the following lines:

- There is no preprocessing of source files in Java.
- In Java there is no split between the interface or header (.h) and the implementation (.cpp) file; there is only one source file (.java).
- Everything in Java is an object in the form of a class. In C++, you can revert to C and start writing code that does not involve classes, even to the point of creating global variables. In Java, you cannot define global variables (values that exist outside a class).
- Java has no autocasting of types; you have to be explicit.
- Java has a simplified object model and patterns; there is no support for multiple inheritance, templates, or operator overloading.

For general application development, Java has far outdistanced C++ as the preferred language. However, C++ still commands a strong position as a server-side programming language and in the world of console game development. C++ programs execute much faster than Java programs, and C++ also provides programmers control over execution and memory. Such capabilities prove useful in some game-development contexts or contexts in which optimized performance is essential. Still, Java applications developed for general enterprise prevail. Java programs often perform better, have fewer bugs, and prove easier to develop and maintain. Moreover, there is no comprehensively unified enterprise or mobile development environment in C++. In this respect, the J2EE platform is the world's standard for development of end-to-end enterprise information systems.

Multiple Editions

The Java language has evolved over the years. The first major edition, now known as the Java 2 Standard Edition (J2SE) was aimed at the development of GUIs, applets, and other standalone applications. A few years ago Sun expanded the Java suite with the Java 2 Enterprise Edition (J2EE), which was built for use in server-side development. This version included expanded tools for database access, messaging, content rendering, inter-process communications, and transaction control.

Sun didn't stop there, though. Desperate to satisfy every programmer on the planet, Sun set its sights on handheld or portable devices. The version of Java Sun designed for these devices is designated Java 2 Micro Edition (J2ME). The current version of Java has been incremented beyond the first release, so Sun often refers to it simply as Java ME.

Mobile Information Devices Everywhere

Mobile information devices are generally small enough to carry in your pocket or purse. The most popular such devices are cell phones, iPods, and iPhones. Sun manufactures special versions of its Java virtual machine to allow your Java programs to execute on such devices. Since such devices are available in every description, the virtual machine approach to application deployment enjoys the same advantage with MIDs that it enjoys with the Internet. You can write an application on one operating system and deploy it to many others.

The purpose of portable Java programs is often to provide an interface for the user. Device manufacturers create operating systems that manage such things as games, telecommunications, or music. The user of such devices browses the Internet, answers a phone call, receives a text message, manages and selects tunes, or plays games. The games you find on such devices are often fairly basic, but with each new day, as the memory, speed, and virtual machine profiles of the devices improve, the software built to run on them increases in complexity.

Applications once considered too large for portable devices are now becoming common features of them. What is significant about this is the sheer magnitude of the market calling for this transformation. Cell phone manufacturers deal with a market that includes billions of possible users. Cell phones are so inexpensive that they are often given away as part of a telecommunications package. The device becomes trivial. The interface and services become much more significant. What applies to cell phones applies in general to all mobile devices. As the hardware decreases in significance, the software and services become more important.

It is generally not at all unreasonable to imagine a world (of over six billion people to date) in which everyone from childhood on is equipped with one or two portable devices. Picture a cell phone and an iPod to start with. In time these might be merged into a single device (like the BlackBerry or iPhone), but the general market for applications to run on such devices remains the same.

As a slight digression, it is important to remember that mobile devices often have very specific and somewhat humble market niches. Consider, for example, a device that is responsible for monitoring the output of a microtransmitter embedded in an automobile tire. By pressing a few buttons, a mechanic can see the tread depth and tire pressure of the tire. This basic information is then fed to a PC with an Internet connection. Someone in a back office can then monitor the status of the tire. This technology can be extended to the shoes of runners in a marathon. If a transmitter is clipped to each running shoe, as runners run by given auditing points, their names and times can be fed into a central database and displayed on a website. All the applications involved might be developed with Java. All involve MID development.

Micro Devices and Software

MIDs are often referred to as micro devices. As you will see in Chapter 2, the support for such micro devices broadens as different devices come into the picture. Figure 1.5 shows several categories of micro devices.

Generally, large corporations can afford (at least to an extent) to create and deploy proprietary development platforms for the devices they produce. In most cases, Java ME provides you with the ability to make use of some of the features of the proprietary development platforms. To use some of these development platforms, you must pay a license fee. In other cases, you can obtain the software for free, but you must integrate software modules with your Java code.

Over the past two decades, micro-device manufacturers have provided programmers and other content creators with various sets of tools to build software applications. This approach to development has met with greater and lesser degrees of success. Generally, the trend now favors open approaches like Java,

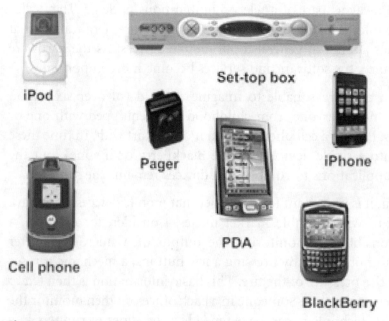

Figure 1.5
The broad categories of micro devices.

Table 1.1 Non-Java Development Tools

Tool	Description
Manufacturer SDK	The most common development platform initially was device-manufacturer SDKs (software development kits) or operating system (such as Palm, Windows CE, and EPOC/Psion) SDKs. In most cases, developers used C/C++.
WAP/WML	WAP (wireless application protocol), a standard communications protocol used in mobile devices, is used in a similar way to HTTP and TCP. An early Internet system developed by mobile phone operators used WAP as transport for WML (wireless markup language), which serves as a replacement for the more complex HTML (hypertext markup language) used by web browsers. Unfortunately, the end result was nothing like the "mobile Internet" promised by promoters.
Web/HTML	Available only to the higher-level devices, the web was sometimes used as a content delivery tool. Content was usually cosmetically modified to suit the characteristics of micro devices.
Other Middleware	Many vendors have also tried to create content-creation middleware and tools such as iMode and BREW, with varying degrees of success.

and almost every major device manufacturer has made a strong effort to incorporate Java ME. The tendency in this respect is toward standardization of hardware and software. Device manufacturers realize that their surest path to the broadest market is through the interoperability Java provides. Table 1.1 lists some of the categories into which proprietary efforts have fallen.

Conclusion

With millions of programmers and worldwide distribution, Java is an enormously popular development platform. As a language, it is easy to learn. Given the extraordinary store of libraries and other supplements that exist for Java, mastery of it is probably no longer a possibility for any lone individual. Still, if you can learn how to work with the basic development environment, whether it is the general JDK or a specialized version of the JDK such as Java ME, you are probably on your way to a lifetime of work.

Developing software for portable devices is one of the key areas of development for Java programmers. The programs they produce often center on user interfaces, which vary according to the device on which the interface is deployed and the market the device manufacturer or service provider targets. One of Java's strengths is that it allows developers to provide software that is both portable and safe for deployment on different devices.

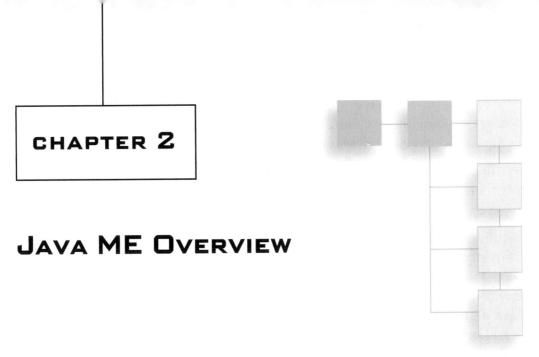

CHAPTER 2

JAVA ME OVERVIEW

In this chapter, you explore the role of Java ME's configurations and profiles. Toward this end, you explore the Connected Limited Device Configuration (CLDC) and the Mobile Information Device Profile (MIDP). These complementary components of the Java ME form the basis of much of what you do to develop software for mobile information devices (MIDs). In this book, your development efforts begin with the CLDC 1.1 and the MIDP 2.0, but it remains that the applications you develop are largely backward compatible with the CLDC 1.0 and the MIDP 1.0. Using the older, simpler functionality gives you a simpler, clearer view of what you can do with the current technology. In addition to investigating features of the CLDC and the MIDP, you also look at a few practical concerns, such as how JAR and JAD files work in relation to mobile information device applications and suites of such applications. Such preliminaries provide the groundwork for efforts in chapters that follow.

A Comprehensive Toolkit

MID programming constitutes one of the most dynamic branches of today's software industry. The number of portable devices requiring software development increases daily. As a developer, you have to cope with this proliferation of devices and the broad range of functionality that characterizes the mobile application market. You also face different software development kits (SDKs) provided by the companies that create the hardware for the devices. Developing software for multiple versions of a given device is hard work; creating it for completely different devices is even harder.

Writing the software isn't the only problem. Delivering it to the device requires a platform capable of installing new software on demand, along with the channels to receive new code. Further, after installation, you must consider security issues.

Although it cannot be said to make the work simple, Java ME renders such work fairly straightforward. Among other things, it provides you with a comprehensive set of tools that allows you to do most of the work required to develop and deploy device-oriented software. While the tools you use reside in different areas of the Java development platform, they all work together to let you work in a fairly seamless way.

Java ME Architecture

As was noted in Chapter 1, Sun creates different versions of Java to suit different development environments. From the enterprise development tools designed for use in servers to those that address mobile systems, each version has its own place in the Java landscape.

It's important to note that the division between platforms can become blurry. Java ME development sometimes requires the use of different platforms. For example, when you're developing a multiplayer game, you use Java ME for the client-side device software, but you also benefit from the power of J2SE and J2EE when you implement the backend server systems.

As Figure 2.1 shows, the various editions of Java suit distinctly different development settings. The three virtual machines overlap but apply to different areas of development. The Java HotSpot VM is the most comprehensive virtual machine supplied by Sun. It incorporates the full-scale version of Java. The Compact Virtual Machine (CVM) and Kilobyte Virtual Machine (KVM) are smaller virtual machine implementations designed to run within the constraints of the limited resources available on micro devices.

When Sun developed the Java ME, it was obvious that the larger version of the VM needed to be reduced in size to fit onto mobile information devices. While the power and memory of chips have increased tremendously since then and might conceivably accommodate a large VM, much that the J2SE offers is not needed in even a complex mobile information device.

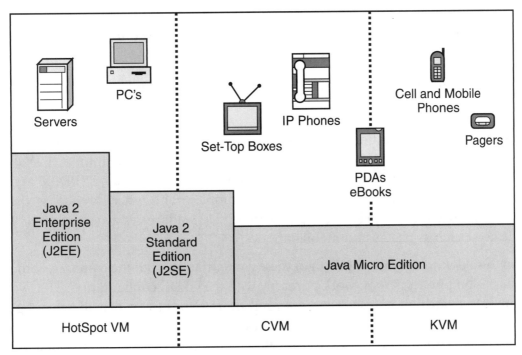

Figure 2.1
The different editions of Java suit different hardware platforms.

The designers of Java ME came up with a solution based on a revised Java architecture that excludes specific platform components, including components that address such areas as language, tools, the JVM, and the API. On the other hand, certain components are added. Among these are components that address features of specific devices.

Configurations and Profiles

A *configuration* defines the capabilities of a Java platform designed for use on a series of hardware devices. A configuration begins with conceptual overview of the services that a given type of device requires. Such services represent a subset of the overall set of services that the Java VM might provide. Among other things, a given J2SE configuration might require removing or adding architectural features along the following lines:

- Language components that are unlikely to be used to develop software that runs on devices.

- Specific types of functionality that address hardware requirements for mobile information devices, such as the memory, screen size, and processor power for the family of devices.

- Java libraries that can be included or excluded arbitrarily during development.

Given such considerations, Sun created two initial configurations to suit the mobile information world. One, the Connected Device Configuration (CDC), addresses slightly limited devices, such as personal digital assistants (PDAs) and set-top boxes (digital TV receivers, for example). The other, known as the Connected Limited Device Configuration (CLDC), addresses general classes of devices, such as pagers and mobile phones.

In this book, you work with both of these configurations, but the emphasis at the start is on phones, so you work primarily with the CLDC configuration. The two are interrelated, of course. The important thing right now is that these configurations let you move forward, confident of the functionality of the underlying target platform. In most cases, you develop for at most a few platforms, not a few hundred.

Configurations define categories of devices and the services provided to them. They merely limit Java to a suitable target platform's capabilities. In other words, they limit the number of classes you work with and orient your development efforts toward the functionality required for a given range of devices.

A *profile* is a description of a given type of device. The profile of a given device makes it a phone, for example, or a PDA. To a great extent the profile determines the API you can use with a device. You might be working with a 2D or a 3D game, for example.

With respect to the API, a central focus of the profile is the user interface (UI) for mobile phones (see Figure 2.2). The CLDC that covers this type of device excludes many of the classes you find in Java UI libraries, the Abstract Windows Toolkit (AWT), and Swing. Consider, for example, that since the screens of most MIDs are small, you are not in a position to develop software with extensive display and menu options. There is little point in providing a profile that includes classes that support features the MID cannot include. The profile that has been developed provides a UI suited to the specific requirements of the MID's LCD screen. The resulting LCD UI is included in the CLDC profile that targets MIDs. This is generally known as the Mobile Information

Figure 2.2
Configuration and profile provide the context in which you create applications for MIDs.

Device Profile (MIDP). In this book, you deal largely with the MIDP 2.0. However, most of the code in this book is backward compatible with the MIDP 1.0.

As Chapter 7 reveals, the LCD UI implementation shown in Figure 2.2 exemplifies the role that profiles play in adding device-category-specific functionality. The keyboard and screen shown have limited dimensions and display characteristics. When a profile presents such features, the components in the API can be limited, and the development activities you perform can be streamlined.

Figure 2.3 shows how the functionality of a game that runs on a phone depends on a device profile (which can be understood as a set of UI classes), a configuration (a range of devices and services addressed by Java), and the capabilities of the Java VM. At the bottom is the operating system of the device. The Java VM

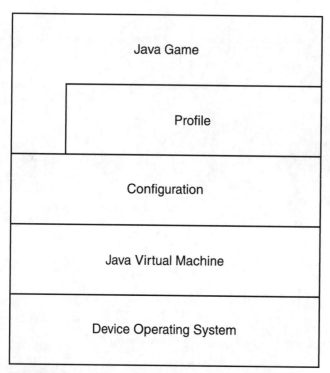

Figure 2.3
Java ME consists of layers of components.

interfaces with the configuration, which in turn provides functionality to the profile and application layers.

The CDC

The Connected Device Configuration (CDC) can be viewed as the generalized set of Java ME configurations. It addresses almost any device you care to name for about any application you wish to develop. The CDC addresses smaller devices, such as phones, and larger devices, such as digital TV set-top boxes and PDAs. It contains a single profile (the Foundation profile) and the high-performance Compact Virtual Machine (CVM). The Java language implementation and the API for the CDC have largely the same capabilities as the J2SE.

Because the CDC provides more capabilities than are needed for most mobile phones, Sun provides the Connected Limited Device Configuration (CLDC). In this book, you use the CLDC (1.1) for the programs you create. This config-uration enables you to work with a smaller, more convenient version of Java as you develop applications for MIDs.

The CLDC

The Connected Limited Device Configuration (CLDC) provides a definition of devices that includes mobile phones and many other devices. Its scope is much broader than the Mobile Information Device Profile (MIDP). To use it, you download a separate configuration package from Sun. (Chapter 6 briefly discusses the CLDC package with respect to the NetBeans.) Over the past few years, different versions of the CLDC have emerged. This book uses version 1.1.

Versions represent the findings of conventions or consortiums of companies that are involved in the Java Community Process (JCP). The JCP provides a formal context in which developers in a given community can submit recommendations concerning standardized platform features. These are known as Java Specification Requests (JSRs). Each collection of requests is identified with a number. The Java Community Process's complete list of JSRs is available online at **http:// jcp.org/en/jsr/all**.

For the CLDC 1.1, JSR 139 is central. If you click on the link for JSR 139, under Section 2.0, you see discussion that includes the following topics:

- Target device characteristics
- The security model
- Application management
- Language differences
- JVM differences
- Included class libraries

CLDC Specification

The JSR for any given version of a CLDC involves contributions from a multitude of companies involved in the mobile device industry. As an example, consider the Java Community Process participants responsible for the development of the JSR for the CLDC 1.0. Table 2.1 provides a partial list.

Table 2.1 CLDC Specification Contributors

America Online	Bull	Ericsson
Fujitsu	Matsushita	Mitsubishi
Motorola	Nokia	NTT DoCoMo
Oracle	Palm Computing	RIM (Research In Motion)
Samsung	Sharp	Siemens
Sony	Sun Microsystems	Symbian

CLDC Target Device Characteristics

The CLDC provides a description of the characteristics of a supported device. Each version of the CLDC changes this description to accommodate increased device capabilities or new technologies. Table 2.2 lists target device characteristics as defined by the CLDC 1.0 specification. These have been extended to the CLDC 1.1.

Note

One thing you might notice right away is that the characteristics of the CLDC don't mention any input methods or screen requirements. That's the job of a particular device profile, which in this book centers on the Mobile Information Device Profile (MIDP). A configuration offers only the core Java system requirements.

CLDC Security Model

J2SE's existing security system was too large to fit within the constraints of the CLDC target platform. A revised model eliminates many of the features but requires far fewer resources. There are two main sections to the CLDC security model. The first involves virtual machine security; the second involves application security. The security model for the CLDC lays some important groundwork for application execution models discussed later in this book.

Virtual Machine Security

The goal of the virtual machine security layer is to protect the underlying device from damage executable code might cause. Under normal circumstances, a

Table 2.2 CLDC Target Platform Characteristics*

Characteristic	Description
Memory	160 KB to 512 KB devoted to the Java platform (minimum 128K available to a Java application)
Processor	16-bit or 32-bit
Connectivity	Some form of connectivity, likely wireless and intermittent
Other	Low power consumption, typically powered by battery

*For more information, see http://java.sun.com/products/cldc/faqs.html.

bytecode verification process carried out prior to code execution takes care of this. This verification process validates class-file bytecode, ensuring that it is correct for execution. The most important result of this process is the protection it offers against the execution of invalid instructions and the creation of scenarios in which memory outside the Java environment is corrupted.

The standard bytecode verification process used with J2SE requires about 50 KB of code space, along with up to 100 KB of heap. While this is negligible on larger systems, it can constitute a sizable portion of the memory available to Java on many micro devices.

The resulting verification implementation within the virtual machine of the CLDC requires around 10 KB of binary code space and as little as 100 bytes of run-time memory.

The reduction in available resources essentially comes from the removal of the iterative dataflow algorithm from the in-memory verification process. The price of the reduction is an additional step known as *pre-verification* that must be undertaken to prepare code for execution on the JVM. The pre-verification process inserts additional attributes into the class file.

Note

Even after undergoing the process of pre-verification, a transformed class file is still valid Java bytecode; the verifier automatically ignores the extra data. The only noticeable difference is that the resulting files are approximately five percent larger.

A tool supplied with the Java ME development environment carries out the process of pre-verification. It's all rather painless. As Figure 2.4 illustrates, the

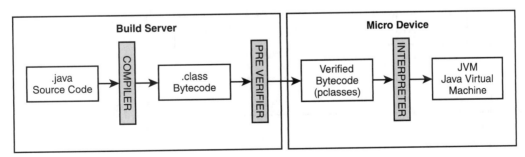

Figure 2.4
A pre-verification process reduces the resources used for the typical class-file verification.

important point is that the resource-intensive part of the verification process is carried out on your (overpowered) development PC (the build server).

Note

Post-verified class files are commonly called *pclasses*.

Application Security

The class-loader verification process discussed previously is pretty limited. Basically, it just confirms that bytecode is the legitimate result of the Java compilation process. Although this is helpful, a further level of security is required to protect a device's resources.

The full J2SE security model is too large for the devices addressed by the CLDC. For this reason, the CLDC incorporates a simplified security model based on the concept of a *sandbox:* your Java code can play (operate) only within the confines of a small, controlled environment. Anything outside is completely out of bounds.

Note

If you've done any applet development (applets are Java programs executed inside a web browser), you're already familiar with the concept of sandbox security. The CLCD implementation is similar.

As Figure 2.5 reveals, your code restricts what's available in the sandbox environment. The CLDC defines a list of exactly what you can execute, and that's all

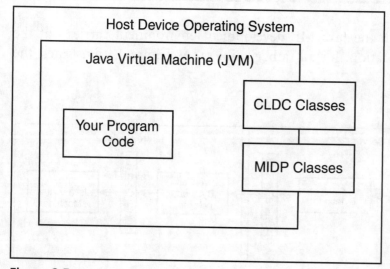

Figure 2.5
The Java sandbox security model provides access to core classes while protecting the underlying device.

you get. Protection is also in place so you can't change the base classes that make up the installed API on the device—the *core classes*. The CLDC specifications mandate protection for these classes.

Application Management

Managing applications on mobile information devices is different from managing applications on PCs. When you work on MIDs, quite often there is no concept of a file system, let alone a file browser. Most of the time, especially on typical MIDs, users have a limited amount of application space in which to store programs. To manage these applications, the device should provide a basic ability to review the installed applications, to launch an application, and to delete an application if the user so desires.

While the CLDC doesn't mandate the form the application manager should take, the capabilities it fosters imply that typical implementations of device software should furnish simple menu-based tools to browse and launch programs.

Restrictions

Fairly significant differences exist between the standard J2SE version of Java and the version you use when programming for micro devices. The differences relate only to limitations, not to changes in syntax. The primary areas involve finalization and error handling.

Finalization

To improve performance and reduce the overall requirements, the CLDC leaves out automatic object finalization. If you have a background in Java, you know that this means that the CLDC does not provide an `Object.finalize` method. When using the J2SE under normal circumstances, the garbage collector process calls this method for an object it is about to discard from memory. You can then free any open resources that explicitly require you to do so (such as open files).

The lack of an `Object.finalize` method doesn't mean the garbage collector doesn't run. It's just that the garbage collector process does not call your finalize method. Because this method is not available, you need to rely on your own application flow to carry out an appropriate resource cleanup process. This is generally a good practice anyway. You should free resources as soon as they

Table 2.3 java.lang.Error Exceptions

Exception	Description
java.awt.AWTError	Because there is no AWT in the CLDC, this isn't required.
java.lang.LinkageError	An error relating to class compilation inconsistencies. There are many subclasses of this exception, such as java.lang.No-ClassDefFoundError.
java.lang.ThreadDeath	This type of error is not listed in the CLDC. The application is not able to do much which such an error.
java.lang.VirtualMachineError	Such errors are often of the types OutOfMemoryError and StackOverflowError. Most devices cannot handle such errors.

become available; don't leave the timing of this process to the notoriously strange behavior of the garbage collector.

Error Handling

Some restrictions apply to error handling. The CLDC does not include support for run-time errors. If an error occurs, the best approach is to terminate the operation of the application. With respect to the java.lang.Error exception class hierarchy, Table 2.3 provides a summary of a few of the issues related to error handling. In some cases, there is little chance of recovering from an error, so the error type is not in the CLDC list. In other cases, the best approach to handling an error is to inform the device OS and have the device OS proceed from there. If an error occurs only in situations in which your application cannot recover, there's no need for the CLDC to provide you with access to them.

Old and New Versions

The Java ME class does not include connectivity classes such as those found in the java.net.* hierarchy. Because of the interdependencies in the current communications library, connectivity classes could not be included without breaking the migration rules. Instead of such classes, the CLDC includes a framework for a new communications class hierarchy known as the *connection framework*. The cut-down framework of the CLDC design is exactly that—a design. There are no included classes that actually implement it. For that, you look to the world of profiles.

CLDC 1.1 adds a number of features not provided with CLDC 1.0 and improves several existing features. Among these are the following:

- Floating point support

- Weak reference support (small subset of the J2SE weak reference classes)

- `NoClassDefFoundError` class

- Attributes and method:
  ```
  Boolean.TRUE, Boolean.FALSE
  Date.toString()
  Random.nextInt(int n)
  String.intern()
  String.equalsIgnoreCase()
  Thread.interrupt()
  ```

- Classes `Calendar`, `Date`, and `TimeZone` have been redesigned to be more J2SE-compliant.

- Minimum memory has been raised form 160 to 192 KB.

JVM Differences

As mentioned briefly at the beginning of this chapter, Java ME uses the Kilobyte Virtual Machine (KVM), which is a limited version of the Java VM. At the same time, it is comprehensive with respect to the CLDC. The primary features excluded from the KVM are as follows:

- Weak references—lets you keep a reference to an object that is still garbage collected

- Reflection—the power to "look into" code at runtime

- Thread groups and daemon threads—advanced thread control

- The Java Native Interface (JNI)—lets you write your own native methods (this is not appropriate for sandbox development)

- User-defined class loaders

Reflection is the Java feature that lets your program inspect the code being executed at runtime. This means you can inspect the code in classes, objects, methods, and fields. The KVM does not support reflection in any form, which also means that you have no access to features that inherit their functionality from the reflection core, such as the Java Virtual Machine Debugging Interface (JVM DI), Remote Method Invocation (RMI), object serialization, and the profiling toolset.

When you develop games for micro devices, you can live without most of these features. For example, RMI lets you execute methods across a network. The RMI proves too heavy to use effectively. You can achieve the same level of functionality by coding a simpler system on your own. Object serialization is something that would be useful for saving and loading game states. However, you can code this for yourself without too much trouble.

While the profiling toolset is also not available, not having the profiling tools just means you can't write your own profiling system. Likewise, you won't be able to create your own debugging system.

User-defined class loaders are another feature that is omitted from the KVM. These were used primarily to reconfigure or replace the class-loading mechanism with one that you supply. Unfortunately, the sandbox security model does not work very well if you implement a class loader and circumvent the security entirely.

CLDC Packages and Class Libraries

Despite restrictions, an extensive library of classes is included in the CLDC. In determining which classes to deploy, the designers of the CLDC faced a number of issues. The first was the key driver behind everything—resources. They had less free space. Some things had to go, and that naturally meant they couldn't please everyone.

This also raised the issue of compatibility. The goal was to retain as much as possible the similarity to and compatibility with the J2SE libraries. To facilitate this, the designers divided the CLDC libraries into two logical categories—classes that are a subset of J2SE and classes that are specific to the CLDC.

These classes are differentiated by the prefix of the library. First are Java ME classes that are based on a subset of equivalent J2SE subset classes. For example, `java.lang.String` has the same name in the Java ME and the J2SE. It's just a reduced version. CLDC-specific classes appear under the java extensions hierarchy `javax.*`. This is reserved for classes that do not normally appear in J2SE.

Note

CLDC-specific classes sound great, but in reality they don't exist. The CLDC specifies a single group of classes relating to connectivity, but it's not the role of the CLDC to implement these; that's the job of a profile, such as the MIDP.

To discern how the classes implemented for the CLDC differ from or resemble those in the J2SE implementation, you can apply the following rules:

■ The package name must be identical to the corresponding J2SE counterpart.

■ There cannot be any additional public or protected methods or fields.

■ There cannot be changes to the semantics of the classes and methods.

To emphasize the third point, a J2SE class implemented in Java ME can only have methods removed. Methods are not added. Further, there can be no change in the interface (use and arguments) of the existing methods.

Note

One thing you might notice when looking through the CLDC class libraries is the distinct lack of a few key elements, such as user interface and access to device-specific functions. That's the job of a given device category's profile. Later in this chapter discussion is provided about these profile-specific libraries.

Here is the list of packages for the CLDC.

■ java.io

■ java.lang

■ java.lang.ref

■ java.util

■ javax.microedition.io

Following is a list of some of the available CLDC classes. If you are familiar with the J2SE implementation of the classes, keep in mind that in several instances methods are removed. For a comprehensive list, access **http://java.sun.com/ javame/reference/apis/jsr139/**.

System classes

- `java.lang.Object`
- `java.lang.Class`
- `java.lang.Runtime`
- `java.lang.System`
- `java.lang.Thread`
- `java.lang.Runnable`
- `java.lang.Throwable`

Input/output classes

- `java.io.InputStream`
- `java.io.OutputStream`
- `java.io.ByteArrayInputStream`
- `java.io.ByteArrayOutputStream`
- `java.io.DataInput` (interface)
- `java.io.DataOutput` (interface)
- `java.io.DataInputStream`
- `java.io.DataOutputStream`
- `java.io.Reader`
- `java.io.Writer`
- `java.io.InputStreamReader`
- `java.io.OutputStreamWriter`
- `java.io.PrintStream`

Collection classes

- `java.util.Vector`
- `java.util.Stack`
- `java.util.Hashtable`
- `java.util.Enumeration` (interface)

Type classes

- `java.lang.Boolean`
- `java.lang.Byte`
- `java.lang.Character`
- `java.lang.Class`
- `java.lang.Double`
- `java.lang.Float`
- `java.lang.Integer`
- `java.lang.Long`
- `java.lang.Short`
- `java.lang.String`
- `java.lang.StringBuffer`

Date and Time classes

- `Calendar`
- `java.util.Date`
- `java.util.TimeZone`

Exception classes

- `java.lang.Exception`
- `java.lang.ClassNotFoundException`
- `java.lang.IllegalAccessException`
- `java.lang.InstantiationException`
- `java.lang.InterruptedException`
- `java.lang.RuntimeException`
- `java.lang.ArithmeticException`
- `java.lang.ArrayStoreException`
- `java.lang.ClassCastException`
- `java.lang.IllegalArgumentException`
- `java.lang.IllegalThreadStateException`
- `java.lang.NumberFormatException`
- `java.lang.IllegalMonitorStateException`
- `java.lang.IndexOutOfBoundsException`
- `java.lang.ArrayIndexOutOfBoundsException`
- `java.lang.StringIndexOutOfBoundsException`
- `java.lang.NegativeArraySizeException`
- `java.lang.NullPointerException`
- `java.lang.NoClassDefFoundException`
- `java.lang.SecurityException`
- `java.lang.VirtualMachineException`
- `java.util.EmptyStackException`
- `java.util.NoSuchElementException`
- `java.io.EOFException`
- `java.io.IOException`
- `java.io.InterruptedIOException`
- `java.io.UnsupportedEncodingException`
- `java.io.UTFDataFormatException`

Error classes

- `java.lang.Error`
- `java.lang.NoClassDefFoundError`
- `java.lang.VirtualMachineError`
- `java.lang.OutOfMemoryError`

MIDP

As mentioned previously in this chapter, the CLDC does not provide user interface components for specific applications. User interface components are device-specific. Implementation of software for them is made possible by a *profile.* The Mobile Information Devices Profile (MIDP) specification designates a target platform that can serve a broad range of handheld devices, especially mobile phones. The Mobile Information Devices Profile 2.0 (MIDP 2.0) provides the set of packages you work with directly in this book. Using the MIDP 2.0, you can implement the MIDlet class so that, among other things, you can work with a device emulator using such tools as the Java Wireless Toolkit and other development aids.

Target Hardware Environment

The characteristics of some target devices can be extremely limited. The screens are tiny, and the memory is only barely adequate. In some cases the CPUs perform relatively slowly. On the other hand, recently it has become more common for MIDs to exceed minimum specifications. Among other things, devices in recent days sport relatively large color screens, more RAM, expanded I/O capabilities, and next-generation networking.

The games you develop on powerful devices in some ways cross boundaries of design into domains once reserved for consoles and PCs, but it is still a good idea to plan for limited resources. Even on low-end hardware, you can still make some great games. Table 2.4 provides the recommended minimum MIDP device characteristics.

Target Software Environment

Like the target hardware environment, the software that controls MIDs can vary significantly in both functionality and power. At the higher end of the market,

Table 2.4 Device Characteristics

Characteristic	Description
Display	96 × 54 pixels with 1 bit of color with an aspect ratio (pixel shape) of approximately 1 to 1
Input types	One-handed keyboard or keypad (like what you see on a typical phone)
	Two-handed QWERTY keyboard (resembling a PC keyboard)
	Touch screen
Memory	128 KB of nonvolatile memory for MIDP components
	8 KB of nonvolatile memory for application-generated persistent data
	32 KB of volatile memory for the Java heap (run-time memory)
Networking	Two-way wireless, possibly intermittent, connectivity
	Usually quite limited bandwidth

Table 2.5 Software Characteristics

Characteristic	Description
Memory	Access to a form of nonvolatile memory (for storing things like player name and high scores)
Networking	Sufficient networking operations to facilitate the communications elements of the MIDP API
Graphics	Ability to display some form of bitmapped graphics
Input	A mechanism to capture and provide feedback on user input
Kernel	Basic operating system kernel capable of handling interrupts, exceptions, and some form of process scheduling

MIDs are similar to small PCs. At the low end, however, some components, such as file systems, are not available. As a result of the varying descriptions of MIDs, the MIDP specifications mandate basic systems software capabilities. Table 2.5 lists the most relevant of these capabilities.

Note

Volatile memory is also known as dynamic memory, heap memory, or RAM. It stores data only as long as the device remains powered on. Nonvolatile memory is known as persistent or static memory. It typically uses ROM, flash, or battery-backed SDRAM and stores information even after the device has been powered down.

MIDP Specification

Like the CLDC, the Mobile Information Device Profile (JSR 37) development effort was part of the Java Community Process expert group. Table 2.6 lists some of the companies involved in the specification effort.

Table 2.6 MIDP Specification Contributors

America Online	Bull	DDI
Ericsson	Espial Group, Inc.	Fujitsu
Matsushita	Mitsubishi	Motorola
NEC	Nokia	NTT DoCoMo
Palm Computing	RIM (Research In Motion)	Samsung
Sharp	Siemens	Sony
Sun Microsystems	Symbian	Telcordia Technologies

MIDP Packages and Class Libraries

The MIDP does a good job of locking down the hardware characteristics of MIDs for you, but there is more to developing applications than describing the hardware. The MIDP also delivers the real guts of the Java ME mobile software solution—the libraries.

The MIDP libraries provide tools designed specifically for the idiosyncrasies of development on MIDs. This includes access to the following packages:

- java.io
- java.lang
- java.util
- javax.microedition.io
- javax.microedition.lcdui
- javax.microedition.lcdui.game
- javax.microedition.media
- javax.microedition.media.control
- javax.microedition.midlet
- javax.microedition.pki
- javax.microedition.rms

Starting in Chapter 7, you find a review of the details of the API. For now, here is a list of some of the available classes. The list provides a summary view of the MIDP 2.0. For a complete list for the MIDP 2.0, access **http://java.sun.com/ javame/reference/apis/jsr118/index.html**.

General utility
- `java.util.Timer`
- `java.util.TimerTask`
- `java.lang.IllegalStateException`

Language and type classes
- `java.lang.Byte`

- `java.lang.Character`
- `java.lang.Double`
- `java.lang.Float`
- `java.lang.Integer`
- `java.lang.Long`
- `java.lang.Math`
- `java.lang.Runtime`
- `java.lang.Short`
- `java.lang.String`
- `java.lang.StringBuffer`
- `java.lang.System`
- `java.lang.Thread`
- `java.lang.Throwable`

User interface classes

- `javax.microedition.lcdui.Choice` (interface)
- `javax.microedition.lcdui.CommandListener` (interface)
- `javax.microedition.lcdui.ItemStateListener` (interface)
- `javax.microedition.lcdui.Alert`
- `javax.microedition.lcdui.AlertType`
- `javax.microedition.lcdui.Canvas`
- `javax.microedition.lcdui.ChoiceGroup`
- `javax.microedition.lcdui.Command`
- `javax.microedition.lcdui.DateField`
- `javax.microedition.lcdui.Display`
- `javax.microedition.lcdui.Displayable`
- `javax.microedition.lcdui.Font`
- `javax.microedition.lcdui.Form`
- `javax.microedition.lcdui.Gauge`
- `javax.microedition.lcdui.Graphics`
- `javax.microedition.lcdui.Image`
- `javax.microedition.lcdui.ImageItem`
- `javax.microedition.lcdui.Item`
- `javax.microedition.lcdui.List`
- `javax.microedition.lcdui.Screen`
- `javax.microedition.lcdui.StringItem`
- `javax.microedition.lcdui.TextBox`
- `javax.microedition.lcdui.TextField`
- `javax.microedition.lcdui.Ticker`

Application classes

- `javax.microedition.midlet.MIDlet`
- `javax.microedition.midlet.MIDletStateChangeException`

Record management classes

- `javax.microedition.rms.RecordComparator` (interface)

- `javax.microedition.rms.RecordEnumeration` (interface)
- `javax.microedition.rms.RecordFilter` (interface)
- `javax.microedition.rms.RecordListener` (interface)
- `javax.microedition.rms.RecordStore`
- `javax.microedition.rms.InvalidRecordIDException`
- `javax.microedition.rms.RecordStoreException`
- `javax.microedition.rms.RecordStoreFullException`
- `javax.microedition.rms.RecordStoreNotFoundException`
- `javax.microedition.rms.RecordStoreNotOpenException`

Networking classes
- `javax.microedition.io.Connection` (interface)
- `javax.microedition.io.ContentConnection` (interface)
- `javax.microedition.io.Datagram` (interface)
- `javax.microedition.io.DatagramConnection` (interface)
- `javax.microedition.io.HttpConnection` (interface)
- `javax.microedition.io.InputConnection` (interface)
- `javax.microedition.io.OutputConnection` (interface)
- `javax.microedition.io.StreamConnection` (interface)
- `javax.microedition.io.StreamConnectionNotifier` (interface)
- `javax.microedition.io.Connector`
- `javax.microedition.io.ConnectionNotFoundException`

Game classes
- `javax.microedition.lcdui.game.GameCanvas`
- `javax.microedition.lcdui.game.Layer`
- `javax.microedition.lcdui.game.LayerManager`
- `javax.microedition.lcdui.game.Sprite`
- `javax.microedition.lcdui.game.TiledLayer`

MIDP 2.0 Game Package

In this book, the focus is on the use of the classes included in the MIDP 2.0. One of the MIDP's most significant assets for game developers is the Game package (detailed in Table 2.7). Table 2.7 provides a summary of the Game package. The classes that make up the Game package are discussed in greater detail later on, but in this context, it is appropriate to note that they address some basic and important programming activities. Specially, they allow you to easily implement such things as painting, message processing for game events, layering, collision detection, and transformation. The GameCanvas class specializes the Canvas class. The Sprite and TiledLayer classes are specializations of the Layer class.

Table 2.7 The Game Package Classes

Class	Description
GameCanvas	This class allows you to lay out the basic user interface of a game. It provides a variety of features, such as buffering and query capabilities.
Layer	You can use a Layer object to represent a Sprite or a TiledLayer object. It allows you to work with attributes relating to the location, size, and visibility of such objects. This is an abstract class.
LayerManager	This class enables you to control what the user sees of the game. It provides comprehensive services for rendering and allows you to control several Layer objects.
Sprite	A Sprite is a Layer characterized by animation and usually involves a set of graphical frames of equal size. An Image object furnishes the frames. Normally, the frames are displayed sequentially, but the Sprite class also allows for them to be displayed in an arbitrary way. In addition to displaying frames, the Sprite class provides methods for flipping and rotating images and for detecting collisions.
TiledLayer	A TiledLayer object provides a substitute or extension of Image objects. Rather than storing images in single extended area, the TiledLayer object provides a grid of cells. Each cell displays one of several tiles provided by a single Image object.

MID Applications

Generally, a Java program written to be executed on a mobile information device is called a MIDlet. Obviously, the name is a play on "applet." The MIDlet is subject to some rules regarding its run-time environment and packaging. The next few sections provide a general discussion of these topics. Chapter 4 shows you how to work with JAR, JAD, and other files in detail.

To develop a MIDlet, in addition to the Java file that contains the implementation of the MIDlet class, you use a manifest and a JAR file, as you do with any Java application. You add to this a *Java application descriptor* (JAD) file. The JAD offers a few extended configuration options as you work with the MIDlet. You use the JAD file to formally identify one or more MIDlets for inclusion in your application.

When you include one or more MIDlets in an application, you create a *MIDlet suite*. When you develop a suite, you then see each MIDlet in the suite displayed in the MID display area. Each can be executed as separate program. Among other things, you can use the suite to set display values. Chapter 4 provides a simple example of how to implement both a single MIDlet and a MIDlet suite.

MID Run-Time Environment

It is the role of the device's built-in application manager to start and stop the execution of a MIDlet. To accomplish this, the application manager must access the following resources:

- The Java files that provide the MIDlet

- The contents of the MIDlet descriptor file

- Classes made available as part of the CLDC and MIDP libraries

With respect to the packaging of the application, the JAR file should contain all the classes required to run the application, along with all the resources, such as image files and data. To set application execution options, you name properties within a plain text MIDlet JAD file. JAD allows you to include a given MIDlet multiple times or to exclude a MIDlet as you assemble a MIDlet suite.

MID Suite Packaging

As mentioned previously, a MIDlet application typically takes the form of a JAR file. This JAR file should contain all of the class and resource files required for your application. It should also contain a manifest file with the name `manifest.mf`.

The manifest is a text file containing attribute-value associations separated by a colon. Here is an example of an attribute-value association:

```
MIDlet-1: TestProps1, ,test.TestProps2
```

If your manifest file contains information on multiple MIDlets (a MIDlet suite), you should use the `MIDlet-<N>` attributes to specify information on each of the individual MIDlets within the package. Here are some examples:

```
MIDlet-1: TestProps1, ,test.TestProps2
MIDlet-2: TestProps2, ,test.TestProps2
```

The first argument after the colon identifies the name of the MIDlet. The second argument is optional and is used to identify the icon associated the MIDlet. The third argument names the class file for the MIDlet. Typically, your package has one application. Table 2.8 lists the required and optional attributes included in a manifest file.

Table 2.8 MIDlet JAR Manifest Attributes

Attribute	Description
Required Attributes	
MIDlet-Name	Descriptive name of the MIDlet suite.
MIDlet-Version	Version number of the MIDlet suite.
MIDlet-Vendor	The owner/developer of the application.
MIDlet-<n>	The name, icon filename, and class of each of the MIDlets in the suite.
	For example:
	MIDlet-1: SuperGame,/supergame.png,com.your.Super-Game
	MIDlet-2: PowerGame,/powergame.png,com.your.Power-Game
MicroEdition-Profile	The name of the profile required to execute the MIDlets in this suite. The value should be exactly the same as the value of the system property microedition.profiles. For MIDP version 1, use MIDP-2.0.
MicroEdition-Configuration	The name of the configuration required to run the MIDlets in this suite. Use the exact name contained in the system property microedition.configuration, such as CLDC-1.1.
Optional Attributes	
MIDlet-Icon	Name of a PNG image file that serves as a picture identifying this MIDlet suite.
MIDlet-Description	Text describing the suite to a potential user.
MIDlet-Info-URL	URL pointing to further information on the suite.
MIDlet-Jar-URL	The URL from which the JAR can be downloaded.
MIDlet-Jar-Size	Size of the JAR in bytes.
MIDlet-Data-Size	Minimum number of bytes of non-volatile memory required by the MIDlet (persistent storage). The default is zero.

In addition to those listed in Table 2.8, you can add your own attributes to the manifest file. The only rule is that they cannot begin with the MIDlet- prefix. Also, keep in mind that attribute names must match exactly, including case.

You might wonder what the point of the MIDlet-Jar-URL attribute is. Given that the manifest file has to be included within a JAR, why bother having a URL to download a JAR when you obviously must have the JAR to know the URL in the first place? The answer involves the Java application descriptor.

You don't need to have the JAR attribute in your manifest file. It's intended for use in the JAD file (which is reviewed in the next section). The attribute is in the list because the manifest file also serves as the default for any attributes not contained within the JAD. The creators of the specifications for MIDP elected to create a single set of attributes for both the manifest and JAD files. A reasonable thing to do, but it still left me confused the first time I read the specifications.

Tip

MIDlet version numbers should follow the standard Java versioning specifications, which essentially specify a format of `Major.Minor[.Micro]`, such as 1.2.34. One approach is to use the major version to indicate a significant functional variation, the minor version for minor features and major bug fixes, and the micro for relatively minor bug fixes.

Here is an example of a manifest file:

```
MIDlet-Name: Super Games
MIDlet-Version: 1.0
MIDlet-Vendor: Your Games Co.
MIDlet-1: SuperGame,/supergame.png,com.test.SuperGame
MIDlet-2: PowerGame,/powergame.png,com.test.PowerGame
MicroEdition-Profile: MIDP-1.0
MicroEdition-Configuration: CLDC-1.0
```

Again, note that working examples of this type of file are provided in Chapter 4. The discussion here is intended to provide only a conceptual framework.

Java Application Descriptors

In addition to a manifest and a JAR file, you work with the Java application descriptor (JAD). This file allows users to view the details of a MIDlet JAR without actually having to download the whole thing. The application descriptor file contains nearly the same attributes as those in the manifest, and it exists independently of the JAR file. Figure 2.6 shows the relationship between all the components of a MIDlet suite and a JAD file.

There is a close link between the JAD and the manifest files. Think of the JAD as a mini-version of the manifest. The following attribute values must be the

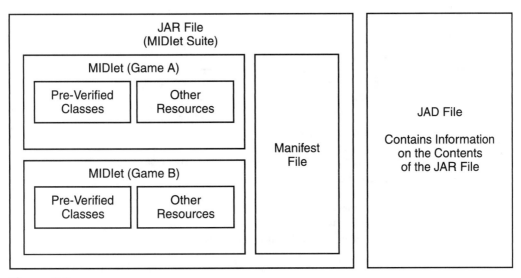

Figure 2.6
A single JAR file lists multiple MIDlet applications, along with their resources, and a manifest and JAD are included to describe the details of the contents.

same in both files, or else the MIDP application manager rejects the MIDlet suite:

- MIDlet-Name

- MIDlet-Version

- MIDlet-Vendor

For all other attributes, the values in the JAD file take precedence.

Here is an example of a JAD file:

```
MIDlet-1: HelloMIDletWorld, , net.test.HelloMIDlet
MIDlet-Description: HelloMIDlet
MIDlet-Jar-URL: helloMIDlet.jar
MIDlet-Name: Hello MIDlet World
MIDlet-Permissions:
MIDlet-Vendor: home.net
MIDlet-Version: 2.0
MicroEdition-Configuration: CLDC-1.0
MicroEdition-Profile: MIDP-2.0
MIDlet-Jar-Size: 3201
```

Table 2.9 MIDP 2.0 Features

Category	Features
Networking	Support for HTTPS
	Incoming data can now "awaken" your MIDlets
Audio	Play polyphonic tones (MIDI) and WAV samples
UI	Improved layout tools
	Better placement control
	New controls, including the power to build your own controls
Games	Support for graphics layers
	Enhanced canvas tools
	Integer arrays as images
	PNG image transparency
Security	Improved permission-based security system

The primary difference between the JAD and manifest examples is the inclusion of the two MIDlet-Jar attributes. Using these attributes, the application manager can determine the download and device storage requirements for your game.

MIDP 2.0 and MIDP 1.0

As you will see in Chapter 4, this book uses the JDK 1.6.x and the MIDP 2.0. With the release of the MIDP 2.0, Sun has added significant functionality. Examples provided early in the book are backward compatible with the MIDP 1.0. As the chapters advance, however, so does the functionality, so some of the code is not backward compatible. Table 2.9 provides a summary view of some of the features of the MIDP 2.0 that are not in the earlier version.

The classes in the MIDP 2.0 expand support for quality sound, transparent images (by default), and a game-oriented API. In addition to all this, the hardware requirements for a MIDP 2.0-compatible device are less restricted. Your application can now be as large as 256 KB (up from 128 KB), and the available run-time memory is now 128 KB (up from 32 KB). This is great news because memory capacity, especially the package size, was a severe limitation in MIDP 1.0.

With the MIDP 2.0 and the CLDC 1.1 (both used in this book), you have access to floating-point support. Generally, the functionality most device users expect to see cannot be attained without using MIDP 2.0 (and CLDC 1.1), which is why, beginning in Chapter 4, work commences with CLDC 1.1 and MIDP 2.0. Even if the functionality you develop is limited to backward-compatible programs, you are still in an excellent position to develop more advanced features.

Conclusion

This chapter reviewed the motivations, design, and inner workings of Java ME. You saw how the CLDC and MIDP specifications provide a solid foundation upon which you can confidently develop games for MIDs. It also provided you with an overview of some of the tools available to you as an application programmer. In addition, it touched on the Java components that are not available when you use Java ME.

The limitations of the CLDC and MIDP platform are in many ways significant. Memory, processors, networking, and graphics capabilities restrict your development activities relative to "big box" game efforts. This is where the real difference between programming for micro devices and PCs or consoles arises. However, as device capabilities improve, newer versions of the CLDC and the MIDP incorporate corresponding functionality.

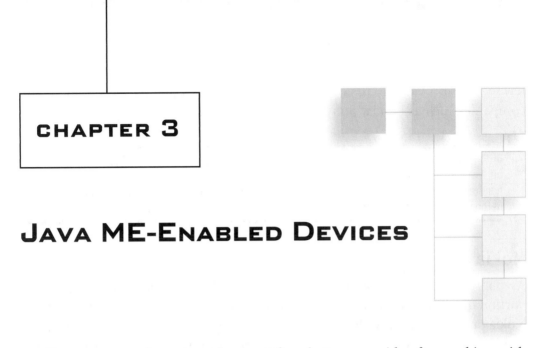

CHAPTER 3

JAVA ME-ENABLED DEVICES

In Chapter 2, you investigated some of tools Java provides for working with mobile information devices (MIDs). If you are wholly new to software development for MIDs, keep in mind that the number and variety of such devices is extraordinary. Many companies are developing such devices, and each company provides a variety of specific types of devices that range widely in supported features. In a book of this type, it is not possible to touch on more than a few conversational points concerning MIDs. For additional details, you must visit various Internet sites. This chapter refers to a few of those sites and provides you with some basic vocabulary you can use to compare and assimilate the information you find on the Internet.

MID Overview

To gain some insight into the types of devices that have characterized the MID market over the past few years, you can begin by considering the role of price. Lower-priced MIDs have tended to dominate the market. MIDs that cost more provide more features but are less popular. The Nokia 3410 might be considered the classic low-end device. Low-end devices offer limited screen sizes, resolution, and memory. Examples of high-end devices are those in the Nokia Series 60 to 90 range and the Sony Ericsson P800/P900. More expensive devices offer fairly sizable screens, relatively large memory stores, and faster processors. The next few sections provide discussions of a few of the devices that have been offered by companies such as Nokia, Sony Ericsson, and Motorola.

Tip

> In the context of this book, development begins with the devices supported by Java ME. To find out what devices Java ME supports, go to **http://wireless.java.sun.com/device**. This page lists hundreds of devices. Although it is not a comprehensive list, it is still a good starting place for getting a sense of the number and variety of Java ME–supported devices.

Nokia

As one of the largest manufacturers of MIDs, Nokia represents a significant portion of the world's MID user base, so spending a little time understanding the Nokia product range is well worth your while. A good site for information about Nokia products is **http://forum.nokia.com**. Although Nokia offers a great number of different phone models, its devices fall into the categories listed in Table 3.1.

Having all models follow a given series provides a convenient framework for developers. You can develop a game for a particular series and be confident that it works on all phones that conform to the specification for the series. The following few sections provide further discussion of some of the series mentioned in Table 3.1.

Series 30

When you examine Nokia devices, you often see references to Series 30, but the Series 30 has been superseded in some respects. The Series 30 devices at one time represented the mass-market for Nokia. They proved successful because of their price, and demonstrated that a low price is the key to the mass-market.

Table 3.1 Nokia Series Devices

Series	Screen	Type	Input Use
Series 30	96×65	Monochrome/Color	One-handed
Series 40	128×128	Color	One-handed
Series 60	176×208	Color	One-handed
Series 80	640×200	Color	Two-handed
Series 90	640×320	Color	Two-handed

Figure 3.1
The low-end Nokia 3410 offered a 96 × 65 monochrome screen and a maximum JAR size of 50 KB.

Economy usually implies that features are relatively few. The original Series 30 phones were all monochrome (2-bit grayscale), with a maximum MID JAR size of 30-50 KB and heap memory of around 150 KB. In later versions, Series 30 phones provided 96 × 65 pixels and a 4,096-color screen. The JAR size grew to 64 KB. All Series 30 phones used the regular phone keypad layout you see in Figure 3.1. A more advanced version, the 3510i, is shown in Figure 3.2.

Tip

Even though devices in the lower ranges, such as Series 30, are limited in what you can do with them, it is important not to dismiss such devices as vehicles for game development. While low-end devices tend to restrict options with respect to things like JAR size, they are advantageous because they achieve large markets due to their low price. When you reach a large market, the game you develop achieves greater visibility. That leads to a number of possibilities, such as redevelopment in more involved versions.

Series 40

Devices in the Nokia Series 40 constitute what might be viewed as a Java ME gaming heartland. Devices in this range have taken the position once occupied by the Series 30 devices. They remain inexpensive and extremely popular, and they

Figure 3.2
The Nokia 3510i, a second-generation Series 30, added a color display and a 64 KB JAR size.

offer enough power to make for fun gaming. They have become one of the most widely supported and targeted phone classes for Java ME developers.

Tip

> The details on different phone models can vary. For Nokia products, see Forum Nokia (**http://www.forum.nokia.com**). There you find detailed information on the capabilities of the devices in series Nokia currently supports. Keyboard characteristics, resolution, memory, and a variety of other features comprise the full description of a device.

Series 40 devices have a 128 × 128-pixel 4,096-color screen. They support a minimum MID JAR size of 64 KB and heap memory of 200 KB. Several of the devices exceed these capabilities. The input layouts can vary, as you can see in Figures 3.3 and 3.4. The Nokia 3300 (Figure 3.3) is one device that involves *form features*. A form feature is any characteristic of the design of the chassis of a mobile device that gives it a distinctive appearance and operational character-istics. A form feature does not usually extend beyond how the device looks, but with variations in I/O characteristics, form features can certainly affect how you program the device. The Nokia 3300 has been marketed with packages that allow its users to acquire music and interact with their PCs.

Figure 3.3
The creative Nokia 3300 has a distinct form factor but still follows the Series 40 specification.

Figure 3.4
The Nokia 6820 is a typical Series 40 device.

In contrast to form features, devices are often characterized by the skins designed for them. A *skin* involves only the color and art that characterizes a given phone. To get an idea of the multiplicity of skins any given phone or device might be sold with, visit **http://www.skinit.com**. In this respect, the Nokia 6820 represents standardized form features but leaves the option of a multitude of skins (see Figure 3.4).

Figure 3.5
The Nokia 3650 is a typical Series 60 device.

Series 60

The Nokia Series 60 is an example of one of the advanced devices Nokia offers. The standard screen size jumps to 176×208. The color depth begins as 12-bit (4,096) color. The JAR size is 4 MB. Heap memory is also up considerably, to 1 MB or more. Devices in this series include the 3600, 3650 (shown in Figure 3.5), 6600, 7650, and N-Gage.

Figure 3.6 shows an N-Gage device. N-Gage devices are thoroughly associated with games (or game decks) and have been marketed primarily as gaming devices that provide users with access to downloadable games. Sites such as **http://www.n-gage.com/** provide a view of the games and activities associated with the N-Gage culture.

Series 80

The Nokia Series 80 devices are at the higher end of the range of series. They are suitable for personal digital assistants (PDAs). As Figure 3.7 reveals, such devices fold. A device that folds once is known as a bi-fold device. Folding devices allow

Figure 3.6
The Nokia N-Gage is a device often associated with gaming culture.

Figure 3.7
The Nokia 9290 provides a QWERTY keyboard and a phone keypad.

for larger screens, among other things; the screen on the device shown is
640×200. Its keyboard, on the other hand, is a small QWERTY keyboard. The
JAR size for such a device is 14 MB or larger.

Note

The QWERTY keyboard is what you find on a standard laptop. This type of keyboard dates from the 1800s and is named for the position of the keys. Originally, typewriter keys were arranged alphabetically. The letters of a QWERTY keyboard are arranged for efficient typing. This is significant for MIDs, because many devices that serve as dictionaries and planners have alphabetical keyboards.

As mentioned previously, the higher-end devices reach smaller markets. For this reason, developers often prefer to develop for lower-range devices and then port their software to the higher-range devices. As is probably fairly evident, porting from higher range devices to devices in the lower range is not practical. Figure 3.7 shows a Series 80 device.

Series 90

The Nokia Series 90 devices are also suitable for PDAs. However, they differ from the Series 80 devices in that they do not include the keyboard. Instead, users use a pen to input data. While this adds the need for an input pen, it also means Series 90 devices are smaller. A typical Series 90 device offers a 640×320 16-bit (65,536-color) display and accommodates a MIDlet of 64 MB. Like the Series 80, Series 90 devices reach a limited market. Cost is the primary limiting factor. Figure 3.8 shows a Series 90 device.

Figure 3.8
The Nokia 7700 provides a variety of programs.

Sony Ericsson

Ericsson deals largely with mobile communications technologies. Sony is famous for many other things that often involve packaging and design superiority. Together Sony and Ericsson have introduced a broad range of phones that incorporate strong support for Java ME. For more details about developing for Sony Ericsson, visit **http://www.sonyericsson.com/developer**. If you click on the Phones tab at this site, you can see a gallery that features images of a few dozen of the Sony Ericsson devices designed primarily as phones. The next few sections provide details on a few of these devices.

K310

Sony Ericsson phones and devices are arranged in D, J, K, W, and Z ranges. The ranges describe differences in capabilities from screen resolution, keyboards, and memory size to a variety of other concerns. The Sony Ericsson K310 device allows for viewing, storing, and sharing images on its 128 × 160-pixel screen. It provides email support, Internet browsing, and storage of around 15 MB. Its JAR capacity is unlimited, but depends on available storage. Figure 3.9 shows the K310.

Figure 3.9
The Sony Ericsson K310 is often compared to T616 and is associated with an extensive array of add-ons.

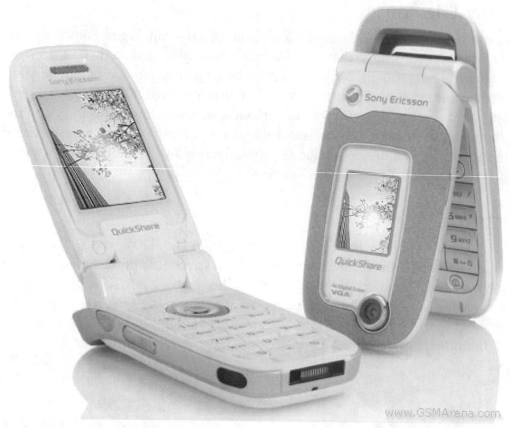

Figure 3.10
The Sony Ericsson Z520 provides a number of high-end features.
Photo Source: http://www.gsmarena.com/.

Sony Ericsson Z520

The Sony Ericsson Z520 (shown in Figure 3.10) has two display screens. The main screen has a resolution of 128×160 pixels. It offers 16 MB of memory. A secondary screen, on the cover of the phone, is of lower resolution and can display the time and other text data. This type of device provides users with the ability to take still or video pictures. Such capabilities represent fairly standard features. Given the increased memory and enhanced screen capabilities, the Z520 is suitable for 3D game development.

Motorola

Motorola offers a wide variety of devices that it categorizes into A, E, I, T, V, and other groups. To view the devices, access **http://developer.motorola.com/** and click on Handsets. If you then click on View All, you can see the dozens of devices

Motorola supports. The vast majority of these support Java ME. When you go to the site and log in, you can filter the devices by using the APIs: Java ME option and then selecting, for example, CLDC 1.0 or MIDP 2.0.

Note

Motorola provides a development suite called Motodev Studio. The design of this integrated development environment (IDE) resembles Eclipse, a popular IDE for Java and other developers. In some cases, a version of Java is not available for Motodev Studio, but where it is available, it provides a way to implement software for Motorola devices quickly and allows you to work with Java ME.

Motorola A830

Among other features on Motorola's developer website are specification sheets in PDF form for devices such as the A830, which is shown in Figure 3.11. This

Figure 3.11
The Motorola A830 is an example of a midrange MID.

device provides storage of 1 MB. The maximum compressed JAR size is 100 KB. The display resolution is 176 × 220 pixels.

iDEN Phones

All Motorola phones that have a model number starting with *i* are within the iDEN range, starting with the lower-range i85s. It offers a 119 × 64 monochrome screen and a MIDlet size of 50 KB. Like most of the lower-end iDEN phones, its memory is limited to 256 KB. Figure 3.12 shows the Motorola iDEN i85s.

The i730 shown in Figure 3.13 is a slightly higher-level iDEN device. It includes a 130 × 130 16-bit color screen and can accommodate a MIDlet of 500 KB.

Figure 3.12
The Motorola iDEN i85s.

Figure 3.13
The Motorola iDEN i730 is fairly modest in some respects but has enjoyed popularity due to its price.

Motorola E550

As a final example of Motorola's devices, Figure 3.14 shows the E550. This device provides a main screen with 176×220 resolution. Its maximum MIDlet size is 100 KB, with MIDlet storage of up to 5 MB.

Conclusion

You can use Java ME to develop software (games) for a multitude of devices. The devices offered by Nokia, Sony Ericsson, and Motorola represent a significant but by no means comprehensive view of the spectrum of such devices. In each instance, to understand why a given device has been developed, a good place to

Figure 3.14
The Motorola E550 provides main and secondary screens and supports 5 MB of storage.

start is price. Low-end devices often provide limited capabilities, but because they are low end, they usually enjoy greater market. Higher-end devices represent greater specialization in some cases but also offer more in terms of screen resolution and input options.

PART II

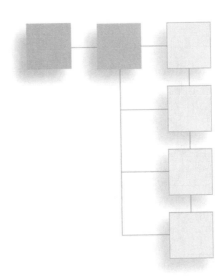

SETTING UP FOR DEVELOPMENT

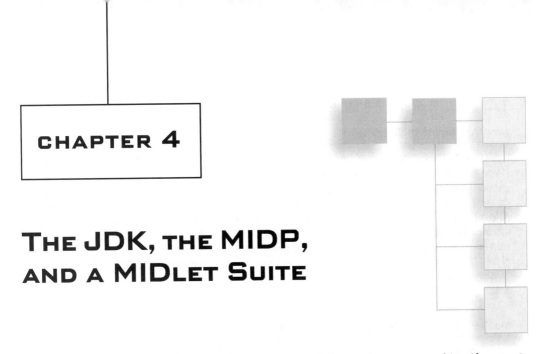

CHAPTER 4

The JDK, the MIDP, and a MIDlet Suite

In this chapter, the discussion returns to some of the topics presented in Chapter 2, where JAR and JAD files were presented. To allow you to go to work, this chapter begins with a short review of how to download and install the JDK 1.6.x and the MIDP 2.0. These are two of the primary tools you use in this book. Once you have the JDK and the MIDP, you can compile, pre-verify, and package the MIDlets you develop. The two MIDlet classes you develop here are `hello.java` and `hello2.java`, which you can use to create a MIDlet suite. All of your work is performed on the command line or using a simple editor. The preferred editor is Notepad. To assemble the MIDlet suite, you create a JAD file and a JAR file for the MIDlets. As you go, you make a manifest file. The work you perform in this chapter establishes a basic understanding of the essentials of compiling MIDlets. Gaining a clear view of the fundamentals puts you in an excellent position to move on to the more advanced activities or to more clearly understand automated processes such as those you are exposed to in Chapter 5, where you work with the Java Wireless Toolkit.

Getting the Tools

To get started, you need some tools. You require two sets of software. The first is the Java JDK. As of the writing of this book, the JDK 1.6 is available, and the software in this book has been created using it. In addition to the JDK, you require the MIDP; version 2.0 is used in this book. You can work with this or

Table 4.1 Sun JDK and MIDP Software

Java Development Kit (JDK)

If you do not have a version of Java Development Kit installed already, use version 1.5.11 or above. You can access the JDK for this version at **http://java.sun.com/javase/downloads/index.jsp**.

Instructions for how to download and install the JDK are given in the next section, "Installing and Setting Up the JDK." If you already have a later version installed, stick with that. There is always a chance that different version numbers can result in problems, but every effort has been made to keep the software in this book as general as possible. If you are given the option of downloading NetBeans with your JDK, do so. It is installed with the JDK. Note that the NetBeans 5.5 IDE requires that you have version 5.0 or above of the JDK installed on your computer. (Note that in this text, reference is made of 1.5.x as "version 5.x" or "version 5," and version 1.6.x as "version 6.x" or "version 6.") Chapter 6 deals with the specifics of installing the NetBeans IDE.

Mobile Information Device Profile (MIDP 2.0)

If you have not yet installed the MIDP, use version 2.0. As with the JDK, different versions introduce the possibility of errors, but the code in this book is written to be as generic as possible. According to Sun, the code for version 2.0 is backward compatible with version 1.0, so you can use that as a starting point. You can access the MIDP software at **http://java.sun.com/javame/index.jsp**.

Instructions for how to download and install the MIDP 2.0 are given in this chapter under the heading "Installing and Setting Up the MIDP." The name of the Zip file you download for version 2.0 is midp-2_0-src-windows-i686.zip. It is approximately 8 MB. (The assumption here is that you are working on a Windows operating system.)

the 1.0 version. All of the code in this book has been written to address the 1.0 or 2.0 versions.

The next section, "Installing and Setting Up the JDK," addresses specific download activities. When you access the Sun site to obtain the software, note that you must register as a Sun developer. If you are not familiar with this routine, click the Register link and fill in the blanks. There is no charge, and you can deselect options that allow Sun to send you updates and product information. Table 4.1 provides essential information needed to access the JDK and MIDP software from Sun.

Keep in mind that this book focuses on functionality that is supported by MIDP 2.0. Many of the classes can be compiled using MIDP 1.0, but if the classes include floating-point values or incorporate newer Game API features, then compiler errors result. This is a book intended to introduce the technology, not to explore its advanced features, but it remains that mobile device technology grows in leaps and bounds almost daily, so using the latest version of the associated development software remains essential.

Installing and Setting Up the JDK

Many readers can skip this section. It is included for readers who are relatively new to Java and need a refresher on installation procedures. If you already know how to install the JDK or already have it installed on your computer, skip to the section titled "Installing and Setting Up the MIDP."

The JDK has gone through many versions. Currently, Sun has released version 6 of the JDK. This book uses this version. If you are still working with version 1.5.x, the programs are likely to compile without problems, but earlier versions cannot be used. Among other things, MIDP 2.0 is not supported by earlier versions; if you use NetBeans, you must begin with version 1.5.x. (NetBeans is discussed in Chapter 6.)

Note

Recall that Sun designates versions with three basic numbers (there can be several more). Version 5.x is represented by Sun as version 1.5.x. Version 6.x is sometimes represented as 1.6.x.

Also remember that as a developer you use the Java Development Kit (JDK). Chances are that your computer already has a version of the Java Runtime Environment (JRE). To see your version of the JRE, select Start > Control Panel and then find the Java icon in the program set in the Control Panel dialog. Click on it. After a moment, you see the Java Control Panel. Click the About button. This shows you the current version of your JRE.

As for the JDK, one quick way to learn whether you have it installed and what version you are working with is to go the Program Files directory in Windows Explorer. In the Program Files directory, search for Java. In the Java directory, if the JDK is installed, you see two folders, one for the JRE named something like `jre1.6.0_01`, and one for the JDK called `jdk1.6.0_01` or something similar. If your versions are 5.0 or later, there is no need to install or reinstall.

Obtaining the JDK

Before you proceed with the activities in this section, you need a place to store downloaded files. Create a directory on your computer in Windows File Explorer like this one:

`C:\downloads`

If you need to install a version of the Java Development Kit (JDK), then access the Sun download site first to obtain the installation executable. As is indicated in Table 4.1, this site is at **http://java.sun.com/javase/downloads/index.jsp**.

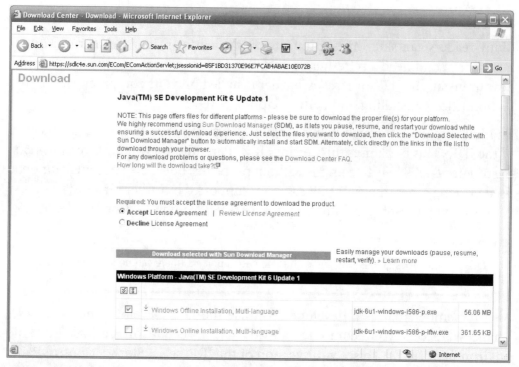

Figure 4.1
Select JDK for the Windows platform and save it to your downloads directory.

Navigate to the download page on the Sun site. Figure 4.1 shows the download page for the JDK 1.6.x. The box for the Windows version is checked. To complete the download you must accept the license terms. Beneath the black bar in Figure 4.1, you see a line for the win (Windows) executable. Check this and click the link. After you click the version download, you see a dialog box with open and save options. Save the file to your downloads directory. The zipped file for the SDK is roughly 135 MB.

Starting Your Windows JDK Installation

When you finish the download of the JDK for the Windows platform, you see a file with roughly the following name:

```
jdk-1_5_0_06-windows-i586-p.exe
```

This is a self-contained installation executable for the JDK. Here are steps for proceeding with the installation:

1. After you download the JDK Windows installer program (jdk-1_5_0_ 11-nb-5_5-win-ml.exe, for example), select Start > Control Panel > Add or

Remove Programs. In the Add or Remove Programs dialog, click Add New Programs. Then click CD or Floppy.

2. In the Install Program from Floppy Disk or CD dialog, click Next. Then click Browse and navigate to your download directory. From the Files of type drop-down list, select All Files. You then see the `j jdk-1_5_0_11-nb-5_5-win-ml.exe` file (or something similar). Select this file and click Open.

3. In the Run Install Program dialog, click Finish.

4. You then see an Open File – Security Warning dialog. Click Run. This starts the Sun installation routine.

5. At this point, you see the J2SE Development Kit Update dialog. Now go to the next section.

JDK Installation and Setup Continued

After the Sun installation program begins, follow these steps.

1. In the J2SE Development Kit dialog, click Next. You then see a license dialog. Click the I Accept option. Then click Next. For the directories dialog, leave the default options. Click Next.

2. You then see a dialog for verification. Click Next.

3. The installation might take several minutes. When the installation is complete, you see the complete dialog. Click Finish.

Copying Path Information

This section requires that you first install the Java JDK. If you have not yet done so, refer to the previous section, titled "Starting Your Windows JDK Installation." In the current section, you begin by gathering two pieces of information required later in the chapter for configuration purposes: the path to the JDK bin directory and the path to the JDK lib directory. You use this information to complete the installation of the JDK and to configure the MIDP files. (This procedure is documented later in this chapter.)

To gather the needed information, use the following steps:

1. Open Windows Explorer and navigate to the following directory:

`C:\Program Files\Java`

2. You see two folders if you have just installed only one version of the JDK. (More appear if you have updated your JDK since installing it.) One of the folders is for the JDK. The other is for the JRE. Note the exact name of the JDK. For example, you might see:

```
jdk1.6.0_01
```

3. Click on this folder. You see a bin directory. With the bin folder selected, look at the Address field in Windows Explorer; you see a path similar to the following:

```
C:\Program Files\Java\jdk1.6.0_01
```

The only information that might differ for you is the version number.

4. Copy exactly what you see on the Address line of Explorer to a piece of paper or copy and paste it into a text file. (One approach is to copy it to Notepad.) For the line in step 3, you copy a path similar to this one:

```
C:\Program Files\Java\jdk1.6.0_01\bin
```

5. Next copy the path to the lib directory. To accomplish this, use the same procedure as in step 3 to navigate to the lib directory, which is a subdirectory of the JDK (jdk1.5.0_11) directory. The path appears roughly like this:

```
C:\Program Files\Java\jdk1.6.0_01\lib
```

As before, copy it to a convenient text file or piece of paper. Now proceed to the next section.

Setting the Path and CLASSPATH Variables

This section assumes that you have performed the tasks detailed in the previous section, "Copying Path Information." If you have not completed the steps described in the previous section, do so before beginning the tasks in this section.

After the Sun installation completes, you need to set a system variable for the path of the JRE when you want to run a Java program. To set the system variable, follow these steps.

1. Select Start > Control Panel. In the Control Panel window, double-click System. The System Properties dialog appears. Click the Advanced tab.

Click the Environment Variables button in the Advanced tab. The Environment Variables dialog appears. (See Figure 4.5 later in this chapter.)

2. In the Environment Variables dialog, inspect the System variables pane. It is the lower of the two panes. In the System variables pane, scroll down until you see the Path line.

3. Double-click the Path line. The Edit System Variables dialog appears.

4. Carefully click to activate the Variable value field. Then use the right arrow to move the cursor to the beginning of the text in the field. At the beginning, type a semicolon (;). Then paste or type the path you copied or wrote down earlier. Confirm that the line ends with a slash and the word `bin`. The path designates the Java bin directory. For example:

   `;C:\Program Files\Java\jdk1.5.0_06\bin`

   You add the semicolon at the beginning of the text to separate this path from others in the list.

5. After confirming you have the correct path, click OK to exit the Edit System Variables dialog.

6. Now scroll to the top of the System variables pane and find the `CLASSPATH` system variable. Click on the `CLASSPATH` variable and then click the Edit button. In the Edit System Variables dialog, activate the cursor in the Variable value field and carefully arrow to the right end of the field. Append the path you copied earlier to the JDK lib directory. Again, separate the new path from those already in the field by prefixing with a semicolon. For example:

   `;C:\Program Files\Java\jdk1.5.0_11\lib`

7. After confirming you have the correct path, click OK to exit the Edit System Variables dialog.

8. You have now set the `PATH` and `CLASSPATH` path environment variables. Click OK to exit the Environment Variables dialog and again to exit the System Properties dialog. Then close the Control Panel window.

9. When you finish with this set of actions, select Start > Turn Off Computer > Restart. Generally, it is a good practice to restart your computer to make new configurations take effect.

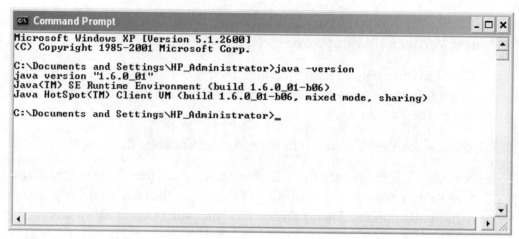

Figure 4.2
Type `java -version` to verify the JDK installation.

Testing Your Installation

To test your installation of the JDK, you can issue the `-version` command at the command (DOS) prompt. To do so, select Start > All Programs > Accessories > Command Prompt. You then see a Command Prompt dialog. As shown in Figure 4.2, type `java -version` at the prompt. The report that follows tells you the status of your Java installation.

Installing and Setting Up the MIDP

If you have not already done so, begin by creating a directory for your downloads from Sun. Here's an example of a download directory path:

`C:\downloads`

As is indicated earlier in Table 4.1, to reach the Sun site for the MIDP, you can access this link: **http://java.sun.com/javame/index.jsp**.

Figure 4.3 provides a screenshot of the Sun page for the MIDP 2.0 software. The Windows version is clicked. Sun asks you to register as a developer and also to accept its license agreements. After you have completed these activities, click the version of the MIDP 2.0 you want to download. As shown in Figure 4.3, this is listed in the download page as

`midp-2_0-src-windows-i686.zip`

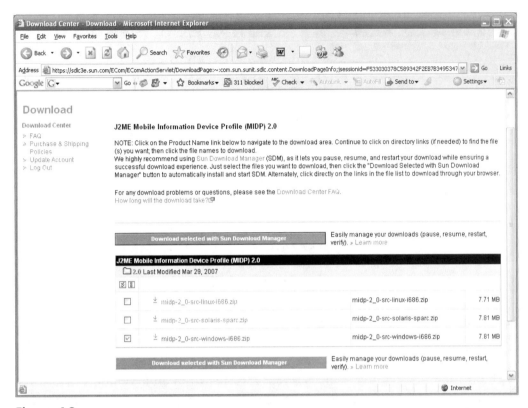

Figure 4.3
For version 2.0, register and then navigate to the MIDP download page.

After you check the version, click the link. When the Download dialog appears, click the Save option rather than the Open option. Select your downloads directory for the target directory of the download.

After you download the MIDP zip file, it appears in your downloads directory as

```
C:\downloads midp-2_0-src-windows-i686.zip
```

Copying the MIDP to a Directory

To install the MIDP, you unzip the file you downloaded from Sun. You copy the files that constitute the MIDP into a directory of your choosing. Toward this end, before you unzip the MIDP file from Sun, first create a directory into which to copy the unzipped files:

```
c:\j2me
```

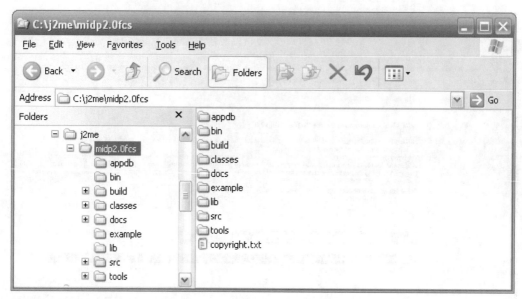

Figure 4.4
Copy the MIDP folders into a directory of your choosing.

Click on the `midp-2_0-src-windows-i686.zip` file to open a Windows Explorer directory window. In this window, you see one folder. The name of the folder is as follows: `midp2.0fcs`. Copy this entire folder into the directory you have created for the MIDP files. If you have created a directory called `j2me`, you see the following directory path in Windows Explorer:

`c:\j2me\midp2.0fcs`

The copy operation is not trivial, so it might take a while even on a fairly robust computer. The unzipped files require roughly 24 MB. In Windows Explorer, when you are done, you see the directory structure shown in Figure 4.4.

Table 4.2 lists the MIDP directories and provides brief descriptions of each. Some are beyond the scope of the current discussion.

Copying the Paths of the MIDP

To complete the tasks in this section, you first install the files for the MIDP. If you have not yet done so, refer to the section titled "Installing and Setting Up the MIDP."

Table 4.2 MIDP Directories

Directory	Description
\appdb	Graphical files of the `*.png` type.
\bin	The command line tools, `preverify.exe`, and the `midp.exe` emulator.
\build	Makefiles for building MIDP for Microsoft Windows.
\classes	MIDP classes. You'll compile using these as a base.
\docs	Comprehensive documentation of the MIDP; includes guides, reference materials, and release notes.
\example	Example JARs and JADs for demonstration purposes.
\lib	Configuration files.
\src	Example source code.
\tools	Primarily the JAD tool, which you use for MIDlet suites.

After you complete the installation of the MIDP, your next task is to retrieve information to set the PATH and CLASSPATH environmental variables of Windows. To do so, use the following steps:

1. Open Windows Explorer and navigate to the following directory:

```
C:\j2me\midp2.0fcs
```

2. Click on the folder for this directory. You see a bin directory. In the bin directory, you see a file named `preverify.exe`. With the `bin` folder selected, if you look at the Address field in Windows Explorer, you see a path similar to the following:

```
C:\j2me\midp2.0fcs\bin
```

3. Copy exactly what you see in the Address field of Explorer to a text file or piece of paper. You use this information to set the PATH environment variable. Here's what you copy:

```
C:\j2me\midp2.0fcs\bin
```

4. Now navigate to the `classes` directory of the MIDP directory. The path is roughly as follows:

```
C:\j2me\midp2.0fcs\classes
```

You use this path to set the CLASSPATH environment variable of Windows. Copy what you see on the Address line of Windows Explorer to a file or piece of paper. Now proceed to the next section.

Setting the PATH and CLASSPATH Variables

This section assumes that you have performed the tasks detailed in the previous section, "Copying the Paths of the MIDP." In this section, you employ the information you collected about the MIDP paths to set Windows environment variables. If you have not completed the tasks described in the previous section, do so before beginning the tasks in this section.

The first environmental variable you set is the PATH variable, which allows Windows to automatically locate and execute the preverify.exe program. To set the PATH variable, follow these steps.

1. Select Start > Control Panel. In the Control Panel window, double-click System. The System Properties dialog appears. Click the Advanced tab. In the Advanced tab, click the Environment Variables button. The Environment Variables dialog appears (see Figure 4.5).

2. In the Environment Variables dialog, inspect the System variables pane, which is the lower of the two panes. In the System variables pane, scroll down until you see the Path line.

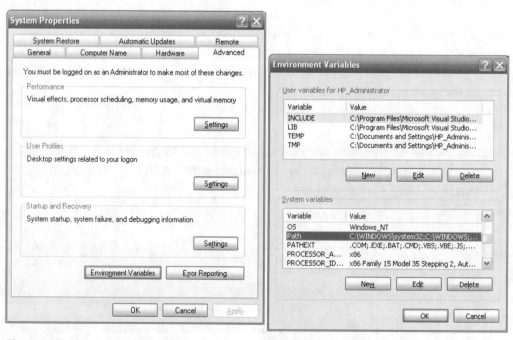

Figure 4.5
The System Properties dialog allows you to set environment variables.

3. Double-click the Path line. The Edit System Variables dialog appears.

4. Carefully click to activate the Variable value field. Then use the right arrow to move the cursor to the end of the text in the field. At the end, type a semicolon (;)—this separates the path you are inserting from other paths in the list. Then paste or type in the path you copied or wrote down earlier. Confirm that the line ends with a slash and the word `bin`. The path designates the MIDP bin directory.

5. At the end of the line, append a semicolon and a period. *If you do not add the semicolon and the period, the MIDP does not function properly.* The text should look like this:

   `;C:\j2me\midp2.0fcs\bin;.`

6. After confirming you have the correct path, click OK to exit the Edit System Variables dialog.

7. Now set the `CLASSPATH` environment variable. To accomplish this, click on the `CLASSPATH` line in the System variables pane. Then click the Edit button.

8. In the Edit System Variables dialog, activate the Variable value field and carefully arrow to the end of the line. At the end of the line, append the path to the MIDP classes directory. Precede it with a semicolon to separate it from previously inserted paths. It appears roughly as follows:

   `;C:\j2me\midp2.0fcs\classes;.`

9. After confirming that the CLASSPATH information is correct, click OK to exit the Edit System Variables dialog. Click OK to exit the Environment Variables dialog, and again to exit the System Properties dialog. Then close the Control Panel window.

10. Optional: when you finish with this set of actions, select Start > Turn Off Computer > Restart. Generally, you need to restart your computer to make new configurations take effect.

Tip

To check the value of your `CLASSPATH`, you can enter `set` at the command line. This shows the current values of all environment variables. Changes to system variables made through the Control Panel do not take effect until you open a new command line (Command Prompt) after making changes to your computer's environment variables.

Setting MIDP_HOME

Some environment variables, such as PATH, already exist. You access them and then update the information associated with them. Other system variables you add on your own. For the MIDP executable, you add an environmental variable named MIDP_HOME. To accomplish this, use the following procedure:

1. Select Start > Control Panel. In the Control Panel window, double-click System. The System Properties dialog appears. Click the Advanced tab. Click the Environment Variables button in the Advanced tab. The Environment Variables dialog appears.

2. In the Environment Variables dialog, inspect the System variables pane. Click the New button.

3. The New System Variable dialog appears.

4. In the Variable name field, type the following:

   MIDP_HOME

5. In the Variable value field, type the following:

   ;C:\j2me\midp2.0fcs

6. After confirming that the MIDP_HOME information is correct, click OK to exit the New System Variable dialog. Click OK to exit the Environment Variables dialog, and again to exit the System Properties dialog. Then close the Control Panel window.

7. Optional: when you finish this set of actions, select Start > Turn Off Computer > Restart. Generally, it is a good idea to restart your computer to make new configurations take effect.

Note

To check the value of environment variables, open a Command Prompt window. (You can enter cmd in the Run field of the Start > Run path.) Enter set in the command line. This shows the current values of all environment variables. System variables take effect when you open a Command Prompt after you have made changes.

Verifying the MIDP Configuration

To test whether you have correctly installed and configured the MIDP, enter a few commands in the Command Prompt window. First, open a Windows

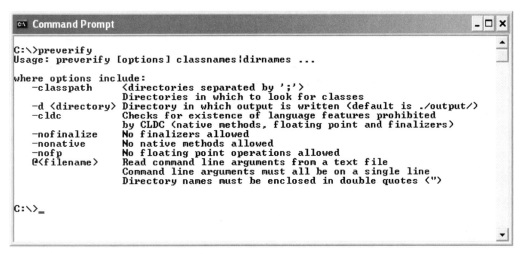

Figure 4.6
Enter `preverify` at the prompt.

Figure 4.7
Enter `midp -version` at the prompt.

Command Prompt window by selecting Start > Run. In the Run field, type `cmd`. After the Command Prompt window opens, type `preverify` at the prompt, as Figure 4.6 illustrates. The preverify command is a primary token for the MIDP. It invokes the program that checks the syntax of the code for your MIDlets.

After issuing the preverify command, check for the version of the MIDP. To accomplish this, as shown in Figure 4.7, type `midp -version` at the prompt. After you issue this command, you should see three lines of output. This verifies your version of the MIDP and the CLDC.

N o t e

If you see an error message, it is likely that you have not concluded one or more lines in the environment variable Value fields with a semicolon and a period. Go back and check the CLASSPATH, PATH, and MIDP_HOME values in the System dialog for environment variables (see Figure 4.5). Environment variables are usually identified in system messages with a dollar sign ($).

Setting Up a Working Directory

If you have followed the directions given so far in this chapter, your MIDP files reside in a directory called j2me. After you use this directory path to define the MIDP_HOME environment variables, it becomes a permanent feature of your development activities. You can now create a working project directory that makes use of the path. Accordingly, use Windows Explorer to create a project directory that is consistent with the MIDP_HOME path:

```
C:\j2me\projects
```

For the projects you develop, add subdirectories to the projects directory. Now each subdirectory becomes what you might recognize as a standard Java package name. For the first project, create a directory named hello. Then add a java file to this directory called hello.java. The next section provides instructions for creating the hello.java code.

N o t e

When you move back and forth between Windows Explorer and the Command Prompt window, to eliminate the need to repeatedly type long paths, you can click on a folder in Windows Explorer and drag it across your desktop to the Command Prompt window. The path appears at the prompt. To change directories, first type cd after the prompt in the Command Prompt window. Follow this with a space. Then drag and drop a folder from Windows Explorer. If you try this with the directory structure suggested for the current chapter, you end up with a series of commands along the following lines. Start with the given prompt:

```
C:\>
```

Then drag and drop the folder from Windows Explorer:

```
C:\>C:\j2me\projects\hello
```

Insert the cd command. Use the arrow keys and type the command at the beginning of the directory path:

```
C:\>cd C:\j2me\projects\hello
```

Creating a MIDlet

In this section, you create a MIDlet, which is a micro device application (or applet). As mentioned in the previous section, before you begin work on this project, create a projects directory:

```
C:\j2me\projects
```

In the projects directory, create a subdirectory called hello:

```
C:\j2me\projects\hello
```

At this point, open Notepad or some other editing application. Save the file as hello.java. For Notepad and other generic editors, set the Encoding field to ANSI and the file type as *.java. The source code for hello.java is available on the CD in the Chapter 4 code folder. You can access it there and copy it into your projects directory, or type it as follows:

```java
/**
 *  Chapter 4 \ hello.java
 */
import javax.microedition.midlet.*;
import javax.microedition.lcdui.*;

public class Hello extends MIDlet
        implements CommandListener{
   protected Form form;
   protected Command quit;

   /**
    * Constructor for the MIDlet
    */
   public Hello(){
      // Create a form and add our components
      form = new Form("Hello MIDlet");
      form.append("Hello, Micro World!");

      // Create a way to quit
      form.setCommandListener(this);
      quit = new Command("Quit", Command.SCREEN, 1);
      form.addCommand(quit);
   }
```

```java
/**
 * Called by the Application Manager when the MIDlet is
 * starting or resuming after being paused.
 */
protected void startApp() throws MIDletStateChangeException{
    // Display the form
    Display.getDisplay(this).setCurrent(form);
}

/**
 * Called by the MID's Application Manager to pause the MIDlet.
 */
protected void pauseApp(){
}

/**
 * Called by the MID's Application Manager when the MIDlet is
 * about to be destroyed (removed from memory).
 */
protected void destroyApp(boolean unconditional)
        throws MIDletStateChangeException{
}

/**
 * Called to execute the quit command
 */
public void commandAction(Command command, Displayable displayable){
    // Check for our quit command and act accordingly
    try
    {
        if (command == quit)
        {
            destroyApp(true);
            // Tell the Application Manager of quitting
            notifyDestroyed();
        }
    }

    // Catch even if not thrown
    catch (MIDletStateChangeException me){
    }
}
}
```

Compiling Your Application

To compile the `hello.java` program, use the DOS CD command to change directories to reach the directory that contains the file `C:\j2m2\projects`:

```
cd \j2me\projects\hello
```

You then see this prompt:

```
C:\j2me\projects\hello>
```

N o t e

A file called `MIDletCC.txt` is included in the Chapter 4 directory. This file contains the lines for the compile, preverify, and run commands. Copy and paste the lines from these commands to the DOS prompt to more quickly get through the initial phases of learning how to compile the code.

To compile the `hello.java` file, enter the following command at the prompt:

```
javac -target 1.6 -bootclasspath %MIDP_HOME%\classes Hello.java
```

The `-target 1.6` argument relates to the current version of the JDK. Use of the version number indicates to the Java compiler to output class files in 1.6 version format. (You can also leave this argument out.)

The `-bootclasspath %MIDP_HOME%\classes` argument forces the compiler to use only the classes in the MIDP classes directory, which contains the core MIDP and CLDC class files. This ensures that what you are compiling is compatible with the intended run-time target.

The compiler generates a class file named `Hello.class`. Use the DOS DIR command to view the `*.class` file. You see the following files:

```
C:\j2me\projects\hello>dir/B
Hello.class
hello.java
C:\j2me\projects\hello>
```

Using Preverify with the Class File

The next step is to preverify the class file. Work again from the prompt you used before:

```
C:\j2me\projects\hello>
```

Issue the following command:

```
preverify -cldc -classpath %MIDP_HOME%\classes;. -d . Hello
```

Although this looks complicated, it is a relatively simple command. First, the -cldc option checks to see that you're not using any language features not supported by the CLDC.

The classpath argument points to both the MIDP class library and the location of your project class files. The -d argument sets the destination directory for the resulting post-verified class files. Hello is the name of the file you want to verify. When you issue the preverify command, you overwrite your original class file with the new one. Later on, this approach can be altered.

Running Your MIDlet

To run the MIDlet, continue to work from the Command Prompt you worked with in the previous sections:

```
C:\j2me\projects\hello>
```

Issue the following command:

```
midp -classpath . Hello
```

When you issue this command, the MIDP window opens on your desktop. Figure 4.8 illustrates what you see.

At this point, you can interact with the emulator in two ways. You can click the standard red control button in the upper right of the MIDP window to close the window. You can also click the button with the horizontal phone icon to the right of the SELECT button (see Figure 4.8). If you have executed your program from the Command Prompt window, use the up arrow key to invoke the run command to experiment with the MIDlet.

Creating the Full Package

To complement the development activity involved in a single MIDlet, the next step is to create a MIDlet suite. As was discussed in Chapter 2, a MIDlet suite consists of two or more MIDlets. Toward this end, in this section, you create a second MIDlet, Hello2.

Figure 4.8
The Sun emulator displays the Hello MIDlet.

Hello, Again

Using the following code example, create a second MIDlet in a file named hello2.java. To implement the code for this file, you can type it or use the code in the Hello2.java file in the Chapter 4 folder. Place it in your projects/hello directory. Use the procedure you used before. If you create it yourself, name it hello2.java. This MIDlet makes use of the hello.java file, so for now the simplest approach to working with it is to place it in the same package (or directory) as the hello.java file.

```
/**
 * Chapter 4 \ hello2.java
 * This MIDlet is used to demonstrate how multiple MIDlets make
 * up a MIDlet suite. This class extends the Hello class and overides
 * the constructor so it displays different content in the form.
```

```
     *
    */
    import javax.microedition.midlet.*;
    import javax.microedition.lcdui.*;

    // #1 Extends the Hello class
    public class Hello2 extends Hello
    {
      // If you want to run this class alone, remove the comment:
      // Form form;
       public Hello2()
       {
          // #2 Create a form and add text
          form = new Form("Hello2 Midlet");
          form.append("Hello Twice to Micro World!");

          // Create a way to quit
          form.setCommandListener(this);
          quit = new Command("Quit", Command.SCREEN, 1);
          form.addCommand(quit);
       }
    }
```

As the comments reveal, the Hello2 class extends the Hello class. Discussion of the fundamentals of inheritance (extending one class from another) is a bit beyond the scope of this chapter. Still, as the class signature following comment #1 reveals, the use of the extends keyword allows you to make use of the functionality implemented in the base class, Hello. Rather than completely rewriting the code for a second MIDlet, by extending the Hello class, you are able to use the previously implemented code. In the derived class, as the line following comment #2 shows, you revise the title and text components in the constructor.

Note

Looking at the code for your first MIDlet, you might notice that the three attributes—display, form, and quit—are in protected, not private, scope. This way, when you derive Hello2, you have access to these fields inside its constructor.

Building the Class

When you have the hello2.java file ready, use the procedures you used in the previous section to compile, preverify, and test the class. Accordingly, first compile it by opening the Command Prompt and changing directories until the prompt shows the hello directory:

```
C:\j2me\projects\hello>
```

At this prompt, issue the compile command for the hello2.java file:

```
javac -target 1.6 -bootclasspath %MIDP_HOME%\classes Hello2.java
```

After you compile, the hello2.class file is generated. Then issue the preverify command:

```
preverify -cldc -classpath %MIDP_HOME%\classes;. -d . Hello2
```

Recall that the preverify operation writes over the hello2.class file. You can then issue the run command:

```
midp -classpath . Hello2
```

Figure 4.9 illustrates the emulator. Note that, as before, the name of the MIDlet appears in the title bar of the device screen. As before, the button with the phone icon to the right of the SELECT button can be clicked to close the emulator.

Figure 4.9
Adding a second MIDlet forms a suite.

Creating the Manifest and JAR

Now that you have compiled, preverified, and tested the `hello.java` and `hello2.java` files, you create a Java Archive (JAR) file for them. As mentioned in Chapter 2, to create a JAR file, you begin by creating a manifest.

JAR Files

A JAR file is an archiving system used to wrap and compress the components of a Java application package, such as class, image, sound, and other data files. The file format is based on the Zip format, with a few extras such as a manifest, which contains information on the contents of the JAR.

You can create or modify a JAR file using the `jar` command-line tool that comes with the JDK. What's also cool is that you can manipulate JAR files using the `java.util.jar` API.

Table 4.3 provides a short list of some useful JAR commands.

Table 4.3 Useful JAR Commands

Command	Description
`jar -cvf my.jar *`	Creates a new JAR named `my.jar`, which contains all of the files in the current directory.
`jar -cvfm my.jar manifest.txt *`	Creates a new JAR named `my.jar`, which contains all of the files in the current directory. Also, it creates a manifest file using the contents of the `manifest.txt` file.
`jar -xvf my.jar *`	Unpacks all of the files in the `my.jar` into the current directory.
`jar -tvf my.jar`	Allows you to view the table of contents for `my.jar`.

As you can see, most commands revolve around the `-f` argument, which specifies the JAR file to work on, and the `-v` argument, which asks for "verbose" output. Combine these with the `c`, `x`, and `t` switches, and you've covered the most common JAR operations.

The manifest file resides in your projects\hello directory. To create the manifest file, first open a new file in your text editor. Save the file as `manifest.txt` in the projects/hello directory. In the file, type the following lines:

```
MIDlet-Name: MegaHello
MIDlet-Version: 1.0
MIDlet-Vendor: J2ME Game Programming
MIDlet-1: First Hello, ,Hello
MIDlet-2: Second Hello, ,Hello2
MicroEdition-Profile: MIDP-2.0
MicroEdition-Configuration: CLDC-1.1
```

To create the JAR file, open a Command Prompt window and change directories until you are in the projects/hello directory.

`C:\j2me\projects\hello>`

To create the JAR file for the suite, issue the following command:

`jar -cvfm hellosuite.jar manifest.txt *.class`

The basic command is `jar`. As Table 4.3 discusses, the `-cvfm` argument creates a JAR file with all the `*.class` files in the current directory, along with a manifest based on the `manifest.txt` file. The resulting JAR file name is `hellosuite.jar`. The manifest file is named `manifest.txt`. Figure 4.10 illustrates the output of the JAR-creation activity.

After running the `jar` command, you can see the compression percentages for the files. To do so, issue the following command:

`jar -tvf hellosuite.jar`

Figure 4.11 shows the output you see when you issue the `-tvf` command.

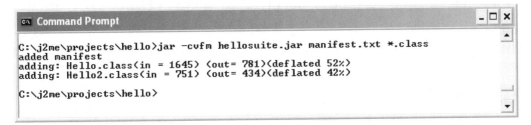

Figure 4.10
Create the JAR file.

```
C:\j2me\projects\hello>jar -cvfm hellosuite.jar manifest.txt *.class
added manifest
adding: Hello.class(in = 1626) (out= 772)(deflated 52%)
adding: Hello2.class(in = 751) (out= 435)(deflated 42%)

C:\j2me\projects\hello>jar -tvf hellosuite.jar
     0 Sat Mar 31 16:44:38 MDT 2007 META-INF/
   291 Sat Mar 31 16:44:38 MDT 2007 META-INF/MANIFEST.MF
  1626 Sat Mar 31 15:25:24 MDT 2007 Hello.class
   751 Sat Mar 31 15:11:26 MDT 2007 Hello2.class

C:\j2me\projects\hello>
```

Figure 4.11
You see compression and content information as you create the JAR file.

Note that the jar command creates a file named manifest.mf, not manifest.txt. This is a common point of confusion. The name of the manifest file you supply, manifest.txt, designates the file that contains information needed to create the actual manifest, manifest.mf.

Creating the JAD

As mentioned in Chapter 2, after you create a JAR file, you create a corresponding JAD file to represent your suite. To accomplish this, in the same directory you have been working in to create the JAR file, create a new file named hellosuite.jad. Most of the lines you include in the JAD file are the same as those in the JAR file. However, there are a few differences.

For the contents of this file, you need to know the size of the JAR file you have just created. Accordingly, use the DIR command to view the contents of the projects\hello directory. Figure 4.12 shows you the directory content thus far. As Figure 4.12 reveals, the size of the hellosuite.jar file is 1909.

For the text of the hellosuite.jad file, type the following lines. Note that the size of the JAR file (which appears in bold type) as shown in Figure 4.12 is used.

```
MIDlet-1: First Hello, ,Hello
MIDlet-2: Second Hello, ,Hello2
```

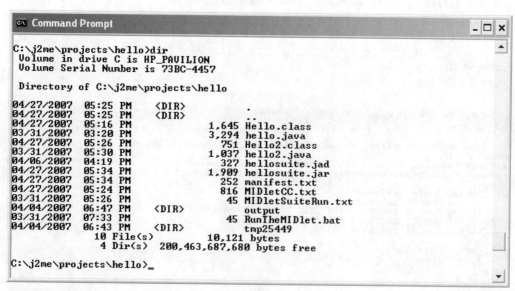

Figure 4.12
Obtain the precise JAR file size from the directory list.

```
MMIDlet-Description: HelloMIDlet
MIDlet-Jar-URL: helloMIDlet.jar
MIDlet-Name: MegaHello
MIDlet-Permissions:
MIDlet-Vendor: home.net
MIDlet-Version: 2.0
MicroEdition-Configuration: CLDC-1.1
MicroEdition-Profile: MIDP-2.0
MIDlet-Jar-Size: 1909
```

In this file, MIDlet-Jar-Size is used to specify the size in bytes of the corresponding JAR file. Additionally, MIDlet-Jar-URL specifies location of the JAR file. These variables allow the user of the JAR file to see its size and to determine the site from which to acquire the JAR file. The MIDlet-1 and MIDlet-2 lines identify the MIDlets you have created. Each appears as a menu item in the emulator.

Note

The JAD file must be updated each time you alter the files for the MIDlet. If you use an IDE like NetBeans, much of this activity is automated for you. See the discussion in Chapter 6. For now, note that it is important to track the size of the JAR files. If you encounter problems with your builds, check the file sizes you set for JAR size. Discrepancies create build and run problems.

Running the MIDlet Suite Package

At this point, you can use the JAD file to execute the MIDlet suite in the emulator. The result of this activity is that the emulator provides you with an application in which you can perform a few navigational activities.

To create the MIDlet suite for the two classes you have created thus far, as you have done before, use a Command Prompt window to work in the projects\hello directory:

```
C:\j2me\projects\hello>
```

Issue the following command:

```
midp -classpath . -Xdescriptor hellosuite.jad
```

Note

Take care with the spaces when entering things on the command line. Mistyping them can sometimes result in errors. The MIDletSuiteRun.txt file in the Chapter 2 directory provides the text for this command.

Figure 4.13
When loading a JAR containing multiple MIDlets, the emulator asks which one to execute.

You do not compile the JAD file. Instead, you specify only that the JAD file is to be executed. The emulator loads everything it needs from the JAR file named in the JAD file. No class files need to be named in the JAD file. Figure 4.13 illustrates the resulting executable.

As Figure 4.13 illustrates, the Java Application Manager (JAM) presents a list of the MIDlets available in the suite. To operate the emulator, start with the following steps:

1. Click the up and down arrows on the SELECT button. Notice that the bar shifts up and down.

2. Position the selection bar on Second Hello. Click in the center of the SELECT button. The Hello2 class executes. You see the output of the

form.append() method, which is the text message, "Hello Twice to Micro World!"

3. Click the button with the red phone icon to the lower right of the SELECT button. This restores the full JAM list.

4. Position the selection bar on the First Hello item and click SELECT. The Hello class executes.

5. Click the On/Off button to exit.

Using a *.bat File to Run Your MIDlet

The Chapter 4 folder provides you with a Windows/DOS *.bat file (RunTheMIDlet.bat) that gives you an easy way to execute the JAD file. To use it, just click on it in Windows Explorer (or if you are using the Command Prompt window, type the name of the file). You can edit the file using Notepad. To edit it, either you must first open your editor and then open the file using the File Open menu, or you can use the Command Prompt to navigate to the projects\hello directory and then type the following command at the prompt:

```
notepad MIDletSuiteRun.txt
```

Also, see the note earlier in this chapter on how to move back and forth between the Command Prompt window and Windows Explorer.

Modifying the JAD

Modify the JAD file so that it redundantly adds classes to the JAM list. Each shows up as a unique item in the JAM menu. To accomplish this, modify the hellosuite.jad to add two more lines. Here is how the modified file appears:

```
MIDlet-Name: MegaHello
MIDlet-Version: 1.0
MIDlet-Vendor: Java ME Game Programming
MIDlet-1: First Hello, ,Hello
MIDlet-2: Second Hello, ,Hello2
MIDlet-3: Third Hello, ,Hello2
MIDlet-4: Fourth Hello, ,Hello
MIDlet-Jar-Size: 1909
MIDlet-Jar-URL: hello.jar
```

This change does not require that you in any way change the hellosuite.jar file. Leave that as is. This experiment shows that the JAD file serves to call the resources named in the JAR file and allows you to designate names for them in the JAM list. This is because the entries within the JAD file always take precedence over those in the JAR file.

This concludes the grand tour of the J2ME command-line development environment. In the next chapter, you look at the alternative that Sun's J2ME Wireless Toolkit offers.

Conclusion

In this chapter, you reviewed how to download and install the JDK 1.6.x and the MIDP 2.0. You then put these tools to work to create two Java classes for MIDlets. You used a JAR file to compress the Java *.class files and then developed a JAD file that allows you to configure a MIDlet suite. The resulting MIDlets allow you to manipulate basic menu items. The work in this chapter was performed from a command line and involved only Notepad or a text editor of your choice. This approach to development lets you glimpse how MIDlets are created from the ground up. In the next chapter, you continue along the same lines using the Java Wireless Toolkit, which allows you to automate much of the activity that you performed manually in this chapter. In Chapter 6, you take yet another step, to the NetBeans IDE. Whether you adopt a given IDE is your choice. However, the tools you worked with in this chapter remain in place for this rest of this book.

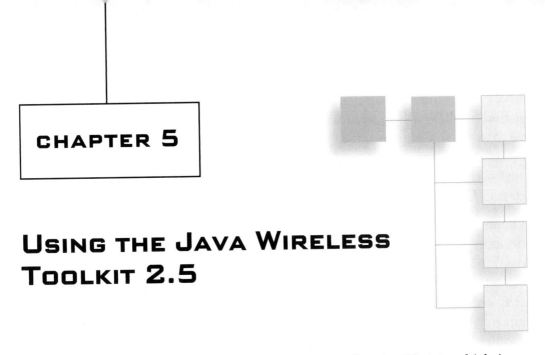

CHAPTER 5

USING THE JAVA WIRELESS TOOLKIT 2.5

In this chapter, you explore the Java Wireless Toolkit (JWT) 2.5, which is an essential tool for many developers who do not want to adopt a full IDE for MIDlet development. The virtue of the Java Wireless Toolkit is that it allows you to develop without having to repeatedly change JAR and JAD files to test your applications. The Java Wireless Toolkit does the work for you. You need only provide the Java code. To use the Java Wireless Toolkit 2.5, you require the JDK 1.5.x or higher, and for this book, you use the Mobile Information Device Profile (MIDP) 2.0 and the Connected Limited Device Configuration (CLDC) version 1.1. This chapter takes you through acquisition and installation procedures for the JWT 2.5 and provides a starter MIDlet, HelloToolkit, to use for initial experiments.

Development Settings

In Chapter 4, Table 4.1 provides a summary view of the two sets of software you require to develop MID applications in the Java ME setting. These are the Java Development Kit (JDK) and the Mobile Information Device Profile (MIDP). This book makes use of the JDK 1.5.x and the MIDP 2.0. Chapter 4 addressed the acquisition and installation of these items and provided a brief tutorial on creating a MIDlet suite consisting of two MIDlets. In that setting, you worked from a Command Prompt window and Notepad, and the primary goal was to show the commands and development activities involved in developing a MIDlet from as close to the essentials as possible. Knowledge gained from such experiences remains invaluable in your development efforts.

At the same time, if you are a developer who works in a given setting for any period at all, you begin writing applications or creating scripts that automate your work. In Chapter 4, for example, a DOS shell script made its way into the effort almost inevitably. It was much easier to place the JAD run command in a shell script and then to execute the script than it would have been to repeatedly retype the command.

In this respect, almost all of the major manufacturers of mobile information devices (MIDs) have in one way or another offered tools that let developers develop software for their devices more expeditiously. For several years now, Sun has offered the Java Wireless Toolkit (JWT) for MIDs, which is the topic of this chapter. The JWT is what its name implies: a set of tools. It is not a fully deployed integrated development environment (IDE). More recently introduced and in another league altogether is the NetBeans IDE, which is discussed in Chapter 6. Packages in the NetBeans IDE make use of the JWT. Table 5.1 provides essential information on the WTK (wireless toolkit) and the NetBeans IDE.

Table 5.1 Development Tools

The Java Wireless Toolkit 2.5

The Java Wireless Toolkit gives you development tools for mobile devices and networked games. It is associated with the CLDC, and its current version level is 2.5. It can be incorporated into the NetBeans IDE 5.5 if you upload a mobility package. (This is covered in Chapter 6.) The JWT is a standalone set of tools, however, and you can at access it at **http://java.sun.com/products/sjwtoolkit/download-2_5.html**. The JWT possesses value for developers in a multitude of respects. Perhaps most significantly, it is associated with Nokia's Scalable Network Application Package (SNAP), which allows developers to work with the server software used for multiplayer games. You can find more information on SNAP at **http://www.forum .nokia.com/games/snapmobile**. The release levels of the JWT (2.2 and 2.5) that appear in this book require that you have version 1.5.x or above of the JDK.

NetBeans IDE 5.5

The NetBeans IDE 5.5 is a comprehensive development environment for anything you want to create using Java. You can readily fold the JWT into it if you install a mobility package for the IDE. Chapter 6 discusses this activity. The NetBeans IDE allows a much larger scope of development that the JWT. For starters, it allows you to use both Java and C++. Using Java, you can develop applets, applications, and MID software by choosing different NetBeans menu items and working from there. You can also use JUnit for testing, and make use of other packages for things like XML development. The architecture of the NetBeans IDE is similar in many ways to the Microsoft Studio IDE, which allows you choose a project type and then makes available a multitude of tools specific to that type. With MIDs, the two primary project types are CDC and Mobile, which Chapter 6 addresses in more detail. Compilation, testing, documentation, and deployment tools are built in to the IDE, or if not, then a vast assortment of Internet resources are available. The NetBeans IDE has emerged as one of the premier development environments for Java developers. To download the NetBeans IDE, access **http://www.netbeans.org**. If you are installing version 1.5.0 of Java, then Sun allows you to obtain, download, and install the NetBeans IDE along with it. The NetBeans IDE requires the JDK 1.5.x or higher.

The Java Wireless Toolkit

To review a few points made in Chapter 2, the CLDC provides definitions of programming interfaces and a virtual machine (VM) for MIDs. It is the foundation of the MIDP. For this reason, the JWT addresses the CLDC in the same general way that the MIDP addresses it. The CLDC is the foundation, and the JWT allows you to work with it. The JWT provides these tools, among others:

- A host of device emulators on which to test your MIDlets.

- An application profiler, which provides facilities to analyze method execution time and use frequency.

- A memory tool that lets you see your application's memory use.

- A network monitor, which shows traffic across a simulated network (including tools to vary the simulated performance).

- Speed emulation tools, which let you adjust the device's operating performance, including slowing bytecode execution.

In this respect, the JWT is a specific set of tools that addresses MIDlet (or MID programming) concerns. It is not, like NetBeans, an IDE designed to facilitate all your activities as a Java programmer. On the other hand, because the JWT is a set of tools, you can work with it independently or fold its capabilities into an IDE like NetBeans.

Installing the Toolkit

You can download the Toolkit from the Sun website at **http://java.sun.com/ products/sjwtoolkit/download-2_5.html**. From that page, you can access the download page depicted in Figure 5.1. The download executable for the JWT 2.5 is named sun_java_wireless_toolkit-2_5-windows.exe. As I suggested in Chapter 4 for the JDK and the MIDP, it is a good idea to create a downloads directory and to save installation packages there.

Figure 5.2 provides you with a view of the downloaded files used thus far in this book, along with the installer file for the JWT 2.5.

To initiate the installation of the JWT 2.5, use the Windows Add or Remove Programs dialog in the Control Panel. Click Add New Programs and then CD or Floppy. Navigate to your downloads directory and, after changing the setting for

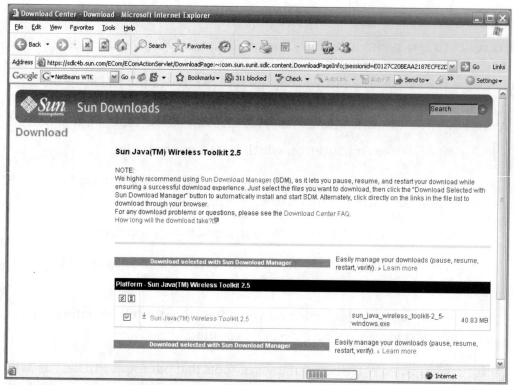

Figure 5.1
From the download page, select the JWT 2.5 for Windows.

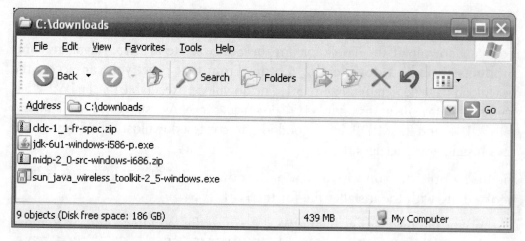

Figure 5.2
Java software can be stored temporarily in a downloads directory.

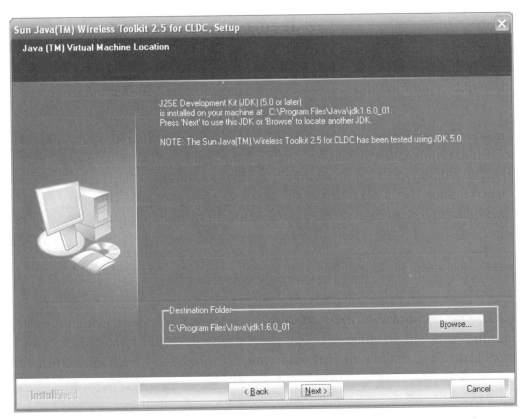

Figure 5.3
Install the JWT to the directory in which the JDK is installed.

file types to All Files, select sun_java_wireless_toolkit-2_5-windows.exe. (An alternative approach is to navigate to the downloads directory and click on the *.exe file for the JWT.)

After you initiate the installation, you encounter the JVM Location dialog, shown in Figure 5.3. This is the first of two locator dialogs you visit during the JWT 2.5 installation. Click the Browse button and navigate to the JDK directory. In Figure 5.3, this is shown as C:\ProgramFiles\Java\jdk1.6.0_01. The JWT installer can then verify that you have an appropriate version of the virtual machine. Keep in mind that the JTW requires the JDK 1.5.0, shown as 5.0 in Figure 5.3.

After you have located the JDK (or VM) in the JVM Location dialog, click Next to go the Choose Destination Location dialog. This dialog is shown in Figure 5.4. It identifies the location to which the files constituting the JWT 2.5 can be written. Use the default location (C:\WTK25) unless you have a specific reason to prefer another directory. If you choose another directory, make certain that its

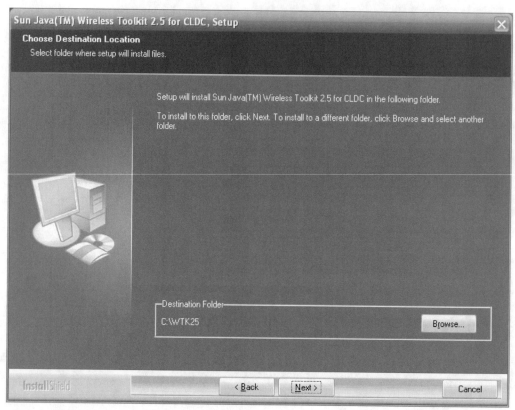

Figure 5.4
Accept the default location for the JWT installation.

path and name do not contain spaces. Spaces in the path can generate errors. Click Next to proceed.

After you designate the JVM and JWT directories, you are asked to designate a directory in which to place JWT icons. For standard Windows installations, the Accessories directory is the first default. Use this. Click Next to see the Start Copying Files dialog. This dialog provides you with a summary of the three directories the JWT uses. The information the dialog provides appears as follows:

```
Destination Directory
        C:\WTK25
Program Folder
        Sun Java(TM) Wireless Toolkit 2.5 for CLDC
JVM Folder
        C:\Program Files\Java\jdk1.6.0_01
```

The Basic WTK 2.5

After you have installed the JWT, you are ready to begin using it. To follow up on some of the activity in Chapter 4, it's possible, for starters, to work with a simple MIDlet. Select Start > All Programs > Sun Java (TM) Wireless Toolkit for CLDC > Wireless Toolkit 2.5. You then see the Sun Java (TM) Wireless Toolkit for CLDC dialog, as shown in Figure 5.5. (The JWT window is often designated the KToobar. This name is a holdover from previous versions of the JWT.)

From the File menu, select Open Project. You then see a number of MID software applications, as shown in Figure 5.6. You can select from among them and run

Figure 5.5
The Sun Java (TM) Wireless Toolkit for CLDC provides you immediate access to testing and development tools.

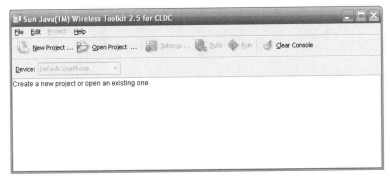

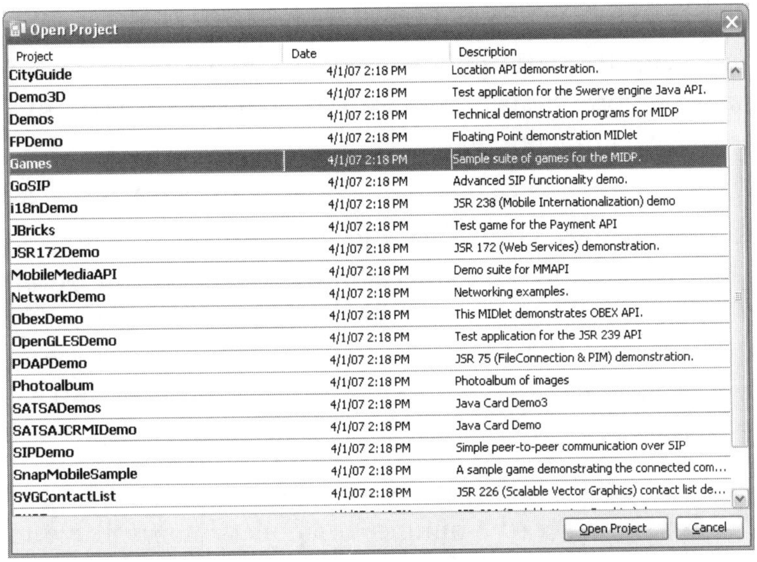

Figure 5.6
Select the Games listing and click Open Project.

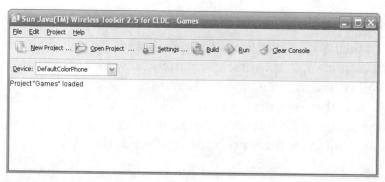

Figure 5.7
After you select one of the MIDlets from the list, click the Run icon on the toolbar.

them in the JWT emulator. Scroll down until you see "Games . . . Simple suite of games for the MIDP." Select this listing and click the Open Project button at the bottom of the window.

After you click the Open Project button, the JWT loads the MIDlet you have selected, as shown in Figure 5.7. At this point, you can select from a small set of standard device skins in the Device field's drop-down list. One is a QWERTY device. The others represent numbered keyboards. For now, leave the Default-ColorPhone as the Device field selection. To execute the application and see the emulator at work, click the Run icon on the toolbar.

After you click the Run icon, the MID phone emulator shown in Figure 5.8 appears. For the Games selection, the Java Application Manager (JAM) shows three MIDlets, each providing a different game.

To close the emulator, click on the close button on either the window or the emulator. When the emulator closes, you are back in the main JWT application window. Notice that the run data for the application is given. At this point, you can select a different device skin. For example, if you select the QWERTY skin and click the Run icon, the MIDlet you have selected (Game) generates a bi-fold device, as shown in Figure 5.9. As before, the JAM displays the MIDlet suite.

Most of the phone emulators have the same general appearance as those shown in Chapters 3 and 4. Generally, however, the number of applications available to you in the Open Project list of the JWT is large. If you are new to device programming, take some time to load and run them.

Figure 5.8
The phone emulator shows a suite of three MIDlets.

Creating a New Project

To create your own MIDlet application, start in the main JWT dialog (the Ktoolbar) and select File > New Project, or click the New Project icon on the toolbar. You see the New Project dialog. In the Project Name field, type Hello Toolkit. In the MIDlet Class Name field, type HelloToolkit again. Figure 5.10 shows the results. Click Create Project.

After you click Create Project in the New Project dialog, you see the API Selection dialog, which Figure 5.11 shows. In the Target Platform field near the top of the API Selection dialog, select JTWI. The dialog refreshes, and you see the Profiles and Configurations labels. Click the button for CLDC 1.1 under Configurations. Note that under Profiles, the profile is MIDP 2.0. Leave the Additional APIs checkboxes with their default values. (If you accidentally close the API Selection dialog, select Project > Settings from the main JWT menu and click the API Selection icon on the left.)

Figure 5.9
Select QWERTY from the Device drop-down list and click Run, and the Game MIDlet generates a bi-fold device emulation.

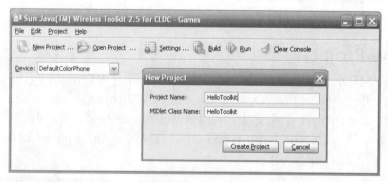

Figure 5.10
Name your Project and the MIDlet class.

On the right side of the API Selection dialog (Figure 5.11), just beneath the API Selection icon, is the Required icon. Click the Required icon. The dialog is refreshed, and you see the table shown in Figure 5.12. At this point, it is not necessary to do anything with this information. Note, however, that these settings represent the JAR, JAD, and manifest attributes you saw at work in Chapter 4.

Figure 5.11
Select the target platform and the MIDP 2.0 and CLDC 1.1.

Next, click on the User Defined icon. Figure 5.13 illustrates the resulting view. If you are accessing the project values for the first time, you see blank Name and Value fields. The Name and Value pair allow you to set up properties to use for testing.

In this case, add the Name property and its associated value. To add the property, click the Add button. The Add Property dialog appears (not shown here). In the Property Name field of the Add Property dialog, type Message. In the Property Value field, type Hello World. Click the OK button. The new property and its associated initial value are added. Note that you can change the name and the value by activating the fields associated with them. Figure 5.13 shows the User Defined pane with the Name property and its associated value added. When you develop the MIDlet later in this chapter, you can retrieve the Value text for display in the MIDlet. To close the dialog, click the OK button. You again see the

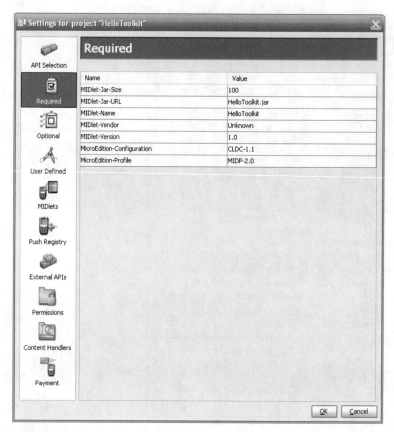

Figure 5.12
The Required view confirms the basic profile of your project.

main JWT window. To develop the code for your MIDlet, proceed to the next section.

Creating the HelloToolkit Source Code

This section assumes that you have completed the previously described tasks for the HelloToolkit MIDlet. If you have not done so, return to the previous section and start there. If you have set up the HelloToolkit MIDlet, then you are ready to implement the code for it.

When you use the JWT to develop the code for a MIDlet, you do not perform the same activities that you performed in Chapter 4 when you developed and ran the hello.java and hello2.java files. More specifically, when you use the JWT, you build and run a MIDlet without issuing preverify commands or creating

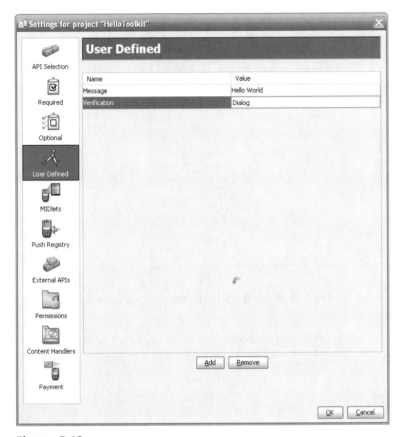

Figure 5.13
Click the Add button to add a new property and value pair.

manifest, JAR, and JAD files. Your activities are limited to typing a `*.java` file and then placing it in a directory where the JWT can find it.

Before typing the code for the MIDlet, consider that when you use the JWT to create the `HelloToolkit` project, the JWT automatically spawns a directory for the project. Figure 5.14 shows this directory in Windows Explorer. In this figure you can also see a `HelloToolkit.java` file. To proceed with your efforts, create this file. For example, you might use Notepad to save an empty file named `HelloToolkit.java` to the `apps\src` directory in the `WTK25` directory structure. As Figure 5.14 illustrates, the path is `C:\WTK25\apps\HelloToolkit\src`.

To implement the code for the file, you either type it or access the `HellToolkit.java` file in the Chapter 5 source code directory. The `HelloToolkit.java` code creates a MIDlet that closely resembles those you worked with in Chapter 4. With the `HelloToolkit` code, the only significant difference is that a call is made to the `getAppProperty()` method (see comment #1). This method retrieves the value

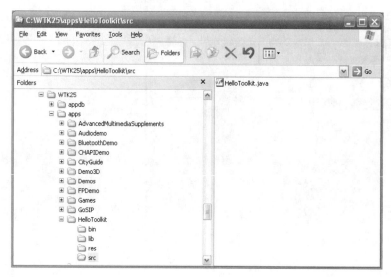

Figure 5.14
Place your source code file in the src directory, which the JWT spawns for your project.

associated with the `Message` property created in the User Defined dialog. Here is the code for the class:

```
/**
 * Chapter 5 \ HelloToolkit.java
 */
import javax.microedition.midlet.*;
import javax.microedition.lcdui.*;

public class HelloToolkit extends MIDlet
        implements CommandListener{
    protected Form form;
    protected Command quit;

    /**
     * Constructor for the MIDlet
     */
    public HelloToolkit(){
        // Create a form and add our components
        form = new Form("Hello JWT MIDlet");

        // #1 define the message attribute
        String msg = getAppProperty("Message");
        if (msg != null)
            form.append(msg);
```

```
    // Create a way to quit
    form.setCommandListener(this);
    quit = new Command("Quit", Command.SCREEN, 1);
    form.addCommand(quit);
}


/**
 * Called by the Application Manager when the MIDlet is starting
 */
protected void startApp() throws MIDletStateChangeException{
    // Display the form
    Display.getDisplay(this).setCurrent(form);
}


/**
 * Called by the MID Application Manager to pause the MIDlet.
*/
protected void pauseApp(){
}


/**
 * Called as the MIDlet is destroyed (removed from memory)
 */
protected void destroyApp(boolean unconditional)
        throws MIDletStateChangeException{
}


/**
 * Called when the user executes a command
 */
public void commandAction(Command command, Displayable displayable){
    // Check for our quit command and act accordingly
    try{
        if (command == quit){
            destroyApp(true);
            // Tell the Application Manager to exit
            notifyDestroyed();
        }
    }
    catch (MIDletStateChangeException me){
    }
}
}
```

Building and Running HelloToolkit.java

After you have placed the `HelloToolkit.java` file in the src directory in the JWT25 directory path, you can then build and run the MIDlet it creates. To accomplish this, in the main JWT window, click the Build icon on the toolbar. If you have correctly entered the code, you see the following message in the text area:

```
Project settings saved
Building "HelloToolkit"
Build complete
```

The build operation automatically runs the preverify command to check the validity of the syntax of your code. If there are errors, the error report appears in the text area of the JWT. Figure 5.15 illustrates a Java error message generated by a missing semicolon at the end of line 16 of the source code.

The JWT makes it convenient to debug your code, even if you are working with only the most elementary text editor. If you are working with Notepad, for example, you can use the Alt + Tab option to switch back and forth.

When the JWT reports that the build is successful, click the Run icon in the JWT toolbar. You then see the emulator with your MIDlet displayed in the JAM. Figure 5.16 illustrates the `HelloToolkit` MIDlet. Click the navigation button at the top of the keyboard to see the text associated with the `Message` property displayed.

Note that when you choose the emulator, as Figure 5.17 reveals, useful diagnostic information appears in the JWT text area.

As an experiment, click the Settings icon of the JWT window. Click the User Defined icon. Click the Value field that corresponds to the `Message` property. Change the text in the Value field to "Message from home." If you click on the

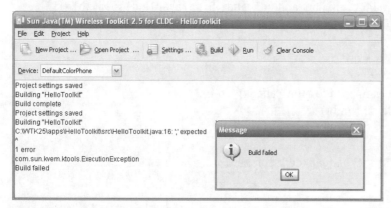

Figure 5.15
The Build process detects a syntax error.

Figure 5.16
The JWT runs the HelloToolkit MIDlet in the emulator.

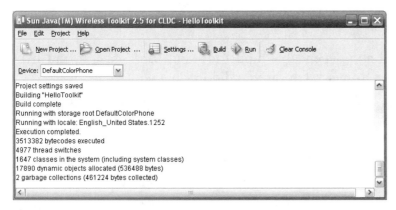

Figure 5.17
Useful information appears in the toolkit console after executing a MIDlet.

field, it is activated for change. When you finish, click the OK button of the User Defined view. Now rebuild and run the HelloToolkit MIDlet. Click the navigation button on the keyboard to see the text newly assigned to the Message property.

Creating JAD, JAR, and Manifest Files

Once your MIDlet Java file builds and compiles without problems, you can use the JWT to generate a manifest, a JAR file, and a JAD file. To accomplish this, select Project > Package > Create Package.

The JWT creates manifest, JAR, and JAD files for you and places them in the bin directory of your application. You then find them along this path:

```
C:\WTK25\apps\HelloToolkit\bin
```

After you have generated the package files, navigate to your bin directory. You should see the following files:

```
04/06/2007    04:37 PM      275 HelloToolkit.jad
04/06/2007    04:37 PM    1,310 HelloToolkit.jar
04/06/2007    04:37 PM      198 MANIFEST.MF
```

Use Notepad to open the `HelloToolkit.jad` file. The contents are as follows:

```
MIDlet-1: HelloToolkit, HelloToolkit.png, HelloToolkit
MIDlet-Jar-Size: 1310
MIDlet-Jar-URL: HelloToolkit.jar
MIDlet-Name: HelloToolkit
MIDlet-Vendor: Unknown
MIDlet-Version: 1.0
Message: Hello MIDlet World
MicroEdition-Configuration: CLDC-1.1
MicroEdition-Profile: MIDP-2.0
```

This provides a useful and dependable model for your `manifest.txt` and JAD files if you are working from scratch (as you did in Chapter 4).

If you issue the following command, the emulator runs, but it also generates an error.

```
midp -classpath . -Xdescriptor HelloToolkit.jad
```

The error tells you that the emulator cannot find the `HelloToolkit.class` file. You see this error if you click the Select button on the emulator.

To solve this problem, copy the `HelloToolkit.class` file from the HelloToolkit\ class directory to the HelloToolkit\bin directory.

To test your `Message` property through the JAD file, change the text as follows for the Message line:

```
Message: Hello MIDlet World once again
```

Save and close the JAD file and reissue the MIDP command. The message you see when you click the Select button reveals that text assigned to the property has been changed.

JWT Options

A few additional notes regarding the use of the JWT 2.5 might be helpful. First, to save the output of the build and run actions, you can select File > Save Console. This action lets you save a text file to the sessions subdirectory of the JTW25 directory. If you select File > Open Project, the Open Project dialog appears, and as Figure 5.18 indicates, you find your newly created project listed among the others.

To remove a project from the project list, navigate to the src file and remove the folder that contains the project. In this instance, for example, you would remove

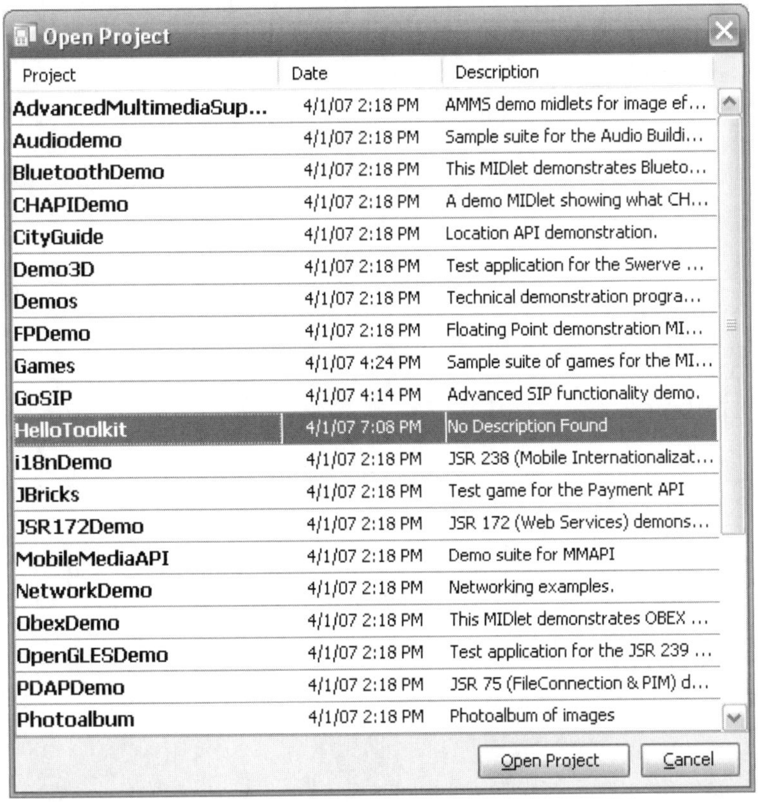

Figure 5.18
Your MIDlet project appears in the project list.

HelloToolkit. For now, leave the project as it is so that you can return to it in subsequent exercises.

Conclusion

In this chapter, you have worked with the Java Wireless Toolkit 2.5. This application allows you to test the code in your Java MIDlet files by building and running the MIDlet. You install the JWT 2.5 application to its own directory, and as you use it, it generates directories for each project you create. To use the JWT, you must configure an API Selection dialog to indicate the version of the CLDC you are using (in this case, version 1.0). As you work toward a more advanced understanding of MIDlet development, you can make greater use of the configuration options. In the User Defined pane of the Settings dialog, you can create properties that you can then use for testing. The getAppProperty() method allows you acquire the property through your code for display in the JAM. The JWT 2.5 does not provide a comprehensive IDE, but even if you employ it in conjunction with a simple text editor, it expedites your development efforts tremendously.

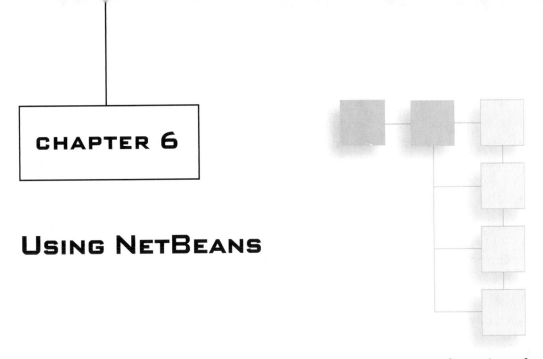

CHAPTER 6

USING NETBEANS

In this chapter, you explore the NetBeans 5.5 IDE. A summary discussion of NetBeans was presented in Chapter 5, in Table 5.1. As Table 5.1 indicates, the NetBeans IDE is an integrated development environment (IDE) for Java developers. NetBeans is an open source application, so you are not obligated to pay for it. It executes on Windows, Linux, Mac OS, and Solaris systems, and you can use it to develop with languages other than Java, notably C and C++. Its default language is Java, and you add language packages to it to make it work with other languages. These packages are free from the NetBeans website (**NetBeans.org**). You can also add packages that support mobile device development. Two of these are especially important in this chapter. One supports basic MID software development and is comparable to the Java Wireless Toolkit. The other is a much more enhanced package that allows you to use a graphical user interface (GUI) to create device display layouts from scratch. While the focus of this book is on basic MID software, in this chapter you review how to access, download, and install the additional packages for MID software development. You also make use of a slightly modified version of the MIDlet code presented in Chapter 5 to develop a MIDlet using the NetBeans IDE.

The NetBeans IDE

This book is not meant to leave you dependent on any given toolset or IDE. However, as the discussion in Chapter 5 reveals, the Java Wireless Toolkit provides a ready way for you to test and refine your Java MID code without having to repeatedly update manifest, JAR, and JAD files. NetBeans extends this capability into a comprehensive development setting. With NetBeans, while you have access to the advantages afforded by the Java Wireless Toolkit, you also have the support of many project management, configuration, and debugging tools that cover most of your development activities. If you download the JDK 1.5.x (or the JDK 1.6.x), you can elect to include the download of the NetBeans IDE and easily install it from there. After the installation, you are in a position to program, compile, and run your Java programs without having to perform any configuration work at all. A second point is that the documentation for the NetBeans IDE is comprehensive and easy to access. In many respects it compares well with the Microsoft Studio IDE and its documentation, which in its Express editions is also now available at no charge.

To make use of the NetBeans IDE for MID development, you must attend to the installation of the JDK and MIDP software. Chapters 4 and 5 provide routines to aid with such activity. This book makes use of the JDK 1.5.x and the MIDP 2.0. It also documents the NetBeans 5.5 IDE, which requires that you install version 1.5.x or later of the JDK.

The primary advertised features of NetBeans IDE are the following:

- It provides an excellent IDE for Java programmers, and it is certainly the best such IDE in the open source world.

- For activities involving MID development, it provides a variety of applications that allow you to develop, test, and deploy MIDlets and MIDlet suites.

- It comprehensively supports web development activities, providing an extensive set of default components while making it easy to upload many others from other sources.

- It fully addresses enterprise development efforts involving programming using such protocols and standards as XML Schema, Web Services Description Language (WSDL), Business Process Execution Language (BPEL), and secure web services.

- For modelling and architectural efforts, it provides access to capabilities that support application development based on Service Oriented Architecture (SOA).

- It supports C/C++ development on largely the same level that it supports Java development and includes capabilities that address memory management.

Installing NetBeans

To download the NetBeans IDE, you have two general options. As previously noted, if you download version 1.5.x or higher of the JDK, you have the option of including it with your download. If you have already installed the JDK but do not yet have the NetBeans IDE, then you can access it at the NetBeans home page at **http://www.netbeans.org**.

As Figure 6.1 illustrates, the NetBeans home page gives you immediate access to both the NetBeans IDE and the primary services or packages associated with the NetBeans IDE. To download the current version of the NetBeans IDE, click the Download NetBeans IDE button.

You then see the NetBeans IDE 5.5 download page, as shown in Figure 6.2. To continue with the download, immediately click one of the mirror links. This action invokes a File Download dialog. Prior to initiating the download, create a download directory on your local drive. If you have followed the routines discussed in Chapter 4 and Chapter 5, you have already created a directory called downloads.

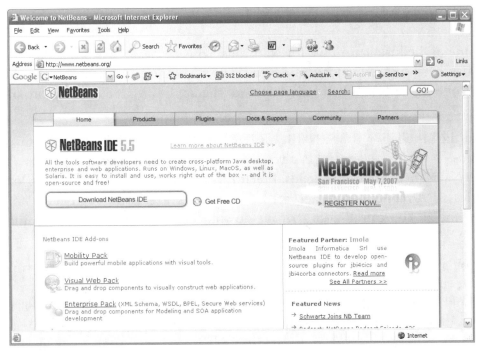

Figure 6.1
On the download page, click the Download NetBeans IDE button.

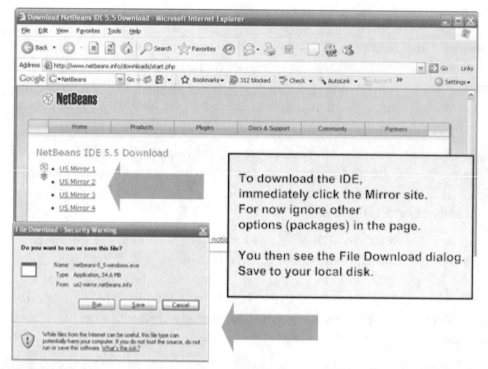

Figure 6.2
Click on a mirror site, and the Download dialog for the NetBeans IDE appears.

The name of the installation file for NetBeans 5.5 is `netbeans-5_5-windows.exe`. Save this file to your downloads directory. The size of the download is roughly 55 MB for version 5.5. When fully installed, the application takes up approximately 225 MB.

To start the installation of the NetBeans IDE, use the Windows Add or Remove Programs dialog in the Control Panel. Click Add New Programs and then CD or Floppy. Navigate to your downloads directory and, after changing the setting for file types to All Files, select `netbeans-5_5-windows.exe`. (Although it is not recommended, you can also go to your downloads directory and click on the *.exe file.)

After you initiate the installation program, it provides a dialog that lets you designate a directory in which to place the NetBeans IDE (see Figure 6.3). By default on Windows the installer places the application in the Program Files directory under a subdirectory identifying the current version of NetBeans. If you have a previous version, the installer does not write over it. You can install different versions without problems, but they must be in unique directories.

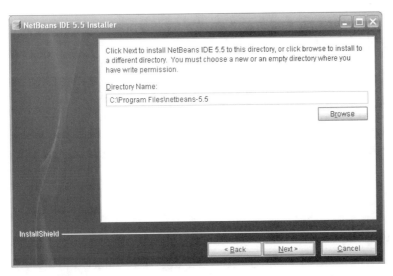

Figure 6.3
The IDE installs to a unique directory.

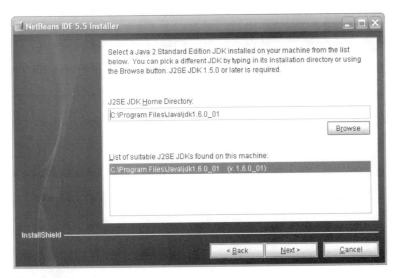

Figure 6.4
For the projects in this book, select JDK version 1.5.x or greater.

After you designate the target directory, you select the version of the JDK that you want to use with the NetBeans IDE. As Figure 6.4 illustrates, the version used for this book is 1.6.0_01. NetBeans readily works with version 1.4.x, but 1.5.x is necessary for use with the mobile software discussed in this book. If you have version 1.5.x of the JDK installed, you should not have any problems with the software in this book, but keep in mind that the software has been developed with the version shown in Figure 6.4.

After you select the version of the JDK you want to associate with your installation of the NetBeans IDE, click Next. The installation proceeds from there, and when it concludes, you can go directly to the Start menu to test a Java program. At this point, you have a few more tasks to perform before you can develop MIDlets using the NetBeans IDE. Subsequent sections of this chapter detail how you download the packages for the IDE you require to equip it to facilitate your MIDlet development efforts.

Sanity Check the IDE

To verify that you have correctly installed the NetBeans IDE, select Start > All Programs > NetBeans 5.5 and open the NetBeans IDE. Figure 6.5 illustrates your

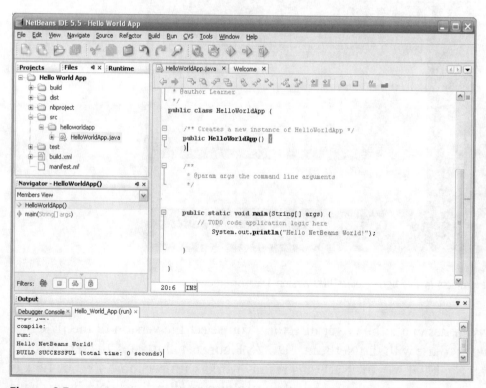

Figure 6.5
Confirm that your installation of the NetBeans IDE was successful.

first view of the application. A starter project, Hello World App, is set up for you, and as you might expect, a HelloWorldApp class is the main class in the project. This class is ready to compile and run. Here are a few starter points:

- In the Chapter 6 code folder is a project called HelloWorldApp. To open this project, select File > Open Project. Navigate to Chapter6MIDlets. Open the folder and click on HelloWorldApp. Then click on Open Project Folder.

- Notice in Figure 6.5 that the Files tab has been clicked and that the path to the HelloWorldApp.java file has been opened. Also, a word has been added to the standard Hello World! output in the println() method ("Hello NetBeans World!"). The lower pane on the left profiles the class, revealing the class constructor and the main() function. If you double-click an item, the cursor moves to the appropriate line. This way, you can easily change your own starter message.

- To build projects, select Build > Build Main Project, or press F11.

- To run the program, select Run > Main Project, or press F6.

- To invoke the debugger only, select Run > Debug Main Project, or press F5.

The NetBeans IDE provides hundreds of services that supplement your development activities. Specific discussion of these lies outside the scope of the current chapter, but an effort is made to review those that are essential to MIDlet development.

A couple of other items might prove interesting as starter activities:

- Notice that after you build the application (press F11), the Output window tells you that the IDE has generated a JAR file for the HelloWorldApp class. As an experiment, you can copy the given command to the Command Prompt window and execute the JAR file from there.

```
java -jar "C:\Documents and Settings\Hello World
App\dist\Hello_World_App.jar"
```

- If you want to access starter information about the IDE, select Help > Quick Start Guide. This tutorial shows you how to set up HelloWorldApp for yourself.

Adding Mobility

After you have installed the NetBeans IDE, you can add two supplemental packages to fully equip yourself to work with MID programs. This book does not make full use of both, but it is worthwhile to install them now. The two packages you install are as follows:

- **Basic Mobility Package**. This package is associated with an executable named `netbeans-mobility-5_5-win.exe`. In the NetBeans download page, as shown in Figure 6.6, click the NetBeans Mobility 5.5 Installer link. Mobility is a primary package that equips the IDE with some services similar to those provided by the Java Wireless Toolkit. You require this package if you want to see the Mobility folder when you select Project > New in the NetBeans Project options.

- **CDC Mobility Package**. This package is associated with an executable named `netbeans-cdc-5_5-win.exe`. In the download page, as shown in Figure 6.7, click the NetBeans Mobility CDC Pack 5.5 Installer link. This is an extremely powerful package that allows you to develop almost any

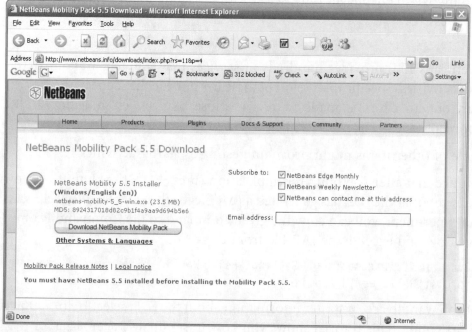

Figure 6.6
Navigate to the download page.

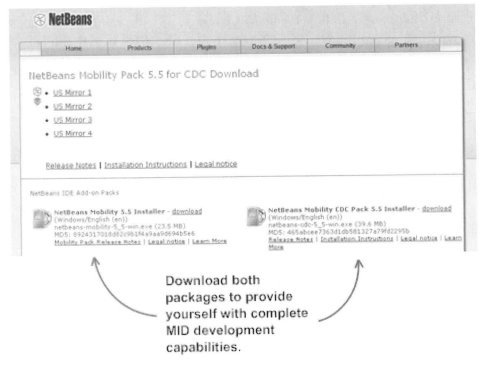

Figure 6.7
Start with the CDC package and click the package link before the mirror link.

type of MID application you can name. Its full capabilities lie beyond the scope of this book. You require this package if you want to see the CDC option when you select Project > New.

After you complete your installation of the mobility packages, you can carry out the activities this book describes without needing to further configure the Net-Beans IDE.

Note

For other platforms, however, additional installations are necessary. For example, special packages are available for Sony Ericsson and Nokia. These installation activities lie beyond the scope of this book, as do development activities geared specifically toward such platforms.

Downloading Mobility Packages

As mentioned in the previous section, you download two packages that allow you to work with MID software development using the NetBeans IDE. These packages are often referred to as *mobility packages*. To access the NetBeans mobility packages, go to the NetBeans Internet site: **http://www.netbeans.org**.

In the NetBeans page, you see a Mobility Pack link. Click this. It takes you to the main Mobility Pack page. In the main Mobility Pack page (not pictured), click the button labeled Download NetBeans Mobility Pack for CDC. This takes you to a page titled NetBeans Mobility Pack 5.5 Download, as shown in Figure 6.6.

Click the Download NetBeans Mobility Pack button pictured in Figure 6.6. This takes you to the download page shown in Figure 6.7. You then see a page with a number of mirror links. Observe that in the lower part of the page there are two packages associated with MID development. As Figure 6.7 illustrates, these are the NetBeans Mobility 5.5 Installer and the NetBeans Mobility CDC Pack 5.5 Installer.

To start, download the mobility package that includes CDC in the title. This is the larger of the two packages. To initiate the download, first click the download link for the CDC package; the page refreshes. Then click one of the mirror links. Note that the links refresh according to the download link you click, so do not click one of the mirror links without first clicking the download link for the package you want to access.

When the File Download dialog appears, you see `netbeans-cdc-5_5-win.exe` (or the executable for the version current for you). Click the Save option and save the file to your downloads directory. The size of the file is approximately 40 MB.

Now return to the NetBeans download page (as shown in Figure 6.7) and click the download link for the NetBeans Mobility 5.5 Installer. Remember to click the download link before clicking the mirror site link. When the File Download dialog appears, you should see the `netbeans-mobility-5_5-win.exe` (or the executable for the version current for you). Click the Save option and save the file to your downloads directory. The size of the file is approximately 25 MB.

Installing the CDC Mobility Package

The installation of the mobility packages require that you first install the JDK 1.5.x or higher and NetBeans 5.5 or higher. If you have not done so, revisit the start of this chapter and Chapter 4 for instructions on how to install these two items.

To install the CDC mobility packages, use the Windows Add or Remove Programs dialog in the Control Panel. Click Add New Programs and then CD or Floppy. Navigate to your downloads directory and, after changing the setting for file

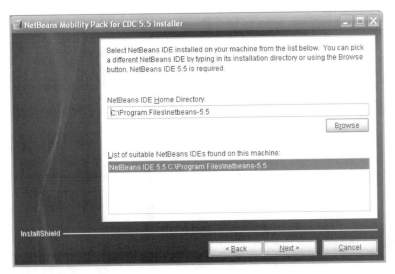

Figure 6.8
Associate the mobility package with a version of NetBeans.

types to All Files, select the `netbeans-cdc-5_5-win.exe`. (Although it is not recommended, you can also go to your downloads directory and click on the *.exe file.)

As Figure 6.8 illustrates, after you initiate the installation of the NetBeans Mobility Pack 5.5 for CDC, the installer allows you to associate a version of NetBeans with your mobility package. Any version that is 5.5 or greater is suitable. Choose a version and click Next.

In the next dialog, the installer allows you to associate the mobility package with a version of the JDK. Any version that is 1.5.x or greater is suitable. Choose your version and then click Next. You see a dialog that identifies the path of a currently installed JDK, as Figure 6.9 illustrates.

You then see the statistics on the installation. The NetBeans Mobility Pack 5.5 for CDC requires around 140 MB of memory. The default installation location is `C:\Program Files\netbeans-5.5\cdc2`. Click Next to initiate the file installation process. When the installation completes, click Finish in the dialog that appears.

Installing the Basic Mobility Package

Before you can install the basic mobility package, you must have installed the JDK 1.5.x or higher and NetBeans 5.5 or higher. If you have not done so, revisit

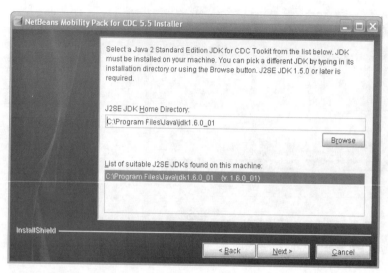

Figure 6.9
Associate the mobility package with a version of the JDK.

the start of this chapter and Chapter 4. At this point, it is also assumed that you have downloaded the basic mobility package and installed the CDC mobility package. If you have not done so, revisit the previous section.

To install the basic mobility package, you can use the Windows Add or Remove Programs dialog, or you can go to your downloads directory and click on the *.exe file. Generally, it is recommended that you install through the Add or Remove Programs dialog. Select the netbeans-mobility-5_5-win.exe file for installation.

Like the CDC mobility package, the basic mobility package's installation program first allows you to associate the package with a version of the JDK and a version of NetBeans. Associate the basic mobility package with the same versions you selected for the CDC mobility package. The JDK must be version 1.5.x or greater. The version of NetBeans must be 5.5 or greater. As Figure 6.10 illustrates, the package is installed to the Program Files directory. The size of the package is approximately 40 MB. Proceed to the final dialog of the installation. Click Finish in the final dialog to conclude the installation.

Confirming Mobile and CDC

After you have installed the basic mobility and the CDC mobility packages, open the NetBeans IDE. Select File > New Project. In the New Project window, shown

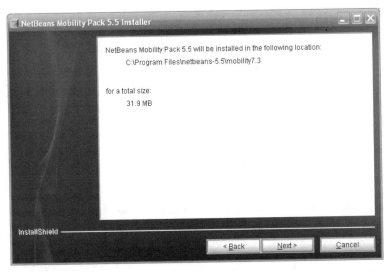

Figure 6.10
The basic mobility package is smaller than the CDC package.

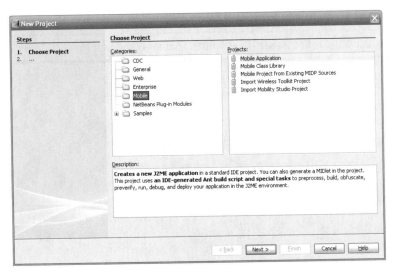

Figure 6.11
The `Mobile` and `CDC` folders are added with your installation of the two mobile packages.

in Figure 6.11, you see folders for CDC and Mobile. Mobile represents the basic package. CDC represents the CDC package. The presence of these two folders (project types) indicates that your installations have been successfully completed. You can now proceed to create a MIDlet.

Creating a MIDlet Project

To create a MIDlet, open the NetBeans IDE. Close any files that might be open in the IDE. Then choose File > New Project.

You see the New Project Dialog, as shown previously in Figure 6.11. In the Categories pane of the New Projects dialog, click the Mobile folder.

In the Projects pane of the New Project dialog, you see several types of project. In this instance, click Mobile Application. Then click Next. You then see the Name and Location dialog, as shown in Figure 6.12.

For the Project Name field, type `HelloNetBeansMIDlet`. For the Project Location field, click Browse and select the projects folder under the J2ME directory you created in Chapter 3: C:\j2me\projects.

For the Set as Main Project checkbox (as shown in Figure 6.12), check the checkbox. For the Create Hello MIDlet checkbox, uncheck the checkbox. Now click Next.

Note

For reference, you can find a `HelloNetBeansMIDlet` in the Chapter 6 code folder.

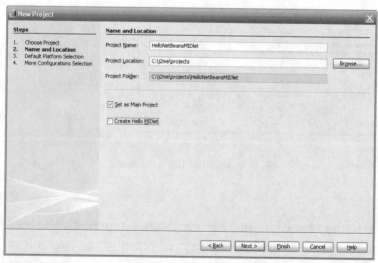

Figure 6.12
Populate the Name and Location fields.

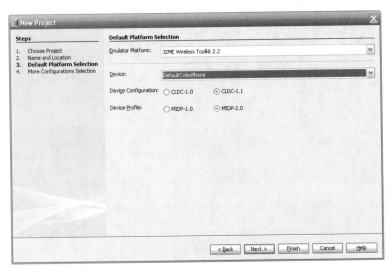

Figure 6.13
Accept the default version of the emulator and verify the Configuration and Profile settings.

Figure 6.13 reveals the Default Platform Selection dialog you see next. If you worked through Chapter 5, you might immediately notice that the version of the Java Wireless Toolkit you see is not version 2.5. The version you see depends on what has been used with the NetBeans mobility packages. In this case, for example, the version level is 2.2. Leave the Emulator Platform as is. For the Devices setting, select DefaultColorPhone. For the Device Configuration, select CLDC-1.1. For the Device Profile, select MIDP-2.0. With the exception of the version level for the JWT, these settings are the same as those you used for the Java Wireless Toolkit emulation in Chapter 5. Click Finish.

If you now click on the Files tab in the pane on the left side of the IDE window, you see that the HelloNetBeansMIDlet project has been created (see Figure 6.14). Likewise, if you access Windows Explorer, you see that subdirectories have now been set up in the J2ME path in a project directory called HelloNetBeansMIDlet. The subdirectories correspond to the folders shown in the left pane in Figure 6.14.

In the directory tree in the left pane of the NetBeans IDE window, right-click the HelloNetBeansMIDlet folder. You see a pop-up menu, as shown in Figure 6.15. Select New > File\Folder . . . .

Next you see the Choose File Type dialog, as shown in Figure 6.16. This dialog resembles the New Project folder, but the two panes are now titled Category and

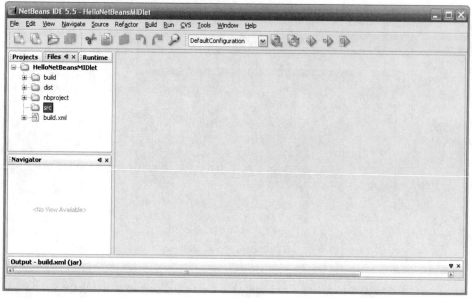

Figure 6.14
The NetBeans IDE provides you with standard project and file panes.

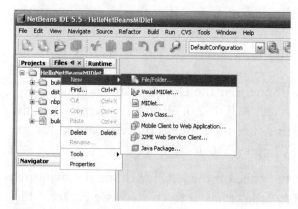

Figure 6.15
Create a new folder for the project.

File Type instead of Category and Project Type. Under Category, click the MIDP folder. Under File Type, click MIDlet. Then click Next.

You now see the New File dialog. In the MIDlet Name field, type Hello-NetBeansMIDlet. As shown in Figure 6.17, the IDE automatically populates the MIDlet Class Name field for you with the same name. Click Finish.

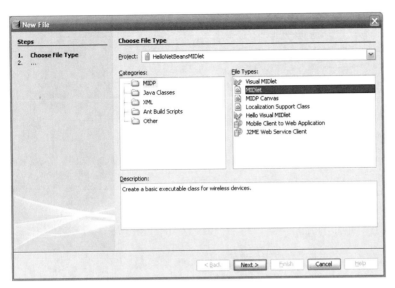

Figure 6.16
Select MIDP and MIDlet.

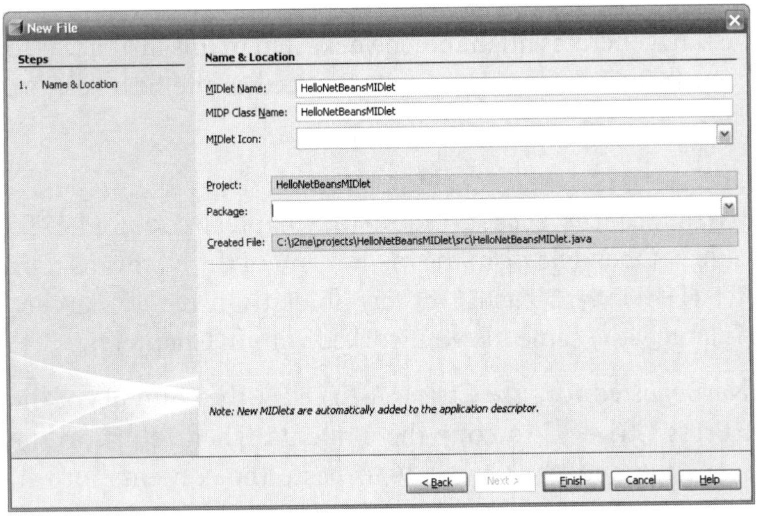

Figure 6.17
Type the name of the MIDlet.

The NetBeans IDE now creates the `HelloNetBeansMIDlet.java` file, as Figure 6.18 shows. To locate the file, click the `src` folder in the left pane of the IDE. When you click on the file name, you see a profile of its methods in the Navigator pane. If you save the code in the file, you see that it provides basic MIDlet methods, a constructor, and essential import statements.

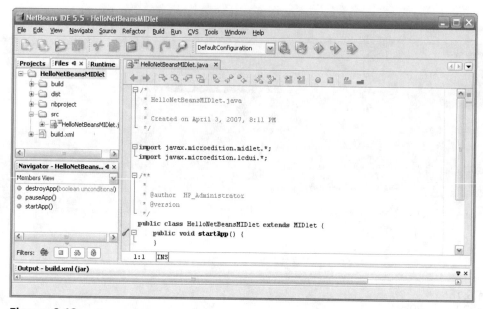

Figure 6.18
The IDE creates the shell of the new class.

As useful as the code the IDE generates might be, the next step in this instance is to delete it and add the code from a previous exercise. Proceed to the next section.

Adding Code

To create a MIDlet, access the `Starter_Code.txt` file in the Chapter 6 code folder. To accomplish this, select File > Open File from the main menu of the NetBeans IDE. Navigate to the Chapter 6 `HelloNetBeansMIDlet\src` folder. Open the `Starter_Code.txt` file. This file is largely the same file you worked with in Chapter 5.

Now, working in the NetBeans editor, use Ctrl + A to select the contents of the `Starter_Code.txt` file. Press Ctrl + C to copy the contents. Then return to the `HelloNetBeansMIDlet.java` file and use Ctrl + V to paste the contents into it. When you finish, close the `Starter_Code.txt` file by clicking the x on the file tab at the top of the IDE edit area.

Note

As a precaution, do not try to copy a *.java file into the src directory of your NetBeans project and then make it compile as a part of the product. NetBeans does not yet support such activity. You must use the New > File/Folder or File > New File options to add a new file to a project. Use the menu options to add a file of the appropriate name. After that, delete the contents of the new file and copy the contents from the source file into it.

While the code for HelloNetBeansMIDlet.java is largely the same as the code you worked with in Chapter 5, there are a few differences. At comment #1, an attribute of the String type (msg) is declared. Following comment #2, the constructor of the String class is used to create an instance of the String class, which is assigned to the msg attribute. In the next line, the Form::append() method is called so that you can see the text assigned to the msg displayed by the MIDlet.

N o t e

Beginning in Chapter 9, such classes as Form, Command, and String are dealt with in greater detail. For now, the task focuses on demonstrating the use of NetBeans. For this reason, comments in the code and elsewhere are kept to a minimum.

Here is the code for the HelloNetBeansMIDlet.java file. You can find this file in the Chapter 6 HelloNetBeans project folder, along with the Starter_Code.txt file:

```
/*
 * Chapter 6 \ HelloNetBeansMIDlet.java
 *
 */

import javax.microedition.midlet.*;
import javax.microedition.lcdui.*;

public class HelloNetBeansMIDlet extends MIDlet
                            implements CommandListener{
    // Attributes to display the message
    protected Form form;
    // process the Quit command
    protected Command quit;
    // #1 Process the message written to the Form (display)
    protected String msg;

    public HelloNetBeansMIDlet(){
        form = new Form("Hello NetBeans MIDlet");

    // #2 Assign a value -- change to experiment
        msg = new String("NetBeans is at Work!");

        // Write to the display
        form.append(msg);
```

```
        // Calls to register the Quit command
        form.setCommandListener(this);
        quit = new Command("Quit", Command.SCREEN, 1);
        form.addCommand(quit);
    }
    //End of constructor

    protected void startApp() throws MIDletStateChangeException{
        // Display the form
        Display.getDisplay(this).setCurrent(form);
    }

    protected void pauseApp(){
    }

    protected void destroyApp(boolean unconditional)
            throws MIDletStateChangeException{
    }

    public void commandAction(Command command, Displayable displayable)
    {
        // Check for the quit command and act accordingly
        try{
            if (command == quit){
                destroyApp(true);
                // Tell the Application Manager to exit
                notifyDestroyed();
            }
        }
        catch (MIDletStateChangeException me){
        }
    }
}
```

After you have typed or copied the code into the edit area of the IDE, press F11 to build the project. To run the MIDlet, press F6.

Figure 6.19 illustrates the output of the MIDlet you create with the Hello-NetBeans.java file. To operate the MIDlet, click the SELECT button. To quit the MIDlet, click the soft button beneath click. (You can also press F2 or F1 for the soft keys.) The text assigned to the msg attribute is displayed. To experiment,

Figure 6.19
The emulator is invoked, and you see your MIDlet.

change the text message (see the line following comment #2). Rebuild the project by pressing F11 as you make your changes. To debug your code, right-click on the name of the file in the Projects pane and select Compile File.

The JAD and JAR Files

Recall from Chapter 5 that the Message property was defined in the dialog that corresponded to the JAD file in the JWT interface. The getAppProperty() method retrieved the defined value. By changing your code and a line in the JAD file for your NetBeans MIDlet, you can restore the getAppProperty() method to your source code and again see the effect of processing the Message property.

The NetBeans IDE incorporates the functionality of the Java Wireless Toolkit (JWT), and just as the JWT generated JAR and JAD files, the NetBeans IDE also

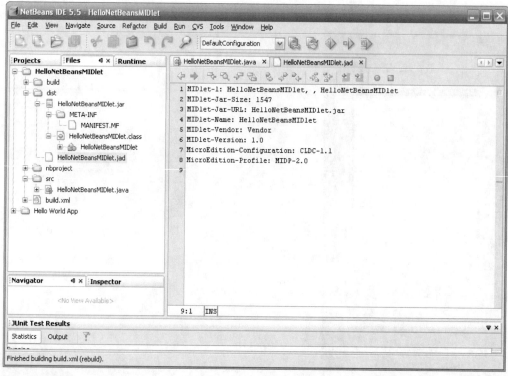

Figure 6.20
The IDE generates JAD and JAR files by using the JWT capabilities.

generates such files. To locate these files, first Select Window > Files from the main menu of the NetBeans IDE. You then see the JAR and JAD files. Click the dist folder, as shown in Figure 6.20. Click the JAD file. You see the contents of the HelloNetBeansMIDlet.jad file displayed in the NetBeans edit window.

As the text of the HelloNetBeansMIDlet.jad file shown in Figure 6.20 reveals, the Property-Value pair that establishes the Message property you used in Chapter 5 is missing from the JAD file. To make it so that a message you provide from the JAD file appears, you can make a few modifications to the file. The next section guides you through this activity. Close HelloNetBeansMIDlet.jad. Proceed to the next section before changing the JAD file.

Adding the Message

At this point, you can alter the code so that it can accommodate a message. To perform this task, begin by making a backup copy of the code in your HelloNetBeansMIDlet.java file. To accomplish this, select Window > Files so that you see the File pane of the `HelloNetBeansMIDlet` project. Then right-click on the name of the project at the top of the File pane. Select New Empty File. In the New Empty File dialog, type `HelloNetBeansMIDlet.txt`. Verify that you have included the `txt` file extension. Click Finish.

A file named `HelloNetBeansMIDlet.txt` appears in the edit pane. If the File pane vanishes, click on it in the left margin of the IDE to restore it. Click `Hello NetBeansMIDlet.java` under the `src` folder and select its contents using Ctrl + A and then Ctrl + C to copy. Then use Ctrl + V to paste the contents of the source file into `HelloNetBeansMIDlet.txt`.

Having made a backup, modify the code in `HelloNetBeansMIDlet.java` so that beginning at comment #1 it reads as follows:

```
// #1 And process the message written to the Form (display)
 protected String msg;
 public HelloNetBeansMIDlet()
 {
   form = new Form("Hello NetBeans MIDlet");

  // #2 Assign a default value
    msg = new String("NetBeans is at Work!");
    form.append(msg);
  // Assign a new one if there is one there to assign
    msg = getAppProperty("Message");
    if(msg != null){
      //Remove the default message
      form.deleteAll();
      //Display the Message value from the JAD file
      form.append(msg);
    }
  }
  //End of constructor
```

Build and run your project to verify that your code contains no errors. The goal now is to edit the JAD file the project has generated.

Note

The alternative code is provided in the "`Constructor with Message.txt`" file in the `Hello-NetBeansMIDlet src` folder in the Chapter 6 source directory.

Changing the JAD File

The NetBeans IDE creates difficulties if you try to edit a JAD file. For this reason, luse Windows Explorer to locate the `C:\j2me\projects\HelloNetBeansMIDlet\dist` directory. You find the JAD and JAR files there. Use Notepad, not the NetBeans editor, to open the `HelloNetBeansMIDlet.jad` file. Modify it by adding one ine for the `Message` property. The new text you add is shown in bold:

```
MIDlet-1: HelloNetBeansMIDlet, , HelloNetBeansMIDlet
MIDlet-Jar-Size: 1547
MIDlet-Jar-URL: HelloNetBeansMIDlet.jar
MIDlet-Name: HelloNetBeansMIDlet
MIDlet-Vendor: Vendor
MIDlet-Version: 1.0
Message: This is a new message
MicroEdition-Configuration: CLDC-1.1
MicroEdition-Profile: MIDP-2.0
```

Save but do not close the JAD file.

Now use Windows Explorer to open the preverified folder of your NetBeans project. The project path is `HelloNetBeansMIDlet\build\preverified`. In this folder, you find the version of the `HelloNetBeansMIDlet.class` file that the pre-verify command has generated. Copy this file to the dist directory:

```
C:\j2me\projects\HelloNetBeansMIDlet\dist
```

Now navigate to the dist directory using the Command Prompt. (To accomplish this, use the routine described in the sidebar, "Drag and Drop Navigation.") After you have navigated to the dist directory, your prompt reads as follows:

```
C:\j2me\projects\HelloNetBeansMIDlet\dist>
```

Issue the following command:

```
midp -classpath . -Xdescriptor HelloNetBeansMIDlet.jad
```

The emulator starts, and you can click the Select button to see the value assigned to the `Message` property, as shown in Figure 6.21. You now have a number of windows open, so you can easily move back and forth to change the values in the JAD file if you want to continue to experiment.

Figure 6.21
Alter the JAD file to see changing values of the Message property.

Note

When NetBeans builds your MIDlet, it erases the changes you make to the JAD file.

Drag and Drop Navigation

To make it easier to work with some of the obscure directory paths you deal with in this chapter, open a Command Prompt and Windows Explorer, as shown in Figure 6.22. In the Command Prompt window, type CD at the prompt. Type a space afterward. Click on the name of the directory that contains the file in Windows Explorer. Drag it and drop it into the Command Prompt window. Press Return.

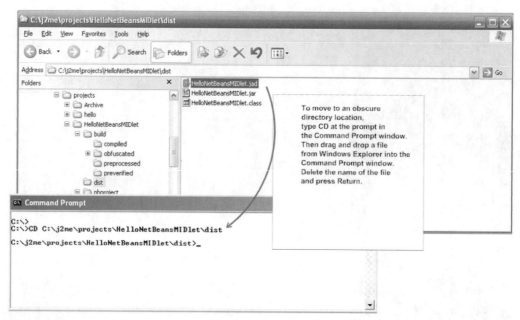

Figure 6.22
To make it easier to navigate, drag and drop.

Conclusion

In this chapter, you downloaded and installed the NetBeans IDE 5.5. You then downloaded and installed the NetBeans Mobility 5.5 Installer and the NetBeans Mobility CDC Pack 5.5 Installer. These two packages provide you with comprehensive capabilities for developing mobile device software in the Net-Beans IDE. Using these packages, you then created a project for a MIDlet and a Java file to define the MIDlet. You replaced the code automatically generated for the MIDlet with code taken largely from the project discussed in Chapter 5. Using the work previously completed with the Java Wireless Toolkit, you have been able to explore how the NetBeans IDE can facilitate your MID software development efforts. You can now see that the work of the JWT is included in the NetBeans mobility packages. The different versions of the JWT in this and the previous chapter present no problems with the code being used. The code was originally compiled with one version of the JWT. When you move to another version, such as the 2.2 version, you see a different emulator. From this point, the prospect opens to include examination of the classes and algorithms involved in developing MID game software.

PART III

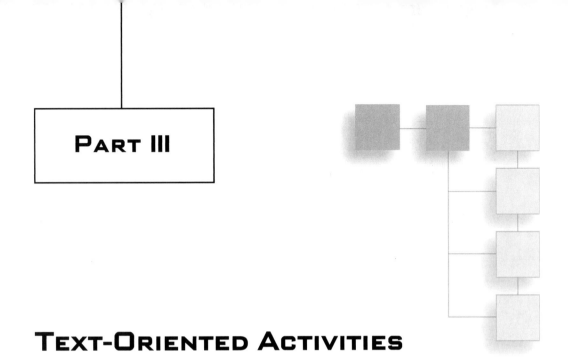

TEXT-ORIENTED ACTIVITIES

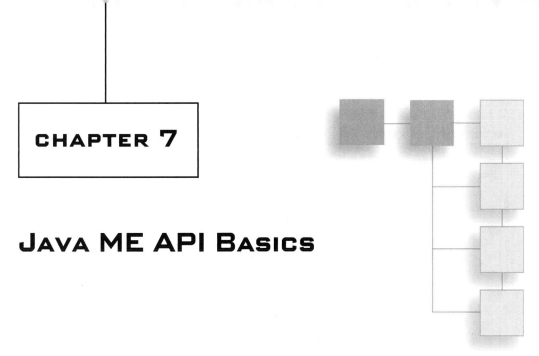

CHAPTER 7

Java ME API Basics

This chapter introduces you to the implementation of the classes and interfaces in the MIDP and CLDC packages. It is the first of four chapters that deal with the classes and interfaces on a general level. Depending on your approach to this book, you might use the next four chapters for reference only. However, they provide short programs intended to introduce the basics of using the classes and interfaces, so exploring these chapters might be effective preparation for the activities in Chapter 11, which focuses on the specifics of game development. In the current chapter, you investigate the MIDP application programming interface, which can be understood as the overall collection of classes and interfaces you access as you create MIDlets. In this chapter, the focus is on the classes and methods that support the basic lifecycle of the MIDlet, the classes that support thread or timer use, and the classes that provide networking capabilities. In subsequent chapters, other aspects of the API are examined.

MIDP API Overview

When you use the MIDP, you access its application programming interface (API). As used in this book, the API consists of the public methods the classes in the MIDP offers. Some of these classes and methods have appeared in previous chapters. In this and the next few chapters, the goal is to examine them much more

Table 7.1 MIDP API Support

Section	Description*
Application	Classes in this collection support devices so that they can run multiple MIDlets.
Utilities	Includes the essential `Timer` and `TimerTask` classes, in addition to such things as the `Stack`, `Vector`, `Calendar`, and `Random` classes.
Networking	Provides support for connectivity, sockets, HTTP connectivity, and streams.
Persistence	Allows you to store and retrieve data. Its functionality centers on the Record Management System (RMS), a basic database.
Audio	Includes a variety of classes that address the playing and listening of audio.
Gaming	Provides classes for tiling, layer management, canvas development, and sprites.
User Interface	The largest collection of classes. It covers images, data, screen management, text display, font, groups, and a number of other UI items.

* See **http://java.sun.com/javame/reference/apis/jsr118/** for a comprehensive review of the packages that constitute the API of the MIDP.

closely. Table 7.1 provides a review of the MIDP with respect to the general categories of its functionality. The largest set of functionality is in the User Interface (UI) classes. These are often referred to under the heading of Liquid Crystal Display User Interface (LCDUI). In addition to the LCDUI classes, the networking interfaces are of central importance, as are those related to threads and timing.

The MIDlet Class

When you develop a MIDlet, you extend the class you create for your MIDlet from the `MIDlet` class, which you can find in the `javax.microedition.midlet` package. It is an abstract class, and in previous chapters you have seen several examples of how to extend classes from it. It provides what is generally referred to as a "profile" application, which means that while it supplies the basic services that characterize a MIDlet, you must implement the control mechanisms relating to the specific device you are working with. Profile services include those necessary for the MIDlet to start, pause, resume, and stop. Table 7.2 provides a list of the methods that supply these services.

As the descriptions in Table 7.2 indicate, the methods of the `MIDlet` class interact heavily with the application management software. The application management software initiates many of the actions to which the methods respond, but it is also the case that the methods allow you to initiate actions that are directed to the

Table 7.2 MIDlet Methods

Method	Description
`String getAppProperty(String key)`	Returns the property value associated with the string key in the JAR or JAD.
`abstract void destroyApp()`	Gives you a chance to attend to actions such as saving state and releasing resources before your application closes. The argument to this method is of the `Boolean` type and is identified as *unconditional*. An unconditional `Boolean` value always generates an action. If it is true, the MIDlet cleans up and releases its resources. If it is false, the MIDlet throws an exception of the `MIDlet-StateChangeException` type to temporarily forestall its destruction.
`abstract void pauseApp()`	Calls on the MIDlet when the user has paused the game.
`abstract void startApp()`	Signals that the user wants the game to start again.
`abstract void notifyDestroyed()`	Informs the application management software that the player has decided to exit the game.
`abstract void notifyPaused()`	Tells the application management software that the player has paused the MIDlet.
`abstract void resumeRequest()`	Tells the application management software that the MIDlet is to be started again after being paused.

application management software. The interaction is in both directions and continuous. What applies to the methods of the `MIDlet` class applies to most of the classes that constitute the API as represented in Table 7.1.

Note

The API classes use standard methods inherited from the `Object` class. The methods used are as follows: `equals()`, `getClass()`, `hashCode()`, `notify()`, `notifyAll()`, `toString()`, `wait()`.

As I mentioned, you can view the lifecycle of a MIDlet in fairly basic terms and trace its actions back to the methods listed in Table 7.2. As Figure 7.1 shows, the lifecycle of the MIDlet begins with its construction. After it is constructed, it is automatically placed in a paused state by the application management software. The `startApp()` method can then be called to set the MIDlet in a running state. After it is running, it can be paused. This can happen if the user of a device switches to another MIDlet. If an application is paused, it can be restarted once again with the `startApp()` method. On the other hand, the user might close it, in which case the `destroyApp()` method is called. Other methods, such as `notifyPaused()` and `notifyDestroyed()`, supplement these efforts.

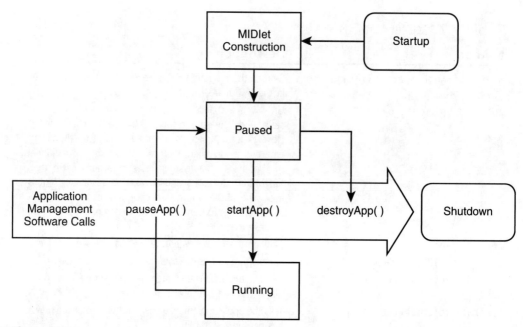

Figure 7.1
Interactions with the user and the application management software characterize the MIDlet lifecycle.

When it is running, a MIDlet can be paused at any time, and when this happens, the application management software immediately calls the pauseApp() method. Consider two applications, A and B. If the user pauses application A and switches to application B, then the pauseApp() method is called for A and the startApp() method is called for B. When the pauseApp() method is called, resources for application A are released. When the user wants to start application A again, the application management software calls the startApp() method for A and the pauseApp() method for application B, and resources are released for application B.

Destruction of a MIDlet works the same way. For example, if the user elects to close application A, then the application management software invokes the destroyApp() method for application A. With the destroyApp() method, the MIDletStateChangeException class comes into play. This exception indicates that an attempt has been made to close the application but that some of the resources for the application have not been released, thus blocking a clean exit.

Projects with NetBeans

The programs in this and subsequent chapters have been developed using the NetBeans IDE. For this reason, you find a NetBeans subfolder in the source directory for Chapter 7 and subsequent chapters of this book. Chapter 6 describes how to get started with the NetBeans IDE.

If you do not want to use NetBeans, the code folders provide duplicate code files that you can copy and work with from the command line or using the Java Wireless Toolkit. For help working with these files in these contexts, review the discussions provided in Chapters 4 and 5.

To access the NetBeans projects provided with this chapter, from the main menu of the NetBeans IDE, select Project > Open Projects and navigate to the directory location where you copied the Chapter 7 code samples. You can find this project in the NetBeans subfolder. Click the Chapter 7 MIDlets selection in the Open Projects dialog. Then click Open Project Folder. At this point, you can build (F11) and run (F6) the MIDlets in the project.

If you want to create your own project, follow the directions given in Chapter 6 for creating a MIDlet project. Then, to add files, select File > New File. In the New File dialog, click MIDP under the Categories label. Click MIDlet under the Files Types label. Then Click Next.

In the New File dialog, type the name of the class (LifecycleTest, for example). Then click Finish. At this point, you see the default starter code for the class you have created. Delete the automatically generated code and copy and paste the code from the appropriate example file into the text area for the class.

You can include several MIDlet classes in any given project. When the IDE builds and runs them, they are displayed in a typical device list in the emulator, as Figure 7.2 illustrates. Use the SELECT key to navigate through the list.

The LifecycleTest Class

The LifecycleTest class is located in the Chapter 7 code folder. See the sidebar, "Projects with NetBeans," for a discussion of how to access and run it. The LifecycleTest class illustrates the actions of some of the methods in the MIDlet class. Among these are the constructor, and the startApp(), destroyApp(), and notifyDestroyed() methods. The pauseApp() method is also shown, but in this case you see no output from it. In addition, the LifecycleTest class explores the CommandListener:: commandAction() method. Here is the code for the LifecycleTest class. Discussion of the LifecycleTest class follows with references to the numbers (#1 for example) that appear in the code.

```
/*
 * Chapter 7 \ LifecycleTest.java
 *
 */

import javax.microedition.midlet.*;
import javax.microedition.lcdui.*;

public class LifecycleTest extends MIDlet
                    implements CommandListener{
```

Select File > New File. Use MIDP for the Category.
Use MIDlet for the File Type. Each class in a project must be
uniquely named.

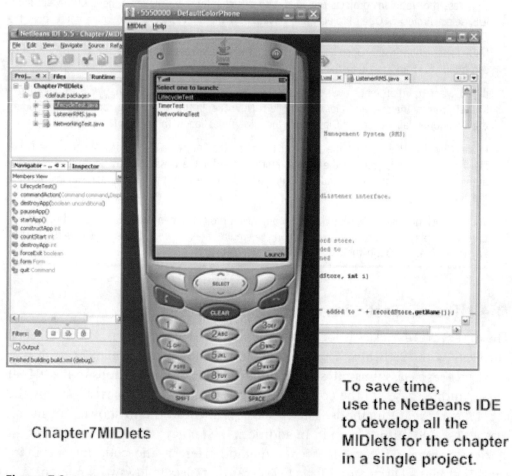

Chapter7MIDlets

To save time,
use the NetBeans IDE
to develop all the
MIDlets for the chapter
in a single project.

Figure 7.2
The NetBeans IDE allows you to use a single project for the files in a given chapter.

```
private Form form;
private Command quit;
private boolean forceExit = false;
//Test attributes to show values as they are generated
private static int countStart,
                    constructApp,
                    destroyApp;
```

```java
// #1 Construct the MIDlet
public LifecycleTest(){
    System.out.println("The constructor is called: " + constructApp++);
    form = new Form("Basic MIDlet Lifecycle.");
    form.append("The MIDlet starts and waits.");
    form.setCommandListener(this);
    // Create and add a command to close the MIDlet state
    quit = new Command("Quit", Command.SCREEN, 1);
    form.addCommand(quit);
}

// #2 Called by the application management software to start
protected void startApp() throws MIDletStateChangeException{
    System.out.println("Select clicked. The startApp() method is called: "
                        + countStart++);
    Display.getDisplay(this).setCurrent(form);
}

// #3 Called by the application management software to pause
protected void pauseApp(){
    System.out.println("pauseApp() called.");
}

 // # 4   Called by the application management software to destroy
protected void destroyApp(boolean unconditional)
                          throws MIDletStateChangeException{
    System.out.println("The destroyApp(" + unconditional
                        + ") method is called: " + destroyApp++);

    if (!unconditional){
        // Once using unconditional, next time forced.
        forceExit = true;
    }
}

// #5 Called when the user executed a command
public void commandAction(Command command, Displayable displayable){
    System.out.println("commandAction(" + command + ", " + displayable +
                        ") called.");
    try{
        if (command == quit){
            destroyApp(forceExit);
            notifyDestroyed();
```

```
        }
    }

    catch (MIDletStateChangeException me){
        System.out.println(me + " caught.");
    }
  }
}
```

Figure 7.3 reviews the primary actions the LifecycleTest class supports. The SELECT button invokes the constructor and the startApp() method of the class. The disconnect phone button to the lower right of the SELECT button invokes the destroyApp() method. You can repeatedly construct and destroy objects of the class to see the output of the methods in it.

Run the application and click the SELECT and disconnect buttons, as shown in Figure 7.3. You invoke the constructor for the class object, the startApp() method, and then the destroyApp() method. Subsequent sections of this chapter discuss the code in detail. The output shown is generated by the NetBeans IDE:

```
Copying 1 file to C:\j2me\projects\Chapter7MIDlets\dist\nbrun#30652
Starting emulator in execution mode
Running with storage root DefaultColorPhone
The constructor is called: 0
Select clicked. The startApp() method is called:0
The destroyApp(true) method is called: 0
The constructor is called: 1
Select clicked. The startApp() method is called:1
The destroyApp(true) method is called: 1
The constructor is called: 2
Select clicked. The startApp() method is called: 2
The destroyApp(true) method is called: 2
Execution completed.
```

Imports and Construction

Consider first the lines preceding comment #1 in the definition of the LifecycleTest class. You see the import directives that are needed in order to include the basic MIDP classes. You have seen these before, but notice in this context the midlet and lcdui packages. As mentioned previously, the midlet package allows you to define the basic profile activities of the application. The

SELECT invokes
the constructor and
the startApp() method.

When you close the
application, the
destroyApp() method is
called.

Figure 7.3
The output from the test MIDlet demonstrates the application termination process.

lcdui package contains the classes that provide the primary components of the user interface, such as the Form, CommandListener, and Canvas classes.

Following the import statements, you see the signature line of the class. To define the class, you extend the MIDlet class, which gives you access to the core MIDlet application functionality. In addition, you implement the CommandListener interface, which lets you handle messages from the events that the commands generate.

Having presented the import directives and the class signature line, you proceed to declare Form and Command objects and a few test attributes of the boolean and int types. The forceExit attribute is used as a toggle to allow you to exit the MIDlet. The Form (form) and Command (quit) objects are central UI objects. The

Form object allows you to display messages. The Command object provides a number of defined properties for keys. Among these are those for SCREEN, STOP, and EXIT. In addition, solely for testing purposes, a few static attributes are declared: countStart, constructApp, destroyApp. You can increment the values of these attributes to more clearly show the cycle of the primary MIDlet methods.

In the lines following comment #1, you implement the constructor for the LifecycleTest class. The constructor makes use of the System.out.println() method to issue test messages to the command line (or Output area). Within the constructor, you call the constructor for the Form class. The Form constructor takes one argument, a string that provides a name for the MIDlet. After that, you assign the Form object to the form identifier and use the form identifier to call the Form::append() method, which writes a text message to the display as the Form object is being constructed. Following that, you call the Form::setCommandLisener() method, which equips the Form with the functionality needed to process messages. The argument for this method is a reference to the LifecycleTest class object, which is provided through the this keyword.

In the closing lines of the LifecycleTest constructor, you call the constructor of the Command class to create an instance of a Command object, which you assign to the quit identifier. Creation of Command objects receives more discussion further on, but for now notice that the Command constructor takes three arguments. The first is the label for the command ("Quit"), the second is the field value that identifies the type of command (SCREEN), and the last is an integer to designate the level of priority you want to assign to the command. The Form::addCommand() method then adds the Command object (quit) to the Form object (form).

Starting and Stopping

Following comment #2 in the LifecycleTest class, you define the startApp() method. When this method is called, it causes the state of the application to change from paused to running. It also provides a place in which you can initialize or refresh objects used for display. In this respect, the Display::getDisplay() method is called statically to return the screen (Display object) of the MIDlet, and you then use this object to call the setCurrent() method to set the next object (form) to be displayed. This action is invoked when the application starts initially or is paused and then started again. The result of this action for the current application is that when you click the SELECT button, you see a console message, and the value of the static `countStart` attribute allows you to see a change as you exit and restart the application.

In the lines trailing comment #3, you define the `pauseApp()` method. When you switch from one MIDlet to another, the `pauseApp()` method clears unneeded resources. It is a frequently used method, for it is necessary to free as many resources as possible when you switch between MIDlets. Clearing resources (destroying them) requires you to reinitialize them when the application is resumed. While initializing resources causes a delay, programmers generally regard the tradeoff as justified, and players seldom object if a short pause precedes resumption of game or other activities. In this case, no action results from this method, but in anticipation of work further on in this chapter, the `println()` method is used to provide a brief test report to the command line. The application management software invokes the `pauseApp()` method only when the application transitions between states. Since this condition is achieved in this class only when the MIDlet starts, the `pauseApp()` method is not called.

Closing

Trailing comment #4 in the `LifecycleTest` class, you implement the `destroyApp()` method. The application management software calls this method as the MIDlet is being closed. The method serves to establish that permission is granted for the MIDlet to close safely. A MIDlet can close safely when this method can process a change of state. The change of state in this case requires that the MIDlet be able to destroy allocated resources no longer needed and save those that are persistent. If this is not possible, then it throws an error of the `MIDletStateChangeException` type, which notifies the system that the application cannot make the change that has been requested. If the argument to this function is true, then the state of the MIDlet transitions to destroyed and a final method called `notifyDestroyed()` can be called. The definition of the method in this case is set up so that if the first attempt to exit fails, then the next attempt sets the value of `forceExit` to true, and the MIDlet can be forced to close.

Command Actions

In the lines following comment #5, you implement the final code for the `LifecycleTest` class. You define the `CommandListener:: commandAction()` method, which you can access directly in this context because the `LifecycleTest` class implements the `CommandListener` class. As with the previous methods, you provide a `println()`

statement for testing purposes. After that, you provide a `try...catch` block in which you implement the code that processes the `quit` message and destroys the MIDlet.

The `commandAction()` method takes two arguments. The first is the command to be performed. The second argument is of the abstract `Displayable` type (concrete subclasses are `Canvas` and `Screen`). Within the `try...catch` block, you provide a selection statement that tests whether the value of the command argument equals the value assigned to the `quit` identifier. If so, then you call the `destroyApp()` method with the `forceExit` attribute as an argument. As pointed out previously, the `forceExit` attribute is a toggle, and its initial value is set to `false`. The first pass, then, invokes the `destroyApp()` method. If the MIDlet can release or save resources without problems, then the flow of the program proceeds to the `notifyDestroyed()` method, and the MIDlet closes. If not, then the `MIDletStateChangeException` message is issued, and the `catch` block is entered. In this case, the only result is that the `println()` method prints a message to the console.

Using Timer and TimerTask Objects

A `Timer` object enables you to schedule tasks for execution. It makes use of a background application thread, and the tasks that you schedule using it can execute either once or multiple times at determined intervals. You can implement several `Timer` objects in a given MIDlet. Each `Timer` object has its own thread within the application. The `Timer` class is supported by the `TimerTask` class, which allows you to specify tasks. Both of these classes are in the `java.util` package, as Table 7.1 indicates. Two exceptions are associated with `Timer` methods. One of these is the `IllegalArgumentException`, which indicates that the period or delay assigned to a task is negative. Another is the `IllegalStateException`, which indicates that an attempt to access a terminated `Timer` object has been made. Table 7.3 summarizes the methods you find in the `Timer` class. Table 7.4 summarizes the `TimerTask` class.

Notice that the arguments for some of the methods in Table 7.3 include the terms *delay*, *period*, and *fixed*. When a method has a delay, the delay designates a period after the `Timer` object is instantiated. Different execution schemes apply to the delay. One centers on the period. The other centers on the delay.

When the execution centers on the period, after the execution starts, first a scheduled task is executed. If a `Timer` object designates tasks to be executed within

Table 7.3 Timer Methods

Method	Description
Timer()	Constructs a new Timer object.
void cancel()	Terminates a Timer object and all the tasks associated with it.
void schedule(TimerTask task, long period)	The first argument designates the task to be scheduled. This is a reference to an object of the TimerTask type. The second argument is of the long type and designates the period in milliseconds that elapses before the task executes.
void schedule(TimerTask task, Date time)	The first argument designates the task to be scheduled. This is a reference to an object of the TimerTask type. The second argument is of the Date type, which is specified in milliseconds, and designates precisely when the task is to be executed.
void schedule(TimerTask task, Date firstTime, long period)	The first argument is of the TimerTask type and designates the task to be executed. The second is of the Date type and establishes the first instance of the task execution. The third argument designates in milliseconds the intervals of execution. Note that each execution is scheduled relative to the delay after the preceding execution.
void schedule(TimerTask task, long delay, long period)	The first argument is of the TimerTask type. The second is a long integer that designates the time in milliseconds before the task is to execute. The third argument then establishes the interval of delay. The execution begins after the first delay.
void scheduleAtFixedRate(TimerTask task, Date firstTime, long period)	The first argument is of the TimerTask type. The second is of the Date type and establishes the first instance of the task execution. The third argument designates a fixed interval for execution in milliseconds.
void scheduleAtFixedRate(TimerTask task, long delay, long period)	The first argument is of the TimerTask type. The second designates delay in milliseconds until the first execution. The third argument establishes a fixed interval, in milliseconds, for subsequent executions.

Table 7.4 TimerTask Methods

Method	Description
`TimerTask()`	Constructs a new timer task.
`boolean cancel()`	Terminates the task. This method can terminate a task before it has run or intervene in a `Timer` object's scheduling of tasks to terminate it at that point.
`abstract void run()`	This method is overridden with a method containing the code to be executed when the `Timer` event goes off. This method is provided by the `Runnable` interface and is invoked to initiate the execution of a task.
`long scheduledExecutionTime()`	Returns the exact time at which the task was run last.

fixed periods, then they begin after the specified period of delay. Following that, if they cannot execute after the defined delay, they are crowded into a period with the next task. The period is preserved, even if the delay between the tasks is not. This can mean that events execute in quick succession.

With fixed rate execution, the picture changes. Then the execution of an event is relative to the execution of the previous event. The first task executes. Then regardless of all else, the next task executes. If one event is delayed, then the execution of all events that follow is also delayed.

In Table 7.3, you see that all of the `Timer` methods depend on arguments of the `TimerTask` type. You create an instance of the `Timer` class. Then you create instances of the `TimerTask` class and assign them to it. You can schedule, run, or cancel a `TimerTask` object. Table 7.4 summarizes the methods the `TimerTask` class offers.

The TimerTest Class

The `TimerTest` class provides an example of how to print the time in milliseconds at regular intervals to the MIDlet display. To implement the `TimerTest` class, you extend the `MIDlet` class and then create instances of the `Timer` and `PrintTask` classes. The `PrintTask` is an inner class that extends the `TimerTask`. Here is the code for the `TimerTest` class. The source file is located in the Chapter 7 code folder. Note that if you are working with the NetBeans IDE, you can open the `Chapter7MIDlets` project and access the code that way. See the sidebar "Projects with NetBeans" for more information about using the NetBeans IDE. The code is discussed in greater detail in the sections following.

```
/**
 * Chapter 7 / TimerTest
 *
 */
import javax.microedition.midlet.*;
import javax.microedition.lcdui.*;
import java.util.*;

// #1
public class TimerTest extends MIDlet{
    private Form form;
    private Timer timer;
    private PrintTask task;
    private static int count = 10;
    private static long lengthOfPause = 1000;

    // #2 MIDlet constructor that creates a form, timer and simple task.
    public TimerTest(){
        form = new Form("Timer Test");
        // Setup the timer and the print timertask
        timer = new Timer();
        task = new PrintTask();
    }

    // #3 Start the application and scheulde the task
    protected void startApp() throws MIDletStateChangeException{
        // display our UI
        Display.getDisplay(this).setCurrent(form);

        // schedule the task for execution every 100 milliseconds
        timer.schedule(task, lengthOfPause, lengthOfPause);
    }

    // #4 If the applicaion pauses, stop the task execution
    protected void pauseApp(){
        task.cancel();
    }
    // #5 If there is a problem, exit and stop the timer
    protected void destroyApp(boolean unconditional)
                    throws MIDletStateChangeException{
        timer.cancel();
    }
```

```
//======================
// #6 Define ann inner class that extends the TimerTask class.
class PrintTask extends TimerTask{

    // To implement a task you need to override the run method.
    public void run(){
      taskToRun();
    }//end run

    private void taskToRun(){
       // output the time the task ran at
       form.append("" + scheduledExecutionTime() + "\n");
       if(count >10){
          form.deleteAll();
          count=0;
       }//end if
       count++;
    }//end taskToRun() def
  }//end TimerTask
  //======================
}//end of class definition
```

Imports and Construction

In the lines preceding comment #1 of the TimerTest class, you use an import statement to access the java.util package. This gives you access to the Timer and TimerTask classes. Following comment #1, you define the signature line for the TimerTest class. This involves, as in previous examples in this book, extending the MIDlet class. After the signature line, you declare five class attributes. The first is a Form object (form), which has been discussed already. The next two relate to the timed execution of tasks in the class. The Timer attribute, timer, allows you to create one or more TimerTask objects. In this class, you use only one such object. This is provided by the task attribute, which is of the PrintTask data type. The PrintTask data type is furnished by an inner class that is explained momentarily.

In addition to the other attributes, you also create a static long attribute, lengthOfPause, to which you assign a value of 1000. This attribute can be used to set the task delay and period values. You also define a count attribute of the int type to govern the number of lines written to the display (10).

At comment #2, you define the constructor for the TimerTest object. Construction involves creating an instance of the PrintTask class and assigning it to the timer attribute. Given the construction of the TimerTest object, in the lines trailing comment #3, you move to the implementation of the startApp() method. To define this method, you first attend to setting up the display. This topic has been discussed previously.

You then use the Timer::schedule() method to assign a PrintTask object to the Timer object. The version of the schedule() method used in this instance sets the task, the delay, and then the period for the task. Both of these values are set in milliseconds, so with the initial value assigned to lengthOfPause, the task is executed one second after the instantiation of the task and at one-second intervals after that. (To experiment, change the initial value.)

Canceling Tasks

In the lines associated with comment #3 in the TimerTest class, you define the pauseApp() method. You define this method using only one statement, which involves using the PrintTask attribute, task, to call the PrintTask::cancel() method. (Recall that the PrintTask class is derived from the TimerTask class.) With the use of the cancel() method, when the user switches MIDlets, the Timer action is cancelled. If you implement the TimerTest class using NetBeans, you can see this happen when you switch between the MIDlets for Chapter 7.

In the lines following comment #5, you again call the Timer::cancel() method. The result of this call is to cancel the Timer object, but as has been discussed previously, if the resources associated with the Timer and the MIDlet generally cannot be destroyed without problems, then the method throws a MIDletState-ChangeException error.

The Inner PrintTask Class

In the lines following comment #6 of the TimerTest class, you create an inner class called PrintTask. To define the PrintTask class, you extend the TimerTask class. To accomplish this, you override one method, the run() method. Overriding the run() method involves inserting one statement into it. The statement is a call to a method that encapsulates a task to be performed, taskToRun().

The run() method executes at the intervals the Task::schedule() method sets for it. In this respect, then, you see the output of the taskToRun () method at

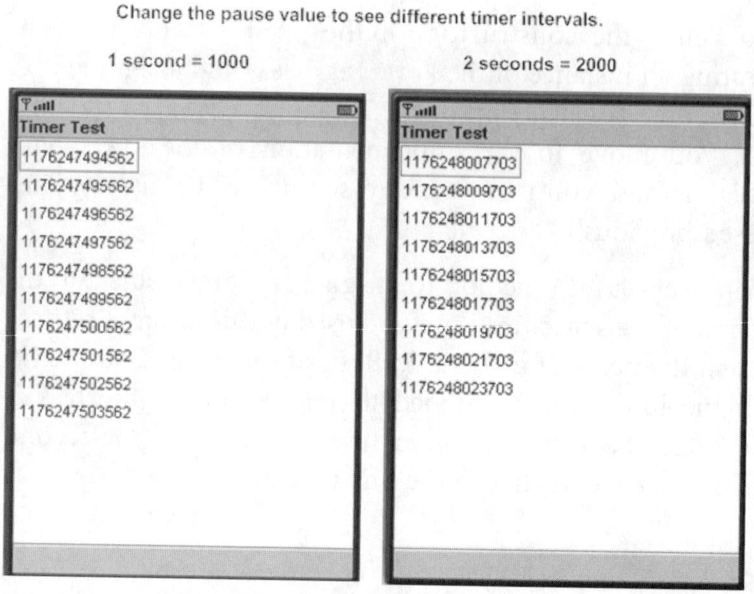

Change the pause value to see different timer intervals.

1 second = 1000   2 seconds = 2000

Figure 7.4
The lengthOfPause setting allows you to see different timer intervals.

intervals determined by the lengthOfPause attribute. The action is made visible with a call to the Form::append() method.

The append() method successively concatenates the millisecond values returned by the TimerTask::scheduledExecutionTime() method. These values report the calculated times of execution given the arguments provided to the Timer::sehedule() method. These times are converted into strings, and as each string is appended to the output, it is terminated by a line return (\n). A selection statement audits the value of the count attribute. When the value of count is greater than 10, the Form::deleteAll() method is called, clearing the MIDlet display and allowing another sequence of time values to be displayed. As Figure 7.4 illustrates, if you set the lengthOfPause attribute at 1000 and then 2000, you can see different intervals represented in the display.

Networking

The MIDP includes support for the Generic Connection Framework (GCF). The GCF provides a fairly straightforward approach to extending connectivity for MIDlets indefinitely. Creating connections using the GCF involves using a

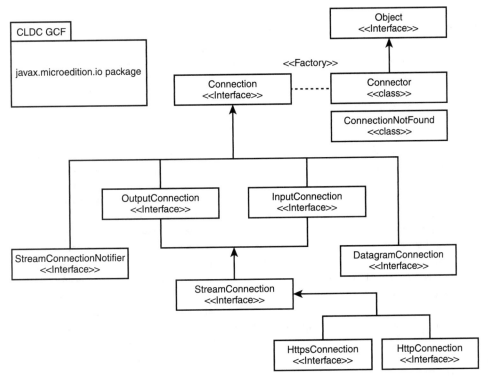

Figure 7.5
The Generic Connection Framework provides a full spread of general-purpose communications classes.

concrete class named Connector. The Connector class is a factory. You employ the factory to create specific types of connections using interfaces derived from the Connection interface hierarchy, illustrated in Figure 7.5. The Connector class and the Connection interface hierarchy are both given by the javax.microedition.io package.

As Figure 7.5 illustrates, I/O based on the DatagramConnection interface employ packets. The others are stream based. This chapter illustrates the use of a stream connection. Note also that the Connector class works in conjunction with the ConnectionNotFound exception class.

The Connector Class

As mentioned previously, the Connector class is a factory class that makes use of the interfaces provided by the Connection hierarchy to create stream and packet connections. Factory activity begins with the use of the open() method of the

Table 7.5 Connector Methods and Modes

Method	Description
`static Connection open(String name)`	Constructs, opens, and returns a new connection to the specified URL name.
`static Connection open(String name, int mode)`	Constructs, opens, and returns a new connection to the specified URL name and access mode.
`static Connection open(String name, int mode, boolean timeouts)`	Constructs, opens, and returns a new connection to the specified URL name, access mode, and a Boolean indicating whether you want to see timeout exceptions being thrown.
`static Connection openDataInputStream(String name)`	Opens a connection and then constructs and returns a data input stream.
`static Connection openDataOutputStream(String name)`	Opens a connection and then constructs and returns a data output stream.
`static Connection openInputStream(String name)`	Opens a connection and then constructs and returns an input stream.
`static Connection openOutputStream(String name)`	Opens a connection and then constructs and returns an output stream.
`static int READ`	Designates the READ mode.
`static int READ_WRITE`	Designates the READ_WRITE mode.
`static int WRITE`	Designates the WRITE mode.

Connector class. As Table 7.5 illustrates, there are several overloaded forms of the open() method. All of these are static. The most simple approach, as an argument to the open() method, is to pass in the name of the resource to which you want to connect. For example, here is how you connect to an HTTP resource:

```
Connector.open("http://java.sun.com");
```

The HttpConnection Interface

In the Connection interface hierarchy depicted in Figure 7.5, you find a partial description of the interface that addresses HTTP connections involving low-latency network tasks. This is the HttpConnection interface. For games, you can use it to download content on demand, update scores or meta-game data, or implement interplayer communications. Table 7.6 reviews a few of the methods and properties this class provides.

Table 7.6 HttpConnection Methods and Properties

Method	Description
long getDate()	Retrieves the date header value.
long getExpiration()	Retrieves the expiration header value.
String getHeaderFieldKey(int n)	Retrieves the header key by index.
String getHeaderField(int n)	Retrieves the header value by index.
String getHeaderField(String name)	Retrieves the value of the named header field.
long getHeaderFieldDate(String name, long def)	Retrieves the value of the named header field in the format of a date long. If the field doesn't exist, the def value is returned.
int getHeaderFieldInt(String name, int def)	Retrieves the value of the named header field as an integer. If the field doesn't exist, the def value is returned.
long getLastModified()	Returns the last modified header field.
String getURL()	Returns the URL.
String getFile()	Returns the file portion of the URL.
String getHost()	Returns the host part of the URL.
int getPort()	Returns the port part of the URL.
String getProtocol()	Returns the protocol part of the URL.
String getQuery()	Returns the query part of the URL.
String getRef()	Returns the ref portion of the URL.
int getResponseCode()	Returns the HTTP response status code.
String getResponseMessage()	Returns the HTTP response message (if there was one).
String getRequestMethod()	Returns the request method of the connection.
void setRequestMethod(String method)	Sets the method of the URL request. Available types are GET, POST, and HEAD.
String getRequestProperty(String key)	Returns the request property value associated with the named key.
void setRequestProperty(String key, String value)	Set the request property value associated with the named key.
HTTP_OK	A request has succeeded.

The NetworkingHTTPTest Class

The NetworkingHTTPTest class provides a MIDlet that allows you to use the Connector class to open a stream for data from a website. To open the connection, you use a static call to the Connector::open() method. You use HTTPConnection interface to establish a connection and then feed the data from this connection to an InputStream object to receive the stream. Using the getResponseCode() and openInputStream() methods lets you confirm and

effect the transfer of data. Here is the code for the `NetworkingHTTPTest` class.
You can find it in the Chapter 7 folder. If you have not yet built and run the
code, review the sidebar titled "Projects with NetBeans."

```
/**
 *   Chapter 7 / NetworkingHTTPTest
 *
 */
import java.util.*;
import java.io.*;
import javax.microedition.midlet.*;
import javax.microedition.lcdui.*;
import javax.microedition.io.*;

// #1
public class NetworkingHTTPTest extends MIDlet
{
    private Form form;
    final int MAXLEN = 521;
    String httpText;

    public NetworkingHTTPTest() throws IOException{
        form = new Form("Http Test Connector");
    // #2 Create a HTTP connection to the java.sun.com site
        String url =  "http://java.sun.com/";
        HttpConnection connection
                = (HttpConnection)Connector.open( url, Connector.READ );

        if (connection.getResponseCode() == HttpConnection.HTTP_OK) {
          InputStream inStream = connection.openInputStream();

          // #3 Open the stream and read data
          byte[] buffer = new byte[MAXLEN];
          int total = 0;
          while (total < MAXLEN) {
            int count = inStream.read(buffer, total, MAXLEN - total);

            if (count < 0) {
              break;
            }
            total += count;
          }//end while
          // #4 Close the stream
```

```
        inStream.close( );
        httpText = new String(buffer, 0, total);
    }
}
protected void startApp( ) throws MIDletStateChangeException{
    Display.getDisplay(this).setCurrent(form);
    form.append(httpText);
}

protected void pauseApp( ){
}

protected void destroyApp(boolean unconditional)
                            throws MIDletStateChangeException{
}
}//end class definition
```

When you run the `NetworkingHTTPTest` MIDlet, you see a security notification to which you must respond. As Figure 7.6 shows, after you click to approve the

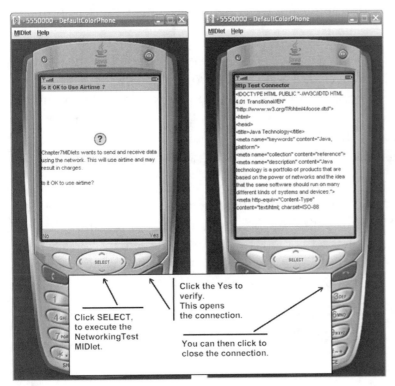

Figure 7.6
A message indicates that the connection is to be opened.

connection, it opens and you see the HTML text of the page to which you have connected.

Preceding comment #1 in the NetworkingTest class, you see the import directives needed to support the networking functionality. This includes the classes and interfaces in the javax.microedition.io package, which supplied the Connection class and the HttpConnection interface. There is also an include statement for the java.io package, which supplies the InputStream and IOException classes. Following comment #1, you declare a final class attribute, MAXLEN, to govern the length of the stream read by the MIDlet. You also make use of the String attribute, httpText, which allows you to display the data string in the Form::append() method.

In the lines following comment #2, you create a local String identifier, url, to which you add the URL shown for the Sun site. You then proceed to use the Connector class to statically call the open() method. The first argument to the open() method provides the location of the data sought. The second establishes the type of stream. The READ_WRITE property of the Connector class stipulates that the connection is for both reading and writing. In this context, the READ property also works without problems.

You then call the HttpConnection::getResponseCode() method to verify that the connection has been established. The HTTP_OK property of the HttpConnection interface definition provides a value to use to check the code. Assuming the connection succeeds, you then call the openInputStream() method. This method is inherited by the HttpConnection interface from the Connection interface. You assign the stream to the inStream identifier, which is of the InputStream type.

In the lines trailing comment #3, you create an array of the byte type (buffer) and call the InputStream::read() method to retrieve the stream. The first argument to the read() method is the array into which the data is placed, the second is the offset, and the last is the length of the stream. The reading action is terminated by the InputStream::close() method.

After the entire stream has been read, it is assigned to the String httpText attribute. As you see in the lines following comment #4, you call the Form::append() method to write the data to the display.

Conclusion

The MIDlet, Timer, TimerTask, and Connector classes are but four of a multitude of classes provided by the API, and the programs provided in this chapter represent only a brief introduction to their capabilities. In the Connection interface hierarchy, the HttpConnection interface works with many others to allow you to develop a variety of connections. In the next few chapters, you continue to examine the classes in the API. Chapter 8 deals with persistence, for example. As you go, refer to Table 7.1 to review the API at a high level. Generally, with respect to the MIDP 2.0, it is a good idea to create a ready link to the MIDP site **http://java.sun.com/javame/reference/apis/jsr118**. This site provides you with an immediate view of the classes, interfaces, fields, and other items covered in this and subsequent chapters.

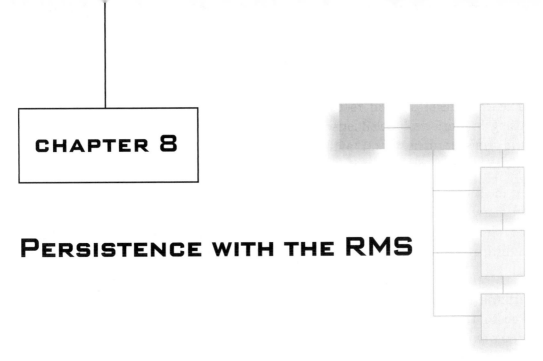

CHAPTER 8

PERSISTENCE WITH THE RMS

In this chapter, you continue to explore the topics introduced in Chapter 7. The topics dealt with in this chapter center on the RecordStore class. This class is complemented by four interface classes: RecordEnumeration, RecordFilter, RecordComparator, and RecordListener. Two key methods from the RecordStore class allow you to add the capabilities the interfaces offer for managing records. These are the enumerateRecords() and addRecordListener() methods. Both of these methods are part of the RecordStore class interface. The activities you can perform using the RecordStore class and its accompanying interface classes are extensive and in many ways are comparable to those characteristic of a database engine. RecordStore objects exist in isolation from the MIDlets in which they are defined, so they can be accessed by other MIDlets if they share the same suite. The RecordStore class and its accompanying interface classes are included in the microedition.rms package.

Persistence

When you develop a MIDlet, you often use persistent data. Persistent data is data that you retain between executions of a MIDlet, such as scores, personal information that is displayed when you access a given MIDlet, or phone data. The means by which you can store and retrieve such data is the Record Management System (RMS). The record management system is a set of components designed to provide services that resemble those of a database engine.

The RMS stores data as records. A record is an array of bytes, and is identified using an integer value that is automatically assigned to the record as you add it to the persistent data store. You then assign this to the data store. It is analogous to the index of an array, but its values begin at 1, not 0.

At the center of the RMS activities is the RecordStore class. The RecordStore class in many ways resembles a standard Java Collection class. It is distinct from a collection object, however, because RecordStore objects are allocated storage in a distinct memory location that is visible to all MIDlets in a given MIDlet suite.

Each RecordStore object is identified with a unique name that can be assigned arbitrarily when the object is created. If the MIDlet associated with a given RecordStore object is removed, the RecordStore object must also be removed. In other words, while a RecordStore object exists in its own space, it is still associated with an application.

Four primary interfaces are associated with the RecordStore class. The Record-Enumeration interface allows you to iterate (or enumerate) through the items. The RecordComparator interface allows you to compare items in a RecordStore. The RecordListener interface allows you to audit changes in an item. The RecordFilter interface provides a match() function, which works like a regular expression to allow you to test whether items in a RecordStore are the same. Several exception classes are associated with the RecordStore class and the associated interfaces. Table 8.1 provides a summary view of the components provided by the javax.microedition.rms package.

The RecordStore Class

As mentioned previously, a RecordStore object provides a memory area in which RMS records are stored. As Figure 8.1 illustrates, a RecordStore object is persistent (nonvolatile) and exists within the scope of a MIDlet suite. As the solid lines in Figure 8.1 indicate, a given RecordStore object is associated with a specific MIDlet, but it can also be accessed by any other MIDlet in the suite.

A RecordStore object is in some ways analogous to a Collection interface in the java.util package (Vector, HashTable, or Stack, for example). On the other hand, it is an entirely distinct entity. A RecordStore object is not, for example, only an attribute of a MIDlet. When it is created, as Figure 8.1 suggests, it shares a common scope with the MIDlet, but it occupies a unique address space, and it can be accessed outside the MIDlet in which it is created.

Table 8.1 The RMS Package

Class	Description
RecordStore	This is a concrete class. It is a collection of records. A key method of this class is the addRecord() method.
RecordComparator	This is an interface. It allows you to compare two records stored in a RecordStore object.
RecordEnumeration	This is an interface. It provides a way to iterate through RecordStore objects.
RecordFilter	This is an interface. It provides a method, matches(), that tests the value assigned to a record to determine whether it matches a specified value.
RecordListener	This is an interface. It gives you the ability to audit record operations involving adding, changing, or removing records. You use it in conjunction with the RecordStore::addRecordListener() method.
Exception	There are several exception classes associated with this package. These include InvalidRecordIDException, RecordStoreException, RecordStoreFullException, RecordStoreNotFoundException, and RecordStoreNotOpenException.

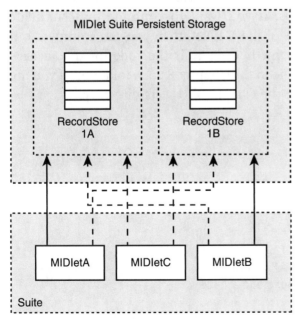

Figure 8.1
A MIDlet has access to RecordStore objects created in the MIDlet suite of which the MIDlet is part.

Table 8.2 summarizes the interface of the `RecordStore` class. A `RecordStore` object is created using the `openRecordStore()` method. Records are added to it using the `addRecord()` method. A `RecordStore` object is deleted using the static `delete-RecordStore()` method. While a record exists, a number of methods provide information about it. Among these are the `getNumRecords()`, `getSize()`, and `get-Name()` methods. Examples of how to use these methods (and others) appear in the `RecordStoreTest` class, which is presented in the next section of this chapter.

The RecordStoreTest Class

The `RecordStoreTest` class allows you to open a `RecordStore` object, assign the names of a few of the months of the year to it, and display the assigned months. After completing these actions, when you switch to another MIDlet, you also close and destroy the `RecordStore` object. You can easily change this so that you do not destroy the object. The `RecordStoreTest` class contains several custom functions—`createRecordStore()`, `populateRecordStore()`, `updateRecord()`, and `displayRecordStore()`—which refactor the primary activities of the class. However, it is also important to note that the `RecordStore` object is closed and deleted in the `destroyApp()` function. The destruction of the `RecordStore` object allows you to repeatedly execute the `RecordStoreTest` MIDlet without accumulating a large number of records. If you want to continue to accumulate records through repeated executions of the MIDlet, then you can comment out the call to the `deleteRecordStore()` method. Here is the code for the `Record-StoreTest` class. You can find this code in the Chapter 8 code folder or, if you are using NetBeans, you can access it in the Chapter8MIDlets directory.

```
/*
 * Chapter8 \ RecordStoreTest
 *
 */
import java.io.*;
import javax.microedition.midlet.*;
import javax.microedition.rms.*;

public class RecordStoreTest extends MIDlet{
    // #1 Declare a RecordStore attribute and a name
    private RecordStore rs;
    private static final String STORE_NAME = "Test RecordStore Object";
```

Table 8.2 RecordStore Methods

Method	Description
`static RecordStore openRecordStore (String recordStoreName, boolean createIfNecessary)`	Opens a record store or creates one if it does not exist.
`void closeRecordStore()`	Closes a record store.
`static void deleteRecordStore (String recordStoreName)`	Deletes a record store.
`long getLastModified()`	Gets the last time the store was modified.
`String getName()`	Gets the name of the store.
`int getNumRecords()`	Returns the number of records currently in the store.
`int getSize()`	Returns the total bytes used by the store.
`int getSizeAvailable()`	Returns the amount of free space. (Keep in mind that records require more storage for housekeeping overhead.)
`int getVersion()`	Retrieves the version number of the `RecordStore` object. This number increases by one every time a record is updated.
`static String[] listRecordStores()`	Returns a string array of all the record stores on the MIDlet to which you have access.
`int addRecord(byte[] data, int offset, int numBytes)`	Adds a new record to the store.
`byte[] getRecord(int recordId)`	Retrieves a record using an ID.
`int getRecord(int recordId, byte[] buffer, int offset)`	Retrieves a record into a byte buffer.
`void deleteRecord (int recordId)`	Deletes the record associated with the `recordId` parameter.
`void setRecord(int recordId, byte[] newData, int offset, int numBytes)`	Changes the contents of the record associated with `recordId` using the new byte array.
`int getNextRecordID()`	Retrieves the ID of the next record when it is inserted.
`int getRecordSize(int recordId)`	Returns the current data size of the record store in bytes.
`RecordEnumeration enumerateRecords (RecordFilter, RecordComparator, keepUpdated)*`	Returns a `RecordEnumeration` object, which is used to enumerate through a collection of records.
`void addRecordListener (RecordListener listener)*`	Adds a `listener` object that is called when records in a `RecordStore` object are changed (added, deleted, changed).
`void removeRecordListener (RecordListener listener)*`	Removes a listener previously added using the `addRecordListener` method.

* These methods are dealt with more extensively in the sections on RecordEnumeration, RecordFilter, and Record-Comparator. See the sections of this chapter dealing with these topics for further discussion.

```
//The openRecordStore() method requires that an exception be handled
public RecordStoreTest() throws Exception{
    // #2 Create an instane of the RecordStore object
        //See "Problems Caused by Deletions""
        //RecordStore.deleteRecordStore(STORE_NAME);
      createRecordStore();
    // Define a String array and assign elements
    String[] months = {"April", "May", "June", "July", "August"};

    // #2.1  Write records to a RecordStore object
    //Use the length propraty to iterate through the array
    for (int itr=0; itr < months.length; itr++){
        populateRecordStore(months[itr]);
    }
    // #2.2 Retrieve records from a RecordStore object
    int len = months.length+1;
    for (int itr=1; itr < len; itr++){
      // if(itr < rs.getSize())
      displayRecordStore(itr);
    }
    /* #2.3 Remove a record using an index
     * Uncomment to show results
     * Warning! Call this method only if the line
     * following #6.1 is not commented out.
     */
      removeRecord(3);

    // #2.4 change the value of a record
      updateRecord(2, "October");


}// End of constructor

// #3 Create the RecordScore
private void createRecordStore()throws RecordStoreException{
    // Create an instane of the RecordStore object
    rs = RecordStore.openRecordStore(STORE_NAME, true);
    System.out.println("The current number of records: "
                                + rs.getNumRecords());
    System.out.println("Name of the current RecordStore object: "
                                + rs.getName());
}//end createRecordStore
```

```java
// #4 Create the RecordScore
private void populateRecordStore(String word)throws RecordStoreException{

    int newRecordId = 0;
    byte[] rec = word.getBytes();
    if(word.length()==0){
        rec = new String("none").getBytes();
    }
    try
    {

        newRecordId = rs.addRecord(rec, 0, rec.length);
    }
    catch (Exception ex)
    {
      System.out.println(ex.toString());
    }

    System.out.println("Record store now has " + rs.getNumRecords()    +
                       " record(s) using " + rs.getSize() + " byte(s) " +
                       "[" + rs.getSizeAvailable() + " bytes free]");
}//end populateRecordStore

 // #5 Display the records in the RecordStore object
private void displayRecordStore(int index)throws Exception{

    // Determine the size of each successive record
    int recordSize = 0;
    if(index < rs.getSize()){
      recordSize = rs.getRecordSize(index);
    }
    // Check for the existence of the record
    if (recordSize > 0)
    {
      String value = new String(rs.getRecord(index));
      // Report progress to the console
      System.out.println("Retrieved record: "
                         + index + " Value: " + value);

    }
}//end displayRecordStore
```

```
protected void startApp() throws MIDletStateChangeException{
    destroyApp(true);
    notifyDestroyed();
}

protected void pauseApp(){
}

// #6 Close and delete the RecordStore object
protected void destroyApp(boolean unconditional)
                                throws MIDletStateChangeException{
    //Close the RecordStore and then Remove it
    try{
        rs.closeRecordStore();
        // #6.1 Comment out out to
        // persist between sessions
        RecordStore.deleteRecordStore(STORE_NAME);
    }catch(RecordStoreException rse){}
}

// #7 Do not use this option if line after #6.1 is commented out
private void removeRecord(int recID)throws Exception{
    String record;
    int recordNum = 0;
    try{
        record = new String(rs.getRecord(recID));
        System.out.println("Store size: " + rs.getNumRecords());
        if(rs.getRecordSize(recID)>0){
            // #7.1 Use the record id to delete
            rs.deleteRecord(recID);
            System.out.println("Record removed: " + record);
            System.out.println("New store size: " + rs.getNumRecords());
        }
    }catch(RecordStoreException rse){
        System.out.println("Record " + recID + " not found.");
        System.out.println(rse.toString());
    }
}//end removeRecord

// #8 Update a record
private void updateRecord(int recID, String newValue)throws Exception{
    String record;
     try{
```

```
            record = new String(rs.getRecord(recID));
            System.out.println("Old   record ("+ recID+ ") data: " + record);
            if(rs.getRecordSize(recID)>0){
                rs.setRecord(recID, newValue.getBytes(), 0, newValue.
length());

                record = new String(rs.getRecord(recID));
                System.out.println("Changed.New record ("+ recID
                                                   + ") " + record);

            }
        }catch(RecordStoreException rse){
            System.out.println("Record " + recID + " not found.");
            System.out.println(rse.toString());
        }
    }//end removeRecord


}//end RecordStoreTest
```

Construction

Figure 8.2 shows the first few lines of RecordStoreTest class's output when the class is executed in the NetBeans IDE. The activities shown reflect those of the createRecordStore() method as called in the constructor of the RecordStoreTest class. Later sections deal with further actions performed by the class.

In the lines preceding comment #1 of the RecordStoreTest class, you see that the io and rms packages have been imported. The rms package provides the classes for the RecordStore object and the interfaces related to it. The io package provides services related to data streams. In the lines following comment #1, the RecordStore data type is used to create a class attribute, rs. After that, an attribute to supply the name of the RecordStore object is defined (STORE_NAME). Note that it is of the String type and is made final and static.

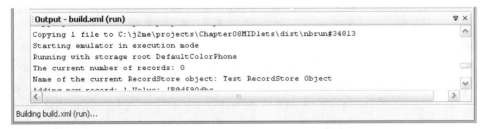

Figure 8.2
The output shows the construction and state of the RecordStore object.

In the lines accompanying comment #2, the `RecordStoreTest` constructor is defined. The constructor is defined so that it can throw an exception of the generic `Exception` type. This level of exception handling is used so that subtypes of the `Exception` class can be handled. The most important in this context is the `RecordStoreException` type.

Four custom methods are called in the context of the constructor: `create-RecordStore()`, `populateRecordStore()`, `displayRecords()`, and `removeRecord()`. The first activity within the constructor involves a call to the `createRecordStore()` method, which contains code that creates a record store. After a record store is created, the next step is to create a `String` array, `months`, to which the names of five months are assigned. This array is then used in the lines following comment #2.1 as an argument to the `populateRecordStore()` method. The argument to the method consists of an element from the `months` array identified by the counter (`itr`). Each element of the `months` array is added to the `RecordStore` object.

In the lines following comment #2.2, the `displayRecords()` method is called. In this instance, the `RecordStore::getNumRecords()` method is used to retrieve the number of records in the `RecordStore` object. The `getNumRecords()` method returns an integer value, and this value is increased by one to shift the range for the repetition statement that follows. The repetition statement calls the `displayRecords()` method, which successively retrieves each record in the `rs` `RecordStore` object.

Trailing comment #2.3 is the `removeRecord()` method. This method demonstrates deletion of a record from a `RecordStore` object. As given in the sample code, this method is initially assigned an invalid record number. To see it run, before making changes, first read the section titled "Deleting Records," later in this chapter. At comment #2.4 is the `updateRecord()` method. As arguments, the method requires the record number and new value for the record.

In the lines trailing comment #3, the `createRecordStore()` method is defined. This method makes use of the static `openRecordStore()` method of the `Record-Store` class, and for this reason, it must be defined so that it can handle an exception generated by the `openRecordStore()` method. The `RecordStore-Exception` type covers the exception. The version of `openRecordStore()` method used requires the first argument to name the `RecordStore` object (`STORE_NAME`). The second argument (`true`) forces the construction of the object if it does not already exist. The instance of the `RecordStore` object returned by the method is then assigned to the `rs` attribute.

The next few lines call the `getNumRecords()` and `getName()` methods. The `get-NumRecords()` method returns an integer revealing the number of records in the `RecordStore` object. The `getName()` method returns the name of the `DataStore`. Its return type is `String`. These returned values are used as arguments for the `println()` method. As the lines in Figure 8.2 illustrate, the values retrieved reveal that the name of the `DataStore` object is "The DataStore Object" and that the number of records currently assigned is 0.

Adding Records

In the lines following comment #4 in the `RecordStoreTest` class, the `populate-RecordStore()` method is defined. The signature line of the method provides that an exception of the `RecordStoreException` type can be thrown. This type of exception can be thrown by the `RecordStore::addRecord()` method. To implement the method, a local variable, `newRecordID`, is declared and initialized to 0. Then the `String::getBytes()` method is used to convert the string supplied by the `String word` identifier from the method's argument to a `byte` array suitable as an argument to the `addRecord()` method. A check of the arguments submitted to the method is then performed. If an empty string has been submitted, then a default value of "none" is inserted into the record. The `String` constructor is used to create the default value, and the `String::getBytes()` method is used to convert the `String` object to a `byte` array, which is required for working with the `RecordStore` object. The result is assigned to the `rec` identifier.

Within the `try...catch` block of the `populateRecordStore()` method, a call to the `RecordStore::addRecord()` method adds a record to the `RecordStore` object (rs). The `RecordStore` object expands automatically to accommodate the new record. The first argument to the `addRecord()` method is the `byte` array, `rec`. The second argument is the index of the first significant character of the `rec` array (index 0). The last is the number of bytes of a given element to be added, and this is retrieved from the `length` property of the `rec` array. The value returned by the `addRecord()` method is an integer that indicates the position (or record ID) of the newly added record in the `RecordStore` object. This integer is assigned to the `newRecordID` identifier. As Figure 8.3 reveals, the values returned begin at 1.

Upon completion of the process that adds the record, the `println()` method is used to print the status of the record and the `RecordStore` object. In the first call to the `println()` method, the value of the `newRecordID` identifier is displayed. After that, three `RecordStore` methods are called and the `println()` method is used to display the values they return. The `getNumRecords()` method returns an

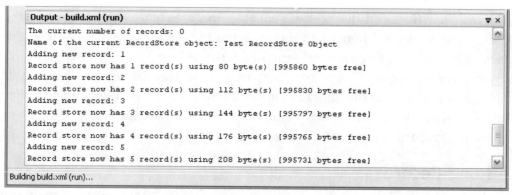

Figure 8.3
As records are added, their indexes and storage requirements can be retrieved.

integer revealing the number of records. The `getSize()` method indicates the size of the `RecordStore` object in bytes. The `getSizeAvailable()` method reveals the number of bytes remaining free for use by the `RecordStore` object. Figure 8.3 shows the change in the values with each of the newly added records.

Retrieving and Displaying Records

In the lines associated with comment #5 of the `RecordStoreTest` class, the `displayRecordStore()` method is defined. This method retrieves and displays the values stored in the `RecordStore` object. This method takes one argument, an integer indicating the index of the record to be retrieved. Because the method calls the `RecordStore::getRecord()` method, it must be able to handle exceptions. The `Exception` type satisfies this requirement.

With the first line in the body of the method, a call to the `RecordStore::getRecordSize()` method returns an integer that indicates the size, in bytes, of a record. The record itself is identified using the `index` argument supplied by the `displayRecordStore()` argument list. The value retrieved in this way is assigned to the local `recordSize` identifier, which is then used in a selection statement to test the validity of a record. A record must be at least 1 byte in length.

To retrieve the value stored in a record, the `DataStore::getRecord()` method is called. This method returns a `byte` array, so to format the returned data for display, it is made the argument of the `String` constructor. The `String` instance is then assigned to the local `String` identifier, `value`, which is used as an argument to the `println()` method, which renders the names of the months as illustrated in Figure 8.4. The `index` identifier provides the index of each record and the value assigned to the record.

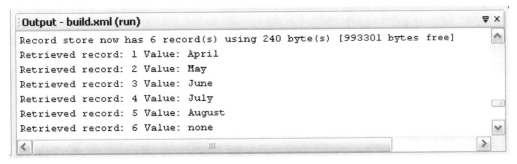

Figure 8.4
The `DataStore::getRecord()` method allows you to retrieve values you have assigned to a `RecordStore` object.

Note

In Figure 8.4, notice that as a test to the `populateRecordStore()` method, for this run only, an empty string (,"") has been inserted at the end of the list of months used to define the month list in the RecordStoreTest constructor:

`String[] months = {"April", "May", "June", "July", "August", ""};.`

Closing and Destroying

In the lines accompanying comment #6 of the `RecordStoreTest class`, the `destroyApp()` method is defined. In the line preceding comment #6.1, you call the `closeRecordStore()` method. This method locks the `RecordStore` object and allows you to switch back and forth between MIDlets without generating errors or corrupting data. It does not delete the data in the `RecordStore` object. On the other hand, following comment #6.1, the static `deleteRecordStore()` method is called, and this method *does* delete the `RecordStore` object. As an argument to this method, you supply the name of the `RecordStore` object (`STORE_NAME`). To call the method, you must place it in a `try...catch` block. The argument type for the `catch` block is `RecordStoreException`. If the `RecordStore` has not been created or cannot be destroyed, then this data type can handle the generated exception.

The lines in the `destroyApp()` method allow you to make a few easy adjustments to the class to explore different options. The `RecordStoreTest` class focuses on the generation of persistent data, which is data that continues to exist between executions of an application. For convenience, the class is initially set up to delete the persistent data it creates so that you can more readily explore concepts. To see the accumulation of persistent data, comment out the line containing the

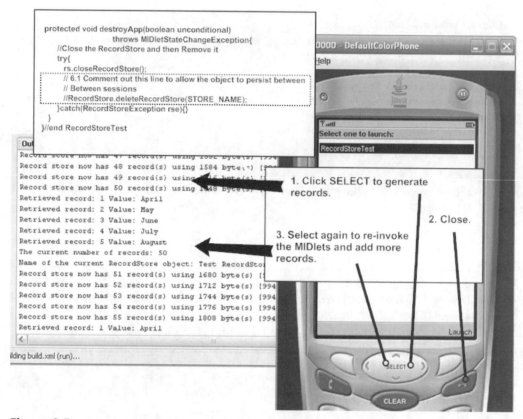

Figure 8.5
By changing the code that deletes the RecordStore, you can see data that persists across builds and runs of the RecordStoreTest class.

deleteRecordStore() method, as shown in Figure 8.5. Unless you remove the comment from the deleteRecordStore() method, records continue to accumulate in the RecordStore object, and rebuilding the class does not remove them. Although it is difficult to discern in Figure 8.5, with a few clicks of the SELECT button, 55 records have been generated.

Deleting Records

For deleting records, the removeRecord() method is called in the lines associated with comment #2.3 in the RecordStoreTest class. To proceed with this section, perform the following tasks:

1. Verify that the lines following comment #6.1 appear exactly as follows:

   // #6.1 Comment out this line to allow the object to

```
// persist between sessions
RecordStore.deleteRecordStore(STORE_NAME);
```

2. Supply a valid number other than 2 to the call to the method after comment #2.3:

```
deleteRecord(2);
```

3. Rebuild and compile your program.

4. Refer to the sidebar "Problems Caused by Deletions" for further details.

The removeRecord() method allows you to delete a record you designate using the record ID (or index) of the record in the RecordStore object. The definition of the method follows comment #7. In the definition of the method, the signature line designates that an exception of the Exception type can be thrown.

The argument of the removeRecord() method is an int value (recID). The value of recID is passed to the RecordStore::getRecord() method, which returns a byte array. The String constructor is used to convert the array to the String type, and then it is assigned to the record identifier. This identifier is passed to the println() method to display the name of the month from the record stores. Next, the getNumRecords() method is called to obtain the initial number of records. This is returned as an int value and concatenated with the output string.

After the validity of the record is established, the deleteRecord() method is called. This is the central method in the RecordStore class for deleting records. It takes one argument, an integer, which identifies the index of the record to be deleted. It has no return value. After the record has been deleted, the println() method is called two more times, one to show the text of the record removed, and the other to show the new size of the RecordStore object after the removal of the record. The new size is returned by the getNumRecords() method. As Figure 8.6 illustrates, with index 2, "May" is removed, and the record count is reduced by one.

Processing of exceptions is accomplished by placing most of the code in the removeRecord() method in a try...catch block. For the definition of the catch block argument, the RecordStoreException data type is used. This data type provides its own output message, but it is helpful in this context to provide an additional message indicating why a problem has occurred. Figure 8.7 shows what happens if the value of the recID argument is outside the range given for this exercise.

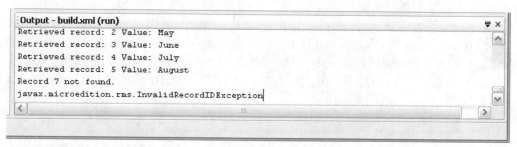

```
Output - build.xml (run)                                                    ▼ ×
Copying 1 file to C:\j2me\projects\Chapter08MIDlets\dist\nbrun#32953
Starting emulator in execution mode
Running with storage root DefaultColorPhone
The current number of records: 0
Name of the current RecordStore object: Test RecordStore Object
Record store now has 1 record(s) using 80 byte(s) [994260 bytes free]
Record store now has 2 record(s) using 112 byte(s) [994230 bytes free]
Record store now has 3 record(s) using 144 byte(s) [994197 bytes free]
Record store now has 4 record(s) using 176 byte(s) [994165 bytes free]
Record store now has 5 record(s) using 208 byte(s) [994131 bytes free]
Retrieved record: 1 Value: April
Retrieved record: 2 Value: May
Retrieved record: 3 Value: June
Retrieved record: 4 Value: July
Retrieved record: 5 Value: August
Store size: 5
Record removed: May
New store size: 4
```

Figure 8.6
The deleteRecord() permanently deletes a record from the RecordStore object.

```
Output - build.xml (run)                                                    ▼ ×
Retrieved record: 2 Value: May
Retrieved record: 3 Value: June
Retrieved record: 4 Value: July
Retrieved record: 5 Value: August
Record 7 not found.
javax.microedition.rms.InvalidRecordIDException
```

Figure 8.7
If 7, which is outside the default range of the record set, is used as an argument to the removeRecord() method, an error is generated.

Problems Caused by Deletions

When you are experimenting with the removeRecord() method, **always uncomment** the line following comment #6.1:

```
RecordStore.deleteRecordStore(STORE_NAME);
```

If you happen to run the program with this line commented out, the program generates an error. The methods of the class do not consistently include functionality that allows detection of removed records. If you encounter problems after deleting records, insert the following line after comment #2 in the constructor and rebuild and run the program. This allows the program to rebuild the data store from scratch.

```
// #2 Create an instance of the RecordStore object
RecordStore.deleteRecordStore(STORE_NAME);
```

Such problems can be remedied in a number of ways. One is with the use of enumerations.

Updating Records

The lines following comment #8 in the `RecordStoreTest` class define the `update-Record()` method. This method takes as its argument an integer (`recID`) that designates the record number and a `String` value (`newValue`) that provides the new data for the record. As with other methods involving records, it processes errors of the general `Exception` type. The lines that implement the method begin with the declaration of a local `String` identifier, `record`. Within a `try...catch` block, the `RecordStore` (`rs`) attribute is used to call the `getRecord()` method, which retrieves the data of the record. The `getRecord()` method takes as its argument the `recID` value from the argument list of the method. The record `byte` value returned by the `getRecord()` method is used as an argument to the `String` constructor, which converts the `byte` value to a `String` value. The value is then assigned to the `record` identifier.

After reporting the old number and value of the record using the `println()` method, the code then uses the `RecordStore` attribute to call the `getRecordSize()` method. Again, the value assigned to `recID` is used as an argument. The size of the record is returned. If this is not greater than zero, then no change is made.

To change the record, the `RecordStore::setRecord()` method is called. This method takes four arguments. The first is the number (`recID`) of the record to be changed. The second is the value to be inserted into the record. This must be a `byte` array. Note that to convert the `String` argument from the method's argument list into a `byte` array, the `String::getBytes()` method is used. The third argument is the offset or starting point from which data in the new string is to be taken. The fourth argument designates the number of characters to be read from the offset point in the new string.

After the new data value has been inserted, the `println()` method is again called. As Figure 8.8 illustrates, the `recID` and `record` identifiers provide the new record value and confirm that the value has been applied to the appropriate record.

Record Enumerations and Record Stores

Using the `RecordEnumeration` object, it is possible to iterate forward or backward through the records in a `RecordStore` object. After you have created a `RecordStore` object and populated it with records, the basic procedure for associating a `Record-Enumeration` object with it involves, first, declaring a `RecordEnumeration` object and then calling the `RecordStore::enumerateRecords()` method to enumerate objects in the `RecordStore` object and initialize the `RecordEnumeration` object.

Figure 8.9 illustrates a basic approach to accomplishing this task. After you have created the `RecordEnumeration` object, you employ it to call such methods

Output – build.xml (run)   ▼ ×

```
Record store now has 5 record(s) using 208 byte(s) [993331 bytes free]
Retrieved record: 1 Value: April
Retrieved record: 2 Value: May
Retrieved record: 3 Value: June
Retrieved record: 4 Value: July
Retrieved record: 5 Value: August
Store size: 5
Record removed: June
New store size: 4
Old  record (2) data: May
Changed.New record (2) October
```

Figure 8.8
The getRecord() method changes the value of a record.

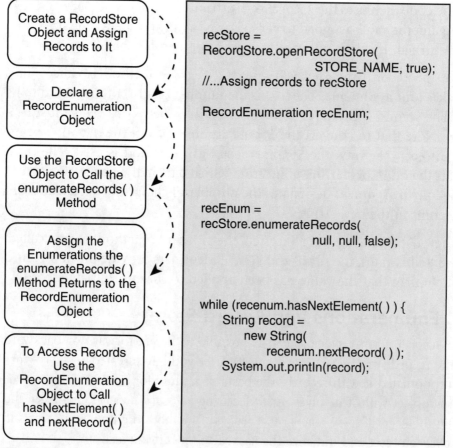

Figure 8.9
The enumerateRecords() method allows you to join the activities of the RecordStore class and RecordEnumeration interface.

Table 8.3 RecordEnumeration Methods

Method	Description
void destroy()	Destroys the enumeration object.
boolean isKeptUpdated ()	Indicates whether this enumeration object is automatically rebuilt if the underlying record store is changed.
keepUpdated (boolean keepUpdated)	Changes the keepUpdated state.
void rebuild ()	Causes the index of the enumeration object to be rebuilt, which can result in a change to the order of entries.
void reset ()	Resets the enumeration back to the state it was in after it was created. In other words, when you increment an enumeration object, it no longer identifies the first element in the RecordStore object. It has been incremented or decremented. This method places it back in its original position.
boolean hasNextElement ()	Tests whether there are any more records in the enumeration in a first-to-last order.
boolean hasPreviousElement ()	Tests whether there are any more records in the enumeration in a last-to-first order.
byte[] nextRecord ()	Retrieves the next record in the store.
byte[] previousRecord ()	Gets the previous record.
int previousRecordId ()	Returns the ID of the previous record.
int nextRecordId ()	Returns the ID of the next record.
int numRecords ()	Returns the number of records, which is important when you are using filters.
enumerateRecords(null, null, false)*	This method is called by a RecordStore object and returns a RecordEnumeration object. The methods listed above can then be called. The arguments by default can be set at null, null, and false. The first argument allows you to add a filter. The second argument allows you to add a comparator. The last indicates whether the Enumeration object should be automatically updated.

* This is a RecordStore method. It is listed here because of its position as the central method linking the RecordStore class and the RecordEnumeration interface.

as hasNextElement() and nextRecord() to navigate through the DataStore records.

The enumerateRecords() method is a member of the RecordStore class. It was listed earlier in this chapter in Table 8.2, which summarized RecordStore methods. I gave it little attention in that context because of its dependency on the RecordEnumeration interface. It deserves extended discussion in the current context, because its use is necessary prior to applying the methods associated with the RecordEnumeration class.

Table 8.3 lists the methods associated with the RecordEnumeration interface. The most visible of these in the current setting are the hasNextElement() and nextRecord() methods. The hasNextElement() method can be used in almost any context in which standard for and while repletion statements are used. It reduces implementation time and produces a safe result. The nextRecord() method returns a byte array, so it is necessary to translate its returned value using such techniques as String construction to be able to use record values for display purposes. The numRecords() and destroy() methods prove useful in situations in which it is necessary to regenerate an enumeration after deletions or additions.

The RecEnumTest Class

A standalone version of the RecEnumTest class is located in the Chapter 8 code directory. You can also access this code by opening the Chapter8MIDlets project with the NetBeans IDE. The RecEnumTest class explores the use of the Record-Enumeration interface and also reviews the standard form of the Enumeration class that allows you to work with, among other things, the Vector class. The Rec-EnumTest class is set up in a manner that closely resembles the RecordStoreTest class. A few improvements have been made. Rather than using repletion statements with controls and incremented counters, it uses only enumerations. Also, rather than an array, it uses a Vector collection. Here is the code for the Rec-EnumTest class. Discussion of it follows.

```
/*
 * @ see Chapter 8 / RecEnumTest.java
 */
import java.io.*;
import javax.microedition.midlet.*;
import javax.microedition.rms.*;
import java.util.*;

public class RecEnumTest extends MIDlet{
    // #1 Declare a RecordStore attribute and a name
    private RecordStore rs;
    private static final String STORE_NAME = "Test RecordStore Object";
    private Vector months = new Vector();


    public RecEnumTest() throws Exception{
        // #2 Set up the data
        setUpVector();
```

```java
      // Construct an empty RecordStore object
      createRecordStore();

      // #2.1 Place items from the Vector object into the
      // the RecordStore object
      Enumeration monthEnum;
      for (monthEnum = months.elements(); monthEnum.hasMoreElements();/**/){
          assignRecord(   monthEnum.nextElement().toString() );
      }

      // #2.2
      displayRecordStore();
}// End of constructor

// #3 Add elements to the Vector class attribute
private void setUpVector(){
      //Add elements to the Vector object
      months.addElement("April");
      months.addElement("May");
      months.addElement("June");
      months.addElement("July");
      months.addElement("August");

      // #3.1 Declare and use local instance of a standard Enumerator
      Enumeration monthEnum;
      // Use the enumerator
      for (monthEnum = months.elements(); monthEnum.hasMoreElements();/**/){
          System.out.println("Vector item: " + monthEnum.nextElement());
      }
}// end setUpVector

private void createRecordStore()throws RecordStoreException{
      // Create an instance of the RecordStore object
      rs = RecordStore.openRecordStore(STORE_NAME, true);
      System.out.println("The current number of records: "
                                    + rs.getNumRecords());
      System.out.println("Name of the current RecordStore object: "
                                    + rs.getName());
}//end createRecordStore

// #4 Assign a record to the DataStore object
public void assignRecord(String record){
      if(record.length()==0){
```

```
              record = "none";
          }
          byte[] rec = record.getBytes();
          try{
            rs.addRecord(rec, 0, rec.length);
            System.out.println("Record assigned. Number of records: "
                                      + rs.getNumRecords());
          }catch (Exception ex){
            System.out.println(ex.toString());
          }
      }//end assignRecord


   // #5 Create and RecordEnumerator and iterate through the records
   public void displayRecordStore(){
      try{
        if (rs.getNumRecords() > 0){
          // #5.1
          RecordEnumeration recEnum;
          recEnum = rs.enumerateRecords(null, null, true);
          while (recEnum.hasNextElement()){
            // 5.2 Retrieve the numbers
            int recNum = recEnum.nextRecordId();
            //Use the record number to get the data
            //For the RecordStore itself
            String record = new String(rs.getRecord(recNum));
            System.out.println(" Record ID: " + recNum +
                               " Record value: " + record);
          }
        }
      }catch (Exception e){
          System.out.println(e.toString());
      }
   }//end displayRecordStore

   protected void startApp() throws MIDletStateChangeException{
      destroyApp(true);
      notifyDestroyed();
   }


   public void pauseApp(){
   }


  protected void destroyApp(boolean unconditional)
```

```
                              throws MIDletStateChangeException{
    //Close the RecordStore and then Remove it
    try{
        rs.closeRecordStore();
        RecordStore.deleteRecordStore(STORE_NAME);
    }catch(RecordStoreException rse){}
  }// end destroyApp

}// end of class
```

Vectors and Enumerations

In the lines preceding comment #1, the import statements are provided. Notice, however, the inclusion of the util package. This package provides the Vector and Enumeration classes, which are used in the RecEnumTest class along with the RecordEnumeration interface. Discussion later on covers the util classes in greater detail. In the lines following comment #1, a Vector attribute is added (months). The Vector class is derived from the Collection class and provides an example of a class that can be used with an Enumeration. In this context, it replaces the array that appeared in the previous example.

Note

If you are familiar with the template constructors used with Collection classes, note that in this implementation, a template form of construction is not used. This version of the MIDP classes does not support the templates. However, to change the declaration to a template form, you use the following form:

```
Vector<String> months = new Vector<String> ();
```

Generally, programmers suggest using ArrayList instead of Vector objects, but ArrayList is not provided in the util package for the MIDP.

In the lines accompanying comment #2, the class constructor for the RecEnumTest class is implemented. First, a call is made to the setUpVector() method, which sets up the data for the class. At comment #3, the setUpVector() method is implemented. In the lines of the method, the Vector object (months) is used to call the addElement() method. This method appends an element to the end of the Vector object. The type of the object is implicitly associated with the Vector, so when it is retrieved from it, it is usually necessary to cast or reassert its type. The Vector expands automatically as the new element is added. In this instance, five names of months are added.

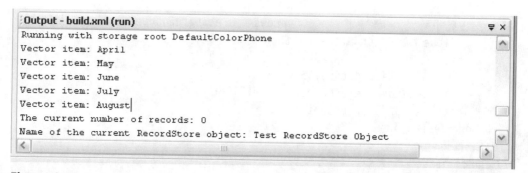

Figure 8.10
The `Vector` object and its associated `Enumeration` object replace arrays and repetition statements that use controls and counters.

In the lines of the constructor following comment #2.1 and also in the lines following comment #3.1, an `Enumeration` object is declared (`monthEnum`). In both cases, the `Vector::elements()` method is called. The `elements()` method identifies the elements in the `Vector` object and returns an `Enumeration` object. Again, in both places, it is assigned to the `monthEnum` identifier.

The `Enumeration` object is then used in a `for` repetition statement. For the first argument of this statement, the `monthEnum` object is used as a counter. The second argument furnishes the control, which in this case is a call to the `hasMore-Elements()` method of the `Enumeration` class. This method returns a value of `true`, so it iterates through the elements stored in the `Enumeration` object until it reaches the last element. At that point, it returns false. The empty comment (`/**/`) appears only to emphasize that no explicit incremental action is required. The `hasNext-Element()` serves to both increment and control the action of the statement.

Given the report that is issued by the `println()` method called immediately after comment #3.2, the output shown in Figure 8.10 appears. At this point, only the `months` Vector object and the `Enumeration` objects have been used. None of the records have as yet been assigned to the `RecordStore` object.

Assignment of the months to the `RecordStore` object occurs in the constructor, in the lines following comment #2.1. The `for` repetition statement uses the `Enumeration` object and the `nextElement()` method repeatedly to supply the `assignRecord()` method with the name of a month. The `assignRecord()` method is defined in the lines that follow comment #4. This method is a refactored version of the `populateRecordStore()` method shown earlier in this chapter.

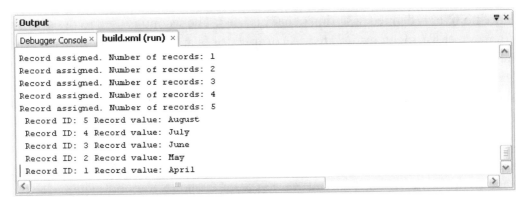

Figure 8.11
The `RecordEnumeration` object allows you to display records with relative ease.

Refactoring isolates the activity of the `RecordStore::addRecord()` method to make it possible to add a single record at a time to the `RecordStore` object (`rs`).

The `nextElement()` method successively retrieves each enumerated month that has been stored in the `Enumeration` object, but since a `String` argument is required, it is necessary to cascade the `toString()` method with the `next-Element()` method. As mentioned previously, calling the `toString()` method is a way of asserting the data type of the elements that have been assigned to the `Vector` object. Figure 8.11 shows the action of the `assignRecord()` method, which issues the message

`Record assigned. Number of records:`

for each month added to the `RecordStore` object.

RecordStores and RecordEnumerations

In the lines associated with comment #5 of the `RecEnumTest` class, the `display-Record()` method is implemented. This version of the method differs from the one seen previously in this chapter in that it makes use of the `RecordEnumeration` interface. Specifically, at comment #5.1, a local `RecordEnumeration` identifier, `recEnum`, is declared. In the next line, the `RecordStore::enumerateRecords()` method is called using the `RecordStore rs` attribute.

The `enumerateRecords()` method takes three arguments. The first argument can be used to designate a filter for the items iterated. A filter is a matching algorithm.

Since no filter is defined, a setting of null is used. The second is used to designate a comparator for the items iterated. A comparator is an algorithm for ordering the items. No comparator is defined, so again the value submitted is null. The third argument is of the boolean type and indicates whether the RecordEnumeration should be automatically updated as it is used. For example, if elements are removed then a true setting automatically updates the Enumeration so that adjustments are automatically made. In this case, the setting is to true.

The enumeration of the records is assigned to the recEnum identifier, and then the recEnum identifier is used to call the hasNextElement() method. The hasNext-Element() method iterates through the records stored in the RecordEnumeration object. Each time it finds a next element, it returns true. When it reaches the last element, it returns false. In this way, it serves to control the while repetition statement.

Within the while repetition statement, following comment #5.2, the recEnum object is used to call the nextRecordId() method. This method successively returns the ID or index number of each enumerated item in the recEnum object. The returned value is of the int type and is assigned to the recNum identifier. The recNum identifier is then used as an argument to the RecordStore::getRecord() method, which returns a byte array holding the value assigned to a record. To be able to alter this returned value so that it can be displayed, a String constructor is employed. The new String object is assigned to the record identifier. The lower five lines of the output shown in Figure 8.11 report the activities of this method.

Clearly, analogies can be made between the actions of the Enumeration::hasMore-Elements() and the RecordEnumeration::hasNextElement() methods. These methods iterate through a collection and then at the end return false. The same applies to the Enumeration:nextElement() method and the RecordEnumeration::nextRecordId() method. These methods return successive elements with each call, incrementing the enumeration. What applies to these methods also applies to the Vector::elements() method and RecordStore::enumerateRecords() method.

Using a RecordComparator Object

As mentioned previously, a comparator is an algorithm for ordering the items. An object of the RecordComparator type is used as the first argument to the RecordStore::enumerateRecords() method. In many cases, a sorting algorithm is not needed for an enumeration, because the order in which items are assigned to a RecordStore can be inspected iteratively with relative ease. On the other hand,

Table 8.4 RecordComparator Methods and Related Details

Method or Property	Description
`int compare(byte[] rec1, byte[] rec2)`	This method is overridden in the specialization of the `RecordComparator` interface used to create a class suitable for filtering. In this method, two records, `rec1` and `rec2`, are compared. By default, if `rec1` comes before `rec2` in the sort order, then the `RecordComparator.PRECEDES` is returned. If `rec1` comes after `rec2` in the sort order, then `RecordComparator.FOLLOWS` is returned. If `rec1` and `rec2` are the same, then `RecordComparator.EQUIVALENT` is returned. The `String::compareTo()` method can be used to customize operations.
`static int EQUIVALENT`	Given the sort order, the two records are the same.
`static int FOLLOWS`	Given the sort order, the second argument in the `compare()` argument list comes after the first argument in the compare argument list.
`static int PRECEDES`	Given the sort order, the first argument in the `compare()` argument list comes after the second argument in the compare argument list.
`enumerateRecords(null, comparator, false)*`	This method is called by a `RecordStore` object and returns a `RecordEnumeration` object. The arguments by default can be set at `null`, `null`, and `false`. The second argument allows you to add a comparator. It is necessary to specialize (implement) the `RecordComparator` interface to create this class.
`String::compareTo(String)`	This method is frequently used in the definition of the conditions set in the `compare()` method. Given two words, *WordA* and *WordB*, if *WordA* is alphabetically prior to *WordB*, then a negative integer value is returned. If *WordA* alphabetically follows *WordB*, then a positive integer value is returned. If *WordA* is alphabetically equal to *WordB*, then zero is returned.

* This is a `RecordStore` method. It is listed here because of its position as the central method linking the `RecordStore` class and the `RecordComparator` interface.

at times being able to order items becomes essential. The `RecordComparator` interface in this respect becomes extremely helpful.

At the core of the interface is the `compare()` method. It is the only visible method in the `RecordComparator` interface. As shown in Table 8.4, this method takes two arguments, both arrays of the byte type. The arguments designate records (rec1 and rec2). The default orders of sorting algorithms are described in Table 8.4, but the three properties (EQUIVALENT, FOLLOWS, and PRECEDES) can be used in selection structures in the definition of the compare() method to create a variety of outcomes. For example, it is possible to reverse orders or to sort alphabetically.

To implement the RecordComparator interface, the standard approach is to implement an inner class using the RecordComparator interface and then to create an instance of this class to use an argument when the enumerateRecords() method is called. Several inner classes can be created if different ordering algorithms are needed. The discussion in this section reviews two implementations.

The ComparatorTest Class

The ComparatorTest class is in the Chapter 8 source folder. As with other classes in this chapter, it is included in the Chapter8MIDlets project folder for the NetBeans IDE. The ComparatorTest class provides two inner classes, RComparator and AComparator. The AComparator class implements a compare() method that sorts the items in the RecordStore object alphabetically. The RComparator sorts them in reverse alphabetical order. The display-RecordStore() method is redefined from its previous version to allow for an argument of the RecordComparator type. Objects of the RComparator and AComparator types can be passed to it because they are each subclasses of the RecordComparator interface.

```
/*
 *   Chapter 8 \ ComparatorTest.java
 *
 */
import java.io.*;
import javax.microedition.midlet.*;
import javax.microedition.rms.*;
import java.util.*;

public class ComparatorTest extends MIDlet{

    // Declare a RecordStore attribute and a name
    private RecordStore rs;
    private static final String STORE_NAME = "Test RecordStore Object";
    private Vector months = new Vector();
```

```
//Construct
public ComparatorTest() throws Exception{
  // Set up the data
   setUpVector();
  // Construct an empty RecordStore object
   createRecordStore();

   // #1 Use Comparators
   RComparator rComp = new RComparator();
   AComparator aComp = new AComparator();
   displayRecordStore(rComp);
   displayRecordStore(aComp);

}// End of constructor

private void setUpVector(){
   //Add elements to the Vector object
   months.addElement("April");
   months.addElement("May");
   months.addElement("June");
   months.addElement("July");
   months.addElement("August");
   months.addElement("September");
   months.addElement("October");
   months.addElement("November");

   // Declare a local instance of a standard Enumerator
   Enumeration monthEnum;
   // Use the enumerator
   for (monthEnum = months.elements(); monthEnum.hasMoreElements() ;) {
      System.out.println(" Vector item: " + monthEnum.nextElement());
   }
}

// Create the RecordScore
private void createRecordStore()throws RecordStoreException{
   // Create an instane of the RecordStore object
    rs = RecordStore.openRecordStore(STORE_NAME, true);
    System.out.println("Name of the current RecordStore object: "
                             + rs.getName());

    //Verify content
    Enumeration monthEnum;
```

```
      for (monthEnum = months.elements() ; monthEnum.hasMoreElements() ;) {
        assignRecord(  monthEnum.nextElement().toString() );
      }


  }//end createRecordStore

  // Assign individual records to the RecordStore object (rs)
  public void assignRecord(String record){
       if(record.length()==0){
          record = "none";
       }
       byte[] rec = record.getBytes();
       try{
         rs.addRecord(rec, 0, rec.length);
       } catch (Exception ex){
         System.out.println(ex.toString());
       }
    }


  // #2 Display the records in the RecordStore object
  // Using one of two comparators
  public void displayRecordStore(RecordComparator compare){
    try{
      if (rs.getNumRecords() > 0){
        RecordEnumeration recEnum;
        recEnum = rs.enumerateRecords(null, compare, true);
        //Retrieve class names
        System.out.println("Order after " +
                           compare.getClass().toString() );
        while (recEnum.hasNextElement()){
          int recNum = recEnum.nextRecordId();
          String record = new String(rs.getRecord(recNum));
          System.out.println(" Record ID: " + recNum +
                            " Record value: " + record);
        }
      }
    }catch (Exception e){
        System.out.println(e.toString());
    }
  }


  // Close and delete the RecordStore object
```

```java
protected void destroyApp(boolean unconditional)
                            throws MIDletStateChangeException{
    //Close the RecordStore and then Remove it
    try{
        rs.closeRecordStore();
        RecordStore.deleteRecordStore(STORE_NAME);
    }catch(RecordStoreException rse){}
}

protected void startApp() throws MIDletStateChangeException{
    destroyApp(true);
     notifyDestroyed();
}

public void pauseApp(){
}

//=====================================================
// #3 Inner class to define a AComparator -- Alphabetical
// Overload one method - compare
 public class AComparator implements RecordComparator{
    public int compare(byte[] rec1, byte[] rec2) {
            String str1= new String(rec1);
            String str2= new String(rec2);
            int cmp = str1.compareTo(str2);
            if (cmp > 0) return RecordComparator.FOLLOWS;
            if (cmp < 0) return RecordComparator.PRECEDES;
            //(cmp == 0)
            return RecordComparator.EQUIVALENT;
            }
 }//End inner class


//=====================================================

// #4 Inner class to define a RComparator -- Reverse
 public class RComparator implements RecordComparator {
     public int compare(byte[] rec1, byte[] rec2) {
            String str1= new String(rec1);
            String str2= new String(rec2);
            int cmp = str1.compareTo(str2);
            if (cmp < 0) return RecordComparator.FOLLOWS;
            if (cmp > 0) return RecordComparator.PRECEDES;
             //(cmp == 0)
```

```
             return RecordComparator.EQUIVALENT;
          }
      }// End inner class


   //=========================================================

}// end of ComparatorTestclass
```

Use with the enumerateRecords() Method

In the lines associated with comment #1 in the ComparatorTest class, two instances of RecordComparator objects are declared and defined. These are the RComparator and AComparator objects. After their declaration, they are passed as arguments to two calls of the displayRecordStore() method. The effect of these two calls to the displayRecordStore() method is to cause the list of months defined in the setUpVector() method to be displayed in ascending and descending alphabetical order.

In the lines following comment #2, the displayRecordStore() method is defined. The method takes an argument of the RecordComparator type (compare). This argument is passed to the enumerateRecords() method, which takes a Record-Comparator object as its second argument. Its first argument is a filter. In this case, no filter has been defined, so the filter argument is set to null. The third argument allows the RecordStore enumeration to be updated. This argument is set to true. The value returned by the enumerateRecords() method is a RecordEnumeration object (recEnum) defined using the RecordComparator object.

The argument provided to the displayRecordStore() method is then used to call the getClass() and toString() methods in a cascading fashion. This allows the names of the RecordComparator classes used to order the enumerations to be named for display. Given this label, the recEnum object is then used as the argument of a while repetition statement to call the RecordEnumeration:: hasNextElement() method. As has been mentioned already, this method returns true until it reaches the end of the enumerated items, at which point it returns false. With a call to the nextRecordId() method, the IDs of the records as sorted by the RecordComparator algorithm are returned, and when used as arguments to the getRecord() method, the values in the records are retrieved. Figure 8.12 illustrates the output of the two calls to the displayRecordStore() method.

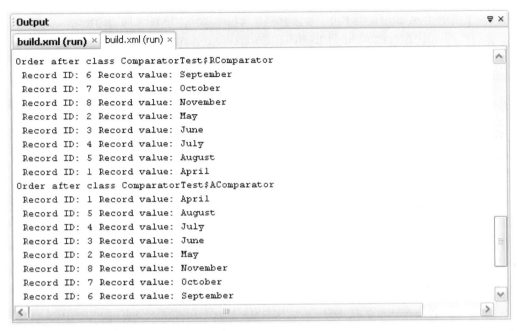

Figure 8.12
The definition of the `compare()` method determines the outcome of the `RecordComparator` action.

Specializing the RecordComparator Interface

To specialize the `RecordComparator` interface, you must redefine the `Record-Comparator::compare()` method. This method allows you to define an algorithm for sorting the items in an enumeration. In the lines following comment #3 of the `ComparatorTest` class, the `AComparator` class is defined. This is an inner class. In the definition of this class, use is made of `String` values derived from the `byte` array arguments of the `compare()` method (`byte[] rec1, byte[] rec2`). To convert the `byte` arrays into `String` objects, the `String` constructor is repeatedly used. `String` objects make it possible to use the `String::compareTo()` method, which compares the calling `String` item with the `String` item submitted as an argument to it. This method returns three values based on the comparison. Here again is a summary of how it works.

- Given two words, *WordA* and *WordB*, if *WordA* is alphabetically prior to *WordB*, then a negative integer value is returned.

- If *WordA* alphabetically follows *WordB*, then a positive integer value is returned.

- If *WordA* is alphabetically equal to *WordB*, then zero is returned.

In the implementation of the AComparator class, the compareTo() method is used to generate an integer that is used to determine how the values of the Record-Comparator constants are to be returned. The selection statements are set up as if statements to make it clearer how the values of the compareTo() method are used. The value returned by the method is assigned to the cmp identifier, and then this identifier is included in the selection statements that follow. The proximity of the two if selection arguments makes it easy to see how items can be sorted in forward or reverse order.

In the lines following comment #3, the forward comparator algorithm is implemented in the AComparator::compare() method. In this context, if the first term is greater than the second (cmp > 0), the value of FOLLOWS is returned. If the first term is less than the second term (cmp < 0), then the value of PRECEDES is returned. If the two are equal, then the value of EQUIVALENT is returned. Using this algorithm, the items in the RecordStore object are sorted alphabetically.

In the lines following comment #4, the RComparator class is implemented. This class implements a version of the compare() method that sorts items in reverse order. In this setting, if the first term is less than the second term (cmp < 0), the value of FOLLOWS is returned. If the first term is greater than the second term (cmp > 0), then the value of PRECEDES is returned. If the two are equal, then the value of EQUIVALENT is returned. Using this algorithm, the items in the RecordStore object are sorted in reverse alphabetical order.

Using a RecordFilter Object

A filter is an algorithm that you can submit to the RecordStore::enumerate-Records() method to direct it to select only specific records from the RecordStore object. To create a filter, you implement a specialized version of the RecordFilter class. To specialize the class, you override the matches() method. After you have implemented a specialized version of the RecordFilter class, you can then use an instance of it as the first argument in the enumerateRecords() method. Table 8.5 provides a summary view of some of the details related to the class.

The FilterTest Class

The FilterTest class is located in the Chapter 8 folder along with the other classes in this chapter. It is also included in the Chapter8MIDlets project for the NetBeans IDE. The class involves code already worked with in this chapter, but

Table 8.5 RecordFilter Details

Method	Description
`boolean matches (byte[] candidate)`	Returns `true` if the candidate record validly passes through the filtering rules. You must define this method when you specialize the `RecordFilter` interface.
`String::indexOf(char, int)`	This method, often used in redefinitions of the `compare()` method, returns an integer that indicates the first location of the character designated by its first argument. The second argument specifies the position in the string from which the search is to start. If a negative number is used for the starting position, the method treats it as though it is a zero. If the number designating the start index is larger than the length of the string, then the method returns −1.
`enumerateRecords(`*filter*`, null, false)*`	This method is called by a `RecordStore` object and returns a `RecordEnumeration` object. You can set the argument for the method at `filter`, `null`, and `true`. The first argument allows you to add a filter. It is necessary to specialize (implement) the `RecordFilter` interface to create the class for the filter.

* This is a `RecordStore` method. It is listed here because of its position as the central method linking the `RecordStore` class and the `RecordFilter` interface.

new features have been added. An inner class named `TextFilter` is implemented; in it the primary method in the `FilterTest` interface is defined so that records containing specific text can be selected from among those in a `RecordStore` object. The constructor for this class accepts as an argument a string to be used as a filter.

The text used for filtering can be any string that might comprise all or part of the elements assigned to the `RecordStore` object. To use the specialized version of the `TextFilter` interface, the `displaySelectedRecords()` method is defined. It accepts as an argument the text to be used as a filter. Its implementation then allows the argument to be used in the construction of a `TextFilter` object. Here is the code for the `FilterTest` class; extended discussion follows.

```
/*
 * Chapter 8 \ FilterTest.java
 *
 */
import java.io.*;
```

```java
import javax.microedition.midlet.*;
import javax.microedition.rms.*;
import java.util.*;

public class FilterTest extends MIDlet{
    // Declare a RecordStore attribute and a name
    private RecordStore rs;
    private static final String STORE_NAME = "Test RecordStore Object";
    private Vector months = new Vector();

    public FilterTest() throws Exception
    {
        // #1 Set up the data
        setUpVector();
        // Construct an empty RecordStore object
        createRecordStore();
        // #1.1
        displaySelectedRecords("none");
    }// End of constructor

    // #2 Set up data so that there are some "none" values
    private void setUpVector(){
        //Add elements to the Vector object
        months.addElement("April");
        months.addElement("May");
        months.addElement("nonentity");
        months.addElement("June");
        months.addElement("none");
        months.addElement("July");
        months.addElement("August");

        // Declare a local instance of a standard Enumerator
        Enumeration monthEnum;
        // Use the enumerator
        for (monthEnum = months.elements(); monthEnum.hasMoreElements() ;){
            System.out.println("Vector item: " + monthEnum.nextElement());
        }
    }

    // Create the RecordScore
    private void createRecordStore()throws RecordStoreException{
        rs = RecordStore.openRecordStore(STORE_NAME, true);
        System.out.println("The current number of records: "
```

```
                                    + rs.getNumRecords());
      System.out.println("Name of the current RecordStore object: "
                              + rs.getName());
      Enumeration monthEnum;
      for (monthEnum = months.elements() ; monthEnum.hasMoreElements() ;){
         assignRecord(   monthEnum.nextElement().toString() );
      }
}//end createRecordStore

// Assign individual records to the RecordStore object (rs)
public void assignRecord(String record){
      if(record.length()==0){
         record = "none";
      }
      byte[] rec = record.getBytes();
      try{
        rs.addRecord(rec, 0, rec.length);
        System.out.println("Record assigned. Number of records: "
                                          + rs.getNumRecords());
      } catch (Exception ex){
        System.out.println(ex.toString());
      }
}

// #3 Use the filter for the records
public void displaySelectedRecords(String textFilter){
   try{
     if (rs.getNumRecords() > 0){
     // Verify the arugument
     String letters = new String(textFilter).trim();
     System.out.println("Filtered with: " + letters);

     // #3.1 Create and instance of the filter
       TextFilter filter = new TextFilter(letters);
     // Use the instance of the filter as an argument
     RecordEnumeration recEnum
              = rs.enumerateRecords(filter, null, true);
     //Retrieve record numbers and data fromthe DataStore object
      while (recEnum.hasNextElement()){
         int recNum = recEnum.nextRecordId();
         String record = new String(rs.getRecord(recNum));
         System.out.println("(Found) Record ID: " + recNum);
         System.out.println(" Record value: " + record);
```

```
              }
            }
        }catch (Exception e){
            System.out.println(e.toString());
        }
    }

    // #4 Define a class for filtering
    //======================================================
class TextFilter implements RecordFilter{

    private String textToFind = null;
    // #4.1
    public TextFilter(String text)
    {
        textToFind = text.toLowerCase();
    }

    // #4.2
    public boolean matches(byte[] value){
        String str = new String(value).toLowerCase();
        // Look for a match
        if (textToFind != null && str.indexOf(textToFind) != -1){
         return true;
        } else{
         return false;
        }
    }// end match
}// end LetterFilter
    //======================================================

    // Close and delete the RecordStore object
    protected void destroyApp(boolean unconditional)
                            throws MIDletStateChangeException{
        //Close the RecordStore and then Remove it
        try{
            rs.closeRecordStore();
            RecordStore.deleteRecordStore(STORE_NAME);
        }catch(RecordStoreException rse){}
    }

    protected void startApp() throws MIDletStateChangeException{
        destroyApp(true);
```

```
        notifyDestroyed();
    }

    public void pauseApp(){
    }
}// end of FilterTest class
```

FilterTest Construction

In the lines preceding comment #1 of the FilterTest class, RecordStore (rs) and Vector (months) attributes are defined for the class. An instance of the Vector class is created. In the line following comment #1, a call is then made to the setUpVector() class. In classes discussed previously in this chapter, this method has been used to define the primary list of records to be used in the RecordStore object. As the lines following comment #3 illustrate, the picture remains the same in this context, with the difference that more records are used and, in a few instances, a string or substring consisting of "none" is appended to the Vector object (months) using the addElement() method.

In the line associated with comment #1.1, the displaySelectedRecords() is called. This method takes an argument of the String type. In this case, the argument is "none". To trace the work of the argument, it is necessary to inspect the code following comment #3, where the displaySelectedRecords() method is defined. The argument for the function is defined using the TextFilter identifier. This argument is then used as the argument to a String constructor and assigned to the letters identifier. The String::trim() method eliminates trailing spaces from the filter text before it is assigned to the letters identifier.

After the println() method writes the value assigned to the letters identifier to the console, in the lines following comment #3.1, the letters identifier is used a second time as the argument to the TextFilter constructor. The constructor takes one argument, which specifies the string to be used as a filter. The instance of the TextFilter class is assigned to the filter identifier.

The filter identifier can then be used as an argument in the enumerateRecords() method of the RecordStore class. The method is called using the rs attribute, and an instance of TextFilter class is used as its first argument. Its second argument is used to designate a comparator. In the current context, no comparator has been defined, so an argument of null is assigned. The last argument designates whether the RecordEnumeration object is to be automatically updated, and this value is set to true. The RecordEnumeration object is assigned to the

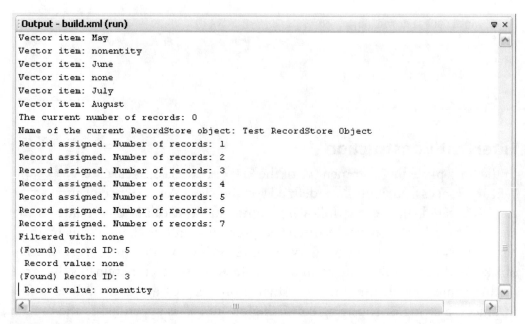

Figure 8.13
Filtering in the `TextFilter` class involves wrapping the `indexOf()` method in the `match()` method.

`recEnum` object, and given the definition of the filter, the `nextRecordId()` method returns only those records that contain the "none" string. Figure 8.13 illustrates the output.

Specializing the RecordFilter Interface

To define a filter to be used in the `RecordStore::enumerateRecords()` method, it is necessary to override the `matches()` method of the `RecordFilter` interface. To accomplish this task, as is shown in the lines trailing comment #4, an inner class, `TextFilter`, is created. The `TextFilter` class implements the `Record-Filter` class.

The class contains one attribute, `textToFind`, which is of the `String` type. As the lines associated with comment #4.1 reveal, for the implementation of the `TextFilter` constructor, one argument is defined (text). This argument is then converted to lowercase characters using the `String::toLowerCase()` method and assigned to the `textToFind` attribute. Converting the string to lowercase letters ensures that they are filtered consistently.

Given this construction sequence, following comment #4.2, the matches() method is implemented. The matches() method takes one argument of the byte array type (value). The value identifier is used as an argument in a String constructor. The constructor calls the toLowerCase() method to convert the resulting string to lowercase letters, and the result is assigned to the str identifier. The identifier is then used in a selection statement that employs a compounded Boolean expression. The first part tests for the existence of the string. The second part tests the value returned by the String::indexOf() method.

As pointed out in Table 8.5, the indexOf() method returns an integer that indicates the first location of the character designated by its first argument. The second argument specifies the position in the string from which the search is to start, and if the number designating the start index is larger than the length of the string, then the method returns –1. Generally, then, the match() in this case wraps the indexOf() method. The result returned is the string the text argument provides. As Figure 8.13 illustrates, the filter allows the enumeration object to examine the list for those records that correspond to the string or substring "none". The indexOf() method can find either.

Using RecordListener Objects

The RecordListener interface provides three methods that allow you to create listeners for RecordStore actions involving adding, changing, and deleting records. A listener is a method that is automatically paired with another method. It reports on the actions of the method with which it is paired. As Figure 8.14 illustrates, the RecordListener interface provides three methods. They work in conjunction with the addRecord(), deleteRecord(), and setRecord() methods of the RecordStore classes. Each time one of these methods is invoked, the recordAdded(), recordChanged(), or recordDeleted() method is also invoked. By taking advantage of this relationship, you can perform background messaging or cleanup activities.

To make it so that such services are provided, one approach is to create an inner class that implements the RecordListener interface. Within this class, the three methods of the RecordStore interface can then be overridden to define specific actions to be performed in conjunction with the three RecordStore messages.

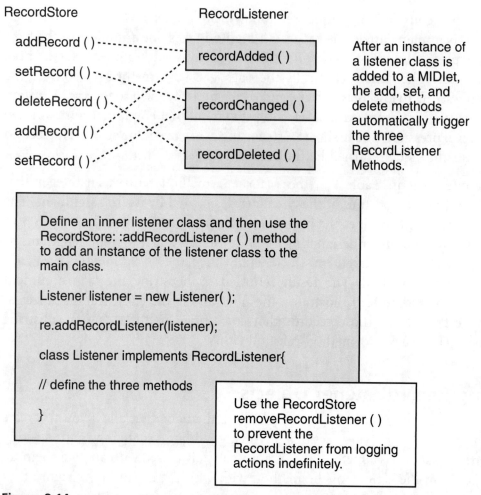

Figure 8.14
One approach to adding a listener to a MIDlet is to use an inner class.

Table 8.6 lists some of the interface features of the RecordListener interface. In addition to the functions the RecordListener interface provides, to use record listeners, it is necessary to call the addRecordListener() method of the RecordStore class. This adds the listener. It is also helpful to call the remove-RecordListener() method to delete items in the listener event list.

The RecordListenerTest Class

The RecordListenerTest class provides an example of how to create a MIDlet class (RecordListenerTest) that features an inner class (Listener). The inner class implements the RecordListener methods so that they can serve as a

Table 8.6 RecordListener and Related Methods

Feature	Method
`void recordAdded(RecordStore recordStore, int recordId)`	This is the `RecordListener` method called when the `addRecord()` of the `RecordStore` class is called.
`void recordChanged (RecordStore recordStore, int recordId)`	This is the `RecordListener` method called when the `setRecord()` method of the `RecordStore` class is called.
`void recordDeleted (RecordStore recordStore, int recordId)`	This is the `RecordListener` method called when the `deleteRecord()` method of the `RecordStore` class is called.
`void removeRecordListener(listener)*`	This is a `RecordStore` method used to remove a record listener from a MIDlet class.
`void addRecordListener(RecordListener listener)*`	This is a `RecordStore` method that adds a listener to the `RecordStore` object so that when records in the `RecordStore` object are changed (added, deleted, changed), the listeners can issue messages about the changes or take other actions.

* These are RecordStore methods. They are listed here because of their position as central methods linking the RecordStore class and the RecordListener interface.

customized set of listeners for the add, delete, and change methods associated with the `RecordStore` class. In this context, the inner `Listener` class defines the `RecordListener` methods so that they issue command line messages. These listeners replace most of the `println()` method calls used to trace events in the classes developed previously in this chapter. To activate the listener methods it is necessary to call the `RecordStore::addRecordListener()` method, which as Table 8.6 mentions, takes a `RecordListener` object as its argument. You can find the `RecordListenerTest` class in both a standalone version in the Chapter 8 source folder and also in the `Chapter8MIDlets` project set up in the NetBeans IDE. Discussion of the code follows.

```
/*
 * Chapter 8 \ RecordListenerTest.java
 *
 */
import java.io.*;
import javax.microedition.midlet.*;
```

```java
import javax.microedition.rms.*;
import java.util.*;

public class RecordListenerTest extends MIDlet{

    private RecordStore rs;
    private static final String STORE_NAME = "Test RecordStore Object";
    private Vector months = new Vector();
    Listener listener = new Listener();
    private final int RECORD_LIMIT = 10;
    private Random random;

    //Construct
    public RecordListenerTest() throws Exception{
        random = new Random(12L);
        // #1 Add a record listener to the class
        rs = RecordStore.openRecordStore(STORE_NAME, true);
        rs.addRecordListener(listener);

        setUpVector();
        // Construct an empty RecordStore object
        createRecordStore();
        // #1.1
        displayRecords();
        // #1.2
        updateRecord(1, randomMonth());
        removeRecord(2);
    }// End of constructor

    // #2 Set up data so that there are some "none" values
    private void setUpVector(){
        //Add elements to the Vector object
        int itr = 0, ctrl = 5;
        while(itr < ctrl){
            months.addElement(randomMonth() );
            itr++;
        }

        Enumeration monthEnum;
        for (monthEnum = months.elements(); monthEnum.hasMoreElements() ;){
            System.out.println("Vector item: " + monthEnum.nextElement());
        }
    }
```

```
// #3 Generate data randomly
private String randomMonth(){
    String changes[] = {"January", "February", "March",
                        "April",   "May",      "June",
                        "July",    "August",   "September",
                        "October", "November", "December"};
    int randInt = 0;
    randInt = random.nextInt(12);
    String val = changes[randInt];
    return val;
}


// 3.1 Create the RecordScore
private void createRecordStore()throws RecordStoreException{
    setUpVector();
    if(rs.getNumRecords()< RECORD_LIMIT){
       for(Enumeration monthEnum = months.elements();
                       monthEnum.hasMoreElements();){
           assignRecord(  monthEnum.nextElement().toString() );
        }
    }

}//end createRecordStore

// #3.2 Assign individual records to the RecordStore object (rs)
public void assignRecord(String record){
    if(record.length()==0){
       record = "none";
    }
    byte[] rec = record.getBytes();
    try{
      rs.addRecord(rec, 0, rec.length);
    } catch (Exception ex){
      System.out.println(ex.toString());
    }
}

// #3.3 Call to the listner with each creation of a record
public void displayRecords(){
   try{
     if (rs.getNumRecords() > 0){
       RecordEnumeration recEnum;
       recEnum = rs.enumerateRecords(null, null, true);
```

```
        while (recEnum.hasNextElement()){
          int recNum = recEnum.nextRecordId();
          String record = new String(rs.getRecord(recNum));
          System.out.println(" Record ID: " + recNum +
                              " Record value: " + record);
        }
      }
    } catch (Exception e){
        System.out.println(e.toString());
    }
}


// #3.4 Call to the listner with each deletion
private void removeRecord(int recID)throws Exception{

    try{
        if(rs.getRecordSize(recID)>0){
          rs.deleteRecord(recID);
        }
    }catch(RecordStoreException rse){
        System.out.println("Record " + recID + " not found.");
        // System.out.println(rse.toString());
    }
}//end removeRecord



// #3.5 Call to the lisener with each update
private void updateRecord(int recID, String newValue)throws Exception{
    String record;
     try{
        record = new String(rs.getRecord(recID));
        if(rs.getRecordSize(recID)>0){
          rs.setRecord(recID, newValue.getBytes(), 0, newValue.
length());
        }
    }catch(RecordStoreException rse){
        System.out.println("Record " + recID + " not found.");
        //System.out.println(rse.toString());
    }
}//end
```

```
// #4 Create a Listener class
//=======================================================
class Listener implements RecordListener
    {

        // #4.1 Reports that a record is added
        public void recordAdded(RecordStore recordStore, int recID){
            String listenerID = "(recordAdded listener)";
            try{
                System.out.println(listenerID  + " Added record " + recID
                                                + " to "
                                                + recordStore.getName());
                System.out.println("(recordAdded listener) Number of records: "
                                                + recordStore.getNumRecords());

            }
            catch(Exception e){
                System.out.println(e);
            }
        }

        // #4.2 Reports that a record is changed
        public void recordChanged(RecordStore recordStore, int recID){
            String listenerID = "(recordChanged listener)";
            try{
                String change = new String(recordStore.getRecord(recID));
                System.out.println(listenerID  + " Changed record " + recID
                                                + " to "
                                                + change);
            }catch (Exception e){
                System.out.println(e);
            }
        }

        // #4.3 Reports when a record is deleted
        public void recordDeleted(RecordStore recordStore, int recID) {
            String listenerID = "(recordDeleted listener)";
            try{
                System.out.println(listenerID  + " Deleted record " + recID
                                                + " from "
                                                + recordStore.getName());
                System.out.println("New store size: " +
                                   rs.getNumRecords() + "\n");
```

```
            }
          catch (Exception e){
              System.out.println(e);
          }
      }
    }// end inner class
  //=================================================

  // #5 Close and delete the RecordStore object
    protected void destroyApp(boolean unconditional)
                                 throws MIDletStateChangeException{
        //Close the RecordStore and then Remove it
        try{
            rs.removeRecordListener(listener);
            rs.closeRecordStore();
            /// #5 Remove the listener
            RecordStore.deleteRecordStore(STORE_NAME);
        }catch(RecordStoreException rse){}
    }


    protected void startApp() throws MIDletStateChangeException{
        destroyApp(false);
        notifyDestroyed();
    }

    public void pauseApp(){
      }
}// end of class
```

RecordListenerTest Construction

As is evident in the lines preceding comment #1 in the RecordListenerTest class, the activity that takes place in the constructor of the RecordListenerTest class involves first declaring a RecordStore attribute (rs) and then initializing an instance of the inner Listener class (listener). Creating an instance of the Listener class is not enough to immediately associate it with the RecordListenerTest class, but it is a necessary preliminary. In addition to the Listener object, the attribute list also provides for a constant value, RECORD_LIMIT, which controls the number of records the class adds to the RecordStore object. This attribute is used in the `createRecordStore()` method (see comment #3.1) to check for the number of records that have been added to the `MIDlet` record store. It is initially set to 10.

After the definition of the `RECORD_LIMIT` constant, an identifier for a `Random` class object is declared (`random`). Then, on the first line within the scope of the constructor, an instance of the `Random` class is created and assigned to the `random` identifier. The argument for the `Random` constructor is a `long` value that sets the range of random numbers that `Random` object generates. To designate a literal constant as a `long`, an `L` is appended to the constant (`12L`). When an instance of the `Random` class is created at the class scope and then initialized in the constructor (as it is here), it can generate new values as it is employed in various contexts later on through calls to the `randomMonth()` method.

Following comment #1, an instance of a `RecordStore` object is created and assigned to the `rs` attribute. After that, the `addRecordListener()` method is called. This method takes as its argument the `listener` attribute created in the attribute list. The `addRecordListener()` method is an important part of the `RecordStore` interface. It is complemented by the `removeRecordListener()` method, which is called in the `destoryApp()` method (see comment #5). Removal of the listener prevents the application from accumulating listener messages if you repeatedly invoke it.

Following the addition of the `RecordListener` object, the `setUpVector()` method is invoked. This method has been presented in several of the classes discussed previously in this chapter. It assigns elements to the `Vector` class attribute (`months`). In this implementation, as is evident in the lines following comment #2, the elements are added to the `Vector` using the calls to the `randomMonth()` method. A `while` repetition statement is used to add records in groups of five. The value for a month is added by using a call to the `randomMonth()` method as an argument to the `Vector::addElement()` method. The `randomMonth()` method returns the name of a month each time it is called.

Assigning Records

Following comment #3, the `randomMonth()` method is defined. It has no arguments, and its return type is `String`. To define this method, the first task involves creating a `String` array (`changes`) consisting of the 12 months of the year. Then the `Random::nextInt()` method is called. The random attribute has been declared at class scope and initialized in the class constructor. When it is used to call the nextInt() method, it returns a pseudorandom number in the range from 0 up to the number set as its argument. In this case, the argument is 12, so the range extends from 0 to 11. The argument defines the limit of the range returned by the method but is not itself within the range. The number returned by the nextInt() is used as an index to retrieve the name of the month from the changes array. This value is returned as a String object by the randomMonth() method. Each call of the method in theory generates a random month name.

RecordListener Actions

In the line preceding comment #1.1, the createRecordStore() method is called. This method is defined in the lines following comment #3.1. At the start of the definition is a call to the setUpVetor() method (see comment #2), which refreshes the list of months that can be added to the RecordStore object. Next, the RECOR-D_LIMIT constant is used to control the number of records added to the Record-Store (rs) object. A record can be assigned to the RecordStore object as long as the value returned by the getNumRecords() method is less than the defined value for RECORD_LIMIT. This element is introduced to this program to limit its capacity to create new records with each new execution. The starting value is 10 but for experimentation this can be set to 50, 500, or any other value. A for repletion statement is then implemented using a compacted implementation of an Enumeration object. Within the repletion block, the assignRecord() method is called.

This proves an important step. Associated with comment #3.2, the assign-Record() method remains largely the same in appearance as in previous classes in this chapter. It serves as a wrapper for the addRecord() method. With each call of this method, a record is added to the RecordStore object, and as Figure 8.15 shows, a message is written to the console. Notice, however, that the println() method that printed such messages is now absent from the assignRecord() method. The messages are now issued by the Listener::recordAdded() method. This listener has been attached to the addRecord() method and generates a message each time it is invoked. Figure 8.15 illustrates the messages issued by the listener as the addRecord() method is called 10 times to create the initial set of records.

The displayRecords() method is called following comment #1.1. This method is defined in the lines following comment #3.3. The only significant feature of the method is that the enumerateRecords() method is set without RecordComparator or RecordFilter objects. The third argument to the method is true, so the RecordEnumeration object can be updated as needed.

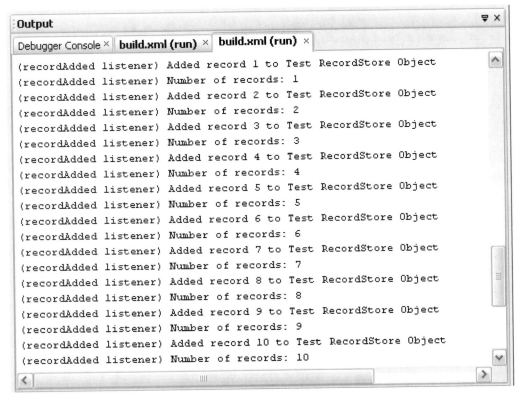

Figure 8.15
A message is generated each time the `addRecord()` method is called.

At comment #1.2, the `updateRecord()` and `removeRecord()` methods are called. These methods, like the `assignRecord()` method, invoke actions from listeners. The `removeRecord()` method (see comment #3.4) invokes the `deleteRecord()` method of the `RecordStore` class. Whenever the `deleteRecord()` method executes, its action triggers the `recordDeleted()` method of the `Listener` class. Along the same lines, the `updateRecord()` method (see comment #3.5) invokes the `setRecord()` method of the `RecordStore` class. This in turn calls the `record-Changed()` method of the `Listener` class. Figure 8.16 in the next section illustrates the messages these methods generate.

Specializing the RecordListener Interface

In the lines trailing comment #4 of the `RecordListenerTest` class, the inner `Listener` class is defined. To define this class, it is necessary to implement the `RecordListener` interface. After that, the three methods of the interface are

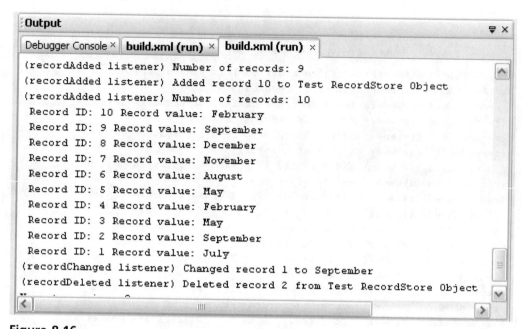

Figure 8.16
The `Listener` class provides messages that accompany actions involving adding, changing, and deleting records.

overridden. As shown in the code following comments #4.1, #4.2, and #4.3, these are the `recordAdded()`, `recordChanged()`, and `recordDeleted()` methods.

You can use the same technique to implement all three of these methods. In the current setting, the approach involves moving the code that was previously embedded in the `RecordListenerTest` class into the methods of the `Listener` class. In the implementation of the `recordAdded()` method, for example, a standard message for the `addRecord()` action — "(recordAdded listener)" — is assigned to a local `String` identifier, `listenerID`. After that, a `try...catch` block is created, and within this a series of calls to the `println()` method reports the action.

As is shown in Figures 8.15 and 8.16, since the `RecordStore` (rs) object lies within the scope of both the outer and inner classes, calls to the `getName()` and `get-NumRecords()` methods report on activities involved in adding, changing, and deleting records.

Exceptions

The classes presented in this chapter have provided examples of exception handling, but the examples are limited. By calling the `toString()` method during

Table 8.7 RMS Exceptions

Exception	Description
InvalidRecordIDException	Indicates that an operation could not be completed because the record ID was invalid.
RecordStoreException	Indicates that a general exception occurred in a record store operation.
RecordStoreFullException	Indicates that an operation could not be completed because the record store system storage was full.
RecordStoreNotFoundException	Indicates that an operation could not be completed because the record store could not be found.
RecordStoreNotOpenException	Indicates that an operation was attempted on a closed record store.

testing sessions you can readily identify the types of exceptions thrown. These are described in Table 8.7. You can use the println() method to channel the default exception text to the command line. In many of the classes shown in this chapter, the general Exception type suffices to handle most of the exceptions.

RecordStoreNotFoundException, RecordStoreNotOpenException, InvalidRecord-IDException, and RecordStoreException can usually be handled without restarting the MIDlet. This is not the case with the RecordStoreFullException, which usually requires that resources be freed up to provide sufficient space for the MIDlet to execute.

Conclusion

In this chapter, you have continued the exploration of the MID API by concentrating on persistent objects. The resources available for working with persistent objects are extensive, but they all center on the RecordStore class. The static RecordStore::openRecordStore() method is used to add a RecordStore object to a MIDlet. The static RecordStore::deleteRecordStore() method is used to remove a RecordStore object. The RecordStore class offers the addRecord(), getRecord(), setRecord(), and deleteRecord() methods to accomplish the basic tasks usually associated with databases. The RecordEnumeration interface makes it possible to create enumeration objects for RecordStore objects. To accomplish this, the enumerateRecords() method of the RecordStore class is used. The RecordEnumeration interface includes the hasNextElement() and nextRecordID() methods. The enumerateRecords() method can also be used to add objects of the `RecordFilter` and `RecordComparator` interfaces to actions associated with the `RecordEnumeration` interface. The `RecordFilter` interface requires that the `matches()` method be overridden. The `RecordComparator` interface requires that the `compare()` method be overridden. Along with these capabilities, one other is also available. This is the use of listeners, which the `RecordListener` interface provides. By defining the `recordAdded()`, `record-Changed()`, and `recordDeleted()` methods of the `RecordListener` interface, automatic actions can be established for the `addRecord()`, `setRecord()`, and `deleteRecord()` methods of the `RecordStore` class.

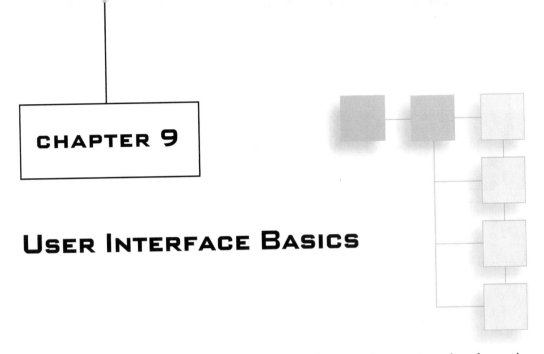

CHAPTER 9

User Interface Basics

This chapter initiates a sequence of several chapters that review the classes in the MIDP that allow you to readily implement user interfaces. The classes that provide these services begin with the Displayable class, which provides a pattern for such classes as Form, TextBox, Alert, and List. By associating Command objects with Displayable objects and using the capabilities provided by the CommandListener interface, you can readily handle the messages generated by the Displayable objects. Processing messages can be accomplished through the commandAction() method of the CommandListener interface. This method allows you to track messages of the Displayable and Command types. Levels of abstraction characterize the user interface components of the MIDP. The higher the level of abstraction, the more readily the components can be implemented.

User Interface (LCDUI)

The MIDP provides what might be viewed as three sets of user interface classes. One set provides a high-level, abstract UI. Another set furnishes a low-level, concrete UI. In a middle level of abstraction is the Game API, which combines features of both of the other two sets. Each set of classes allows you to achieve specific ends. This chapter and the next provide a discussion of high-level classes. Chapter 11 discusses low-level classes. Chapter 13 discusses specific aspects of the Game API classes.

API Characteristics

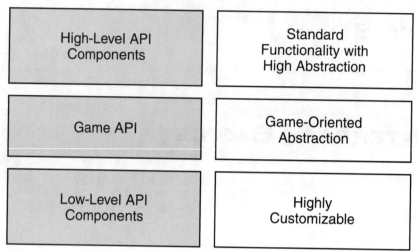

Figure 9.1
Levels of abstraction characterize the ME UI classes.

Figure 9.1 illustrates the differences between the classes with respect to their levels of abstraction. Some features of the software you develop for devices allow few development options. Others allow many. The fewer the options, the more sense it makes to provide highly abstract classes—classes that furnish fairly standardized features. The larger the number of options, the more sense it makes to allow greater flexibility.

At the high level, the UI completely abstracts the device. Consider, for example, that it makes little sense to do things like change the standard operations of keys, buttons, or display options to conform with the characteristics of the thousands of devices that might be targeted. With respect to such features, the MIDP implementation on a particular device determines what the user sees and how the user can respond to it. A standardized set of interactions is sustained.

At the low level, things change because the routines you implement represent the creativity that makes an application or game interesting. It is not practical or even advisable to try to abstract such activities. For this reason, the low-level UI comes in play. It provides components and functionality that allow you to effect a wide variety of different activities in various ways.

The Game API represents what might be viewed as a middle level of abstraction. When you use the Game API, you have access to a small set of classes, such as

GameCanvas, Layer, and Sprite, which provide you with enhanced, standardized, and in some cases abstract features that allow you to implement game behavior.

Class Hierarchy

The group of classes that provides the user interface is usually referred to as the Liquid Crystal Display User Interface (LCDUI). Use of the LCDUI centers on the screen and how the user interacts with it. This approach to the UI simplifies program implementation but is still flexible in the face of a dizzying variety of devices. Table 9.1 summarizes the high-level classes in the LCDUI packages. These

Table 9.1 Selective LCDUI Class Summary

Class	Description
Interfaces	
Choice	Provides the common interface used to manage a selection of items.
CommandListener	Lets you create a listener for command events from the high-level UI.
ItemStateListener	Lets you create a listener for changes to an Item object's state.
UI System and Utility Classes	
Display	Represents the manager of the system's display and input devices.
Font	Obtains font objects along with their metrics.
Image	A class for holding image data.
AlertType	A helper class that defines the types of alerts you can create, such as ALARM, CONFIRMATION, ERROR, INFO, WARNING.
Displayable	An abstract base class for an object that can be displayed.
High-Level UI	
Command	Abstracts a user action on the interface.
Screen Classes	
Screen	Provides a base class for high-level UI components.
Alert	A screen to alert the user to something. An Alert object is a screen. It takes over the entire display, but it cannot have commands like other Screen objects.
List	A screen object that contains a list of choices.
TextBox	A screen object used for editing text. A TextBox object uses the entire screen and has additional features, such as a clipboard and cut, copy, and paste tools.
Forms and Items	
Form	A screen that acts as a container for one or more Items.
Item	A base class for something you can stick on a Form (or an Alert).
Space	An object that is not interactive. It is used to set space between items.

(Continued)

Table 9.1 Continued

Class	Description
ChoiceGroup	Provides a UI component for presenting a list of choices.
DateField	Provides a UI component to get the user to enter a date.
Gauge	Displays a pretty graph bar to show progress.
ImageItem	Provides an Item that is also an Image. (See earlier Item entry for more information.)
StringItem	An Item object for displaying a String.
TextField	An Item used to edit text. A TextField is a simple control you can embed inside a form.
Ticker	An Item that scrolls a band of text along the display.
Low-Level UI	
Graphics	Provides 2D graphics tools.
Canvas	The base class used to create low-level UI graphics.
Game API	
GameCanvas	The primary building block for user interfaces for games.
Sprite	The primary visual element in games.
TiledLayer	A visual element that provides a set of cells.
Layer	An abstract class used to organize the display of visual objects.
LayerManager	An object used to manage the rendering of layers.

classes are provided by the javax.microedition.lcdui and javax.microedition .lcdui.game packages. For a complete view of the classes, access **http://java.sun .com/javame/reference/apis/jsr118/**. As Table 9.1 shows, the classes that provide these objects fall into the following functional categories:

- System or utility classes, such as Display, Font, AlertType, and Ticker.

- Low-level API classes, such as Canvas and Graphics.

- High-level API Screen classes, such as Alert, Form, List, and TextBox.

- Game API classes, among which are GameCanvas, Sprite, and TiledLayer.

- High-level API Form component classes. Such classes are derived from Item. Among them are ChoiceGroup, DateField, Gauge, ImageItem, StringItem, and TextField.

At the heart of the higher-level activities of the LCDUI is the display apparatus of the MID. What appears on the display can be generically referred to as a *screen*. One screen can be displayed at any given point in time. This situation is analogous to looking at the faces of cards in a deck. As you proceed through the deck,

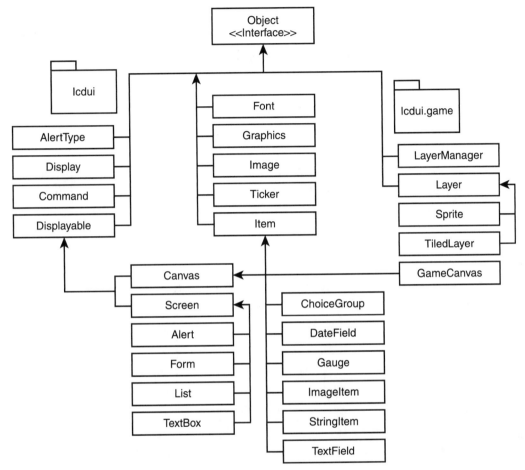

Figure 9.2
The class hierarchy for the LCDUI.

each card is a screen. The classes that provide screens can be viewed in four basic groups:

- **Low-level UI.** Accessible through the Canvas class.

- **Game API.** Activities you implement using the game classes.

- **Form.** Displays groups of UI components.

- **Complex components at a higher level.** Such components are often subclasses of the Screen class. Examples are TextBox, List, and Form.

When you work with a screen, you create features that are seen and features that are unseen. The services the MIDP offers become more visible the more they move in the direction of the high-level components. Figure 9.2 illustrates the

LCDUI class hierarchy for most of the classes listed in Table 9.1. Note that the classes in the Game API are included in the lcdui.game package, while others are in the lcdui package. The class names shown in italics are abstract.

Display and Displayable

The Display class provides the foundation for visual interaction with a MIDlet. There can be one and only one instance of the Display class in a MIDlet. The Display object allows you to communicate with the device and to provide a context in which to display visible screen components. To obtain an instance of the display, you use the getDisplay() method. This method is static and returns an object of the Display type. A call to the getDisplay() takes the following form:

```
Display display = Display.getDisplay(this);
```

The this keyword identifies the current instance of the MIDlet class. Table 9.2 furnishes a summary of a few of the methods in the interface of the Display class.

Table 9.2 Display Methods

Method	Description
void callSerially(Runnable r)	Serially calls a java.lang.Runnable object later.
Displayable getCurrent()	Gets the current Displayable object.
static Display getDisplay(MIDlet m)	Retrieves the current Display object for the MIDlet.
boolean isColor()	Determines whether the device supports color.
int numColors()	Determines the number of colors (or gray levels, if not color).
setCurrent(Displayable)	Designates the next Displayable object to be shown.
void setCurrent(Alert alert, Displayable nextDisplayable)	Displays Alert, and then falls back to display the nextDisplayable object.
setCurrentItem(Item)	Brings the focus to the Displayable object that contains the named Item object.
void setCurrent(Displayable nextDisplayable)	Shows the nextDisplayable object.
getDisplay(MIDlet)	This method returns an instance of the Display class associated with the current MIDlet. It is called statically: Display.getDisplay(this), and the this keyword identifies the current instance of the MIDlet class.
vibrate()	Used to cause the device to vibrate if it is capable of such activity.

The `Display()::getCurrent()` method returns an argument of the `Displayable` type. The `Display::setCurrent()` method renders visible the object you submit to it as an argument. Such actions allow you to work readily with the primary components that appear on the screen.

As shown in Figure 9.2, most of the large visible components you work with are derived from the `Screen` and `Canvas` classes. The `Screen` and `Canvas` classes are abstract and are derived from the `Displayable` class. The `Alert`, `Form`, `List`, and `TextBox` classes are derived from the `Screen` class. To display or manipulate such objects, you often use calls to methods provided in the abstract `Displayable` class.

Since the `Displayable` class is abstract, its interface becomes concrete in classes derived from the `Screen` and `Canvas` classes. As Table 9.3 illustrates, the methods the `Displayable` and other abstract classes furnish are concerned with component

Table 9.3 Displayable Methods

Method	Description
addCommand(Command cmd)	Associates a command to the Displayable object.
int getHeight()	Returns the height of the displayable area available to the application. The measurement is in pixels.
Ticker getTicker()	Returns the Ticker object associated with the Displayable.
String getTitle()	Returns the title of the Displayable.
int getWidth()	Returns the width of the area available for use by objects. The measurement is in pixels.
boolean isShown()	Returns a Boolean value to indicate whether the Displayable object is currently visible.
void removeCommand(Command)	Makes it so that a given command is no longer associated with a Displayable object.
void setCommandListener(CommandListener)	Associates an instance of CommandListener with the Displayable object. A call to this method replaces previously associated instances of CommandListener.
void setTicker(Ticker)	Associates a ticker with a Displayable object. A call to this method replaces previous associations.
void setTitle(String)	Sets the title of the Displayable object.
protected void sizeChanged(int w, int h)	This method must be overridden; it furnishes a way to provide notice that the area available for a Displayable object has been changed.

identification, sizing displayed entities, and associating commands with the entities. In addition, the methods associated with the Ticker class provide a way to ensure that a given Displayable object can be displayed in a timed way.

The DisplayTest Class

The DisplayTest class allows you to work with the basic interactions among the Display, Displayable, Screen, and TextBox classes. You can find this class in the folder for Chapter 9. It is also included in the NetBeans Chapter9MIDlets project. The getDisplay() method first obtains the Display object associated with the device. After that, as Figure 9.3 illustrates, you call the setCurrent() method to change the TextBox object you see displayed. The argument type of the setCurrent() method is Displayable, and since its class is derived from the Screen class, an object of the TextBox type can be used as an argument.

In addition to the screen interactions, the DisplayTest class also makes use of Command objects. Command objects let you associate events and handlers with Displayable objects. In this way, when the MIDlet is invoked, it displays "Albert". (See Figure 9.4.) The text at the top of the screen identifies this as a first name. When you click to invoke the Last Name event, you see "Gore". The title of the display changes with the event. A fuller discussion of the Command class appears in the next section. Here is the code for the DisplayTest class.

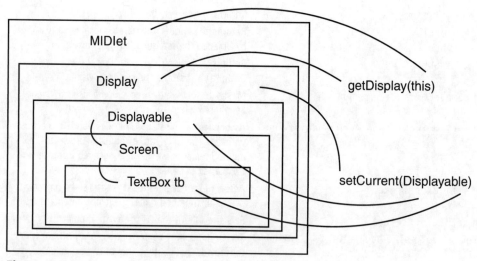

Figure 9.3
Classes derived from Displayable can be used as arguments to the setCurrent() method.

```
/*
 *  Chapter 9 \ DisplayTest.java
 */
import javax.microedition.midlet.*;
import javax.microedition.lcdui.*;
public class DisplayTest extends MIDlet implements CommandListener{
    // #1 Attributes
    private TextBox textBoxA,
                    textBoxB;
    private Command quit,
                    change;
    private Display currentDisplay;
    //Constructor
    public DisplayTest(){
        // #2 Create an instance of TextBox
        textBoxA = new TextBox("Here is the first name:",
                               "Albert", 20, TextField.ANY);
        textBoxB = new TextBox("Here is the last name:",
                               "Gore",   20, TextField.ANY);
        // #2.1 Create instances of Command
        change = new Command("View Last Name", Command.EXIT, 1);
        quit   = new Command("Quit",          Command.EXIT, 2);
        // Associate commands with the textbox
        textBoxA.addCommand(change);
        textBoxB.addCommand(quit);
        // #2.2 Associate the command with the TextBox instance
        textBoxA.setCommandListener(this);
        textBoxB.setCommandListener(this);
    }

    protected void startApp() throws MIDletStateChangeException{
        // #3 set the first TextBox for display
        currentDisplay = Display.getDisplay(this);
        currentDisplay.setCurrent(textBoxA);
    }
    protected void pauseApp(){
    }

    protected void destroyApp(boolean unconditional)
                            throws MIDletStateChangeException{
    }
    public void commandAction(Command command, Displayable displayable){
        try{
```

```
        if (command == change){
            // #4 Cascaded calls to set the second TextBox for display
            currentDisplay.getDisplay(this).setCurrent(textBoxB);
        }

        if (command == quit){
            destroyApp(true);
            notifyDestroyed();
        }
    }catch (MIDletStateChangeException ex){
        System.out.println(ex + " Caught.");
    }
  }//end commandAction
}// end class
```

In the lines associated with comment #1 in the DisplayTest class, you create a set of attributes of the TextBox, Command, and Display types. Declaring the identifiers as class attributes allows them to be used in different methods for purposes of demonstration. In the lines trailing comment #2, the constructor provides two instances of TextBox objects, textBoxA and textBoxB, and these are assigned to the class attributes.

In the lines associated with comment #2.1, instances of the Command class are created and assigned to the two Command class attributes, quit and change. At comment #2.2, the addCommand() and setCommandListener() methods of the TextBox class are called to associate the command events with the current MIDlet (identified with the this keyword).

Given that the two TextBox objects can now generate events, functionality is implemented to make the events cause displayed items to change. The first change is effected in the startApp() method. In the lines following comment #3, you use a static call to the getDisplay() method to retrieve a reference to the current Display object. This is assigned to the class Display attribute, current-Display. The argument for the getDisplay() method is of the MIDlet type, and the this keyword provides a reference to the current instance of its class. You then call the setCurrent() method of the Display class. This takes an argument of the Displayable type, and the textBoxA object is of the TextBox class, a subclass of Displayable. When the MIDlet is invoked, the first item displayed is textBoxA, which furnishes the screen title "Here is the first name" and the TextBox text "Albert".

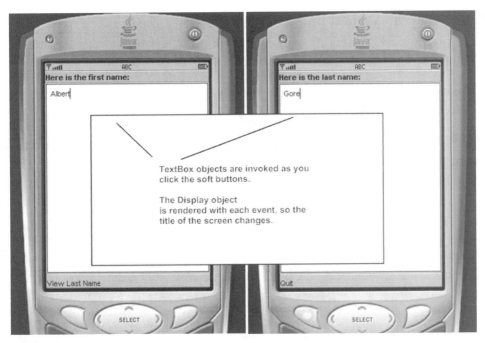

Figure 9.4
As events are processed, the Displayable object (TextBox) is repeatedly rendered.

Within the scope of the commandAction() method, the getDisplay() and setCurrent() methods are called once again. As the lines following comment #4 reveal, in this case a cascading set of calls accomplishes the task of designating textBoxB for the current display. This action is invoked when the user clicks the soft button for the "View Last Name" event. The display then shows "Gore", and the display is refreshed so that the user sees the "Quit" option. Clicking the soft button "Quit" closes the MIDlet. Figure 9.4 illustrates the sequence of changes the Display class facilitates.

Command and CommandListener

The DisplayTest class in the previous section makes use of Command objects to allow you to use the soft buttons to invoke events that render different TextBox images on the display. Command objects can be associated with soft buttons and enable you to assign events to any Displayable object. Such objects are associated with three primary properties:

■ **Type.** The types are BACK, CANCEL, EXIT, HELP, ITEM, OK, SCREEN, and STOP. The Command object type determines how the label of the command is displayed.

- **Label.** These are defined properties of the Command class. As the Display-Test class shows (see Figure 9.4), the label is the test that identifies the command.

- **Priority.** The priority of a Command usually begins at 1 for an event that receives top priority. Levels 2 and higher designate lower priority.

As Table 9.4 shows, the Command class offers two constructions. One constructor is characterized by three arguments. The other is characterized by four. The difference between the two is that the four-argument constructor allows you to

Table 9.4 Command and CommandListener

Type	Description
Command(String, int, int)	Constructs a new Command object. The first argument defines the label for the command. The second argument is the Command object type. The third argument is the priority assigned to the Command object.
Command(String, String, int, int)	Constructs a new Command object. The first argument defines the short label. The second argument defines the long label. The third argument is the Command object type. The fourth argument is the priority assigned to the Command object.
int getCommandType()	Returns the type of the command.
String getLabel()	Gets the label.
int getPriority()	Gets the priority.
BACK	Returns to the previous screen.
OK	Provides a standard way to display OK.
CANCEL	Provides a standard way to display Cancel.
EXIT	Provides a standard way to quit a MIDlet.
HELP	Asks for help.
ITEM	Adds the command to an item list.
SCREEN	Indicates that the command is of a custom type.
STOP	Provides a standard way to issue a stop signal.
void commandAction (Command, Displayable)	This is a method in the CommandListener interface. You implement the CommandListener interface and then override this one method, which is called when an argument of the Command type is executed on any object of the Displayable type.
setCommandListener(MIDlet)	This method is part of the interface of the Displayable class. It allows you to register any object of the Displayable type with the MIDlet so that the events the object generates can be processed.

provide an extended text for the command. Here is an example of how to use the constructor:

```
Command cancelCommand;
cancelCommand = new Command("Cancel", Command.CANCEL, 1);
```

The arguments to the constructor create a Command object with "Cancel" as its label, SCREEN as its display type, and a priority of 1. Table 9.4 provides an overview of the Command class methods and properties. In addition to the Command methods and properties, it also provides information on the CommandListener interface and the setSetCommandListener() method of the Displayable class. You use the CommandListener interface for one purpose: to handle the events Command objects generate. The CommandListener interface provides one method, commandAction().

To associate a class with the CommandListener interface, you implement the CommandListener interface. This interface consists of one method, command-Action(). Here is an abbreviated version of the DisplayTest class that shows the implementation of the Command and CommandListener classes to process an event generated by a TextBox object.

```
// See the DisplayTest class for an executable version of this code.
// This is an essential view of the DisplayTest for discussion only.
// #1 Implement the CommandListener interface
public class DisplayTest extends MIDlet implements CommandListener{
    // #2 Declare identifiers for the Displayable and Command classes
        private TextBox textBoXA;
        private Command change;
    public DisplayTest(){
        // #2.1 Define an object derived from Displayable
        textBoxA = new TextBox("Here is the first name:",
                            "Albert", 20, TextField.ANY);
        // #3 Create an Instance of the Command
        change = new Command("View Last Name", Command.EXIT, 1);
        // #3.1 Associate commands with the textbox
        textBoxA.addCommand(change);
        // #3.2  Register the object that generates the event
        textBoxA.setCommandListener(this);
    }
```

```
        // #4 Override (implement) the one method of the
        //CommandListener interface
        public void commandAction(Command command, Displayable displayable){
              if (command == change){
                //Define an action
              }
        }//end commandAction
}// end class
```

In the lines trailing comment #1, you implement the CommandListener interface. This obligates you to override (define) the commandAction() method. The definition of this method follows comment #4. In this instance, the definition involves processing Command and Displayable arguments to identify the Command object that has generated an event. A selection statement is used to evaluate the event. In this case, only one event is used (change). If it is identified as the change event, then it is processed.

A Displayable object can generate an event. The TextBox class is a subclass (through Screen) of the Displayable class. Given this situation, as the lines following comment #2 reveal, you create an instance of the TextBox class. Then at comment #3 you create an instance of the Command class and assign it to the change identifier. Following comment #3.1, you use the addCommand() method to associate the change command to the TextBox object. Following comment #3.2, you call the setCommandListener() method to register the TextBox object with the this reference to the MIDlet object. Given that each Command object is identified with a unique TextBox identifier (change), in the lines trailing comment #4 you can use a selection statement within the commandAction() method to process the event the TextBox object generates.

TextBox

The DisplayTest class also provides examples of the TextBox class. As has been mentioned, the TextBox class is a subclass of the Displayable class and therefore can be associated with the Command class. In the DisplayTest class, only the most elementary use of the TextBox object appears. In subsequent programs, the TextBox class is revisited in different contexts. For now, it is enough to note that it allows you to copy, cut, and paste to or from a clipboard. You can also type multiple lines of text into it. In addition, you can use a mask to screen the type of text you allow to be entered in it. Table 9.5 provides basic discussion of some of

Table 9.5 TextBox Methods and Properties

Method	Description
TextBox (String, String, int, int)	Constructor. The first argument is of the String type and allows you to furnish the object with a default body of text. The second argument, also of the String type, provides the title. The third argument, of the int type, designates the maximum number of characters the object displays. The last argument designates the appearance mode of the TextBox. Modes are values defined in the TextField class. Here is a summary list: PLANE, ANY, PASSWORD, UNEDITABLE, SENSITIVE, NON_PREDICTIVE, INITIAL_CAPS_WORD, INITIAL_CAPS_SENTENCE.
void delete (int, int)	Deletes characters. The first argument designates the starting position for the deletion. The second argument designates how many characters are to be deleted.
int getCaretPosition()	Returns the current cursor position.
int getChars (char[])	Gets the contents of the TextBox as an array of chars.
int getConstraints()	Returns the TextField constraint value that has been applied to the TextBox object by the setConstraints() method or through construction.
int getMaxSize()	Gets the maximum number of characters that can be stored in this TextBox.
String getString()	Returns the current contents of the text area as a String object.
setString(String)	Replaces the existing text with the String object provided as an argument.
void insert (char[], int, int, int)	The first argument is a character array that provides characters to be inserted into the text area. The second argument indicates the starting index in the character array of characters to be used. The third argument establishes the number of characters to be inserted from the starting index. The last argument designates the index in the text area at which the insertion is to begin.
void insert(String, int)	Inserts text into the text area defined by the String argument into the position indicated by the int argument.
void setChars(char[] data, int offset, int length)	Replaces chars with new values.
void setConstraints(int constraints)	Changes the constraints.
int setMaxSize(int)	Changes the maximum size of the text area.
void setString(String)	Sets the contents to a string.
void setTitle(String)	Sets the string for the title. If you supply a null argument, then the title disappears.
int size ()	Returns the number of chars used.

the primary methods and properties of the TextBox class. See the NameGameTest class further on in this chapter for discussion of and extended uses of the TextBox class.

Alert and AlertType

As Figure 9.2 shows, the Alert class is another class derived from the Displayable class. As a Displayable class, the Alert class can be associated with Command objects, and like the CommandListener class in relation to the Command class, it is complemented by the AlertType class. The AlertType class is derived from the Object class. Properties of the AlertType class allow you to define the type of Alert you invoke.

The Alert class provides what might be viewed as a dialog. Like a dialog, there are two basic forms of Alert object. One is analogous to a modeless dialog. It displays for a set period and does not interrupt the scheduled actions of the application. The other type of Alert object behaves like a modal dialog box. It halts the action of the application until the user responds to it.

There are two basic constructors for the Alert class. As Table 9.6 discusses, the first type takes only one argument, a string that the Alert displays. The second constructor takes four arguments and allows you to designate the title of the

Table 9.6 Alert and AlertType Methods and Properties

Method	Description
Alert (String)	Constructs a simple Alert that automatically disappears after a system-defined period of time. The argument provides the title of the Alert object.
Alert (String, String, Image, AlertType)	The first String argument is the title of the alert. The second argument, also of the String type, provides text for the alert to display. The third argument is null or of the Image type and designates an image to be displayed. The last argument is of the AlertType and sets the type of Alert to be used. See the AlertType properties further on in this table.
int getDefaultTimeout()	Gets the default timeout used by the MID.
Image getImage()	Gets the Alert's image.
String getString()	Gets the Alert's string.
int getTimeout()	Gets the current timeout.
AlertType getType()	Gets the current type.
void setImage(Image)	Sets the image.
void setString(String str)	Sets the Alert message.
void setTimeout(int time)	Sets the timeout.

Table 9.6 Continued

Class	Description
void setType(AlertType)	Sets the type.
void setCommandListener (CommandListener)	There are some complexities associated with this version. It is the same as the Displayable method, but you can also use a null argument to designate that the default listener is to be used.
ALARM	AlertType property that alerts the user to an event for which he has previously requested notification.
CONFIRMATION	AlertType property that confirms a user's action.
ERROR	AlertType property that indicates that something bad happened.
INFO	AlertType property that indicates something informative.
WARNING	AlertType property that warns the user of something.
boolean playSound (Display)	AlertType property that plays a sound associated with an Alert without having to actually construct the Alert.

display, the text of the Alert object, a graphical image for the Alert object, and the AlertType property to be applied to the Alert object. Here's an example:

```
alert = new Alert("Title" , "Alert Text",
                null,   AlertType.CONFIRMATION);
display.setCurrent(alert);
```

The NameGameTest Class

The NameGameTest class allows you to explore a few uses of TextBox, Alert, AlertType, and Command items. It allows you to enter the name of an author in a field and then retrieve information on the author. Three Command objects are associated with a single TextBox object, and when you process the events generated by the objects, you obtain one of two Alert objects. One of these furnishes information on the author whose last name you have typed. The other provides help. If you do not know the name of an author, the help option shows the list of choices. Here is the code for the NameGameTest class. You can find it in the Chapter 9 folder, and it is included in the NetBeans Chapter9MIDlets project.

```
/*
 * Chapter9 \ NameGameTest.java
 *
 */
```

```java
import javax.microedition.lcdui.*;
import javax.microedition.midlet.*;
public class NameGameTest extends MIDlet implements CommandListener{
    // #1 Class attributes
    private TextBox nameTextBox;
    private Alert alert;
    private Command quit, hint, go;
    private String boxText;

    public NameGameTest(){
        boxText = "Name:";
        // #2 Generate a text box
        nameTextBox = new TextBox ("Author Facts",
                                    boxText, 60, TextField.PLAIN);
        // #2.1 Commands
        quit = new Command("Quit", Command.EXIT, 2);
        // #2.2 Create a list
        go =    new Command("View Info", Command.ITEM, 1);
        hint =    new Command("Hint", Command.ITEM, 1);
        // #2.3 Register and add
        nameTextBox.addCommand(go);
        nameTextBox.addCommand(quit);
        nameTextBox.addCommand(hint);
        nameTextBox.setCommandListener(this);
    }

    protected void startApp() throws MIDletStateChangeException{
        // #3 Initial display
        Display.getDisplay(this).setCurrent(nameTextBox);
    }

    protected void pauseApp(){
    }

    protected void destroyApp(boolean unconditional)
                        throws MIDletStateChangeException{
    }

    // #4 Provide information
    protected String getInformation(String authorName){
        String info = new String();
        // # 4.1 Strings contain line returns
        if(authorName.equalsIgnoreCase("Shakespeare")){
```

```
        info = "William Shakespeare (1564-1616)"
                + "\n" +  "Julius Caesar"
                + "\n" +  "Hamlet"
                + "\n" +  "King Lear";
    }else if(authorName.equalsIgnoreCase("Hemingway")){
        info = "Ernest Hemingway (1899-1961)"
                + "\n" +  "A Farewell to Arms"
                + "\n" +  "For Whom the Bell Tolls"
                + "\n" +  "The Old Man and the Sea";
    }else if(authorName.equalsIgnoreCase("Austen")){
        info = "Jane Austen (1731-1805)"
                + "\n" +  "Pride and Prejudice"
                + "\n" +  "Emma"
                + "\n" +  "Sense and Sensibility";
    } else{
        info = "Author not known.";
    }
    return info;
}


// #5 Process the command
public void commandAction(Command command, Displayable displayable){
    try
    {
        if (command == quit){
            destroyApp(true);
            notifyDestroyed();
        }
        if (command == hint){
            // #5.1 Clear the text field
            alert = new Alert("Hint",
                              "Type: Shakespeare, Hemingway, or Austen",
                              null, AlertType.INFO);
            Display.getDisplay(this).setCurrent(alert);
        }
        if (command == go){
            // #5.2 Clear the text field
            nameTextBox.delete(0,boxText.length());
            // #5.3 Create an instance of the alert
            alert = new Alert("Author Info",
                              getInformation(nameTextBox.getString()),
                              null, AlertType.CONFIRMATION);
            Display.getDisplay(this).setCurrent(alert);
```

```
                // #5.4 reset the string
                nameTextBox.setString(boxText);
            }
        }catch (MIDletStateChangeException me){
                System.out.println(me + " caught.");
        }
    }//end commandAction
}//end class
```

Construction and Definition

In the lines preceding comment #1 in the `NameGameTest` class, the class implements the `CommandListener` interface. This makes it necessary to define the
`commandAction()` method. This activity receives attention momentarily. Trailing
comment #1, several class attributes are declared. The first of these are a `TextBox`
attribute, `nameTextBox`; an `Alert` attribute, `alert`; and three `Command` attributes,
`quit`, `hint`, and `go`. In addition, an attribute of the `String` type is declared
(`boxText`).

The constructor of the `NameGameTest` class attends to creating an instance of the
`TextBox` class and associating `Command` objects with it. Accordingly, in the line
preceding comment #2, the `boxText` attribute is initialized with the value of
"Name:", and then in the lines trailing comment #2, the `TextBox` constructor is
used to create an instance of the `TextBox` class that uses the value assigned
`boxText` for its second argument. The second argument is of the `String` type and
establishes the text displayed in the `TextBox`. The first argument is also of the
`String` type and provides the text that appears across the top of the display (or
screen) area. The third argument, of the `int` type, designates the maximum
number of characters allowed in the `TextBox`. In this instance this argument is set
to 60.

The last argument of the `TextBox` constructor designates the appearance mode of
the `TextBox`. As discussed in Table 9.5, the values used to set the mode are defined
in the `TextField` class. In this instance, the `ANY` mode is used. This mode
accommodates line breaks ("\n") and text entry by the user.

At comment #2.1, the definition of a series of three `Command` objects begins. The
mode of the first `Command` object (`quit`) is `EXIT`. The mode is set using the second
argument of the `Command` constructor. The third argument sets the priority of the
`Command` object, and a value of 2 is supplied for it. The first argument provides the

name of the `Command` button, "Quit". The button appears in the lower left corner of the display area, as Figure 9.5 shows.

Following comment #2.2, `Command` objects defined using the `Command.ITEM` mode are created. As shown in Figure 9.5, the `ITEM` mode causes the `Command` object label to be set in a list in a menu in the lower left of the display area. In this case, the "View Info" label is assigned to the `go` `Command` object and the "Hint" label is assigned to the `hint` `Command` object. Both objects are also set with a priority of 1.

In the lines following comment #2.3, the `Command` objects are associated with the `nameTextBox` attribute, which is of the `TextBox` type. As a `Screen` subclass, the `TextBox` class can accommodate different commands and modes of command. The `TextBox::addCommand()` method is called three times to associate the three `Command` objects with it. After that, all that remains is to register the `TextBox` object with the MIDlet. This is accomplished using the `setCommandListener()` method, which takes the `this` keyword as its argument to identify the current `MIDlet` instance.

The TextBox Cycle

The life of the `TextBox` object (`nameTextBox`) in the `NameGameTest` class begins in the constructor, as was discussed in the previous section. Its life after that is fairly basic. As is evident in the line following comment #3, when the MIDlet starts, the static `Display::getDisplay()` method is used to retrieve the current instance of the display. The `nameTextBox` is then set as the current display with a call to the `Display::setCurrent()` method.

After that, the `nameTextBox` attribute is revisited according to its place in the event cycle. One of the first stops in this respect occurs following comment #5.2 in the `commandAction()` method. There, the `TextBox::delete()` method is used to remove the term "Name:" from the text in the `TextBox` field. This is so that the last name of the author can be used to search for the information about the author. The first argument of the `delete()` method is of the `int` type and designates the starting character index of the deletion. The second argument stipulates the number of characters to be deleted. To obtain the number of characters, the `String::length()` method is called using the `boxText` attribute.

After the information about an author is retrieved and displayed, the user is returned to the starting point, where only the implied query of the "Name:" label is visible. To reset the label, in the line associated with command #5.3, the

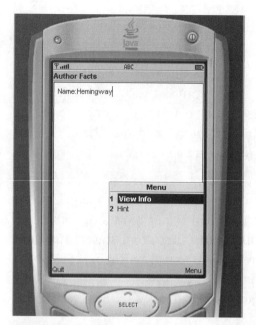

Figure 9.5
The `TextBox` and `Command` classes allow the user to input data and process it.

`TextBox::setString()` method is called. The argument for the method is of the `String` type, and the `boxText` attribute is supplied. Having been removed, the "Name:" text is now restored to the `TextBox` field, and the user can make another query. Figure 9.5 illustrates a search initiated with "Hemingway". When the user selects Menu and View Info, the information on Hemingway's books and life appears.

Alert Processing

In the `NameGameTest` class, the hint and go `Command` objects provide a way to use objects of the `Alert` class in different ways. At the center of this activity, as Figure 9.5 illustrates, are the "View Info" and "Hint" menu items. The messages generated when these items are selected invoke different `Alert` objects. How this is so becomes evident in the lines following comment #5, where the `hint` command is first processed in an `if` selection statement.

In the line preceding comment #5.1, the `hint` identifier is tested against the `command` argument. If the evaluation proves true, then the flow of the program enters the `hint` block and an `Alert` object is created and assigned to the `alert` identifier. The first two arguments of the `Alert` constructor are of the `String` type. The first argument is the title that appears at the top of the display. The second is the message text of the `Alert` field. In this case the message consists of the last names of three authors, Shakespeare, Hemingway, and Austen. The third argument to the `Alert` constructor establishes the mode of the alert. The value for this argument is defined in the `AlertType` class. In this case, the `INFO` property is used, which provides a distinctive, fairly intrusive succession of tones.

With the completion of the construction activity for the `Alert` object, the `Display::getDisplay()` method is called to retrieve the current `Display` object, and the `Display::setCurrent()` is used to make the `alert` object visible. The user who clicks the Hint menu item and then the SELECT button can see the list of names that can be entered in the `TextBox` field. The `Alert` object displays for a few seconds only and closes automatically.

The construction of the `Alert` object in the lines following comment #5.3 involves a call to the `getInformation()` method, which is defined as part of the interface of the `NameGameTest` class. The definition of the method follows comment #4. The method takes a `String` argument, which provides the last name of an author. This is a string that the user types in the text box constructed in the lines accompanying comment #2. The name the user typed is retrieved in the lines following comment #5.3 using the `TextBox::getString()` method.

Fed to the `getInformation()` method, as the definition of the method shows, the string is used in a set of selection statements to retrieve information about an author and assign it to the `info` identifier, which is a local value of the `String` type. The `getInformation()` method returns this value. In the definition of the information returned by the method, several line returns are used to format the text. As Figure 9.6 illustrates, displaying the text reveals that the `Alert` objects can handle multiple lines of text.

The value returned is used for the second argument of the `Alert` constructor associated with comment #5.3. It furnishes the second argument, which is the text the `Alert` object displays. When the `Alert` object appears, it is accompanied by a sound. The tone you hear is established using the third argument of the constructor, which is of the `AlertType` class. The specific property used is `AlertType.CONFIRMATION`. This provides a series of three descending tones. Figure 9.6 illustrates the information as it is displayed by the `Alert` object.

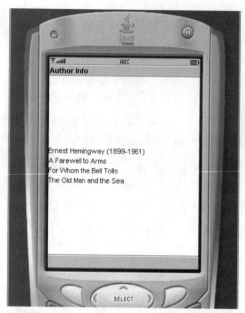

Figure 9.6
The Alert class provides a way to display successive lines of text.

Lists

The List class provides an object that can be used to display a series of elements, each of which can individually invoke a command. There are three modes of List objects. Two of these modes designate List objects that can be selected one at time. Field values obtained from the Choice class are used to identify these two modes of the List object. They are the IMPLICIT and EXCLUSIVE fields. As Table 9.7 indicates, the IMPLICIT mode allows you to display unadorned lists of items. The EXCLUSIVE mode allows you to precede displayed items with radio buttons, as is shown in Figure 9.7. You can select only one item at a time from such lists, and as you do so the radio button is activated. The other mode is MULTIPLE. This mode of list object allows you to select as many items from a list at a time as you want, and with each selection, a checkbox preceding the item is activated. This mode of list is illustrated by Figure 9.8, in which several authors are selected at one time.

Lists with Single Selection

When you create an instance of a list, you usually associate Command objects with it. The Command object then allows you to process messages issued by the list. To process messages for specific items, you can make use of the getSelectedIndex()

Table 9.7 List Methods and Properties

Method or Field	Description
List (String, int)	Constructs a List object. The first argument is the title of the list as shown at the top of the screen. The second argument designates the type of the list: IMPLICIT, EXCLUSIVE, MULTIPLE.
List (String, int, String[], Image[])	Constructs a List object. The first argument is the title of the list as shown at the top of the screen. The second argument designates the mode of the list: IMPLICIT, or EXCLUSIVE, MULTIPLE. The third argument is an array of the String type providing the items that make up the list. The fourth argument is an array of items of the Image type that can be used as elements. For a List object without Image objects, use null for the fourth argument.
int append (String, Image)	Adds an element to a List object and identifies it using an Image* object. The element added can be designated by an object of the String type, the Image type, or both.
void delete (int)	Removes an element from a List object. The argument is of the int type and designates the element to be deleted.
void insert (int, String, Image)	Inserts an element into a List object. The object added can be designated with a String object, an Image* object, or both.
void set (int, String, Image)	Sets or resets an element in List object. The object set can be designated with a String object, an Image* object, or both.
Image getImage (int)	Returns the Image* reference associated with an element. The argument is of the int type and designates the image to be retrieved.
String getString (int)	Returns the String reference associated with an element. The argument is of the int type and designates the element to be retrieved.
boolean isSelected (int)	Returns a Boolean value indicating whether a particular element is currently selected.
int getSelectedIndex ()	Returns the currently selected element index.
void setSelectedIndex (int, boolean)	Sets a selection by element index.
int getSelectedFlags (boolean[])	Fills an array of the Boolean type with true or false values indicating whether the elements in a List object have been selected. This works most readily with lists of the MULTIPLE mode.
void setSelectedFlags (boolean[])	Directly sets the selections based on an array of Boolean values corresponding to the elements to be set.
int size()	Returns the number of elements in the list.
IMPLICIT	Allows one item at a time to generate an event. The items in the List object appear without checkboxes or radio buttons. This field is inherited from the Choice class.
EXCLUSIVE	Allows one list item at a time to generate an event. The items in the List object appear with radio buttons. This field is inherited from the Choice class.

(Continued)

Table 9.7 Continued

Method or Field	Description
MULTIPLE	Allows any number of items to be selected simultaneously. They can generate events individually or as a group. The items in the List object appear with checkboxes. The checkboxes are activated as you select items from the list. This field is inherited from the Choice class.

*Objects of the Image type are dealt with in Chapter 10.

and getString() methods of the List class. The ListTest class provides you with an example of how to process messages issued for lists defined using the EXCLUSIVE and IMPLICIT modes. You can alter the line preceding comment #1 to view the effects of the different modes. The ListTest class is in the Chapter 9 folder and is included in the Chaper9MIDlets project for NetBeans. Here is the code for the class. Discussion of the class appears in the sections that follow.

```java
/*
 * Chapter 9 \ ListTest.java
 *
 */
import javax.microedition.midlet.*;
import javax.microedition.lcdui.*;
import java.util.*;    // for Vector
public class ListTest extends MIDlet implements CommandListener{
    private Form form;
    private Command quit, begin, back, select;
    private Vector authorInfo;
    private List authorList;
    private Alert alert;
    // Create an array for the list
    private String[] choices = { "Shakespeare", "Austen",    "Camus",
                                 "Hemingway",    "Vonnegut", "Grass"};
    public ListTest(){
        // Construct the list
                                    // or List.IMPLICIT
        authorList = new List("Authors", List.EXCLUSIVE, choices, null);
        // #1 Commands for the authorList
        select =   new Command("Select", Command.OK,    1);
        back = new Command("Back",        Command.BACK, 2);
        authorList.addCommand(select);
```

```
      authorList.addCommand(back);
      authorList.setCommandListener(this);

      // #2 Create an instance of a form
      form = new Form("Information on Authors");
      begin =  new Command("Begin",  Command.SCREEN, 1);
      quit = new Command("Quit",      Command.EXIT,   2);
      form.addCommand(begin);
      form.addCommand(quit);
      form.setCommandListener(this);
}// end ListTest

// #3 Set the form and populate the Vector object
protected void startApp() throws MIDletStateChangeException{
      Display.getDisplay(this).setCurrent(form);
      setUpVector();
}

protected void pauseApp(){
}

protected void destroyApp(boolean unconditional)
                         throws MIDletStateChangeException{

}

public void commandAction(Command command, Displayable displayable){
      System.out.println("commandAction(" + command + ", " + displayable +
                     ") called.");
      try{
         // #4 Handle events from the Form object
         if (displayable == form){
            if (command == quit){
               destroyApp(true);
               notifyDestroyed();
            }
            // #4.1
            if (command == begin){
               Display.getDisplay(this).setCurrent(authorList);
            }
         }// end if

         // #5 Handle events from the List object
         if (displayable == authorList){
```

```
            if (command == select){
                String index = new String();
                // #5.1
                index = String.valueOf(authorList.getSelectedIndex());
                String itemOfIndex;
                // #5.2
                itemOfIndex = authorList.getString(
                                        authorList.getSelectedIndex());
                alert = new Alert( getInformation(itemOfIndex),
                                " Index:" + index + "\n"
                                + getInformation(itemOfIndex),
                                null, AlertType.INFO);
                Display.getDisplay(this).setCurrent(alert);
            }
            else if (command == back){
                Display.getDisplay(this).setCurrent(form);
            }
            else{
                System.out.println("Not found.");
            }// end else if
        }// end if
    }catch (MIDletStateChangeException me){
            System.out.println(me + " caught.");
        }//end catch
}//end commandAction

// #6 Access information
protected String getInformation(String authorName){
    String info = new String();
    // # 6.1 Strings contain line returns
    for(int itr =0; itr < authorList.size();itr++ ){
        if(authorName.equalsIgnoreCase(choices[itr])){
            info = authorInfo.elementAt(itr).toString();
        }
    }//end for
    return info;
}// end getInformation

// #7 Add information to the vector
 protected void setUpVector(){
    authorInfo = new Vector();
    String info = new String();
    info = " William Shakespeare (1564-1616)"
```

```
      + "\n" +  " Julius Caesar"
      + "\n" +  " Hamlet"
      + "\n" +  " King Lear";
      authorInfo.addElement(info);
      info = " Jane Austen (1731-1805)"
      + "\n" + " Pride and Prejudice"
      + "\n" + " Emma"
      + "\n" + " Sense and Sensibility";
      authorInfo.addElement(info);
      info = " Albert Camus (1913-1960)"
      + "\n" + " The Stranger"
      + "\n" + " The Plague"
      + "\n" + " The Fall";
      authorInfo.addElement(info);
      info = " Ernest Hemingway (1899-1961)"
      + "\n" + " A Farewell to Arms"
      + "\n" + " For Whom the Bell Tolls"
      + "\n" + " The Old Man and the Sea";
      authorInfo.addElement(info);
      info = " Kurt Vonnegut (1922-2007)"
      + "\n" + " Slaughterhouse-Five"
      + "\n" + " The Sirens of Titan"
      + "\n" + " Cat's Cradle";
      authorInfo.addElement(info);
      info = " Gunter Grass (b. 1927)"
      + "\n" + " The Flounder"
      + "\n" + " The Tin Drum"
      + "\n" + " Dog Years";
      authorInfo.addElement(info);
   }// end setUpVector
}// end class
```

Construction and Definition

In the lines preceding comment #1 of the ListTest class, a number of class attributes are defined. To control the general actions of the MIDlet, the quit and begin attributes are declared. To control and process events from the List object, the back and select attributes are declared. These are all of the Command type. To store the names of authors and information about them, an attribute of the Vector type is declared (authorInfo), and following that, a List attribute, authorList, is declared. To process information, an Alert attribute is then added, and immediately after that, an array of the String type, choices, is defined with the names of six authors.

In the line immediately before comment #1, the constructor for the List class is called. The first argument provides the title of the screen in which the items in the list appear. In this case, the value provided is "Authors", as the right panel of Figure 9.7 reveals. The second argument is the mode value obtained from the Choice class. The List class inherits these values. The two values available for single-choice List objects are EXCLUSIVE and IMPLICIT. In this instance, the EXCLUSIVE value is designated, which provides for radio buttons. The third argument to the List constructor is a reference to an array of String values to be used for the List elements. The choices array is used as this argument. The final argument is also an array, this one of the Image type. In this instance, no Image objects are associated with the items assigned to the List object, so a value of null is supplied.

To process list items, it is necessary to register the List object with the MIDlet. Accordingly, in the lines following comment #1, the select and back attributes are defined. The label used for select is "Select", and this command allows the user to generate an event associated with a given single item in a list. The addCommand() method is used to associate the select attribute with the authorList object. The setCommandListener() method then associates the authorList object with the MIDlet. Following comment #2, the same operations are performed with respect to the begin and quit attributes. In this case, the result is that messages generated by the Form object (form) can be processed.

Using a Vector Object for Data

After the Form and List objects for the MIDlet have been attended to, at comment #3 the startApp() method is defined. In this case, the Display object is associated with the form object using the Display::setCurrent() method. Following that, a call to the setUpVector() method is called. Calling the method at this point defines the authorInfo Vector so that it can be used during the life of the MIDlet.

The setUpVector() method defines the authorInfo so that it contains six elements, each of which furnishes biographical information about a given author. To populate the Vector object, a redundant approach is used. The String identifier info is repeatedly assigned a long string with the desired information, and then info is used as an argument to the Vector::addElement() method.

In this way, with each successive call to the addElement() method, an indexed element providing author information is added to the end of the Vector object. The indexes of the Vector object begin as 0, corresponding to those of the choices array. The information for the choices array, the authorList List object, and the authorInfo Vector object are all the same and represent the same authors.

Processing Messages

To process messages issued by a List object, you retrieve the value associated with the Command object associated with the List object. To process the messages, you override the commandAction() method, which is provided by the Command-Listener interface. In the definition of the ListTest class, there are two groups of Command messages. One group applies to the List object. The other applies to the Form object.

One way to distinguish a Form object message from a List object message is to evaluate the value passed by the Displayable argument of the commandAction() method. The Displayable argument (in this case displayable) allows you to use a selection statement to test for the name of the Displayable object that has issued a message. By using the result of this evaluation, you can then channel the flow of the program into further selection blocks to evaluate the identity of the Command messages. Accordingly, as is evident in the lines following comment #4, a selection statement first handles messages issued by the Form object (form). If the message is found to be from the form object, the flow of the program enters the outer selection block and the Command messages associated with the Form object (quit and begin) can then be processed.

The procedure used to process messages associated with the Form object can also be used to process messages associated with the authorList object. The List class is derived from the Displayable class, as is the Form class, so a selection statement can be used to evaluate the Displayable argument of the commandAction() method with relation to the authorList object. If the Displayable object is identified as authorList, then the flow of the program enters the selection block following comment #5, and specific messages pertaining to the List object can be dealt with.

In the lines following comment #5.1, one approach to processing a List message is shown to involve calling the List::getSelectedIndex() method. This method retrieves the index of the currently selected element in the List object. The value returned is an integer, so to convert it so that it can be displayed, the

`String::valueOf()` method is used. The resulting `String` reference is assigned to the index identifier, which is of the `String` type.

To retrieve the text associated with a given `List` index, the `List::getString()` method can be called. The `getString()` method takes an `int` value as an argument and returns a `String` reference. This is the approach used in the lines following comment #5.2. In this case, the value returned by the `getSelectedIndex()` is used as an argument to the `getString()` method. The value retrieved is assigned to the `itemOfIndex` identifier.

The `itemOfIndex` is used in the first argument for the constructor for the `Alert` object (`alert`). To use the identifier, a call to the `getInformation()` method is made. This method takes an object of the `String` type as its argument, and on the basis of the information provided, returns the name and dates of the author. This information appears in the title of the screen. For the second argument of the `Alert` constructor, as Figure 9.7 illustrates, the index of the selected item is displayed along with the full text of the author's biographical information.

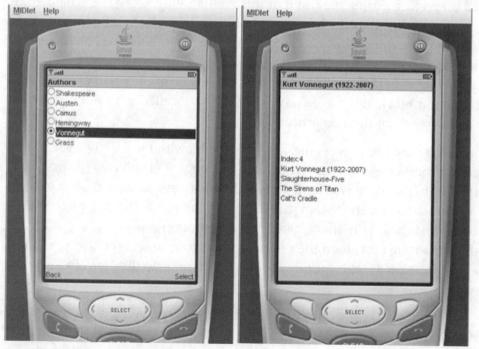

Figure 9.7
The `EXCLUSIVE` option in the definition of a `List` object provides buttons to indicate exclusivity.

The getInformation() method is defined in the lines following comment #6. As the line following comment #6.1 shows, the List::size() method is used to return the highest index value of the authorList object. This value is then used to control the number of times the for repetition block iterates. With the iteration of the for block, the values assigned to the authorName Vector object are compared to those assigned to the choices array. If the comparison proves true, then the Vector::elementAt() method is called to return the indexed object. Since the author information is stored in a Vector object, it is necessary to call the toString() method to make it suitable for assignment to the info identifier, which is of the String type. The method then returns the value assigned to the info identifier.

Lists with Multiple Selection

Since the List and Form classes are derived from the Displayable class, the identity of a specific List can be distinguished from that of the Form or another List object by using a selection statement to process the second argument of the commandAction() method. In the ListWithMultipleTest class, the approach to processing messages is simplified somewhat from the approach used in the ListTest class. The emphasis is on bringing messages that relate to the List object to the forefront. This makes it easier to see how the List::getSelected-Flags() method can be used to retrieve an array of all currently selected items in a List object.

The array the getSelectedFlags() method retrieves is of the Boolean type, and after it has been retrieved, it can then be traversed to identify the selected List elements. Showing this activity is the central focus of the ListWithMultipleTest class. You can find the ListWithMultipleTest class in the Chapter 9 code folder. As with the other classes discussed in this chapter, it is also included in the NetBeans Chapter9MIDlets project. Here is the code for the class. Discussion appears in the section that follows.

```
/*
 * Chapter 9 \ ListWithMultipleTest.java
 *
 */
import javax.microedition.midlet.*;
import javax.microedition.lcdui.*;
import java.util.*;    // for Vector
```

```
public class ListWithMultipleTest extends MIDlet implements CommandListener{
  // #1
  private Display display;
  private Command exit, selectAuthor;
  private List listChoices;
  private Vector authorInfo;
  private Alert alert;
  private String title;
  private String[] choices = { "Shakespeare", "Austen",   "Camus",
                               "Hemingway",   "Vonnegut", "Grass"};

  public ListWithMultipleTest(){
    display = Display.getDisplay(this);
    // #2 Construct the list
    title = "Author Information";
    listChoices = new List(title, List.MULTIPLE, choices, null);
    // Alternatively, use the append() method
    //listChoices.append("Marquez", null);

    exit = new Command("Exit", Command.EXIT, 1);
    selectAuthor = new Command("View", Command.SCREEN,2);
    // Add commands, listen for events
    listChoices.addCommand(exit);
    listChoices.addCommand(selectAuthor);
    listChoices.setCommandListener(this);
  }

  // #3
  public void startApp(){
    display.setCurrent(listChoices);
    setUpVector();
  }

  public void pauseApp(){
  }
  public void destroyApp(boolean unconditional){
  }

  public void commandAction(Command command, Displayable displayable){
    // #4
    if (command == selectAuthor)
```

```
    {
      // Create a Boolean array the size of the listed items
      boolean selected[] = new boolean[listChoices.size()];
      // 4.1 Populate the array with true (selected) and false items
      listChoices.getSelectedFlags(selected);
      // #4.2 Iterate through the array and find the seletected items
      StringBuffer selectedInfo= new StringBuffer();
      for (int i = 0; i < listChoices.size(); i++){
        if( selected[i] == true){
            selectedInfo.append("- - - - - - - - - - - - -\n");
            selectedInfo.append(authorInfo.elementAt(i).toString() + "\n");
        }// end if
      }//end for
      // #4.3
      alert = new Alert(title,
                        selectedInfo.toString(),
                        null, AlertType.INFO);
      Display.getDisplay(this).setCurrent(alert);
    }//end if
    else if (command == exit)
    {
      destroyApp(false);
      notifyDestroyed();
    }
}// end commandAction

  // #5 Add information to the vector
   protected void setUpVector(){
     authorInfo = new Vector();
     String info = new String();
     info = " William Shakespeare (1564-1616)"
     + "\n" + " Julius Caesar"
     + "\n" + " Hamlet"
     + "\n" + " King Lear";
     authorInfo.addElement(info);
     info = " Jane Austen (1731-1805)"
     + "\n" + " Pride and Prejudice"
     + "\n" + " Emma"
     + "\n" + " Sense and Sensibility";
     authorInfo.addElement(info);
```

```
        info = " Albert Camus (1913-1960)"
        + "\n" + " The Stranger"
        + "\n" + " The Plague"
        + "\n" + " The Fall";
        authorInfo.addElement(info);
        info = " Ernest Hemingway (1899-1961)"
        + "\n" + " A Farewell to Arms"
        + "\n" + " For Whom the Bell Tolls"
        + "\n" + " The Old Man and the Sea";
        authorInfo.addElement(info);
        info = " Kurt Vonnegut (1922-2007)"
        + "\n" + " Slaughterhouse-Five"
        + "\n" + " The Sirens of Titan"
        + "\n" + " Cat's Cradle";
        authorInfo.addElement(info);
        info = " Gunter Grass (b. 1927)"
        + "\n" + " The Flounder"
        + "\n" + " The Tin Drum"
        + "\n" + " Dog Years";
        authorInfo.addElement(info);
    }// end setUpVector
}// end class
```

Construction and Definition

In the lines following comment #1 of the ListWithMutipleTest class, most of the attributes defined for the ListTest class are used once again. One difference in the attribute list is the inclusion of title, which provides a way to furnish the screen title for the List object as it is refreshed. Another difference is that no Form attribute appears. To simplify the implementation of this class, all actions are accomplished by refreshing the List object alone. The name of the List attribute is listChoices.

In the lines following comment #2, after assigning a string, "Author Information", to the title attribute, a call is made to the List constructor and the new instance of the List class is assigned to the listChoices attribute. The title attribute is used as the first argument in the constructor. Again, this provides the text for the screen title, as is shown in Figure 9.8.

For the second argument, the MULTIPLE field is used to set the mode of the List object. The List class inherits the definition of this field from the Choice class, which is defined as an interface. Use of the MULTIPLE mode creates a List object that displays items preceded by checkboxes. Checking a box activates the item associated with it, and no limit applies to the number of items that can be checked.

For the third argument to the List constructor, the choices array is provided. This array is of the String type and furnishes the names of a group of authors. The authors' names are the same as those named for the ListTest class. As a matter of interest only, notice that the List::append() method is shown immediately after the construction statement, commented out. This line is included as a reminder that such methods as delete() and append() can be used dynamically to add or remove List elements.

To associate Command objects with the listChoices attribute, the List::addCommand() method is called. In this way, the exit and selectAuthor attributes identify the only two messages the ListWithMutipleTest class processes. The setCommandListener() method is then used to register the selectAuthor attribute with the MIDlet. At comment #3, the listChoices object is set as the current object for the MIDlet as it is started.

Processing Messages

Processing multiple simultaneous messages most centrally involves making a call to the List::getSelectedFlags() method. This method iterates through the items in the currently active List object and identifies those that have been selected. To perform its work, the getSelectedFlags() method requires an array of the Boolean type, so in the lines following comment #4, an array (selected) is defined.

To define the selected array, a call is made to the Boolean constructor, and as an argument to the constructor, the listChoices attribute is used to call the List:size() method. The value returned by the size() method sets the length of the array, so whenever the ListWithMultipleTest class processes a message issued by a List item, it can dynamically determine the number of items in the List.

The next step, shown in the line following comment #4.1, is to call the getSelectedFlags() method and use the selected array as an argument. The getSelectedFlags() method takes a reference to a Boolean array as an argument, and its action is to set the true and false values associated with the items in the array the reference identifies. By default items are set as `false`; they are set to `true` when selected.

The goal then becomes to retrieve the text values associated with the `List` items and to concatenate these values with the biographical information stored in the `authorInfo` `Vector` object. To make it so that the information gathered for concatenation can be processed, a `StringBuffer` object (`selectedInfo`) is defined in the line trailing comment #4.2. A `StringBuffer` object differs from a `String` object because a `StringBuffer` object can grow dynamically after it has been constructed. The means of accomplishing this is the `StringBuffer::append()` method, which takes an argument of the `String` type.

To retrieve selected items and build the text assigned to the `selectedInfo` identifier, a `for` repetition statement is used. The `List::size()` method controls the iteration of the repetition block. As the block iterates, it traverses the `selected` array. With each repetition, an `if` selection statement tests the value of indexed items in the `selected` array against `true`. If the test proves `true`, then the flow of the program enters the selection block. There, a dashed line and the appropriate autobiographical information are appended to the `selectedInfo` object.

To retrieve the biographical information, the `Vector::elementAt()` method is called. Since the index values of the `List` and `Vector` objects identify the same author information, the `elementAt()` method can find the appropriate text for each selected author. However, since the text stored in the `Vector` object is associated with the `Object` type, the `toString()` method must be used to convert it so that it can be appended to the `StringBuffer` object.

After the information associated with all of the selected `List` items has been appended to the `selectedInfo` object, an `Alert` object is used to display it. For the first argument of the `Alert` constructor, no conversion is necessary, because the `title` attribute is used. For this reason, the title of the screen does not change as it is refreshed. Since the second argument of the `Alert` constructor is of the `String` type, the `StringBuffer::toString()` method must be called to convert the text from the `StringBuffer` object (`selectedInfo`) into a `String` object. Figure 9.8 illustrates the information displayed after three authors, Shakespeare, Camus, and Vonnegut, have been selected.

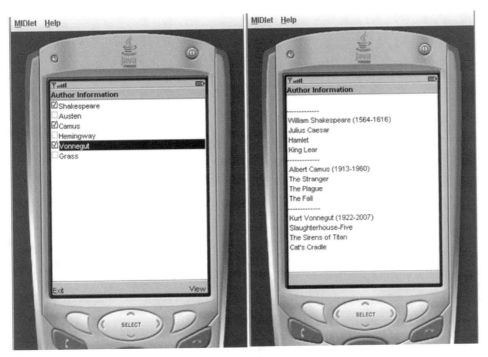

Figure 9.8
The `MULTIPLE` option provides checkboxes.

Conclusion

In this chapter, you have reviewed the first of several classes in the user interface of the MIDP classes. These include the `Display`, `Displayable`, `Command`, `Commmand-Listener`, `Alert`, `TextBox`, and `List` classes. The `AlertType` and `Choice` classes, which are defined as interfaces, provide field values for setting the modes of `Alert` and `List` options. To process messages issued by `List` objects, you can use selection statements that test for both `Displayable` and `Command` arguments. `List`, `Form`, and `TextBox` objects are all of the `Displayable` type. With respect to the `List` class, the key modes are defined by the `EXCLUSIVE` and `MULTIPLE` values. The `EXCLUSIVE` mode allows for the selection of only one item at a time. The `MULTIPLE` mode allows for the selection of several items at a time. For filtering simultaneous messages issued by `List` objects, you can make use of the `getSelectedFlags()` method.

PART IV

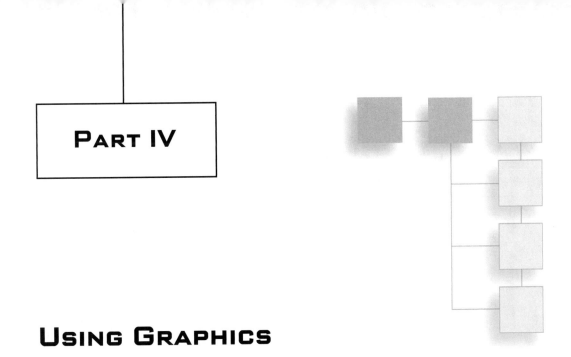

USING GRAPHICS

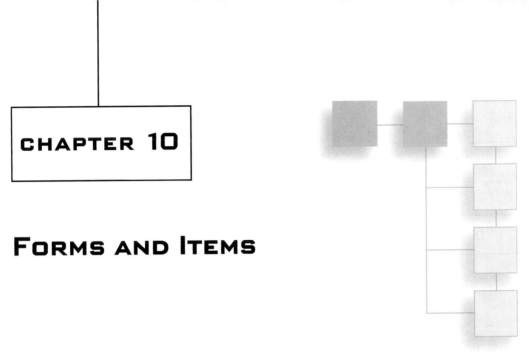

CHAPTER 10

FORMS AND ITEMS

In previous chapters, you have already glimpsed several uses of the Form class. This chapter shows you how to use the Form class in conjunction with the Item classes. The Form class provides a convenient way to organize components for display, and the Item class is the base class of the set of classes that furnish several useful ways of organizing and manipulating text and other types of information to supplement the operations in your display. In this chapter, you concentrate on the TextField and StringItem classes, reviewing work with the CommandListener and ItemStateListener interfaces to process the events that apply to the objects of the classes. You also work with the Spacer, Font, and String classes, investigating how to make use of these resources to enhance your options as you develop displays. Methods and properties provided by the Form and Item classes repeatedly come into play as you work with the layout and formatting activities involved with the Item subclasses. By developing two basic MIDlets that use scenarios drawn from text-oriented games, you explore many of the interface features of the Form and Item classes and at the same time prepare the way for work in Chapter 11 involving the Image, Gauge, and other classes associated with the Form and Item classes.

General Features of the Item and Form Classes

Figure 10.1 illustrates the relationships that exist between the abstract Item class, the classes derived from it, and the ItemCommandListener interface. In addition, it traces the relationship between the Form class, the Item class, and the ItemStateListener

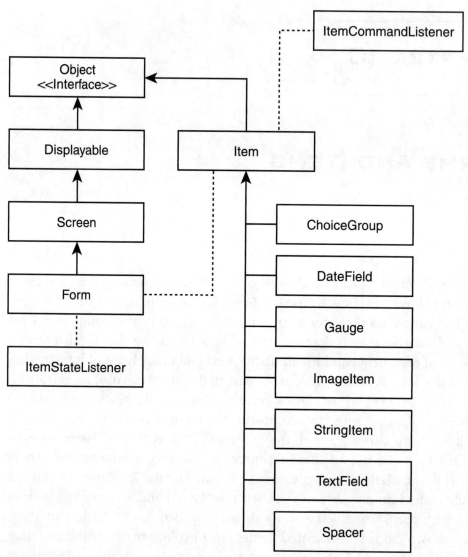

Figure 10.1
Classes derived from the Item class implement the ItemCommandListener interface.

interface. A Form class object can contain instances of the subclasses of the Item class. You call the Form::append() method to add reference to the Item subclasses to the Form object. After adding an Item object to a Form object, to manage the events associated with the Item class objects, your two main options are the ItemStateListener and the ItemCommandListener interfaces. You use the ItemCommandListener most extensively with the Form object. For the classes derived from the Item class, you use the ItemStateListener interface. Even then, if you make use of the notifyStateChanged() method of the Item subclasses, many different approaches to message processing remain open to you.

Note

For a summary of the methods and properties of the Item class, see the sidebar "Overview of the Item Class," which appears toward the end of this chapter.

The Form Class

The Form class allows you to organize and manage objects of types derived from the Item class. An object of the Form class can contain one or more instances of any of the classes associated with the Item class, and you can assign or order these objects in any combination. As Figure 10.1 shows, the classes are as follows: StringItem, ImageItem, TextField, ChoiceGroup, DateField, Gauge, and Spacer. While the Form object serves as a container for the objects of the classes derived from the Item class, how the objects appear after you associate them with the Form is in part dependent on the MID.

In previous chapters, you have used an object of the Form type to process commands. To add a command to a Form object, you employ the addCommand() method, which the Form class inherits from the Displayable class. To process messages related to Item objects, you use a different approach. To start with, to associate objects of the classes derived from the Item class with the Form object, you employ the insert() and append() methods, and after associating them, you can then use the delete() and set() methods to further manipulate them. To process messages, you implement the ItemStateListener interface when you define your MIDlet class. You can then call the itemStateChanged() method. Table 10.1 provides discussion of the Form class. Included in this table is the itemStateChanged() method of the ItemStateListener interface, along with a short review of some of the methods the Form class inherits from the Displayable class. Primary examples of how to use the Form object in association with Item objects are shown in this chapter in the FormTextFieldTest class.

Table 10.1 Form

Method	Description
Form (String)	Constructs a form with a given title. The sole argument is of the String type and provides a name for the Form object.
Form (String, Item[])	Constructs a form with a title. The second argument is an array of the Item type. The array populates the Form object with the elements furnished by the array.
int append (Image)	One of three overloaded versions. Appends an object of the Image type to the Form object. The appended Image reference appears at the bottom of the display.
int append (Item)	One of three overloaded versions. Appends an object of the Item type to the Form object. The object appended appears at the bottom of the display.
int append (String)	One of three overloaded versions. Appends an object of the String type to the Form object. The appended String object appears at the bottom of the display.
void delete (int)	Takes an integer as an argument. The integer designates the index of an element in the Form object. The method deletes the element designated by the argument. When you delete an element from a Form object, the size of the object is decreased by one.
deleteAll()	Completely clears a Form object of all the elements (Item objects) you have assigned to it.
Item get (int)	Takes an integer as an argument. The integer designates the index of an element in the Form object. The method returns the element designated by the argument.
int size()	Returns an integer that tells you the number of elements in the Form object.
void insert (int, Item)	Inserts an Item reference. The first argument is of the int type and designates the index of the Form to be associated with the newly inserted element. The second argument is of the Item type and provides the object to be inserted.
void set (int, Item)	Sets an Item reference at a particular index. The first argument designates the index of object within the Form container. The second argument designates the Item object to be set.
void setItemStateListener (ItemStateListener)	Associates a listener with the Form object so that events generated by elements within it can be handled. Takes an ItemStateListener object as its argument.
ItemStateListener::itemChanged (Item)	This method is not a Form method. It is the sole method of the ItemStateListener interface, and you implement this method to process events generated by Item objects associated with the Form object. It takes an Item reference as an argument and is called whenever an Item object is changed.
Inherited Displayable methods	Among these are addCommand(), getTicker(), getTitle(), isShown(), setCommandListener(), setTicker(), setTitle().

TextField

One of the most commonly used of the Item subclasses is the TextField class. It provides a convenient way to format text as it is entered or displayed. To apply formatting to the text processed by TextField objects, you can use one of several TextField properties. Among these are the DECIMAL and ANY properties, which are reviewed in Table 10.2. Since a TextField object is a subclass of Item, you can store it in an array of the Item type. You can then handle the messages from the TextField object by using the itemChanged() method, which is provided by the ItemStateListener interface.

Table 10.2 TextField

Method	Description
TextField (String, String, int, int)	Constructs a new TextField. The first argument is of the String type and provides a label for the text field. The second argument, also of the String type, provides the initial text for the text field. The third argument is of the int type and provides the maximum length of the text field. The last argument is a TextField property that allows you to control the masking and other properties of the field.
void setConstraints (int)	Allows you to set the Constraints property applied to the TextField object. (See further on in this table for a selected list.)
void insert (char[], int, int, int)	Inserts characters into the field. The first argument is an array of the character type from which the text is to be taken. The second argument is the starting index position in the array from which text is to be taken. The third argument indicates the number of characters to be taken from the array. The fourth argument is the starting index position in the field to which the text is to be copied.
void insert (String src, int position)	Inserts a string into the field. The first argument provides the text to be written to the field. The second argument indicates the starting index position in the field to which the characters are to be written.
void delete (int offset, int)	Removes characters from the field. The first argument is the index position in the field at which the deletion is to begin. The second argument indicates the number of characters to be deleted.
int getCaretPosition ()	Retrieves index of the current cursor position in the field.
int getChars (char[] data)	Gets the current contents of the field as a char array.
void setChars (char[] data, int offset, int)	The first argument is an array of the char type. The second argument is the starting index in the array from which characters are to be taken from the array. The third argument is the number of characters to be taken from the array.
void setString (String)	Sets the text to be displayed in a field.

(Continued)

Table 10.2 Continued

Method	Description
String getString ()	Gets the current contents of the field as a string.
int getMaxSize()	Gets the maximum number of characters allowed in the field.
int setMaxSize(int)	Establishes the maximum number of characters allowed in the field.
int size ()	Gets the current number of characters in the field.
ANY	Allows you to process an alpha or numeric value from a field or to display such a value to a field.
EMAILADDR	Provides a mask for an email address.
NUMERIC	Converts the values in the field into an integer value.
PHONENUMBER	Provides a mask for a phone number, which consists of a mixture of characters.
URL	Provides a mask that accepts the characters for a URL.
DECIMAL	Allows you to process numbers with decimal points.
PASSWORD	Masks the characters so that the value typed does not appear literally.
UNEDITABLE	Prevents values from being entered into the field. It also prevents you from assigning values to the field programmatically.
INITIAL_CAPS_WORD	Forces each new word to be capitalized.
INITIAL_CAPS_SENTENCE	Forces each new sentence to be capitalized.
Appearance Modes	Table 10.3 provides an extended list of the appearance modes that you can use with all objects derived from the Item class.

In addition to the properties and methods that are defined in the TextField class itself, you can make use of properties and methods inherited from the Item class. Among the properties that are important in this respect are those that you use as arguments to the setLayout() method. Use of this method is discussed at greater length in relation to the StringItem class. For information on the Item class and its layout properties, see the sidebar "Overview of the Item Class."

Playing with Numbers

The FormTextFieldTest class provides a simple calculator that can perform multiplication and addition. It offers examples of how to use Form, Item, Text-Field, and StringItem objects to process messages that indicate the type of operation to be performed and display the result of the calculation. It also provides examples of the use of casting and the Double class for retrieving values of the String type from TextField objects and then converting them into float values so that the calculations can be displayed. To process the messages from a

TextField object, the ItemStateListener interface is implemented. The item-StateChanged() method, which is the sole method provided by the ItemStateListener interface, allows you to process messages generated by any of the subclasses of the Item class. The FormTextFieldTest class provides four TextField objects, all of which are assigned to an array of the Item type. You can find the FormTextFieldTest class in the Chapter 10 source directory. It is also included in the Chapter10MIDlets NetBeans project. The code is explicated in the sections that follow. Here is the code for the class.

```java
/*
 * Chapter 10 \ FormTestFieldTest.java
 *
 */

import javax.microedition.midlet.*;
import javax.microedition.lcdui.*;
//import java.io.*;
//import java.util.*;

public class FormItemTextFieldTest extends MIDlet
                            implements CommandListener,
                                         ItemStateListener{
  // #1 Declare attibutes
  private Form form;
  private Display display;
  private TextField textFieldA;
  private TextField textFieldB;
  private TextField textFieldC;
  private TextField textFieldD;
  private StringItem textFieldE;
  // #1.1 create an array of the Item type
  final int COUNT = 5;
  private Item elements[] = new Item[COUNT];
  private String strA, strB;
  private String doAction;
  private Command quit;

  public FormItemTextFieldTest()
  {
      display = Display.getDisplay(this);
      // #2 Construct a Form object
      form = new Form("Form and Item Test");
```

```
                // #2.1 Construct and add textfield objects to an Item array
                textFieldA = new TextField("Num A:", "", 10,   textFieldA.DECIMAL);
                textFieldB = new TextField("Num B:", "", 10,   TextField.DECIMAL);
                textFieldC = new TextField("Operation:", "", 1,    TextField.ANY);
                textFieldD = new TextField("Sum", "",   10, TextField.DECIMAL);
                textFieldE = new StringItem("", "Type num, SELECT Down, num, " +
                                          "SELECT Down, num, " +
                                          "SELECT Down keypad M or A, " +
                                          "and then SELECT Down, keypad 1 " +
                                          "for the Sum field. " +
                                          "Clear clears a field."   );
            elements[0] = textFieldA;
            elements[1] = textFieldB;
            elements[2] = textFieldC;
            elements[3] = textFieldD;
            elements[4] = textFieldE;
            // #2.2 Add the Item object to the array
            for (int itr = 0; itr<COUNT; itr++){
                form.append(elements[itr]);
            }



            quit = new Command("Quit", Command.EXIT, 2);
            form.addCommand(quit);
            form.setCommandListener(this);

            // #2.3   Add a listener for the Item objects
            form.setItemStateListener(this);
    }

    protected void startApp() throws MIDletStateChangeException{
        display.setCurrent(form);
    }

    protected void pauseApp(){
    }

    protected void destroyApp(boolean unconditional)
                            throws MIDletStateChangeException{
    }
```

```java
// #3 Handle events for the Item objects
public void itemStateChanged(Item item){
    // #3.1 variables of the double type
    double dA, dB;
    double total;
    textFieldD.setString("");
    // #3.2 select for the Item objects
    if(item == textFieldA){
      System.out.println("State changed for " + item);
    // #3.3 Retrieving a field value
      textFieldA = (TextField)form.get(0);
      strA = textFieldA.getString();
    }
    if(item == textFieldB){
      System.out.println("State changed for " + item);
      textFieldA = (TextField)form.get(1);
      strB = textFieldB.getString();
    }
    if(item == textFieldC){
      textFieldC = (TextField)form.get(2);
      doAction = textFieldC.getString();
      System.out.println("Action " + doAction);
    }
    if(item == textFieldD){
      dA = 0;
      dB = 0;
      total = 0;
      // #3.4 Processing Double/double values
      textFieldD = (TextField)form.get(3);
      dA = Double.valueOf(strA).doubleValue();
      dB = Double.valueOf(strB).doubleValue();
      System.out.println("D - Action " + doAction);
      // #3.5 Select using the retrieved
      if(doAction.equalsIgnoreCase("M")){
        System.out.println("DM - Action " + doAction);
          total = dA * dB;
      }
      if(doAction.equalsIgnoreCase("A")){
          System.out.println("DM - Action " + doAction);
          total = dA + dB;
      }
```

```
            textFieldD.setString(String.valueOf(total));
        }
    }// end itemStateChance

    public void commandAction(Command command, Displayable displayable)
    {
        try{
            if(command == quit){
                destroyApp(true);
                notifyDestroyed();
            }
        }catch (MIDletStateChangeException me){
            System.out.println(me + " caught.");
        }
    }//end commandAction
}// end class
```

Construction and Definition

In the FormItemTextFieldTest class, in the lines following comment #1, you declare attributes of the Form, Display, TextField, StringItem, Item, String, and Command types. Of these, as Figure 10.1 shows, the TextField and StringItem attribute types are subtypes of the Item class, so you can store references to these classes in the elements array, which is defined to contain five references to objects of the Item subtypes. The Form attribute allows you to add the Item objects to the MIDlet in a sequential manner, as is shown in Figure 10.2. One Command attribute is used to close the MIDlet, but you can handle additional actions from objects of the Item subclasses by making use of the ItemStateListener interface, which you implement as an interface. To define the number of elements in the elements array and also to control repetition statements that make use of the elements array, you declare a final attribute of the int type (COUNT).

In the construction of the class, in the lines following comment #2, you create a new Form object and assign it to the form attribute. After that, in the lines associated with comment #2.1, you create five instances of the Item subclasses, which you assign to the TextField and StringItem attributes. The TextField constructor requires four arguments. The first argument is a literal string object of the String type that provides the label of the TextField object. This value is set with the construction of the TextField object and cannot be changed afterward.

N o t e

It is possible to create and assign TextField objects directly to an array of the Item type, but using the attributes in an intermediary step makes it clearer what is being done. Here is an example showing how you can directly create an instance of one of the Item subclasses and assign it to an array of the Item type:

```
elements[0] = new TextField("Num A:", "",
                        10, textFieldA.DECIMAL);
```

Using this approach, you can eliminate the redundant use of the class attributes.

The second argument of the TextField constructor provides the default value to be displayed by the TextField object in its active field. For all of the TextField objects in the current class, this argument is an empty string. As Table 10.1 reveals, you can use such methods as insert(), setChars(), setString(), and delete() to change the value of the active field.

The third argument for the TextField constructor is of the int type. It establishes the number of characters the TextField object accepts in its display field. In this instance, with the exception of the "Operation" field, which is set to 1, all the TextField objects are defined with active fields that can accept 10 characters.

The last argument of the TextField constructor is of the int type. The acceptable arguments are defined as properties of the TextField class. The properties used are DECIMAL and ANY. The first of these automatically displays and accepts rational values. The second allows for both numerical and alphabetical input.

For the StringItem constructor, two arguments are required. The first is the label of the StringItem object. The label of a StringItem object behaves in largely the same way as the label of a TextField object. The difference is that the active field of the StringItem object is not by default active and is not surrounded with a bordered box. The methods that apply to it are also different than those you use with objects of the TextField class.

N o t e

The StringItem class is covered in greater detail in a subsequent section of this chapter. In this context, it is important only to recognize that it is a subclass of Item and so can be used in ways similar to other Item objects. Its construction and methods differ from those of the TextField class.

To add the Item subclass object to the Form object, you use the append() method of the Form class. To accomplish this, as is evident in the lines following comment #2.2, you use a for repetition statement to add the Item objects to the elements

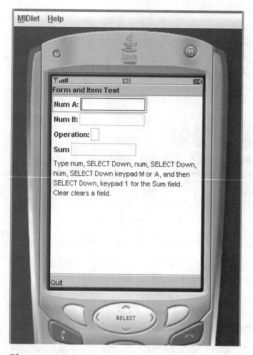

Figure 10.2
The objects derived from the `Item` class appear in sequence after being added to the `Form` object.

array. The repetition iterates five times, associating the `Form` object with four
`TextField` references and one `StringItem` reference. Figure 10.2 provides a view
of the display that results.

Processing Events

In the `FormItemTextFieldTest` class, having populated the `Form` object with references to objects of the `Item` subclasses, you then add the `quit` command to the `Form`
object. To accomplish this, you call the `addCommand()` and `setCommandListener()`
methods. These two methods pertain to messages relating to the `Form` object. For
the `Item` objects, you require a second type of message processing.

In the signature line of the `FormItemTextFieldTest` class, you use the `implements`
keyword to implement both the `CommandListener` interface, which allows you
to process `Form` messages, and the `ItemStateListener` interface, which allows you
to process messages relating to the subclasses of the `Item` subclasses class. As is
shown in the lines following comment #2.3, you call the `Form::setItem-`
`StateListener()` method to set up processing for `Item` messages.

To handle the messages from the `Item` objects, you implement the `itemState-Changed()` method, which is provided by the `ItemStateListener` interface. As is evident in the lines associated with comment #3, this method takes an argument of the `Item` type. To process an argument from one of the `Item` objects, you can use any number of approaches. In this case, a series of `if` selection statements is used. In each case, the approach is the same. You test the `Item` argument for the identity of the object that issues the message. For example, the first selection statement tests for the `textFieldA` object. (You might also test using `elements[0]`.)

If the selection statement renders `true` for `textFieldA`, the flow of the program enters the first selection block. The first statement in this block, preceding comment #3.3, issues a test message to the console. After that, following comment #3.3, you cast the value returned by the `Form::get()` method to retrieve the `TextField` reference. The `get()` method takes an argument of the `int` type. The argument designates the index of the `Item` subclass object you have assigned to the `Form` object. The index values corresponding to the `Item` subclass objects are determined by the order in which you assign the objects. For this reason, the `textFieldA` object corresponds to an index value of 0. The `textFieldB` object corresponds to an index value of 1.

When you use the `get()` method to retrieve an `Index` object, it is necessary to cast the object into its proper type. In this case, you cast `textFieldA` as a `TextField` object, so the argument for the cast is `TextField`. You then assign the object back to its proper identifier (`textFieldA`). Having done this, you are in a position to call any of the methods of the `TextField` class.

For the `textFieldA` object, you call the `TextField::getString()` object, which returns a reference of the `String` type. The value returned is the value currently residing in the active field of the `textFieldA` object. You assign the returned value to a local identifier of the `String` type (`strA`).

The `textFieldA` object returns a string that resembles a rational value. It does so because you have constructed the `textFieldA` object using the `DECIMAL` property. The same approach is used to retrieve the active field value for the `textFieldB` object. As Figure 10.3 illustrates, the objective in both cases is to retrieve strings representing numerical values from the active fields of the two objects so that you can perform calculations using them.

With the `textFieldC` object, you identify the calculation to be performed. For this application, only two calculations apply, multiplication and addition. The

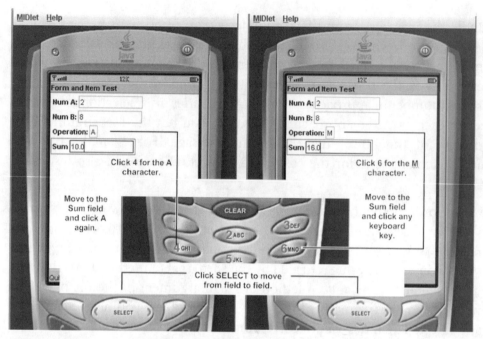

Use CLEAR and SELECT buttons to try different values.

Figure 10.3
Use the `ItemStateListener` interface to process messages issued by the subclasses of the `Item` class assigned to a `Form` object.

statements in the `if` selection block follow the same pattern as those previously implemented, but in this case, you assign the returned value of the `getString()` method to an identifier of the `String` type (`doAction`). The value that you assign is a letter (`A` or `M`). This is possible because you have used the ANY property to define the `textFieldC` object. This property forces the value you enter into the field using the keyboard to be converted into an alphabetical value.

For the final selection statement, you test for the `textFieldD` object. When a message is received from this object, first you initialize the local identifiers, `dA`, `dB`, and `total`, to 0. After casting the `textFieldD` object back to itself, you then revisit the `String` values stored in the `strA` and `strB` identifiers, which you have defined using the values retrieved from the `textFieldA` and `textFieldB` objects. These values must be converted to the `double` type to be processed arithmetically, and to accomplish this, you use the `Double::valueOf()` method to first convert the `String` values to values of the abstract `Double` type. You then call the `String::doubleValue()` method to convert these values to the primitive `double` type.

Given the conversion of the String references to primitive double values, you can carry out the arithmetic necessary to calculate a value for the total identifier. To accomplish this, as the lines following comment #3.5 show, you test the value assigned to the doAction identifier. This identifier is of the String type, and the String::equalsIgnoreCase() method allows you to determine alphabetical equality between String items. If the value is M, then the statement in the selection block multiplies the value of dA by the value of dB and assigns the result to total. If the value is A, then the one value is added to the other and assigned to total.

To display the value assigned to the total identifier, the String::valueOf() method is called. This method is overloaded so that it can accept arguments of any of the primitive types, so in this case, no problem is created with the use of the total identifier. The value is converted to the String type, and the TextField::setString() method is then called to populate the active field of the textFieldD object with the result of the calculation. As Figure 10.3 illustrates, after you move the cursor to the Sum field, you can click any of the keyboard keys to invoke the textFieldD selection statement and see the calculated results.

StringItem

As shown previously in this chapter, the StringItem class provides objects that display text messages. Since it is a subclass of the Item class, you use the append() method to associate it with a Form object. As with the TextField class, the StringItem class inherits several methods from the Item class. In addition to the inherited properties you can use to set its mode of appearance there are also those that you use in relation to the setLayout() method. Table 10.3 provides a partial list of the defined values for the mode of appearance. See the sidebar, "Overview of the Item Class," for information on the layout properties. They can all be used as arguments in one of the StringItem constructors. They allow you to control such things as where the StringItem object appears in the display, whether a new line character follows it, and whether it appears as a hyperlink.

The StringItem class is derived from the Item class, and for this reason, several of the methods that you regularly use with it are covered only in the documentation of the Item class. Since the Item class is abstract, you can use it, for example, as a type for an array or a collection, but you cannot directly instantiate instances of it.

Table 10.3 StringItem

Method	Description
StringItem(String, String)	Creates a new StringItem object. The first argument sets the value for the label. The second argument sets the value for the text area. Use an argument of null to exclude the label or text area from construction.
StringItem(String, String, int)	This constructor is the same as the first with respect to the first two arguments. For the third argument, you use an appearance mode property. A list of these appears later in this table.
String getText()	Returns a reference to a String object with the characters in the text area. It returns null if you have not assigned a value to the text area.
void setFont(int, int, int)	Allows you to set the font for the text area. The arguments for method are all integer values defined in the Font class that designate the face, style, and size of the Font object.
void setPreferredSize(int, int)	The first argument sets the width. The second argument sets the height.
void setText(String)	Allows you to assign characters in the form of a String object or reference to the text area. You can also use a literal string value.
Appearance Modes	Inherited from the Item class. A few examples are BUTTON, HYPERLINK, LAYOUT_BOTTOM, LAYOUT_CENTER, LAYOUT_DEFAULT, LAYOUT_LEFT, LAYOUT_NEWLINE_AFTER, LAYOUT_TOP, and LAYOUT_VSHRINK, PLAIN. See Table 10.4 for further discussion of these values.
Item::setLayout()	This method is a member of the Item class. You use such values as LAYOUT_LEFT, LAYOUT_RIGHT, and LAYOUT_CENTER, and Or them with DEFAULT_LAYOUT to position StringItem objects in the display area.

The ItemPlayTest Class

The ItemPlayTest class reviews some of the methods you use in association with the StringItem class. Some of these are derived from the Item class. The StringItem class works largely the same way as the other classes derived from the Item class, with the difference that the text area or field associated with it cannot be changed through direct interaction. To alter the text you associate with a StringItem object, you have a number of options, however. Among other things, you can use the notifyStateChanged() method. The StringItem class inherits the method from the Item class. Since the notifyStateChanged() method generates an event, you can use the event in conjunction with the setText() method of the StringItem class to dynamically change the text associated with a StringItem object.

Like the other demonstration classes in this chapter, the ItemPlayTest class is in the Chapter 10 source directory. You can also find it in the NetBeans Chapter10MIDlets project. The class allows the user to repeatedly press one of the soft buttons to generate random values that are assigned to the names of cities. The user gets a limited number of tries with each round of play. Numbers are randomly assigned to the cities, and the highest number designates the "winning" city. The MIDlet might be the beginning of a game involving finding a destination for a vacation.

```java
/*
 * Chapter 10\ItemPlayTest.java
 */

import javax.microedition.midlet.*;
import javax.microedition.lcdui.*;
import java.util.*;

public class ItemPlayTest extends MIDlet implements CommandListener,
                                                    ItemStateListener{
    // #1
    private Form form;
    private Display display;
    private StringItem strItemA, strItemB, strItemC,
                       strItemD, strItemE, strItemF;
    private final int CITY_LIMIT = 6;
    private final int NUMOFTRIES = 9;
    private Item elements[] = new StringItem[CITY_LIMIT];
    private TextField textFieldA;
    private Command quit, tryACity;
    private Random random;
    private int randInt;
    private int highScore;

    public ItemPlayTest()
    {
        random = new Random();
        display = Display.getDisplay(this);
        highScore = 1;
        form = new Form("Find your next destination!!!");
```

```
// #2 Construct and add textfield objects to an Item array
strItemA = new StringItem("1. San Francisco", "California", Item.BUTTON);
strItemB = new StringItem("2. Manhattan", "New York",  Item.BUTTON);
strItemC = new StringItem("3. London", "England", Item.BUTTON);
strItemD = new StringItem("4. Paris", "France");
strItemD.setLayout(Item.BUTTON);
strItemE = new StringItem("5. Tokyo", "Japan", Item.BUTTON);
strItemF = new StringItem("6. Sidney", "Australia", Item.BUTTON);

textFieldA =  new TextField("Try: ", "",  12,  TextField.ANY);

elements[0] = strItemA;
elements[1] = strItemB;
elements[2] = strItemC;
elements[3] = strItemD;
elements[4] = strItemE;
elements[5] = strItemF;

// #3 Set set the items left, right, and center
elements[0].setLayout(Item.LAYOUT_LEFT | Item.LAYOUT_DEFAULT);
elements[1].setLayout(Item.LAYOUT_RIGHT | Item.LAYOUT_DEFAULT);
elements[2].setLayout(Item.LAYOUT_LEFT |Item.LAYOUT_DEFAULT);
elements[3].setLayout(Item.LAYOUT_RIGHT |Item.LAYOUT_DEFAULT);
elements[4].setLayout(Item.LAYOUT_LEFT |Item.LAYOUT_DEFAULT);
elements[5].setLayout(Item.LAYOUT_RIGHT |Item.LAYOUT_DEFAULT);
textFieldA.setLayout(Item.LAYOUT_CENTER |Item.LAYOUT_DEFAULT);

for (int itr = 0; itr<CITY_LIMIT; itr++){
   // # 3.1
     StringItem tempItem = (StringItem)elements[itr];
     tempItem.setFont(Font.getFont(Font.FACE_PROPORTIONAL,
                                   Font.STYLE_ITALIC |
                                   Font.STYLE_BOLD,
                                   Font.SIZE_LARGE));
     form.append(elements[itr]);
}
form.append(textFieldA);
form.append(new Spacer(50, 10));
    // #3.2
String introStr =
        new String("\n When the Backlight flashes\n " +
                 "The highest score wins");
```

```
    form.append(introStr);
    form.append("\nYou have ten tries.");
        // #3.3
    int numOfItems = form.size();
    StringItem tempItem  =  (StringItem)form.get(numOfItems-1);
    tempItem.setFont(Font.getFont(Font.FACE_PROPORTIONAL,
                                  Font.SIZE_MEDIUM |
                                  Font.STYLE_BOLD,
                                  Font.SIZE_LARGE));

    // #4
    tryACity =  new Command("Try", Command.OK, 2);
    quit = new Command("Quit", Command.EXIT, 2);
    form.addCommand(quit);
    form.addCommand(tryACity);
    form.setCommandListener(this);
    form.setItemStateListener(this);
}

// #5
public void commandAction(Command command, Displayable displayable){
    try{
       if (command == quit){
          destroyApp(true);
          notifyDestroyed();
       }
       // #5.1
       if (command == tryACity){
          randInt = random.nextInt(CITY_LIMIT);

          if(highScore > NUMOFTRIES){
            display.flashBacklight(3000);
            highScore = 0;
            return;
          }
          highScore++;
          // #5.2
          form.get(randInt).notifyStateChanged();
       }
    }catch (Exception me){
       System.out.println(me + " caught.");
    }
}//end commandAction
```

```
    // #6
    public void itemStateChanged(Item item){
        System.out.println("State changed for " + randInt);
        StringItem tempStItem;
        tempStItem = (StringItem)form.get(randInt);
        // #6.1
        textFieldA.setString(tempStItem.getText());
        tempStItem.setText("Score:" + highScore);
    }

    protected void startApp() throws MIDletStateChangeException{
        display.setCurrent(form);
    }

    public void pauseApp() {
    }

    public void destroyApp(boolean unconditional) {
    }
}// end class
```

Note

When you operate the application for testing, use the F1 and F2 keys on your keyboard to invoke the actions of the left and right soft keys on the Java Wireless Toolkit device emulator.

Definition and Construction

In the lines preceding comment #1 of the ItemPlayTest class, you define the ItemPlayTest class so that it implements the CommandListener and ItemStateListener interfaces. The CommandListener interface obligates you to implement the command-Action() method, while the ItemStateListener brings with it the need to implement the itemStateChanged() method. In lines immediately following comment #1, you declare Form and Display class attributes, and following that, you add six StringItem class attributes. In the next few lines, you attend to defining the elements array. In this case, the array constructor for the array, StringItem[CITY_LIMIT], uses the StringItem type, but you can assign the constructed instance of the array to an identifier of the Item type. This is an irregular approach to constructing an array, but it serves to emphasize that the StringItem class is derived from the Item class. As an experiment, you can change the definition so that it reads as follows:

```
private Item elements[] = new Item[CITY_LIMIT];
```

You might also use this approach, which makes some of the code in the class definition redundant:

```
private StringItem elements[] = new StringItem[CITY_LIMIT];
```

In addition to defining class attributes of the StringItem and Item types, you also declare a class attribute of the Random type (random). To access the Random type, import the java.util package, as is accomplished with the import statements preceding comment #1. Along with the class attribute of the Random type, you declare a class attribute of the int type to store random values used in different methods of the class.

Preceding comment #2, you create an instance of the Random class and assign it to the random class attribute. Constructing the Random object in the constructor of the MIDlet allows you to generate different starting values with each new instance of the MIDlet. Although you can provide a seed value to the Random constructor, in this case the default version of the constructor is used. This ensures that you see a different sequence of values with each execution of the MIDlet.

In the lines trailing comment #2, a somewhat redundant approach to constructing StringItem objects is used. You see both of the overloaded constructors for the StringItem class in use. Most of the construction statements involve the three-argument constructor. The first argument for this constructor is of the String type and provides the label of the StringItem object. The second argument is also of the String type. It provides the text to be written to the text field of the StringItem object. The third argument is of the int type and is populated using one of the defined values provided by the Item class. Generally, this third argument designates what is known as the appearance mode of the object it defines. The appearance mode extends to cover the position of the object in the display and the appearance of the font. Here is an example of the use of the three-argument constructors:

```
strItemA = new StringItem("1. San Francisco",
                          "California", Item.BUTTON);
```

The instance the StringItem class is assigned to one of the class attributes, and a few lines later, this attribute is assigned to the elements array, which is of Item type.

```
elements[0] = strItemA;
```

The instances the StringItem class might be assigned directly to the elements array, but using an extra step involving named class attributes makes the definition activities more visible.

The three-argument StringItem constructor is used for all but one of the construction statements. The one exception occurs with the strItemD attribute. Here the two-argument constructor is used. With the constructor, the first argument is of the String type and provides the initial wording for the label. The second, also of the String type, provides the wording for the text field of the StringItem object.

To provide the strItemD attribute with the same definition that the other attributes are given, a call is made to the setLayout() method. Its sole argument is of the int type and is defined using one or more of the appearance mode properties supplied by the Item class. In this instance, as in the construction statements of the other StringItem objects, you see the Item.BUTTON property:

```
strItemD = new StringItem("4. Paris", "France");
strItemD.setLayout(Item.BUTTON);
```

Using the Bit OR Operator

In the lines following comment #3 of the ItemPlayTest class, after assigning the explicitly constructed instances of the StringItem class attributes to the elements array, you then proceed to call the setLayout() method using the elements array. The StringItem class is a subclass of the Item class, and you have assigned attributes of the StringItem type to the Item array. For this reason, in some cases, it is necessary to *down cast* the references in the elements array to the StringItem type before you can call methods exclusive to the StringItem class. No problem arises from this approach to calling the setLayout() method, because the setLayout() method is a member of the Item class that is inherited by all its subclasses, among which is the StringItem class.

Unlike the arguments supplied in the initial construction and definition statements for the StringItem class, in this case, with the calls to setLayout(), you use the bit OR (|) operation to join the integer values of different properties supplied by the Item class. For example, in each case, you appropriate the Item.LAYOUT_DEFAULT property, which defines the StringItem object so that it accepts the sizing and positioning priorities supplied by the device and also so that the object is displayed horizontally and relative to the left side, right side, or center of the display.

You also make use of the Item.LAYOUT_RIGHT, Item.LAYOUT_LEFT, and Item.-LAYOUT_CENTER properties to designate that the StringItem objects are to appear nestled against the left or right borders of the display area or centered on given lines.

Note

You can leave out the `LAYOUT_DEFAULT` property argument for the `setLayout()` method (`Item.LAYOUT_RIGHT`, instead of `Item.LAYOUT_RIGHT | Item.LAYOUT_ DEFAULT`), but when you do so, you allow the `MIDP` class itself to use a default layout.

Font Definitions, Literal Strings, and Appending

The `Font` class provides an extensive set of options for changing the face, size, and other features of the characters that appear in the display area of the MIDlet. As a way of exploring how to set `Font` values, in the lines associated with comment #3.1 of the `ItemPlayTest` class, you employ a `for` repetition statement to iterate through the `StringItem` references assigned to the `elements` array. With each repetition of the `for` block, these lines are invoked:

```
// # 3.1
StringItem tempItem = (StringItem)elements[itr];
tempItem.setFont(Font.getFont(Font.FACE_PROPORTIONAL,
                    Font.STYLE_ITALIC |
                    Font.STYLE_BOLD,
                    Font.SIZE_LARGE));
```

The first line downcasts the references from the `elements` array and assigns them, using a cast, to a temporary `StringItem` object, `tempItem`. Such an action is necessary because in the next line a call is made to the `StringItem::setFont()` method, which is defined in the `StringItem` class and so cannot be called with a reference stored in an array of the `Item` class, which as a superclass does not support the specialized methods of classes derived from it.

As for the `setFont()` method itself, you call it using the `StringItem` object and then supply as an argument to it a reference of the `Font` type. The `Font` class provides the `getFont()` method, which is static and serves in place of a constructor to allow you to create instances of the `Font` class for use with the `setFont()` and other methods. The `getFont()` method requires three arguments, each taken from a list of defined properties provided by the `Font` class. In this instance, the `FACE_PROPORTIONAL`, `STYLE_ITALIC`, `STYLE_BOLD`, and `SIZE_LARGE` properties are used. You use the bit `OR` (`|`) operator to set both the italic and bold properties of the font. Figure 10.4 shows the difference changing the face, type, and size properties can make. The names of the states represent the newly defined font.

Having defined the `StringItem` objects to include distinct font characteristics, you then call the `Form::append()` method to add the `StringItem` references from

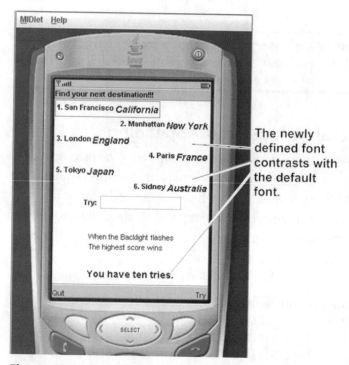

The newly defined font contrasts with the default font.

Figure 10.4
The setFont() method allows you to alter the size, style, and face of the font.

the elements array to the Form object. One of the overloaded versions of the append() method takes as an argument a reference to the general Item class. As an extension of this activity, in the lines preceding comment #3.2, you employ the append() method to add a reference to a TextField object to the Form object. Likewise, in the lines following comment #3.2, you make use of a second overloaded version of the append() method. This version accepts a reference to a String object as an argument.

In addition to using the append() method to add String and StringItem objects to the Form object, you can also use it to directly append literal strings. In the line directly preceding comment #3.3, you use this approach to add the string "You have ten tries" to the display. This is the same thing you add to the Form object. When the string is added to the Form object, it is implicitly stored as an Item object. That being the case, you can then retrieve it from the Form object, cast it as needed, and use the setFont() method to format it for display. How this is accomplished is evident in the lines following comment #3.3. For convenience, here is the code.

```
// #3.3
  int numOfItems = form.size();
  StringItem tempItem  =  (StringItem)form.get(numOfItems-1);
  tempItem.setFont(Font.getFont(Font.FACE_PROPORTIONAL,
                                Font.STYLE_ITALIC |
                                Font.STYLE_BOLD,
                                Font.SIZE_LARGE));
```

The Form::size() method returns an integer value that gives the total number of Item objects you have added to the Form object. To discover the index value of the final element in the array, it is necessary to subtract 1 from the total number. To reduce the complexity of the code, the retrieved reference is cast to a StringItem object and then assigned to the tempItem identifier. On the next line, this identifier is then used to call the setFont() method of the StringItem class, and the same values used before are applied to the final lines of the display. Figure 10.4 illustrates the differences in the font faces, sizes, and styles achieved through the use of the setFont() method.

Spacers and Implicit Appending

Among the classes shown in Figure 10.1 that are derived from the Item class is the Spacer class. The Spacer class provides a constructor that allows you to create a rectangular space that is defined by pixel values. As arguments, the Spacer constructor accepts two positive integer values. The first argument designates the minimum width of the Spacer rectangle. The second argument designates the minimum height of the spacer rectangle. In the lines just prior to #3.2 in the ItemPlayTest class, you see the following activity:

```
form.append(new Spacer(50, 10));
```

In this instance, the spacer constructor is used to create an anonymous reference to a Spacer object 50 pixels wide and 10 pixels high. The size of the rectangle can expand from the values you set to accord with resizing events in the display area. As shown in Figure 10.5, the inclusion of the Spacer object forces the text in the bottom of the display downward from the TextField object identified with the Try label. The box with the dashed border that appears in Figure 10.5 does not represent the Spacer as it actually appears. It is intended only to show you that a spacer is essentially a rectangular space that you can insert into your display.

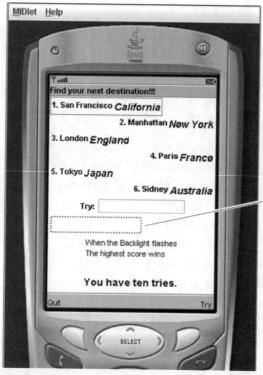

The Spacer object forces a minimum rectangular area into the display. (The box shown is an approximation. Also, the Spacer object does not have a visible border.)

Figure 10.5
Use `Spacer` objects to adjust the positions of the display.

Note

Although it is beyond the scope of the discussion in this chapter, you can add commands to dynamically resize `Spacer` objects using such `Spacer` methods as `addCommand()` and `setMinimumSize()`. For comprehensive discussion of all aspects of the MIDP classes, access **http://java.sun.com/javame/reference/apis/jsr118/**.

Working with Events

In the lines following comment #4 of the `ItemPlayTest` class, you define objects of the `Command` type. One is specified using the `Command.OK` field value and labeled with "Try". This is the `tryACity` attribute. The other is specified using the `Command.EXIT` field value and labeled with "Quit". This is the `quit` attribute. You then call the `Form::setCommand()` method to associate the two `Command` attributes to the `Form` object. Following that, you call the `setCommandListener()` and `setItemStateListener()` methods, both of which use the `this` keyword as their arguments, to initialize the `Form` object so that it can handle events.

As mentioned earlier in this chapter, the setItemStateListener() allows you to handle events associated with the Item references you have added to the Form object. Events affiliated with Item objects are handled by the itemStateChanged() method, which you define when you implement the ItemStateChanged interface. To handle other events, you implement the commandAction() method, which is provided by the CommandListener interface.

The primary events of the ItemPlayTest class are generated by the quit and tryACity commands, both of which are controlled with the soft buttons. The Try button issues the tryACity event, which is caught by the commandAction() method and then processed in the if selection block associated with comment #5.1. When the user activates the Try button, the flow of the program enters the selection block and a random number in the range from 0 to 5 is generated. This number is then assigned to the randInt class attribute. Following the generation of a random number, you then increment the value of a second class attribute, highScore.

Assigned to the randInt class attribute, the randomly generated value is used in the itemStateChanged() method to allow you to select Item objects randomly from the Form object. This is possible because each Item object is associated with an index, and in this case, the indexes 0 through 5 correspond to the names of six cities around the world, all of which are named in the labels of StringItem objects. To complement the names of the cities, the text field of each StringItem object is initialized with the name of the country or state in which the city is located.

When the user generates a Try event, the current value of highScore replaces the name of one of the countries that is identified by the random number. To assign the value, in the lines following comment #6.1, you use the rendInt attribute as an argument to the Form::get() method to retrieve one of the StringItem references from the Form object. After casting the reference as a StringItem object and assigning it to the tempItem identifier, you then use the reference to call the setText() method, which allows you to assign the value of highScore to the text field of the StringItem object. Just prior to assigning the highScore value to the StringItem text field, you call the setString() method of the TextArea object (textFieldA) to display either the name of the country identified by the random number or, if the country has already been identified, a newly assigned value.

As Figure 10.6 illustrates, the game of generating random numbers and identifying a single city as the highest scoring city is limited to 10 try actions. An if selection statement tests the value assigned to the highScore attribute against

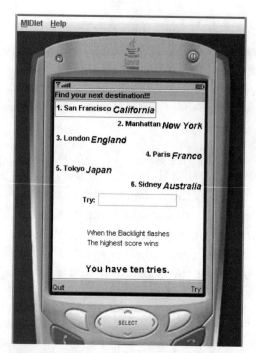

Figure 10.6
The `notifyStateChanged()` method invokes the `itemStateChanged()` method.

NUMOFTRIES. When the value of `highScore` equals NUMOFTRIES, then the keyboard flashes and `highScore` is reset to 0.

Overview of the Item Class

The `Item` class is an abstract class that contains several properties you use as you work with objects of the `StringItem`, `TextField`, `DateField`, and other classes that are derived from it. Table 10.4 provides a summary view of some of the properties and methods provided by the `Item` class. For a comprehensive discussion of the `Item` class, see the MIDP site at **http://java.sun .com/javame/reference/apis/jsr118/**.

Table 10.4 Selected Item Methods and Modes

Class Method or Property	Description
void addCommand(Command)	Adds a context-sensitive `Command` to the `Item` object.
String getLabel()	Returns a `String` reference with the text of the `Item` object.
int getLayout()	Returns the value or values you have used to position the `Item` object in the display.
int getMinimumHeight()	If you have assigned a minimum height to the `Item` object, then this method returns the integer value you have used to designate the minimum height.

Table 10.4 Continued

Class Method or Property	Description
int getMinimumWidth()	If you have assigned a minimum width to the Item object, then this method returns the integer value you have used to designate the minimum width.
void notifyStateChanged()	Induces the Form object that contains an Item object to issue a message that can be handled by the ItemStateLis-tener() method.
void removeCommand(Command)	Removes the context-sensitive command from Item object.
void setDefaultCommand-(Command)	Sets the default Command for this Item object.
void setLabel(String)	Allows you to assign text to the label of the Item object.
void setLayout(int)	Allows you to associate layout directives for this Item object. You often use several values joined using the bit or operator.
BUTTON	Indicates that the Item object should appear as a bordered box or a button.
HYPERLINK	Allows you to designate the Item object as a hyperlink.
LAYOUT_CENTER	Causes the Item object to appear in the center, horizontally, of the display and to be positioned vertically according to the position you have assigned it in the Form object.
LAYOUT_DEFAULT	You can use the bit or operator to join this value with such values as LAYOUT_CENTER. This ensures that the default layout policy of the form (or container) applies when the Item object is positioned for display.
LAYOUT_EXPAND	Causes a given Item object to expand until it fills the space available.
LAYOUT_LEFT	Causes the Item object to appear in the left of the display, positioned vertically according to the place you have assigned it in the Form object.
LAYOUT_NEWLINE_AFTER	If you assign several Item objects to a row, you can use this to force a line return. The Item object that follows then appears on the next row.
LAYOUT_NEWLINE_BEFORE	Forces the Item object associated with it onto a new line.
LAYOUT_RIGHT	Causes the Item object to appear in the right of the display, positioned vertically according to the place you assigned it in the Form object.
LAYOUT_SHRINK	Grants permission to the display to reduce an Item to the minimum width you have defined for it.
LAYOUT_TOP	Lines up the Item object it is affiliated with at the top of the display.
LAYOUT_VCENTER	Lines up the associated Item object at the vertical center of the display.

Conclusion

In this chapter, you have explored the Item, Form, TextField, StringItem, and Spacer classes and have also experimented further with the CommandListener and ItemStateListener interfaces. In addition, you worked with the Font class and such methods as getFont() and setFont() of the StringItem class. Since the TextField and StringItem classes are both derived from the Item class, they share many common features. On the other hand, the ways that you can use them differ slightly. The StringItem class offers label and field properties, as does the TextField class, but processing events with StringItem objects can require a bit more work than objects in the TextField classes.

Still, as is shown in the ItemPlayTest and FormTextFieldTest classes, the Item subclasses allow you to work fairly readily with events to pass text information between objects. In some cases, casting proves essential in this regard. Having recast references after retrieving them from an array, you can then use the restored object to call the methods specific to the subclasses. Along the same lines, while the get() method of the Form class allows you to retrieve subclass references from Form objects, the append() method enables you to add Item objects to the Form objects. The append() method proves especially effective because it is overloaded to allow you to work with different data types as you assign them to the form object. This extends to such classes as String and Item. When you assign a literal string to a Form object, you have the option of retrieving a reference to the string and casting it as a String or StringItem, in which case you can then apply formatting to it.

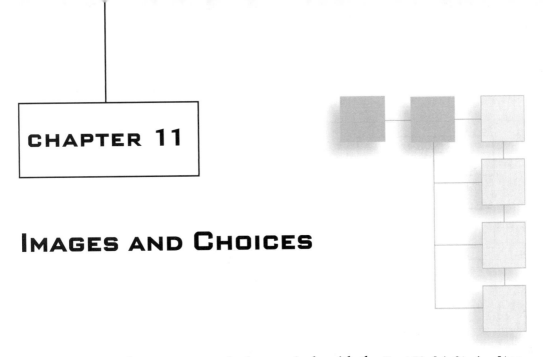

CHAPTER 11

IMAGES AND CHOICES

In the previous chapter, you worked extensively with the TextField, StringItem, and Spacer classes, gaining as you went a sense of how to process messages relating to them after you have placed them in a form. Toward this end, you examined how to use the ItemCommandListener and ItemStateListener interfaces to capture and process events. In this chapter, you will continue your examination of the classes derived from the Item classes. This chapter includes discussion of the ChoiceGroup and ImageItem classes. Discussion of these two classes provides an excellent context to begin examining a class that has become increasingly important as an element in games that involve animations and graphical components. This is the Image class. The Image class allows you to load data from files to create stationary and animated items in your MIDlet games.

Figure 11.1 illustrates the hierarchy of classes dealt with in this chapter.

ChoiceGroup

The ChoiceGroup class provides a way to group a list of selections together so that when you choose one of them, the message you generate can be retrieved using an index that identifies the choice within the group of choices. In many ways, the ChoiceGroup class resembles the List class. As the ComedyChoiceGroup class illustrates, when you create a ChoiceGroup object, one ready option is to make it so that you select one item at a time. Clicking one radio button, in other words,

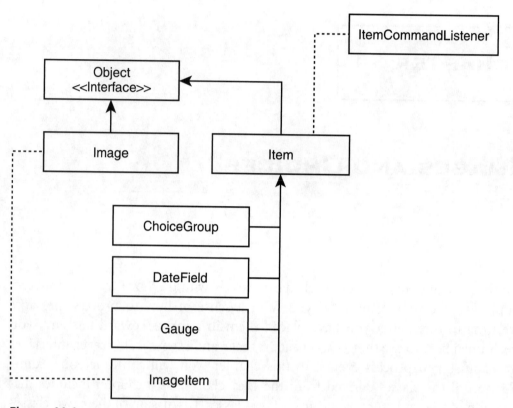

Figure 11.1
The subclasses of the Item class covered in the current chapter are in some respects more complex than the TextField and StringItem classes.

deactivates other selections. This list is created using the EXCLUSIVE property, which is provided by the ChoiceGroup class definition. In addition to single selections, you can also make multiple selections. To set this option, you define the ChoiceGroup object using the MULTIPLE property. Table 11.1 provides a summary of the methods and properties available in the ChoiceGroup class.

The ComedyChoiceGroup Class

You can find the ComedyChoiceGroup class in the Chapter 11 folder in two versions, one standalone, the other included in the Chapter11MIDlets project folder. The PNG files used by the class are in the Chapter11MIDlets\src folder.

Table 11.1 ChoiceGroup

Method	Description
ChoiceGroup(String label, int)	Constructs a new ChoiceGroup. The constructor takes two arguments. The first argument is of the String type and collectively identifies the choices to be included in the group. The second is an integer value supplied by a defined property of the ChoiceGroup class. This value establishes, for example, whether the choice group is to allow multiple choices, single choices, or wrapping lines. (See the descriptions of the properties further along in this table.)
ChoiceGroup(String, int, String[], Image[])	Constructs a ChoiceGroup object. The constructor takes four arguments. The first argument is of the String type and collectively identifies the choices to be included in the group. As indicated previously, the second argument, of the int type, determines whether the list is to process, for example, single or multiple selections. (See the list below.) The third argument is an array of the String type that provides, sequentially, the labels for each of the choices in the group. The fourth argument, an array of the Image type, provides a set of images that can be associated (again sequentially) with the choices.
int append(String, Image)	This is one of the most frequently used methods. After creating the ChoiceGroup object, you use this method to append choices to the object. The index of the choice you append is set according to the order or sequence in which you append it. The first item appended is assigned to index 0. The index is incremented with each subsequently appended choice.
void delete(int)	Deletes a choice from a group. The sole argument is the index of the choice to be deleted.
Image getImage(int)	Returns the image associated with a choice. The sole argument is the index of the choice with which the Image object is associated.
int getSelectedFlags-(boolean[])	Used to process events for choice groups defined using the MULTIPLE property. It works in a fashion similar to the getSelectedIndex() methods, with the exception that it populates the boolean array with the selection values (true or false) corresponding to the selected choices. The element indexes in the boolean array correspond to the indexes in the choice group. The value returned provides the number of items in the choice group.
int getSelectedIndex()	This is perhaps the most frequently used method for processing events from choice groups. It returns the index of the currently selected choice.
String getString (int)	Returns the text associated with a choice. The argument, of the int type, designates the index of the choice in the group.
void insert (int, String, Image)	Allows you to create and assign a choice to a choice group. Inserts a choice. The first argument designates the index of the choice to be created. The second argument provides text to associate with the choice. The final argument provides an Image object you can associate with the choice in addition to or instead of the text.
boolean isSelected (int)	Returns a boolean value of true if the choice has been selected. Otherwise, it returns a boolean value of false.

(Continued)

Table 11.1 Continued

Method	Description
void set (int, String, Image)	Allows you to define or update an existing indexed choice in a group. The first argument designates the index of the choice to be defined. The second argument provides text to associate with the choice. The final argument provides an Image object you can associate with the choice in addition to or instead of the text.
void setSelectedFlags (boolean[])	Used to set all values in a choice group. The argument you provide is an array of boolean values. The first element in the boolean array, index 0, sets the first choice in the choice group, which also has an index value of 0. Subsequent indexes in the array correspond similarly to remaining indexes of the choice group. If the array offers too few index settings, then the choices default to false.
void setSelectedIndex (int boolean)	Often used to set the default choice in the choice group. The first argument is of the int type and designates the index of the choice to be set. The second argument, a boolean value, determines whether the choice is to be shown as selected or not selected. A boolean value of true selects the choice.
int public int size ()	Returns the number of choices.
EXCLUSIVE	With this property, the ChoiceGroup object provides a selection from which the user can choose only one at a time.
MULTIPLE	Inherited from the Choice class. This property allows the user to choose more than one option at a time.
POPUP	Inherited from the Choice class. This property resembles the EXCLUSIVE property, with the difference that unless the user clicks or in some other way activates the choice list, only the currently selected option is visible.
TEXT_WRAP_OFF	Inherited from the Choice class. This property forces the text associated with the choices in the group to be limited to one line each. Text longer than a line is truncated.
TEXT_WRAP_ON	Inherited from the Choice class. This property allows the text that is associated with a choice to continue over multiple lines.
Item Methods and Commands	Note that you often use methods and properties of the Item class with ChoiceGroup objects. Among the properties are LAYOUT_LEFT, LAYOUT_NEWLINE_AFTER, LAYOUT_NEWLINE_BEFORE, LAYOUT_RIGHT. These you identify by using the dot operator to statically associate them with the Item class, for example, Item.LAYOUT_LEFT. Likewise, property values are often or-ed together.

In addition to the primary MIDlet class file, you also make use of the Quotes.java file, which is used in this context in place of a data file or an RMS object. Here, the information used in the application is accessed using arrays, one for the files used to create Image objects, the other for the text displayed after the user selects one of

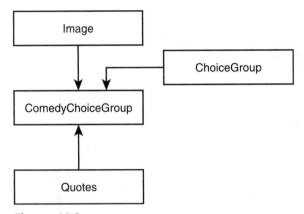

Figure 11.2
The Image, Quotes, and ChoiceGroup classes make it possible to construct and then display messages for the ComedyChoiceGroup listings.

the choices offered by the ChoiceGroup object. The use of Image objects is covered more extensively later on in this chapter. For now, it is important to note only that the static Image::createImage() method is repeatedly used to populate the comedianImage array, which is of the Image type. Figure 11.2 illustrates the relationships between the Image, Quotes, and ChoiceGroup classes as developed for this example.

The Quotes class provides sets of quotes for a group of four comedians named in a choice group. When the user selects a given comedian from the choice group, the display is refreshed, and a quote from the comedian's repertoire is displayed. Figure 11.3 illustrates a user session with the ComedyChoiceGroup MIDlet. The Image objects displayed in the menu are in this case indistinct. In an exercise presented later in this chapter (see the section "The ImageItemFind Class"), larger images of the comedians are presented.

Here is the code for the ComedyChoiceGroup class. Specific discussion of the code follows. Subsequent sections of this chapter discuss the Quotes and Image classes.

```
/*
 * Chapter 11 \ ComedyChoiceGroup.java
 *
 */
```

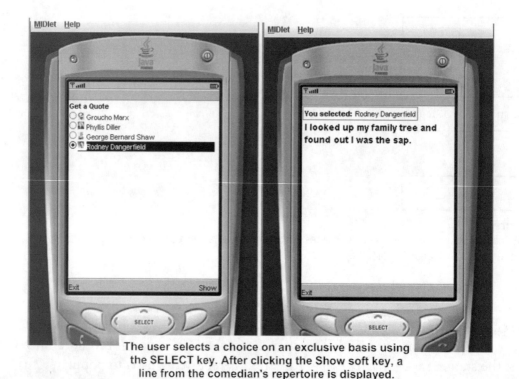

The user selects a choice on an exclusive basis using
the SELECT key. After clicking the Show soft key, a
line from the comedian's repertoire is displayed.

Figure 11.3
The `ChoiceGroup` object provides choices that can be accessed exclusively.

```
import javax.microedition.midlet.*;
import javax.microedition.lcdui.*;
import java.io.IOException;

public class ComedyChoiceGroup extends MIDlet
                              implements CommandListener{
   // #1
   private Display display;
   private Form form;
   private Command exitCmd;
   private Command showCmd;
   private ChoiceGroup choiceGroupA;
   private int indexInGroup;
   private int choiceGroupIndex;
   private Quotes quotes;
   private Image comedianImages[] = new Image[4];

   public ComedyChoiceGroup(){
```

```
// #2
quotes = new Quotes();
loadImages();
display = Display.getDisplay(this);
form = new Form("");

// #3
choiceGroupA = new ChoiceGroup("Get a Quote", Choice.EXCLUSIVE);
// Append options; the second (null) argument is for an image
choiceGroupA.append("Groucho Marx", comedianImages[0]);
choiceGroupA.append("Phyllis Diller", comedianImages[1]);
// Set the default
indexInGroup =   choiceGroupA.append("George Bernard Shaw",
                                          comedianImages[2]);
choiceGroupA.append("Rodney Dangerfield", comedianImages[3]);

// Set the above choice as the initially selected option
choiceGroupA.setSelectedIndex(indexInGroup, true);

// #4
exitCmd = new Command("Exit", Command.EXIT, 1);
showCmd = new Command("Show", Command.SCREEN,2);

choiceGroupIndex = form.append(choiceGroupA);
form.addCommand(exitCmd);
form.addCommand(showCmd);
form.setCommandListener(this);
}

// Called by application manager to start the MIDlet.
public void startApp(){
  display.setCurrent(form);
}

public void pauseApp(){ }

public void destroyApp(boolean unconditional){ }

public void commandAction(Command cmd, Displayable dsp){
    // #5
    if (cmd == showCmd){
        // Build a string showing which option was selected
        StringItem textOfChoice = new StringItem("You selected: ",
```

```
                    choiceGroupA.getString(choiceGroupA.getSelectedIndex())));
            System.out.println(choiceGroupA.getSelectedIndex());
            String selectedQuote = quotes.getQuote(
                                choiceGroupA.getSelectedIndex());

            // Place the String reference in a StringItem object
            StringItem itemForQuote = new StringItem(null, selectedQuote);

            // Apply formatting
            itemForQuote.setFont(Font.getFont(Font.FACE_PROPORTIONAL,
                                            Font.SIZE_MEDIUM |
                                            Font.STYLE_BOLD,
                                            Font.SIZE_LARGE));
            form.append(textOfChoice);
            form.append(itemForQuote);
            // Update the MIDlet to show the choice
            form.delete(choiceGroupIndex);
            form.removeCommand(showCmd);
        }else if (cmd == exitCmd){
            destroyApp(false);
            notifyDestroyed();
        }
    }// end commandAction

    public void loadImages(){
        try{
            comedianImages[0] = Image.createImage("/groucho.png");
            comedianImages[1] = Image.createImage("/phyllis.png");
            comedianImages[2] = Image.createImage("/george.png");
            comedianImages[3] = Image.createImage("/rodney.png");
        }catch(IOException ioe){
            ioe.toString();
        }//end try block
    }//end loadImages

} //end class
```

Class Definition

In the lines associated with comment #1 in the ComedyChoiceGroup class, you first declare class attributes of the Display, Form, and Command types. In the signature line of the class, you implement the CommandListener interface, so the events for the objects in the class are processed through events generated through the Form object using the commandAction() method, which is provided by the Command-Listener interface.

To accommodate a group of choices, you declare a ChoiceGroup class attribute (comedianChoiceGroup). To set the default choice and to process messages from the choice group, you declare two attributes of the int type, defaultChoice and choiceGroupIndex. You also declare an object of the Quotes type, which is a class created to randomly generate quotes attributed to the comedians featured in the choice group. To make it possible to associate small images with each of the choices, you create an array of the Image type (comedianImages).

In the lines associated with comment #2, you create an instance of the Quotes class and assign it to the quotes identifier. You then call the loadImages() method of the ComedyChoiceGroup class, which is defined in the lines trailing comment #6. This method makes use of the comedianImage array to successively load four small images of the *.png type. To load images, you call the Image::createImage() method. Here is an example of one of the construction statements following comment #6:

```
comedianImages[0] = Image.createImage("/groucho.png");
```

The PNG file type is but one of many that the createImage() method can work with. Among others are the GIF, BMP, and JPEG formats. The createImage() method is static and audits the file data as it is loaded. To call the createImage() method, as the lines following comment #6 show, you must use a try...catch() block. The data type used in this context for the catch argument is IOException. To use this class, you must include the java.io.IOException package at the start of the program. A compiler error is generated unless potential IO errors generated by the createImage() method can be handled. In essence, the constructor for the Image class is wrapped in the createImage() method in a way that throws an error of several possible types, including IOException, if the construction statement fails.

Defining the Choice Group Object

Having created the Image objects to be used with the ChoiceGroup elements, in the lines following comment #3, you call the ChoiceGroup constructor to create a new instance of the ChoiceGroup class. This you assign to the comedianChoiceGroup identifier. The constructor for the ChoiceGroup class in this instance requires two arguments. The first is of the String type and sets the title of the ChoiceGroup object. The second argument is of the int type and makes use of one of the properties defined in the ChoiceGroup class. As Table 1.1 discusses, the use of the EXCLUSIVE property designates that the user may choose only one offering at a time from the group.

Following the construction of the ChoiceGroup object, specific choices can be assigned to it. Choices consisting of the names of four comedians are furnished using the append() method. The append() method takes two arguments. Its first argument is of the String type, providing the text for the choice, and its second is of the Image type. In most situations, developers do not assign a reference to an Image to a choice, instead providing null as the second argument. Here is how such a statement might appear if the picture of Phyllis Diller were left out of the display:

```
comedianChoiceGroup.append("Phyllis Diller", null);
```

As it is, all of the calls to the append() method do associate images with the comedians. This call sets up a choice for Phyllis Diller:

```
comedianChoiceGroup.append("Phyllis Diller", comedianImages[1]);
```

The Image references are extracted from the comedianImages array, the indexes of the array identifying successive objects of the Image type that have been assigned to the array.

Note

The size of Image objects the ChoiceGroup can accommodate should generally be around 10 pixels in width and height in a standard display list if you do not alter the default font or layout settings. Figure 11.3 provides an example of what you get with the default settings.

In addition to setting up the choices for the group, you can also set a specific choice as the default. If not defined, the default choice is the first choice in the list. To set a different choice, further use of the append() method can be made. The append() method returns the index value of each new item you assign to a group using it, so in the lines following #3, you see this statement:

```
defaultChoice = comedianChoiceGroup.append(
              "George B. Shaw", comedianImages[2]);
```

This call to the append() method returns the index value associated with the choice for G. B. Shaw, which is assigned to the defaultChoice identifier. A few lines later, the setSelectedIndex() method is called to establish the Shaw choice as the default. You use the value assigned to defaultChoice as the first argument to the method. The second argument, of the boolean type, is used to associate a value of true with the selection:

```
comedianChoiceGroup.setSelectedIndex(defaultChoice, true);
```

If you set the selected index to true, then the button for the choice is activated, as shown in Figure 11.3, and in a choice group defined using the EXCLUSIVE property, the choice you have defined in this way becomes the default choice. Were you to set the value to false, then the ChoiceGroup object would seek any other choice that might be set to true. Finding none, it sets the first choice in the group as the default choice.

Having fully defined the ChoiceGroup object so that each of the choices it represents contains both a text providing the name of a comedian and a small image of the comedian, and also having set G. B. Shaw as the default choice, you now proceed, in the line immediately preceding comment #4, to call the Form::append() method to add the entire choice group to the Form object of the MIDlet. The argument to the method is the comedianChoiceGroup identifier.

Processing Messages

As is shown in the lines following comment #4 of the ComedyChoiceGroup class, the Command constructor is invoked twice to create instances of the Command class to assign to the exitCmd and showCmd attributes. The addCommand() method is then used to add references to these commands to the form. In addition, the set-CommandListener() method is called, establishing general message processing capabilities for the MIDlet's form attribute.

Processing messages for the ComedyChoiceGroup class takes place within the scope of the commandAction(), which is defined in the lines associated with comment #5. In this context, as is evident in the lines immediately following comment #5, you make extensive use of the comedianChoiceGroup object to call two ChoiceGroup methods, getString() and getSelectedIndex(). The getSelectedIndex() method processes the message issued by the Form object to determine the index of the choice in ChoiceGroup that is selected when the showCmd event is triggered. The getSelected() method returns the integer index value of the selection. Since the getString() method takes as its argument an int value designating a choice in the ChoiceGroup object, you have a way to readily retrieve the text that identifies the selected choice.

The getString() method returns a value of the String type. This value is used to create a StringItem object (nameOfChoice) that you use to display the name of the selected comedian. The String argument is the second argument of the constructor for the StringItem class. The first argument is also of the String type, and in this case you provide a literal string, "You selected:".

In addition to using it to retrieve the text that identifies the selected comedian, you call the getSelectedIndex() method to supply an argument to the Quotes::getQuote() method. This method takes as an argument an index identifying the comedian for whom a quote is needed. As set up in this system of classes, the indexes of the comedians as defined in the ChoiceGroup object correspond to the indexes that define the comedians in the Quotes class.

Note

The ComedyChoiceGroup and Quotes classes are closely coupled, so it is necessary to inspect both classes to know the index values corresponding to the comedian names as identified in the ChoiceGroup object and the names of the comedians as identified in the Quotes class. The indexes are the same in both places, of course, but it is clear that the situation provides opportunities for revision, possibly with a lookup using a RMS container.

Formatting the Font and Displaying the Results

As the lines following comment #5.1 reveal, the randomly selected quote from the Quotes class that is assigned to the String object (retrievedQuote) can be used to create a second StringItem object, quoteForDisplay. The StringItem object makes it possible for you to use the setFont() method of the StringItem class to format the font of the message, making it large enough to be easily read, as shown in Figure 11.4.

The setFont() method takes as its argument a reference to a Font object, and to supply such an object, you call the static Font::getFont() method. In this case, the arguments used to define the Font object are the same as those used in Chapter 10. The values used relate to the face, size, and style of the font, and the font that results is larger and darker than the default.

Having formatted the font, it then becomes possible to once again call the append() method of the Form class to append the two StringItem objects (nameOfChoice and quoteForDisplay) to the form identifier. Following this, you then call the Form::delete() method to remove the selected index. You also call the Form::removeCommand() method to remove the showCmd from the Form object.

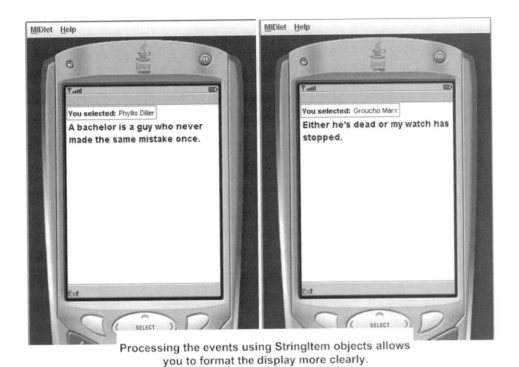

Processing the events using StringItem objects allows
you to format the display more clearly.

Figure 11.4
Messages are retrieved using the indexes of the ChoiceGroup object.

These methods clear the MIDlet after you perform a selection, allowing you to return to the starter menu when you are done viewing the displayed joke.

The Quotes Class

As Figure 11.5 shows, the Quotes class is used on a composition basis with the ComedyChoiceGroup class to provide randomly selected quotes for a specific set of comedians that includes Rodney Dangerfield, Groucho Marx, Phyllis Diller, and G. B. Shaw. The approach used for supplying the quotes involves retrieving an index value representing a comedian in the ChoiceGroup object in the ComedyChoiceGroup class and then using it to identify the same comedian in the Quotes class. In the Quotes class, the quotes are stored in Vector containers. This class, like the ComedyChoiceGroup class, is provided in standalone and NetBeans versions in the Chapter 11 source code folder. Much of the code represents items already covered in previous chapters, but it is included for purposes of review. Extended discussion follows the presentation of the code.

```java
/*
 * Chapter 11 \ Quotes.java
 *
 */
import javax.microedition.midlet.*;
import javax.microedition.lcdui.*;
import java.util.*;

public class Quotes {
    // #1
    private Vector Groucho;
    private Vector Phyllis;
    private Vector George;
    private Vector Rodney;
    private final int NUMSPEAKERS = 4;
    private int randInt;
    private Random random;
    // #2
    public Quotes(){
        random  = new Random();
        Groucho = new Vector();
        Phyllis = new Vector();
        George  = new Vector();
        Rodney  = new Vector();
        makeQuotes();
    }
    // #3
    private String findQuote(Vector vect){
        int ctr;
        ctr = random.nextInt(vect.size());
        return vect.elementAt(ctr).toString();
    }
    // #4
    public String getQuote(int speaker){
        StringBuffer quote = new StringBuffer();
        int ctr;
        if(speaker > NUMSPEAKERS-1 || speaker < 0){
          speaker = 0;
        }
        switch(speaker){
          case 0:
              quote.append(findQuote(Groucho));
            break;
```

```
            case 1:
                quote.append(findQuote(Phyllis));
              break;
            case 2:
                quote.append(findQuote(George));
            break;
            case 3:
                quote.append(findQuote(Rodney));
            break;
              default:
                quote.append("Not found");
        }//end switch
        return quote.toString();
    }//end getQuote


// #5
private void makeQuotes(){
        Groucho.addElement("Either he's dead or my watch has stopped.");
        Groucho.addElement("And I want to thank you for all the " +
                            "enjoyment you've taken out of it.");
        Groucho.addElement("I don't care to belong to a club that " +
                            "accepts people like me as members. ");
        Groucho.addElement("I must confess, I was born at a very early age.");
        Groucho.addElement("I worked my way up from nothing " +
                            "to a state of extreme poverty. ");
        Groucho.addElement("No man goes before his time - " +
                            "unless the boss leaves early. ");

        Phyllis.addElement("A bachelor is a guy who never made " +
                            "the same mistake once.");
        Phyllis.addElement("A smile is a curve that sets " +
                            "everything straight. ");
        Phyllis.addElement("Aim high, and you won't shoot your foot off. ");
        Phyllis.addElement("Any time three New Yorkers get into a cab " +
                            "without an argument, a bank has just been robbed.");
        Phyllis.addElement("Best way to get rid of kitchen odors: Eat out.");
        Phyllis.addElement("Cleaning your house while your kids are still "+
                            "growing is like shoveling the sidewalk before " +
                            "it stops snowing." );

        George.addElement("A government that robs Peter to pay Paul" +
                            "can always depend on the support of Paul. ");
```

```
George.addElement("All great truths begin as blasphemies. ");
George.addElement("Baseball has the great advantage over cricket" +
                " of being sooner ended. ");
George.addElement(
        "If all the economists in the world were laid end to end, " +
        "they wouldn't reach any conclusion. ");
George.addElement("My reputation grows with every failure. ");
George.addElement("One man that has a mind and knows it can "+
                "always beat ten men who haven't and don't.");


Rodney.addElement("When I was born I was so ugly the doctor " +
                "slapped my mother.");
Rodney.addElement("I could tell that my parents hated me. My bath " +
                "toys were a toaster and a radio.");
Rodney.addElement("I get no respect. The way my luck is running, " +
                "if I was a politician I would be honest.");
Rodney.addElement("I have good looking kids. Thank goodness " +
                "my wife cheats on me.");
Rodney.addElement("I haven't spoken to my wife in years. " +
                "I didn't want to interrupt her.");
Rodney.addElement("I looked up my family tree and found " +
                "out I was the sap.");
    }
}
```

Construction and Definition

In the lines accompanying comment #1 of the Quotes class, four attributes of the Vector type are declared, each identified by the first name of a comedian. This informal approach to setting up data retrieval clearly leaves much to be desired in industrial settings, but for the present purposes, the familiarity of terms makes the exercise easier to understand. In addition to a set of Vector objects, you also have a final or constant value, NUMOFSPEAKERS, and an attribute of the Random type. To manage randomly generated values, an attribute of the int type is also defined, randInt.

In the lines in the constructor for the class which follows comment #2, you create instances of the Random and Vector classes and assign them to the class attribute. You also call the makeQuotes() method. The makeQuotes() method is defined in the lines following comment #5, and it consists wholly of repeated calls by the Vector objects to the addElement() method. This method takes a generic object of any type derived from Object, so in this case, the literal strings provided as arguments are implicitly converted into generic objects.

Note

Use of the Vector class differs with recent versions of Java. The Vector class is now defined so that it uses a template constructor. The constructor allows you to designate the type upon construction, so casting data as you retrieve it from the Vector is not required. As mentioned in a previous chapter, the generic collection uses the following type of constructor:

```
Vector<String> vector = new Vector<String> ();
```

At comment #2 in the Quotes class, the findQuote() method is defined. This is not a feature of the public interface of the class. Like the makeQuotes() method, it provides a service used to retrieve quotes randomly. It takes a reference to a Vector as its argument and returns a randomly chosen element from the Vector object. To choose an element, it makes use of the Vector::size() method to ascertain the number of elements contained by the Vector object. The value returned by the size() method is of the int type and serves in this respect to set the range for the Random::nextInt() method, which itself returns a value in the range extending from 0 up to the maximum given by size(). Since the size of the Vector is the number of items in the Vector and not the highest index value, it can serve to establish a range that encompasses all the elements in the Vector, which like an array are identified with indexes beginning at 0. The randomly generated values are assigned to the ctr identifier.

As mentioned in the note on the template form of the constructor, the type of construction statement supported by the MIDP 2.0 for the Vector class stipulates that when you assign a reference to a Vector object, the Vector object accepts it as a subclass of the Object class. For this reason, after retrieving the reference from the Vector object using the elementAt() method (which uses the value assigned to ctr as an argument), you must use the toString() method to convert the retrieved value back into a string. This value is then returned by the findQuote() method.

Aside from the constructor, the only public method provided by the Quotes class is getQuotes(). This method takes an argument of the int type and returns a value of the String type. In this case, a local identifier of the StringBuffer type is defined. Definition of the StringBuffer identifier is in part a precautionary measure. This way, the method always returns a legitimate reference, even if it is empty. To assign text to the quote identifier, the argument to the method is used to select one of the speakers. The switch statement provides a case for each of the speakers. As can be determined after a glance at the set of calls to the append() method used to define the ChoiceGroup object in the ComedyChoiceGroup class, the numbers evaluated by the case statements to identify the comedians are the same as the index values for the ChoiceGroup object.

The StringBuffer::append() method allows you to assign a text string of varying length to the StringBuffer object, which unlike a String object can grow in length after it has been constructed. Next, the flow of the program passes through the case statements, locates the appropriate comedian using the index number, uses the findQuote() method to retrieve a quote from the Vector supplied as an argument, and then stores the retrieved text in the quote identifier. The StringBuffer::toString() method can then be used to convert the text to the String type so that it can be returned by the method.

ImageItem and Image

As Figure 11.5 illustrates, the ImageItem class is associated with the Image class. The primary purpose of the ImageItem class is to provide you with a convenient way to format and display Image objects. This relationship is made clear in Table 11.2, which presents the two overloaded versions of the ImageItem constructor. Both constructors use arguments of the Image type. Generally, the primary purpose of the ImageItem class is to facilitate the management of Image objects as you present them for display. The formatting capabilities they offer in this respect prove invaluable and provide you with a way to separate the activity of preparing an image for presentation (an activity that centers on the Image class) and formatting the prepared image for display in the context provided by a Form object (an activity that centers on the ImageItem class).

As has been demonstrated in part with the ComedyChoiceGroup class, Image objects can be used with ChoiceGroup objects. They can also be used with ImageItem objects and objects generated from such classes as Alert, Choice, and Form. A closer examination of the Image class is therefore in order. Table 11.3 provides a summary discussion of some of the features of the Image class.

Note

With respect to some of the methods and terms used Table 11.3, an Image object is mutable when its pixels are fully opaque. In practical terms this relates to whether an Image can have a transparent background. To have a transparent background, an image must be to some extent immutable. Immutable images can consist of a combination of opaque, transparent, and semi-transparent pixels.

Table 11.2 ImageItem Methods and Properties

Method	Description
ImageItem(String, Image, int, String)	Creates a new ImageItem object using four arguments. The first argument is of the String type and provides a label for the ImageItem object. This label appears just above the Image object the ImageItem displays. The second argument is of the Image type and provides the graphical object the ImageItem object serves to display. The third argument provides a defined value used to format the display of the ImageItem. The last argument provides text that can be displayed in the event that the Image does not.
ImageItem(String, Image, int, String, int)	This version of the constructor allows you to create an ImageItem using five arguments. The first provides a label for the ImageItem object, which appears above the object when it is displayed. The second argument provides a graphical or pictorial item of the Image type for the ImageItem object to display. The third argument is of the int type and is defined in the ImageItem class (see the list below). The fourth argument is of the String type and provides a text alternative if no Image object is available for display. The final argument designates the appearance mode. The appearance mode is an integer value defined in the Item class and consists of such properties as Item.BUTTON and Item.HYPERLINK.
Image getImage()	Returns a reference to an Image object that has been assigned to an ImageItem object.
void setImage(Image)	Allows you to assign an Image object to an ImageItem object. You can also use it to change an Image if one has already been assigned.
int getLayout()	This method returns the integer value corresponding to the ImageItem layout properties you can assign to ImageItem objects.
void setLayout(int)	Allows you to assign layout values to the ImageItem object. These values are defined in the ImageItem class. See the list below.
String getAltText()	Provides the text, if any, that has been supplied as a placeholder for the Image object the ImageItem provides.
void setAltText(String)	Allows you to change the alternative text assigned to the ImageItem object.
LAYOUT_DEFAULT	Causes the default alignment the device provides to be used for the layout positioning of the ImageItem object.
LAYOUT_CENTER	Centers the Image object horizontally.
LAYOUT_RIGHT	Aligns the Image object so that it is positioned against the right border of the ImageItem.
LAYOUT_LEFT	Aligns the Image object so that it is positioned against the left border of the ImageItem.
LAYOUT_NEWLINE_AFTER	Appends a line break after the ImageItem.
LAYOUT_NEWLINE_BEFORE	Inserts a line break before displaying ImageItem.

Table 11.3 Image Class Method and Properties

Method	Description
Image createImage (byte[], int, int)	Creates an immutable image from a byte array in PNG format.
Image createImage (Image source)	Creates an immutable image from another image.
Image createImage (int width, int height)	Creates a mutable image buffer of a set width and height.
Image createImage (String)	Creates an immutable image using the name of a resource file.
Image createImage(Image, int x, int y, int width, int height, int transform)	Allows you to create one Image object from another. The first argument is of the Image type and allows you to identify an immutable image. The subsequent four parameters allow you to designate a region within this Image object that you can copy to a new Image object. The final argument is of the int type and is given by a value defined in the Sprite class.
Graphics getGraphics()	Returns a graphics object that allows you to use Graphics methods on an Image object that calls this method.
int getHeight()	Returns the height, in pixels, of the Image object.
int getWidth()	Returns the width, in pixels, of the Image object.
boolean isMutable()	Determines whether the image is mutable. If it is mutable, you can make it immutable by providing it as an argument to the createImage() method and assigning the returned reference to an Image identifier.
Sprite.TRANS_ROT90	Rotates a selected region of a specified Image object clockwise 90 degrees.
Sprite.TRANS_ROT180	Rotates a selected region of an Image object 180 degrees.
Sprite.TRANS_ROT270	Rotates a selected region of an Image object clockwise 270 degrees.
Sprite.TRANS_MIRROR	Reflects an Image object about its vertical axis.

Transformation, mirroring, rotation, and other such uses of Image objects exceed the scope of the discussion in this chapter. However, in subsequent chapters, where Image objects are used in Sprite objects that are rendered in animated game frameworks, such topics receive extended attention.

Despite the close association between the Image and ImageItem classes, when you construct an ImageItem object, you are not required to supply a reference to an Image object. You can supply the constructor with an argument of null in place of a reference to an Image object, for example, and then furnish a reference at a later time. A call can be made to the setImate() method to supply an Image reference.

Here is an example of the four-argument constructor of an ImageItem supplied with null in place of a reference to an Image. The example is modeled on the code provided in the ImageItemFind class discussed in the next section of this chapter.

```
for(int ctr = 0; ctr < fileNames.length; ctr++ ){
    // #a Construct the Image obect
    imageToLoad = Image.createImage(fileNames[ctr]);
    // #b Constructor with null Image argument
    imageItem = new ImageItem(null, null,
                        ImageItem.LAYOUT_CENTER,
                        String.valueOf(ctr));
    // #c Image object reference provided afterward
     imageItem.setImage(imageToLoad);
    //Assign the ImageItem objects to a Vector object
    images.addElement(imageItem);
}
```

In this instance, to review the ImageItem constructor (see comment #b), the first argument is of the String type and provides a label for the ImageItem object. The second argument is of the Image type and provides the graphical object the ImageItem object serves to display. The third argument provides defined values used to format the display of the ImageItem. The last argument serves as a substitute for the Image object if it is not available for display. This argument is of the String type.

Here, the second argument, which asks for a reference to an Image object, is initially set to null. This creates no problem. In essence, if the ImageItem object were left without an Image object, then it would serve more or less as a placeholder in the Form object. However, as the line following comment #c shows, the ImageItem::setImage() method is called after the construction of the ImageItem object to supply it with the reference to the Image object. As Table 11.2 details, the setImage() method allows you to change the Image object associated with the ImageItem object.

The ImageItemFind Class

An extension of the work begun with the ComedyChoiceGroup, the ImageItemFind class provides examples of further uses of the Image class. In this setting, you add a photograph to the quote, providing the user of the MIDlet with both a view of

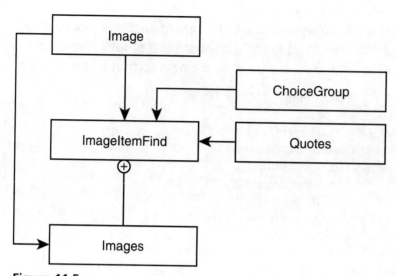

Figure 11.5
The Images class is an inner class for the ImageItemFind class that provides a service similar to the Quotes class.

the comedian and a representative joke from the comedian's repertoire. To implement this class, you again use the Quotes class, but you use an inner class, Images, which provides largely the same service as the Quotes class, except that with this class no random selection is made. This class loads files that provide the data with which to create Image objects, and the Image objects can then be called based on their position within an array.

As with the previous example, being able to retrieve the index of the selected ChoiceGroup listing allows you to retrieve an Image object from the Images class and a String object from the Quotes class. These parallel activities allow you to simultaneously explore the capabilities of the ImageItem, ChoiceGroup, and StringItem classes in relation to the Form object and the CommandListener interface. Figure 11.6 illustrates the interface of the ImageItemFind class at work.

As with other classes in this chapter, you can find the ImageItemFind class in the Chapter 11 source folder. It is also included in the NetBeans Chapter11MIDlets project. Operation of the application involves the same actions performed for the ComedyChoiceGroup MIDlet. You select a comedian from the choice group list and then press F2 or activate the left soft key to see the picture and the quote. Here is the code for the ImageItemFind class. The sections following discuss the code.

Figure 11.6
ImageItem and StringItem objects furnish the basis for depictions of and representative quotes from selected comedians.

```
/*
 * Chapter 11 \ ImageItemFind.java
 *
 */

import javax.microedition.midlet.*;
import javax.microedition.lcdui.*;
import java.io.IOException;
import java.util.*;

public class ImageItemFind extends MIDlet
                           implements CommandListener{
// #1
  private Display display;
  private Form form;
  private Command exitCmd;
  private Command showCmd;
```

```
private ChoiceGroup choiceGroupA;
private int defaultChoice;
private int choiceGroupIndex;
private Images images;
private Quotes quotes;

public ImageItemFind(){
  // #2
  quotes = new Quotes();
  images = new Images();

  display = Display.getDisplay(this);
  form = new Form("Comedians and Their Lines");
  choiceGroupA = new ChoiceGroup("Comedians", Choice.EXCLUSIVE);
  // Append options; the second (null) argument is for an image
  choiceGroupA.append("Groucho Marx", null);
  choiceGroupA.append("Phyllis Diller", null);
  // Set the default
  defaultChoice =   choiceGroupA.append(
                    "G. B. Shaw", null);
  choiceGroupA.append("Rodney Dangerfield", null);

  // Set the above choice as the initially selected option
  choiceGroupA.setSelectedIndex(defaultChoice, true);

  exitCmd = new Command("Exit", Command.EXIT, 1);
  showCmd = new Command("Show", Command.SCREEN,2);

  choiceGroupIndex = form.append(choiceGroupA);
  form.addCommand(exitCmd);
  form.addCommand(showCmd);
  form.setCommandListener(this);
}

// Called by application manager to start the MIDlet.
public void startApp()
{
  display.setCurrent(form);
}
```

```
public void pauseApp()
{ }
public void destroyApp(boolean unconditional)
{ }


// #3
public void commandAction(Command cmd, Displayable s){
  if (cmd == showCmd){
    //Obtain the index value of the selection
    int selectedValue = choiceGroupA.getSelectedIndex();
    // #3.1
    StringItem textOfChoice = new StringItem("Comedian's name: ",
                              choiceGroupA.getString(selectedValue));
    form.append(textOfChoice);

    System.out.println(selectedValue);
    // # 3.2
    ImageItem pictureToShow = new ImageItem(
                        images.getFileName(selectedValue),
                        images.findImage(selectedValue),
                        ImageItem.LAYOUT_CENTER,
                        String.valueOf(selectedValue));

    form.append(pictureToShow);

    StringItem textOfJoke = new StringItem("Quote: \n",
                        quotes.getQuote(selectedValue) );
    textOfJoke.setLayout(Item.LAYOUT_LEFT |Item.LAYOUT_DEFAULT);
    textOfJoke.setFont(Font.getFont(Font.FACE_PROPORTIONAL,
                                Font.SIZE_MEDIUM |
                                Font.STYLE_BOLD,
                                Font.SIZE_LARGE));
    form.append(textOfJoke);

    // Update the MIDlet to show the choice
    form.delete(choiceGroupIndex);
    form.removeCommand(showCmd);
  }
  else if (cmd == exitCmd){
    destroyApp(false);
    notifyDestroyed();
  }
}
```

```
// #4 ================================

    //Inner class
    public class Images{
        private Vector images;
        private final int CHOICES = 4;
        private String[] fileNames = new String[CHOICES];
//    ImageItem imageItem;
        Image imageToLoad;
        // #4.1
        Images(){
            images = new Vector();
            setFileNames();
            try{
             // // #4.2 Construct the ImageItem objects
                for(int ctr = 0; ctr < fileNames.length; ctr++ ){
                    imageToLoad = Image.createImage(fileNames[ctr]);
                    images.addElement(imageToLoad);
                }
            }catch(IOException ioe){
                System.out.println("Unable to load image.");
            }
        }//end ctr

        // #5
        private void setFileNames(){
            fileNames[0] = "/grouchoL.png";
            fileNames[1] = "/phyllisL.png";
            fileNames[2] = "/georgeL.png";
            fileNames[3] = "/rodneyL.png";
        }

        // #6
        public String getFileName(int index){
            StringBuffer fileName = new StringBuffer();
            if(index > fileNames.length || index < 0){
                fileName.append("Not found");
            }else{
                fileName.append( fileNames[index] );
            }
            return fileName.toString();
        }
```

```
    // #7
    public Image findImage(int item){
        return (Image)images.elementAt(item);
    }
}// end Inner class
//=================================
} //end outer class
```

Construction and Definition

In the lines following comment #1 in the ImageItemFind class, you declare attributes of the Display, Form, Command, and ChoiceGroup types. You then declare two attributes that allow you to work with the index values the ChoiceGroup object generates as you select names of comedians from the list the ChoiceGroup object offers in the initial display, as Figure 11.7 illustrates. In this iteration of the interface the small Image objects are no longer included in the ChoiceGroup listing.

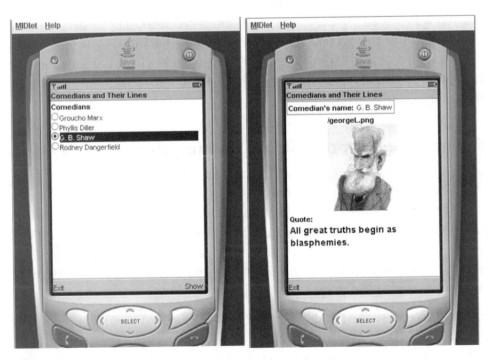

Figure 11.7
A ChoiceGroup object provides the primary form of interaction.

After setting up the basic interface features of the class, you then declare attributes (images and quotes) of the Images and Quotes types. The Quotes class already has been covered in this chapter. The Images class remains to be dealt with. The Images class provides a ready way to acquire Image objects for display in the context provided by ImageItem objects.

In the lines associated with comment #2, you proceed with the construction of the Quotes and Images objects. You then construct the display features of the application. In addition, with the construction of the Form object, you provide a title for the display, "Comedians and Their Lines." The MIDlet includes a ChoiceGroup that provides a list of four comedians. By assigning the value returned by the append() method to the defaultChoice attribute, you capture the value of the index to use as a default setting. To establish the default setting, you call the setSelectedIndex() method, supplying the value assigned to defaultChoice as its sole argument.

After setting up the commands and event handler of the Form object by calling the addCommand() and setCommandListener() methods, you then proceed to process the messages generated by the ChoiceGroup selections. In the lines trailing comment #3, use of two StringItem objects and one ImageItem object allows you to access data provided by the Quotes and Images classes. The code from the previous iteration of the commandAction() method in this instance is refactored. Now, rather than repeated calls to the getSelectedIndex() method, only one call is made, and the returned value is assigned to the selectedValue identifier, which is of the int type.

Retrieving Images and Defining an ImageItem

Beginning in the lines associated with comment #3.1, you make use of the selectedValue identifier as an argument to several methods. First, you provide its value as to the ChoiceGroup::getString() method, where it serves to retrieve the name of the selected comedian. This comedian's name is in the construction of a StringItem object with a label reading "Comedian's name". Next, after calling the println() method to print test output to the command line, you move on to work with methods of the Images class.

The Images class is described in detail in the next section. For now, it is enough to note the getFileName() method of the Images class returns the name of the source file used to create an Image object. As Figure 11.7 illustrates, you see this file name just above the picture of the comedian in the display. As the lines following comment #3.2 show, the getFileName() method takes an argument of the int type, and the selectedValue identifier provides this value. The file name returned becomes the first argument to the constructor of the ImageItem object (pictureToShow) used to display the comedian's picture.

For the second argument of the ImageItem constructor for the pictureToShow object you call the Images::findImage() method, which returns the Image object corresponding to the named comedian. Again, this method takes an argument of the int type, which the value assigned to selectedValue satisfies.

For the last two arguments of the ImageItem constructor, you provide a defined value from the ImageItem class (LAYOUT_CENTER). This value causes the ImageItem object to display the Image object in the horizontal center of the display area. As the final argument, you use the selectedValue identifier as the argument of the valueOf() method of the String class, which returns a String reference that provides text for display as an alternative if the Image object is not available for the ImageItem object to display.

Having completely defined the pictureToShow object, you then call the Form ::append() method to add the pictureToShow object to the form. At this point, you proceed to create an instance of a StringItem object. The constructor used to create the object requires only two arguments. The first argument involves a literal string, "Quote:\n", which introduces the comedian's lines. The second argument is satisfied by the value returned by the Quotes::getQuote() method, which furnishes a randomly selected joke by the comedian. The selectedValue identifier in this case identifies the comedian for whom a random joke is to be retrieved.

To increase the legibility of the text displayed by the second StringItem object, you call the StringItem::setFont() method, supplying it with the same set of parameters used in the previous iteration of the MIDlet. Following construction of the StringItem object, you again call the append() method to add it to the Form object. Having defined the three Item subclass objects, you call the delete() and removeCommand() methods of the Form class to clear the MIDlet display after you perform a selection.

Images as an Inner Class

To provide an easy way to access Image objects for display, you implement Images as an inner class. This class might just as easily be implemented as a separate class, as is the Quotes class, but given the brevity of the class, it works well as an inner

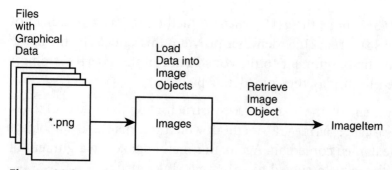

Figure 11.8
An inner class retrieves data from PNG files for display.

class. As Figure 11.8 illustrates, its primary purpose is to provide a way to load files containing graphical data into Image objects.

Implementation of the Images class begins in the lines associated with comment #4. To accommodate a set of Image objects, you declare a class attribute of the Vector type (images). After defining a constant, CHOICES, and assigning it a value of 4, you create an array of the String type, fileNames, which serves to store the names of the files that provide graphical data used to create Image objects. You also define an Image attribute to be used in generic operations needed to create Image references that are stored in the images Vector object.

In the lines associated with comment #4, you construct the Vector object, images, and immediately following that, you call the setFileNames() method. Defined in the lines following comment #5, this method populates the fileNames array with literal strings representing the source files of the data used to create Image objects. In each instance, the files are of the *.png type.

Construction of the Image objects is attended to in the lines following comment #4.2, where a for repetition statement is implemented to iterate through the fileNames array, providing the file names one after the other as an argument to the Image::createImage() method. This is a static method that serves as a constructor. As Table 11.3 reveals, there are several overloaded versions of this method; the one employed in this context is the simplest. It loads the data from the file into an Image object without cropping or otherwise altering it.

As the for block repeats, the flow of the program constructs Image objects and assigns them to the imageToLoad identifier, which is used as an argument to the Vector::addElement() method. In this way, the Vector object is populated,

Figure 11.9
The ImageItem object readily accommodates the images for the display.

beginning at index 0, with Image objects representing the loaded files. This action is enclosed in a try. . .catch block to cover for the errors that the createImage() method can generate. The error type of the catch clause is IOException.

At comment #6, the getFileName() method is implemented. In this case, after checking to confirm that the index is within the acceptable range, the name of the file is retrieved from the fileNames array and returned as a String value. In this way, it is possible to retrieve the name of the source file used to create the Image object. Along the same lines, in the lines associated with comment #7, the findImage() method uses an integer value supplied by the item parameter as an argument to the Vector::elementAt() method. This method returns a reference of the Object type, which must be cast to the Image type prior to being returned. Figure 11.9 provides yet another view of the display.

Conclusion

In this chapter, you have explored the relationships between the Image, the ChoiceGroup, and the ImageItem classes. You can use miniaturized Image objects to enhance the display provided by the listing in a ChoiceGroup object, but the smallness of the images used in this context requires that you restrict their complexity. As an exercise, pictures of comedians were used in this chapter. With respect to larger displays, however, the ImageItem object works readily to provide an easy way to display Image objects. Used in conjunction with StringItem objects, the ImageItem object provides you with a variety of development alternatives. With respect to text-oriented game development, this is an invaluable tool. To implement the MIDlet classes described in this chapter, you made use of the Image class in two distinct contexts. On the horizon are further uses of the Image class involving the Canvas, GameCanvas, Sprite, TiledLayer, and other classes. Subsequent chapters discuss such uses in detail.

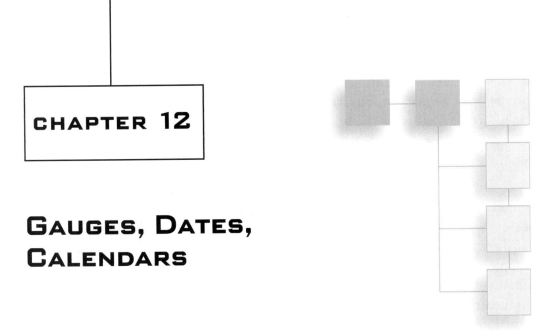

CHAPTER 12

GAUGES, DATES, CALENDARS

Having worked in the previous chapter with the ChoiceGroup, ImageItem, and Image classes, you are in a position in this chapter to extend your explorations to two more Item classes, DateField and Gauge, and to add to this still other experimentation involving the subclasses of the Image class. To supplement your work with the DateField class, it is useful to examine the Date, Calendar, and TimeZone classes. These classes are derived from the Object class, and they make it possible to work in a number of directions as you implement the Image classes. Moving beyond date and time issues, you also explore the Canvas and Graphics classes. Work with these two classes anticipates several classes in the Game API, among which are Sprite and GameCanvas. They likewise provide an excellent way for you to accustom yourself to using the paint() method as you work with graphical activities. The features provided by the Image and Graphics classes provide the basis for your movement away from textually oriented development activities and into the graphical realm.

Calendar and Date

Before discussing the DateField class, it is helpful to review the Calendar class, which is derived from the Object class. The Calendar class is one of the two primary classes you employ as you work with programming activities involving time and date information. The other primary class in this respect is Date. Both of these classes are supplemented by the TimeZone class. The Calendar and Date classes provide fairly complex objects. For example, the Calendar class furnishes you with a calendar you can scroll through to find specific dates far into the past or future. When using the Calendar object, you can activate the day by positioning the cursor on it and then generate an event that you can process in any number of ways.

You can use a reference generated by the Date class to initialize a Calendar object, and by using the TimeZone class, you can adjust for time zones. The CalendarFortune class makes use of the Calendar and Date classes to explore a few of the methods associated with the two classes. Along with the messages, this chapter explores a few of the extensive list of defined values. The defined values allow you to set and retrieve date and time values. Table 12.1 provides a sampling of the Calendar class options along with a list of the defined values. Figure 12.1 illustrates a Calendar object. By using SELECT button, you can change the month, and beneath that, enter the days of a given month. From there you can initiate an event associated with the day, the month, or the year. Generally, you retrieve the information you require from the event message.

Note

The interface of the Date class consists of only a few methods. In contrast, the interface of the Calendar class provides many. For more information, see the full class documentation at **http:// java.sun.com/javame/reference/apis/jsr118/**. This page provides links to the Date and TimeZone classes.

As is emphasized in the CalendarFortune class, you can use constant or dynamic approaches to initializing the date value of a Calendar object. Here is how you can set values using the constants the Calendar class provides.

```
Calendar calendarA = Calendar.getInstance();
calendarA.set(Calendar.YEAR, 1857);
calendarA.set(Calendar.MONTH, Calendar.DECEMBER);
calendarA.set(Calendar.DAY_OF_MONTH, 3);
```

Using this approach, the first calendar you see is set for 1857. The index of December, if you retrieve its corresponding integer value, is 11, not 12. January is 0. The day of the month is set at December 3. This is the novelist Joseph Conrad's birthday.

Alternatively, you can use a reference to a Date object to initialize the date. If you use this approach, then you obtain the current system time. To accomplish this

Table 12.1 Selected Calendar, TimeZone, and Date Methods and Fields

Method/Field	Description
Calendar()	Constructs a Calendar object with default time zone.
int get(int)	Gets the value for a given time field designated by one of the defined values for the Calendar class.
Calendar getInstance()	A static method that returns an instance of a Calendar object. Use this in place of a constructor: Calendar newCal = Calendar.getInstance().
Calendar getInstance (TimeZone)	Takes an argument of the TimeZone type. Provides an instance of a Calendar object using the specified time zone.
Date getTime()	Retrieves the current time of the Calendar object.
TimeZone getTimeZone()	Returns an object of the TimeZone type. It identifies the time zone with which the Calendar object is associated.
set(int, int)	The first argument is a defined value or an integer designating a field defined in the Calendar class, such as MONTH or YEAR. The second argument sets the value for the field.
void setTime(Date)	This method takes a reference to a Date object as its argument. You can use it, among other things, to set the current date.
void setTimeZone(TimeZone)	This method takes a reference to a TimeZone object as its argument.
Defined values	You use theses values to set and retrieve values using, among others, the set() and get() methods: AM, AM_PM, APRIL, AUGUST, DATE, DAY_OF_MONTH, DAY_OF_WEEK, DECEMBER, FEBRUARY, FRIDAY HOUR, HOUR_OF_DAY, JANUARY, JULY, JUNE, MARCH, MAY, MILLISECOND, MINUTE, MONDAY, MONTH, NOVEMBER, OCTOBER, PM, SATURDAY, SECOND, SEPTEMBER, SUNDAY, THURSDAY, TUESDAY, WEDNESDAY, and YEAR.
Date()	Constructor for the Date class. You can use the constructor to initialize Calendar and DateField objects. The value the constructor provides is the number of milliseconds elapsed since January 1, 1970, 00:00:00 GMT. Typical use: calendarObj.setTime(new Date( ).
TimeZone::getTimeZone()	Constructor for the TimeZone class. Like the Date class constructor, this constructor allows you to initialize Date and Calendar objects so that they are identified with specific time zones. Here is an example of its use with the static getTimeZone() method: TimeZone timeZone = TimeZone.getTimeZone("PST").

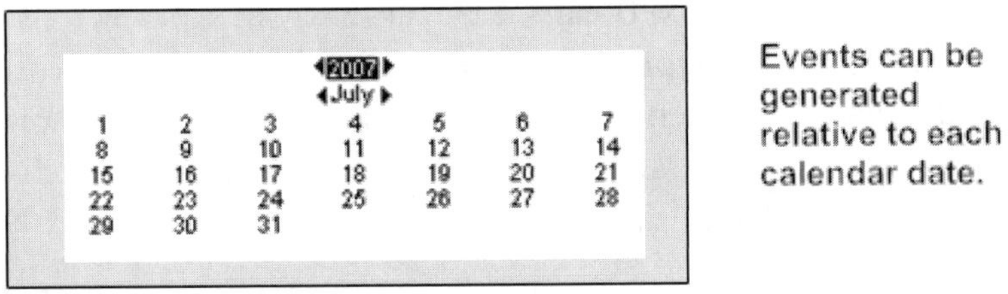

Figure 12.1
The Calendar class generates a substantial object that allows you to find dates extending well into the past or future.

task, you can use the set method and supply a reference to a newly created instance of the Date class. Here is an example.

```
calendarB.setTime( new Date() );
```

DateField

Along with the Calendar and Date classes, the DateField class allows you to readily display and process messages related to time and date events. Derived from the Item class, the DateField class provides an interface that shares many of the features available to the other subclasses of the Item class. The primary difference involves defined values related to setting and formatting date and time information. Formatting the mode of display for the time and date information is accomplished using the setDate() and setInputMode() methods. You can also set the class constructor.

As Table 12.2 indicates, one version of the constructor allows you to set a label and the mode of display for the date or time. A second constructor allows you to designate the time zone in addition to the mode of display. Defined values in the DateField class furnish three modes of display. The DATE value used alone allows you to view the date information alone. The DATE_TIME value provides both time and date information. The TIME property allows you to view the time alone. Figure 12.2 shows a clock generated using the TIME option.

The CalendarFortune Class

The CalendarFortune class allows you to see how a few of the methods of the Calendar and DateField classes work together to make it possible to set, transfer, and retrieve information relating to date and time. In the process, you explore the defined values the two classes provide. Use of the Date class proves important throughout, and to provide a contrast and review, use is made of the StringItem class and some of the formatting capabilities provided by the Item class. You can find the CalendarFortune class in the NetBeans Chapter12MIDlets project file and, in a standalone version, in the Chapter 12 source code file. When you run the MIDlet, you see a calendar. You then use the SELECT arrows and the soft keys to invoke an event. The event generates a specific date and with it a predication or advisory relating to the date.

Table 12.2 DateField Methods and Properties

Method/Property	Description
DateField (String, int)	Constructs a new DateField using the specified label and mode. The first argument is of the String type and provides a label for the field. The second argument is of the int type and is one of the modes presented last in this table.
DateField (String, int, TimeZone)	Constructs a new DateField. The first argument is of the String type and provides the label for the field. The second argument is of the int type and is one of the three defined modes listed last in this table. The third argument is of the TimeZone type.
Date getDate()	Returns the value of the Date type using the display mode assigned to the Date object.
int getInputMode()	Returns the mode that has been applied to the field.
setDate(Date)	Allows you to set the date assigned to the Date object. To set the current date, use dateFObj.setDate(new Date).
setInputMode(int)	Assigns a mode of input to the field.
DATE	A mode of display. Allows you to view calendar dates and generate events related to them.
DATE_TIME	A mode of display. Provides both time and date settings. In other words, you see a clock and a calendar.
TIME	A mode of display. Restricts what you see to a view of the time alone.
Date()	Constructor for the Date class. You can use the constructor to initialize Calendar and DateField objects.
TimeZone::getTimeZone()	Constructor for the TimeZone class. Typical use: DateField date = new DateField ("date", DateField. DATE, TimeZone.getTimeZone("GMT")).

A clock can also
be invoked.

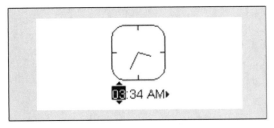

Figure 12.2
Use of the defined values allows you to view information differently.

```java
/*
 * Chapter 12 \ CalendarFortune.java
 *
 */

import javax.microedition.midlet.*;
import javax.microedition.lcdui.*;
import java.util.*;

public class CalendarFortune extends MIDlet
                            implements ItemStateListener,
                                    CommandListener{
// #1
private Display display;
private Form form;
private Command exitCmd;
private DateField currentDate;
private StringItem arbDate;
private StringItem prospect;
private Random random;
private Calendar calendarA;
private Calendar calendarB;

public CalendarFortune(){
    // #2
    random = new Random();
    display = Display.getDisplay(this);
    form = new Form("Calendar Fortune");

    // #2.1
    calendarA = Calendar.getInstance();
    calendarB = Calendar.getInstance();

    // Calendar set() and get()
    calendarA.set(Calendar.YEAR, 1857);
    calendarA.set(Calendar.MONTH, Calendar.DECEMBER + 1);
    calendarA.set(Calendar.DAY_OF_MONTH, 3);

    // #2.2
    // Retrieve string values
```

```java
String month = String.valueOf( calendarA.get(Calendar.MONTH ));
String dayOfMonth = String.valueOf(
                        calendarA.get( Calendar.DAY_OF_MONTH ));
String year = String.valueOf( calendarA.get( Calendar.YEAR ) );
//Display
arbDate = new StringItem("Conrad: \n",
                            month + "/" +
                            dayOfMonth + "/" +
                            year);
arbDate.setLayout(Item.LAYOUT_CENTER | Item.LAYOUT_DEFAULT);

// #2.3
// Set with the current date
calendarB.setTime( new Date() );

//Format StringItem
arbDate.setLayout(Item.LAYOUT_CENTER | Item.LAYOUT_NEWLINE_BEFORE);

// #3
//DateField creation and formatting
currentDate = new DateField("Current date:", DateField.DATE_TIME);
currentDate.setDate(new Date());
currentDate.setLayout(Item.LAYOUT_CENTER |
Item.LAYOUT_NEWLINE_BEFORE);

// #3.1
form.append(arbDate);
form.append(new Spacer(50, 20));
form.append(currentDate);

exitCmd = new Command("Exit", Command.EXIT, 1);
form.addCommand(exitCmd);
form.setCommandListener(this);
form.setItemStateListener(this);
    }

public void startApp(){
    display.setCurrent(form);
}
```

```
public void pauseApp(){
}

public void destroyApp(boolean unconditional){
}

public void commandAction(Command cmd, Displayable dsp){
    if (cmd == exitCmd){
      destroyApp(false);
      notifyDestroyed();
    }
}


// For event from the calendar
public void itemStateChanged(Item item){
    //Clear for new view
    // #4
    form.deleteAll();
    // The date selected from the calendar
    StringItem newSItem = new StringItem("Year of birth: ",
                              String.valueOf(
                              calendarA.get(Calendar.YEAR) ));
    newSItem.setLayout(Item.LAYOUT_LEFT);

    // #4.1
    DateField newDField = new DateField("Date", DateField.DATE);
    newDField.setDate(currentDate.getDate());
    newDField.setLayout(Item.LAYOUT_LEFT);

    // #4.2
    prospect = new StringItem("Today's prospects: ", getProspects());
    prospect.setLayout(Item.LAYOUT_LEFT);
    form.append(newSItem);
    form.append(new Spacer(150, 20));
    form.append(newDField);
    form.append(new Spacer(150, 20));
    form.append(prospect);
}

// #5
protected String getProspects(){
   String prospects[] =
                 {"Indifferent - - Boring? Maybe it is time for a change.",
```

```
            "Promising - - Indeed, so watch for opportunities.",
            "Hazardous - - Yes, it happens. Watch for ice!",
            "Luscious - - Delectable and inviting. Good for you!",
            "Inviting - - Have at it!",
            "Puzzling - - It's always nice to find" +
            " inviting challenges.",
            "Mordant - - Probably best to sit this one out.",
            "Muddled - - It's okay. Just think of it as fog.",
            "Hilarious - - Laugh while the going's good!",
            "Ridiculous - - Don't worry. It'll pass."};
    // #5.1
    int randInt = 0;
    randInt = random.nextInt(prospects.length);
    String val = prospects[randInt];
    return val;
    }
}//end class
```

Construction and Definition

In the lines following comment #1 of the CalendarFortune class, you declare Display, Form, and Command attributes. You then follow with a DateField attribute, currentDate. Following the declaration of the DateField attribute, you then declare two StringItem attributes. This then provides three class attributes derived from the Item class. You then declare two Calendar attributes. As mentioned previously, the Calendar class is derived, like the Date class, directly from the Object class. The Date, Calendar, and TimeZone classes are all provided by the java.util package. One additional attribute, of the Random type, allows you to generate random numbers. This class is also provided by the java.util package and is directly derived from the Object class.

The constructor for the CalendarFortune class is defined starting with the lines associated with comment #2. The first action in this respect is the creation of a Random object, which is assigned to random, a class attribute. You then create instances of the Display and Form classes, assigning them to the display and form attributes.

Following comment #2.1, you begin working with the Calendar attributes. Accordingly, you call the static Calendar::getInstance() method to create instances of the Calendar class. They are assigned to the calendarA and calendarB attributes. The getInstance() method serves as a default constructor for Calendar objects. To assign a value, you call the Calendar::set() method.

The set() method takes two arguments, both of the int type. The first argument allows you to designate a position in a value array associated with the Calendar object. To do so, you first use the Calendar.YEAR property to assign 1857 to the year value associated with the Calendar. Next, you use the Calendar.MONTH property to set the month. For the value assigned, you apply the Calendar. DECEMBER property. The actual value of the DECEMBER property is 11 instead of 12, because the months associated with the Calendar class begin with January set to the 0 index. To make it so that when the value is retrieved the recognized integer value of 12 can be returned, you augment the value of the month by 1.

In addition to the YEAR and MONTH properties, you also draw on the DAY_OF_MONTH property, in this case complementing it with 3. The resulting date, December 3, 1857, is the birthday of Joseph Conrad, author of *Lord Jim* and *Heart of Darkness,* to name two of his novels. As Table 12.1 shows, an extensive list of defined values is provided by the Calendar class, covering all the months of the year and a few additional time and day values.

To complement the use of the set() method, in the lines associated with comment #2.2, you call the get() method. The get() method requires only one argument. The argument is, once again, one of the defined values provided by the Calendar class. In the first call to the get() method, you use the Calendar.MONTH value. In the second, you employ the DAY_OF_MONTH property. In the third instance, you furnish the Calendar.YEAR value. In each case, the value you provide retrieves a value from an array associated with the Calendar class.

To make use of the values you retrieve from the Calendar array, you convert the integer values that the set() method returns into String values. To accomplish this, you call the static valueOf() method of the String class. Overloaded to accommodate all of the primitive data types, the valueOf() method returns a String that you then assign to the month, dayOfMonth, and year identifiers. You then use these three identifiers to form a concatenated string that you provide as the sole argument to the StringItem class constructor. You then assign the instance of StringItem to the arbDate identifier. You can then call the setLayout() method, common to the Item class object, to position the date string for display. In this case, you use the LAYOUT_CENTER property, provided by the Item class, to center the StringItem object horizontally when it is displayed.

Using the Date and DateField Classes

As the previous section revealed, you can set the date associated with a Calendar object by using integer values and the values provided by the Calendar class. In the line associated with comment #2.3, you follow a different approach. This one involves creating a reference to a Date object. The Date object furnishes the Calendar object with the values needed to define the current state of the Calendar using values for the current date. Later in the program, when you retrieve the values assigned to the calendarA and calendarB class attributes, you see both the date associated with Conrad and the current date as generated by the Date class reference.

Further use of the Date class is made in the lines following comment #3. Here, you start by creating a new instance of a DateField object. To create the new instance of the DateField object, you call a version of the DateField constructor that requires two arguments. The first argument provides a label for the Date-Field object. The second argument provides a defined value that specifies the type of date representation you want to see. As Table 12.2 reveals, you have three options in this respect. In this case, you choose the option that provides two representations, one oriented toward a clock, the other toward a calendar representation. In other words, the DATE_TIME value of the DateField class designates that both date and time representations of the data are available to you.

Once the instance of the DateField class is assigned to the currentDate attribute, you call the setDate() method of the DateField class. This method requires an argument of the Date type, and in this case, you supply an anonymously constructed instance of a Date object as the argument. This then provides date and time values to the DateField object that correspond to the current date and time.

Given the assignment of the date to the DateField attribute, you then proceed to call the setLayout() method to format the attribute for display. As with StringItem and the other classes of the Item class, you use the LAYOUT_CENTER value to force the DateField object into the horizontal center of the display.

Beyond formatting, the only activity that remains to be carried out in the constructor involves calling the Form::append() method to append the items you have constructed to the initial display. You use the addCommand() and addCommand-Listener() to set up message processing for the Form object. You call the setItem-StateListener() method to process messages issued by the Item objects. With the invocation of the startApp() method and the accompanying call to setCurrent(), you see the display shown in Figure 12.3.

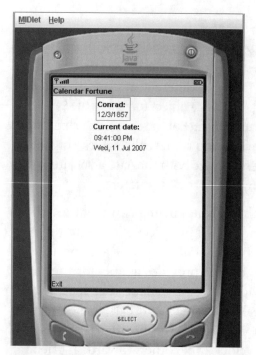

Figure 12.3
Using the `StringItem` and `DateField` classes, two dates are displayed.

Event Processing

The top field in Figure 12.3 is the field you generate using the `String` identifiers and the `StringItem` object. "Conrad:", the label, and 12/3/1857, the date, are both `String` values. On the other hand, the "Current date:" label identifies the result of the assignment of the `Date` object to the `DateField` object. This object differs in significant ways from the `StringItem` object. In the first place, as Figure 12.4 illustrates, if you use the SELECT button, you can toggle between the date and the time values. If you use the soft keys or in another way invoke an action while one or the other is selected, you see different results.

Reviewing the figures shown earlier in the chapter, Figure 12.5 illustrates the two options. Selecting the time, you see the time. Selecting the date, you see a calendar.

The date and calendar displays provide a vehicle for further event processing. With respect to the calendar representation, the state to which you set the object can then be propagated using event processing.

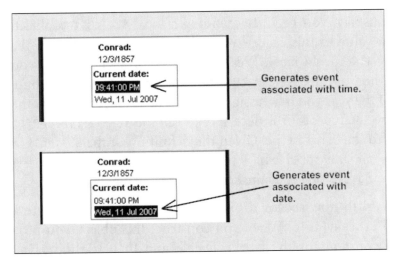

Figure 12.4
Each field generates a different message, allowing you to view a different result.

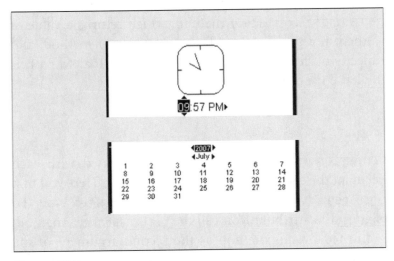

Figure 12.5
Time and date events evoke different responses.

Generating Events from the Calendar

In the code associated with comment #4 of the CalendarFortune class, you implement the itemStateChanged() method of the ItemStateListener interface. In the line immediately following comment #4, call the Form::deleteAll() method to remove features and commands from the MIDlet. You can then reintroduce features as needed, displaying them on a clean slate. To generate content for the new display, you begin by defining a local StringItem object, newSItem. To assign a value to this object, you provide the constructor of the StringItem object with text for the label, "Year of birth:". For the field value, you employ the get() method of the Calendar class to allow the calendarA attribute to retrieve the value of the year you have assigned to it. The value returned by the get() method is of the int type, so it is necessary to call the String::valueOf() method to convert it to the String type. Given the definition of the StringItem object, you can then call the setLayout() method—inherited from the Item class—to post the StringItem object against the left edge of the display.

The year of Conrad's birth now set for display, you can move on to create a second DateField object, newDField. When you construct this object, you provide it with a string constant for the label, "Date", and then use the Date-Field.DATE value to set the mode of the DateField object so that it displays dates alone. In the next line, you call the setDate() method of the DateField to set the date using the date value you retrieve from the calendarA object. To retrieve the date value, you call the Calendar::getDate() method, which returns a value of the Date type. You are then in a position to call the setLayout() method, and with the StringItem object, you format the DateField object so that when it is displayed it rests on the left edge of the display.

Prognostication

To make some predictions or provide some prospects associated with each calendar date, you implement the code that follows comment #4.2. Here you first assign a value to the prospect attribute, which is of the StringItem type. To obtain the value to assign to the attribute, you call the getProspects() method. You assign the value returned by this method as the second argument of the StringItem constructor. For the first argument, which provides the label for the StringItem object, you furnish a string constant, "Today's prospects:".

How the value assigned to the prospect attribute is generated becomes evident in the lines following comment #5, where the getProspects() method is defined. The method provides, first, for the definition of an array of the String type, prospects. The definition of the array involves a comma-delimited set of strings, each of which provides an adjective followed by some type of comment. The list is limited for purposes of the application, but given the use of an RMS component, it obviously could be extended to accommodate many more values, each of which might be retrieved via an identifier corresponding to a given date value.

To make it so that the prognostications can be randomly retrieved by the `getProspects()` method, you use the `Random` object (`random`) to call the `nextInt()` method. As an argument to the `nextInt()` method, you use the value returned by the `length` attribute associated with the array. This returns the number of items in the array. Since the `nextInt()` method returns values extending from 0 up to but not including the number given as an argument to the `nextInt()` method, you are in this way given a range of numbers that corresponds to all the items in the array. Retrieved from the `prospects` array, the prediction is assigned to the local `val` identifier and then returned by the method. This approach to the return value is redundant, so some refactoring could reduce the final three statements to a single line:

```
return prospects[random.nextInt(prospects.length)];
```

For purposes of discussion, however, the less optimized version proves friendlier.

Operations

When you operate the `CalendarFortune` application, you see the work of the `Date`, `DateField`, and `Calendar` classes at work in a number of ways. To review two scenarios, consider first navigating from the date to the calendar, and then invoking the final display with the event generated by the calendar-year date alone. As the sequence shown in Figure 12.6 illustrates, in the end you see the

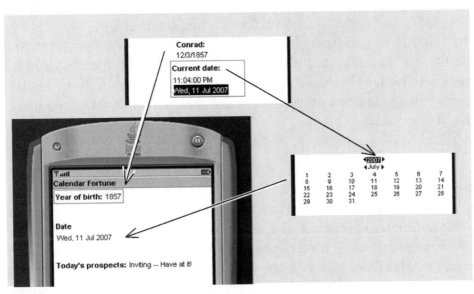

Figure 12.6
The date event invokes the calendar display, and if left on the year, the calendar then furnishes the current date, while the set date remains the same.

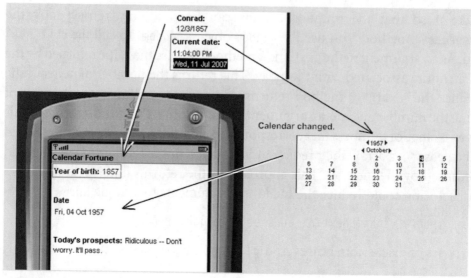

Figure 12.7
Adjusting the date alters the default value set by the Date object reference.

current date supplied by the reference to the Date class, which by default supplies the current date. At the same time, you also see the fixed value representing Conrad's year of birth.

In the second example, as shown in Figure 12.7, the calendar example is set to October 4, 1957, the day the Sputnik became the first artificial satellite to make its way into space. In this instance, by selecting the date from the first screen and then selecting the year, month, and day values from the calendar, it is possible to generate a date value other than the current date. In this case, then, the date furnished by the reference to the Date class is replaced by the date the object generates as you adjust it.

Gauge

The Gauge class provides objects that allow you to audit timed activities, such as the download or retrieval of data. The objects you can generate using the Gauge class can be interactive or noninteractive. As Table 12.3 reveals, the constructor for the Gauge class allows you to name the Timer class and indicate whether it should be interactive or noninteractive. The difference between the two modes is that when a Gauge object is interactive, you can set its counter to a value within the range you have defined for it. As the discussion of the Gauge constructor

Table 12.3 Selected Gauge Methods and Values

Method/Value	Description
Gauge (String, boolean, int, int)	This is the constructor for the Gauge class. The first argument is of the String type and provides a label for the Gauge object. The second argument is of the boolean type and establishes whether the Gauge object is to be interactive—in other words, whether it dynamically responds to events. The third argument is of the int type and establishes the maximum number to which the Gauge object can count. The last argument is also of the int type. It establishes the initial count value of the Gauge object.
int getMaxValue()	Returns an integer that indicates the maximum value assigned to the Gauge object.
void setDefaultCommand(Command)	Accepts a value of the Command type and allows you to associate a Command object with the Gauge object so that events can be handled.
void setMaxValue(int)	This method takes an argument of the int type, which establishes the maximum value of the count the gauge tracks.
void setLayout(int)	Allows you to associate a layout. The sole argument is a defined value provided by the Item class.
void setPreferredSize(int, int)	This method takes two arguments, both of the int type. The first sets the width of the Gauge object as it is displayed. The second sets the height of the Gauge object.
int getValue()	This method returns a value of the int type. The value returned indicates the current value of the count.
void setValue(int)	This takes different values, depending on whether the Gauge is interactive or noninteractive. If it is a noninteractive gauge and has been defined with an indefinite range, then you are restricted to the following values: CONTINUOUS_IDLE, INCREMENTAL_IDLE, CONTINUOUS_RUNNING, or INCREMENTAL_UPDATING. If it is interactive, then the value is set in the range between the minimum and maximum. Negative numbers are set to zero. Numbers larger than the maximum are set at the maximum.
boolean isInteractive()	The value returned by this method indicates whether the gauge is interactive. The returned value is of the boolean type. A value of true establishes that the Gauge object is interactive.
INDEFINITE	Indicates that the Gauge has an indefinite range.
CONTINUOUS_IDLE	Shows that no work is in progress.
CONTINUOUS_RUNNING	After this value is assigned, the Gauge counts automatically. This is continuously updated and shows work in progress.
INCREMENTAL_UPDATING	Provides a Gauge that can accommodate an indefinite incremental count.

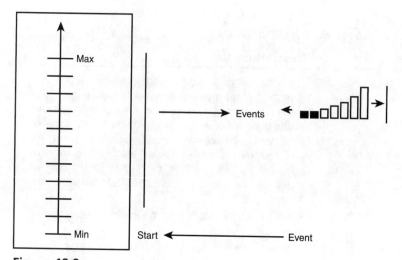

Figure 12.8
The noninteractive Gauge object generates a graphical representation that traces events that involve issuing integer values corresponding to the ticks of a timer or some other traceable process.

provided in Table 12.3 indicates, you set this range with the final two arguments in the constructor. The first of these sets the end or maximum value the Gauge counter accommodates. The last sets the starting value.

In the operation of a noninteractive gauge, the Gauge object provides a graphical representation of a process. In the example provided in the current chapter, this is a series of values generated by a Timer object. This is just one of many possible applications. Figure 12.8 illustrates the general scheme of things. The time is involved and then traces events through a sequence that is defined by its minimum and maximum values. When its maximum is reached, the Gauge object halts, revealing that the process it was defined to trace (a series of integer values, for example) has terminated.

As Table 12.3 shows, the interface for the Gauge class provides methods for setting the maximum value. The method for setting the maximum value is setMax-Value(), which takes an int value as an argument. The method you use to set the minimum or start value is the setValue() method. In addition to the minimum value, you can also use this method to set the counter at any value in the defined range. One other method that proves important is the getValue() method, which allows you to use the Gauge object to mediate or trace an event as it is moderated by the count the object provides. A Gauge object defined with a count of 14 can issue 14 distinct messages.

The SonnetMaker Class

You can find the SonnetMaker class included in the NetBeans Chapter12MIDlets project and as a standalone file in the Chapter 12 source folder. The SonnetMaker class illustrates the use of a noninteractive Gauge object. The noninteractive Gauge object displays status bars to audit the timed process of retrieving lines of a sonnet from an array at intervals of a second each. The timing activity is made possible by the Timer and TimerTask objects, and the lines of the sonnet are provided by a Vector object. To accommodate the TimerTask and Vector activities, two inner classes, CompositionTask and Sonnets, are defined. As its name implies, the CompositionTask class specializes the TimerTask class and provides an object that you can use to control the action of the Gauge object. The Sonnets class wraps the interface of a Vector object and allows you to sequentially retrieve lines of Shakespeare's Sonnet 29.

```
/*
 * Chapter 12 \ SonnetMaker.java
 *
 */

import javax.microedition.midlet.*;
import javax.microedition.lcdui.*;
import java.util.*; //Time and TimerTask
import java.lang.*;


public class SonnetMaker extends MIDlet
                     implements CommandListener{
  // #1
  private Display display;
  private Form form;
  private Command exitCmd;
  private Command stopCmd;
  private Gauge sonGauge;
  private Timer sonTimer;
  private CompositionTask compTask;
  private Sonnets sonnets;

  // #2
  public SonnetMaker(){
    sonnets = new Sonnets();
    display = Display.getDisplay(this);
```

```
    form = new Form("Compose a Sonnet");

    sonGauge = new Gauge("Sonnet Progress", false, 14, 0);
    exitCmd = new Command("Exit", Command.EXIT, 1);
    stopCmd = new Command("Stop", Command.STOP, 1);

    form.append(sonGauge);
    form.addCommand(stopCmd);
    form.setCommandListener(this);
  }

// #3
  public void startApp()
  {
    display.setCurrent(form);
    sonTimer = new Timer();
    CompositionTask compTask = new CompositionTask();
    sonTimer.scheduleAtFixedRate(compTask, 0, 1000);
  }

  public void pauseApp()
  { }

  public void destroyApp(boolean unconditional)
  { }

// #4
  public void commandAction(Command c, Displayable s)
  {
    if (c == exitCmd)
    {
      destroyApp(false);
      notifyDestroyed();
    }
    else if (c == stopCmd)
    {
      sonTimer.cancel();
      form.removeCommand(stopCmd);
      form.addCommand(exitCmd);
      sonGauge.setLabel("Reading cancelled!");
    }
  }
```

```
//- - - - - - - - - - - - - - - - - - - - - - - - - - - - - - - - - - - - - - - - - - - - - - -
// Inner Class for compostion timer
// #5
private class CompositionTask extends TimerTask{

    // # 5.1
    StringItem lineItem;
    CompositionTask(){
        lineItem = new StringItem("", "");
    }

    // #5.2
    public final void run(){
            int currentValue = sonGauge.getValue();
            if (currentValue < sonGauge.getMaxValue()){
                System.out.println("First: \t\t" + sonGauge.getValue());
                currentValue += 1 ;
                sonGauge.setValue(currentValue);
                sonGauge.setLabel("Line: " + currentValue);
                int line = currentValue - 1;
                System.out.println("Second: \t" + sonGauge.getValue());
                // 5.3
                lineItem = new StringItem("", sonnets.getLine(line));
                lineItem.setLayout(Item.LAYOUT_LEFT | Item.LAYOUT_DEFAULT);
                lineItem.setFont( Font.getFont( Font.FACE_PROPORTIONAL,
                                    Font.STYLE_BOLD,
                                    Font.SIZE_SMALL) );
                form.append(lineItem);
            }else{
                // 5.4
                form.removeCommand(stopCmd);
                form.addCommand(exitCmd);
                sonGauge.setLabel("Done!");
                cancel();
            }
    }
}//end inner class

//- - - - - - - - - - - - - - - - - - - - - - - - - - - - - - - - - - - - - - - - - - -
//Inner class for the sonnet
// #6
private class Sonnets{
```

```java
      private Vector sonnet29;
      // #6.1
      public Sonnets(){
        sonnet29 = new Vector();
        makeSonnet();
      }
      // #6.2
      public String getLine(int line){
          String sonnetLine = new String();
          if(line < sonnet29.size() && line >= 0){
             sonnetLine = sonnet29.elementAt(line).toString();
          }else{
             sonnetLine = "-";
          }
          return sonnetLine;
      }
    // #7
     private void makeSonnet(){
          sonnet29.addElement("When, in disgrace with fortune " +
                              "and men's eyes,");
          sonnet29.addElement("I all alone beweep my outcast state");
          sonnet29.addElement("And trouble deaf heaven with my "   +
                              "bootless cries");
          sonnet29.addElement("And look upon myself and curse my fate,");
          sonnet29.addElement("Wishing me like to one more rich in hope,");
          sonnet29.addElement("Featured like him, like him " +
                              "with friends possess'd,");
          sonnet29.addElement("Desiring this man's art and that " +
                              "man's scope,");
          sonnet29.addElement("With what I most enjoy contented least;");
          sonnet29.addElement("Yet in these thoughts myself " +
                              "almost despising, ");
          sonnet29.addElement("Haply I think on thee, and then my state,");
          sonnet29.addElement("Like to the lark at break of day arising");
          sonnet29.addElement("From sullen earth, sings hymns " +
                              "at heaven's gate;");
          sonnet29.addElement("For thy sweet love remember'd " +
                              "such wealth brings");
          sonnet29.addElement("That then I scorn to change my " +
                              "state with kings.");
      }
    }//end Sonnets class
 }//end outer class
```

Construction and Definition

In the lines trailing comment #1 in the SonnetMaker class, you declare Display, Form, and Command attributes. You then declare a Gauge attribute, sonGauge. You also declare attributes of the Timer and CompositionTask classes. The inner CompositionTask class, as is discussed further on, is a specialized version of the TimerTask class. For the last attribute in the list, you create an identifier using the Sonnets data type, which like the Composition data type is made possible by an inner class.

In the lines associated with comment #2, you define the constructor for the SonnetMaker class. As a first statement, you call the constructor for the Sonnets class and assign the instance you create to the sonnets attribute. After that, you create an instance of the Display class, which you assign to the display attribute, and an instance of the Form class, which you assign to the form attribute. From there you move on to work with the constructor of the Gauge class.

The constructor for the Gauge class requires four arguments. The first argument, of the String type, provides the label for the Gauge. The second argument, which is of the boolean type, establishes whether the Gauge object is interactive or noninteractive. A value of false sets the object to be noninteractive, which means that its action cannot be interrupted by the user after it has been initiated. In this case, such a course of action prevents the user from promoting the counter of the Gauge object, allowing it to completely increment through its count and display all the lines of the sonnet.

A sonnet is a poem with 14 lines, and in this instance, the number of lines in the sonnet is anticipated by the final two values provided to the constructor for the Gauge object. The penultimate argument, 14, sets the maximum count value of the Gauge object. This argument is always of the integer (int) type. The final argument, also of the int type, sets the value of the initial count. In other words, when the Gauge object is constructed, its first issued value is 0.

The final statements in the SonnetMaker constructor provide for the creation of the two Command objects (exitCmd and stopCmd) and the use of the Form::append() method to add the Gauge object to the Form object (form). The stopCmd object generates an event that stops the progress of the counter. The exitCmd closes the MIDlet. You call the addCommand() and setCommandListener() methods to fully implement capabilities for handling messages.

CompositionTask

The startApp() method requires a bit more discussion in this exercise than it has in others in this book. The reason for this is that it contains lines that pertain to the generation of events in the context provided by the Gauge application. Accordingly, in the lines following comment #3, you call the constructor of the Timer class and assign the instance of the class to the sonTimer attribute.

Having created a Timer object you then proceed to create a CompositionTask object. This is a specialized version of the TimerTask class. You assign it to the compTask identifier, and then use it as the first argument in the Timer::schedule-AtFixedRate() method. In one of its overloaded versions, this method takes a TimerTask reference as its first argument. Its second argument designates the delay following its construction for its first execution. The last argument is the period between executions. In this case, the period is set at one second (1000 milliseconds).

The definition of the CompositionTask class is presented in the lines following comment #5. As has been repeatedly mentioned, this class extends (specializes) the TimerTask class. To specialize the TimerTask, you must implement the run() method, but in this case, you also add a constructor to the class. The constructor is defined in the lines following comment #5.1. You first define a class attribute, lineItem, which is of the StringItem type. The constructor serves largely to initialize this attribute. It does so by assigning empty character strings to the label and field value of the StringItem object (the first and second arguments, respectively).

The implementation of the run() method begins in the lines following comment #2. There you first define a local identifier, currentValue, to which you assign the current value of the counter of the Gauge object (sonGauge). As an inner class, the CompositionTask class can access all the attributes of the containing SonnetMaker class, and for this reason, the use of the sonGauge attribute in this context creates no problem. To obtain the current value of the counter, you call the Gauge::getValue() method.

After setting the initial value of the currentValue identifier, you then test its value using a selection statement. The test verifies that the counter value returned by the getValue() method is less than the maximum counter value, which is returned by the Gauge::getMaxValue() method. Having verified that the current count is less than the maximum allowed count, the flow of the program then can proceed into the selection block.

The first action performed within the block involves incrementing the value of the count. This is accomplished by incrementing the value assigned to currentValue by 1. You then pass the increment value to the setValue() method, which advances the counter by one. This causes the counter progress bar to move forward.

Advancing the Counter

The run() method is invoked with each tick of the counter. Using this event, you use parallel calls to the getValue() and setValue() methods of the Gauge class to advance the counter. To track the two successive calls, you can uncomment the test code that appears prior to comment #5.3:

```
System.out.println("First: \t\t" + sonGauge.getValue());
currentValue += 1 ;
sonGauge.setValue(currentValue);
sonGauge.setLabel("Line: " + currentValue);
int line = currentValue - 1;
System.out.println("Second: \t" + sonGauge.getValue());
// 5.3
```

Here is the output the two println() methods generate to the output pane of NetBeans:

```
First:      1
Second:     2
First:      2
Second:     3
First:      3
Second:     4
```

Displaying the Lines

To display the lines of the sonnet, you call the setLabel() method of the Gauge class and assign a message to it that consists of a String constant, "Line", concatenated with the value assigned to the line identifier. When you initialize the line identifier, you must subtract 1 from the value of currentValue, because the line you display is identified as an array (or Vector) value, the indexes of which begin at 0.

As the lines following comment #5.3 show, to retrieve the line of the sonnet, you call the Sonnets::getLine() method, which takes as an argument the index of the line you want to retrieve. As just mentioned, these begin at 0. When you retrieve the line, you use it as the second argument of the StringItem constructor. The

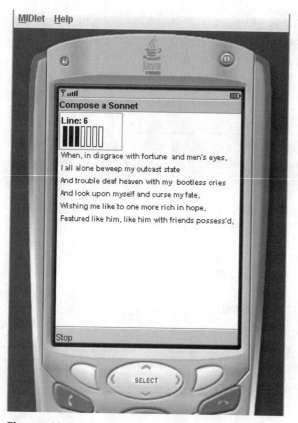

Figure 12.9
As the counter progresses, successive lines appear and a number and the Gauge object display the progress.

first argument, providing the label for the item, you assign an empty character string (""). To make it so that each line of the display requires only one line, you employ the setFont() method of the StringItem class and call the static Font::getFont() method to set the display font face so that it is small, bold, and proportional. You then call the append method of the Form class to display the successive lines. Figure 12.9 illustrates the lines as they are being written with the advance of the counter.

Finishing the Display

In the lines associated with comment #5.4 inside the CompositionTask class, an else statement is defined. The else statement becomes part of the program flow if the selection statement following comment #5.2 proves false. This occurs if the

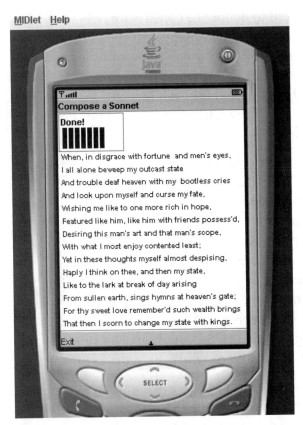

Figure 12.10
With the printing of the fourteenth line, the sonnet is fully displayed.

value of currentValue is no longer less than the maximum value assigned to the Gauge object. In this case, you first disable the stopCmd event, which can be used at any time to stop the progress of the counter. You then add the exitCmd. Following that, you display "Done" in the label of the Gauge object. At this point, the progress bars of the Gauge object are completely filled in, and the sonnet is fully visible. Figure 12.10 shows the messages associated with the complete display of the sonnet.

Sonnets

The second inner class, the Sonnets class, wraps a Vector object and provides a way to access successive lines of the sonnet by calls to the getLine() method. In the line preceding comment #6.1, you define a single attribute, sonnet29, which is of the Vector type. You then proceed to define the constructor, which involves creating an instance of the Vector class and assigning it to the class attribute. Additionally, you call the makeSonnet() method, which is responsible for adding the lines of the sonnet to the Vector object. This method receives its definition in the lines following comment #7, where the Vector::addElements() is called in a somewhat laboriously repetitious way. With each call of the method, a character string is assigned to the Vector object.

To retrieve the lines assigned to the Vector object, you implement the getLine() method, which is defined in the lines trailing comment #6.2. This method takes one argument of the int type, which designates the line to be returned. To deliver the line, you first create a String object, sonnetLine. After affirming the value of the line argument is less than the value returned by the Vector::size() method and greater than zero, you then call the Vector.elementAt() method, using the index value supplied by the line argument, to retrieve a specific line of the sonnet. Since the Vector stores its contents as Object references, it is necessary to convert each retrieved line back into a String reference using the toString() method. The result is then assigned to the sonnetLine object, the value of which is returned in the final line of the method.

As a precautionary measure, an else clause is provided that assigns a character value to the sonnetLine identifier in the event that no line has been retrieved. In this way, the service the Sonnets class provides is slightly more robust than it would be otherwise.

Stop and Exit Messages

In the lines associated with comment #4, the stopCmd and exitCmd messages are processed. With respect to the stopCmd message, the first action is to call the Timer::cancel() method, which destroys the Timer object. This action allows you to prematurely stop the display of the sonnet, and a message to this effect is then issued. You call the removeCommand() method to remove the Stop command label from the display area. You also restore the exitCmd label, allowing the user to exit the MIDlet. As a final action, you call the Gauge::setLabel() method to change the text displayed in the label to "Reading Cancelled!" This is shown in Figure 12.11.

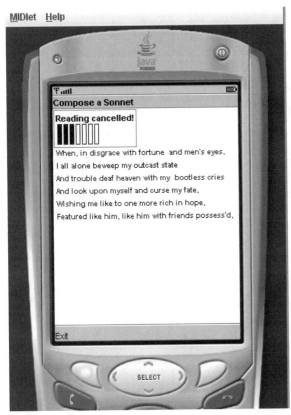

Figure 12.11
The message from the `stopCmd` object terminates the progress by destroying the `Timer` object.

Conclusion

In this chapter, you have investigated the `DateField`, `Calendar`, `Date`, and `Gauge` classes. The `DateField` and `Calendar` classes are derived from the `Item` class; exploration of these classes proves interesting in light of text-based game applications. How this might be so is shown in part with the implementation of the `CalendarFortune` and `SonnetMaker` classes, which allow you to explore chance and sequence in rudimentary ways. Working with these two classes allows you to further explore the possibilities the MIDP classes provide for developing text-based games. As it is, however, exploration of these classes also moves your work with the MIDP classes toward the `Graphics` and `Canvas` classes, the topics of the next chapter. Use of these classes opens the door to many more scenarios for developing games.

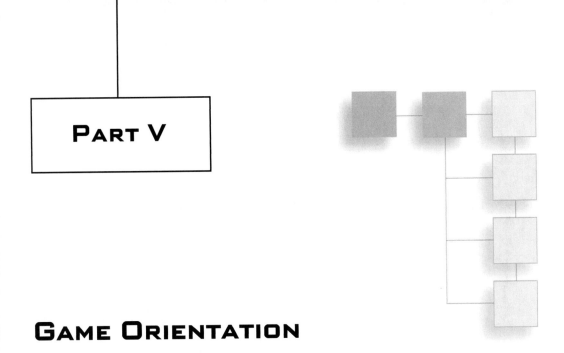

Part V

Game Orientation

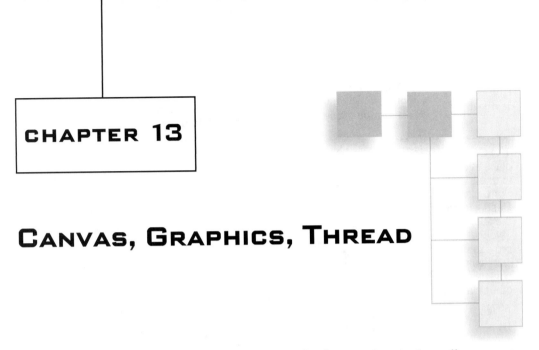

CHAPTER 13

CANVAS, GRAPHICS, THREAD

In this chapter you explore two of the standard GUI classes that allow you to develop a wide variety of interfaces. These are Graphics and Canvas. Many of the topics dealt with in this chapter anticipate the Game API classes. The virtue of not immediately exploring the uses of the Game API classes is that the Canvas class remains a reliable and frequently used class in the MIDP package set, and using the Graphics, Image, Font, and other classes with the Canvas class is a convenient way to learn. In this chapter, you concentrate on two shorter introductory classes and then one longer class. The longer class makes use of a Thread object to control the behavior of the objects displayed. It also makes use of methods for processing events generated by keys. To process such events, it employs defined values provided by the Canvas class. These provide valuable assets you can use to develop action-oriented games for devices.

Canvas

The Canvas class is in some ways analogous to the Form class. You create an instance of the Canvas class and then call the Display::setCurrent() method to make it active. After you have activated the Canvas object, you then have access to the primary method of the Canvas class: the paint() method. The paint() method is defined so that it receives an argument of the Graphics type. Figure 13.1 provides a simplified overview of some of the activities you can perform using Graphics objects.

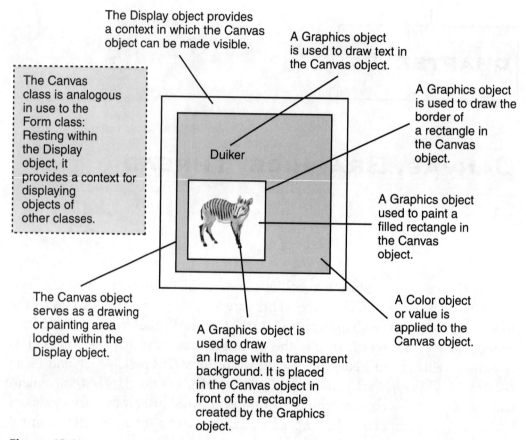

Figure 13.1
The Canvas and Graphics classes allow you to create and display a variety of items.

Table 13.1 discusses several of the features of the Canvas class. Generally, it is beneficial to study the Canvas class if you plan to use the GameCanvas class. The Canvas class is the base class of the GameCanvas class.

CGExplorer

The CGExplorer class provides a rudimentary example of how to combine the Canvas, Graphics, and Image classes to create an essential display. While Table 13.1 provides information on the Canvas class, Table 13.2 explores features of the Graphics class. The CGCanvas class developed later in this chapter provides many more opportunities for discussing in detail a number of the methods provided by the two classes. The CGExplorer class provides only the most essential example of how to implement a Canvas class. It is developed as an inner class, and the paint()

Table 13.1 Canvas Class Methods

Method	Description
int getGameAction (int)	Takes a single argument of the int type. The key codes are defined in the Canvas class. Such events are considered standard to games. Game actions are identified with the constants UP, DOWN, LEFT, RIGHT, and FIRE.
int getKeyCode(int)	This retrieves the values assigned to the keys used for game actions. It returns an integer value that you can then use in a more generalized context. It takes as an argument an integer argument identifying the game action to be handled. Standard key codes can be integer values or defined values, such as KEY_NUM0 or KEY_NUM1.
String getKeyName(int)	This method returns a String reference and uses a defined key code value or an integer value as its argument. Takes an integer argument designating the key that is to be identified.
boolean hasPointerEvents()	This method, which is beyond the scope of the current discussion, verifies whether the device or platform on which you are working supports release and press events produced by a pointer.
boolean hasPointerMotionEvents()	Confirms that the platform you are developing on can support events that involve dragging a pointer across the screen. This is beyond the scope of the current discussion.
boolean hasRepeatEvents()	Verifies that if a user holds down a given key, the action is interpreted as a repeating event.
void hideNotify()	If you remove a given Canvas object from the display, you can use this event to issue a message to this effect.
boolean isDoubleBuffered()	This method verifies that the Canvas object you are using is double buffered, which means that graphical features can be written into a buffer prior to being displayed.
protected void keyPressed(int)	Handles the event that is initiated when a key is pressed. This method takes an integer argument identifying the code of the key that is pressed.
protected void keyReleased(int)	Handles the event that is initiated when a key is pressed. Takes an integer argument identifying the code of the key that is released.
protected void keyRepeated(int)	Called when a key is repeated (held down). Takes an integer argument identifying the key that is repeatedly pressed.
protected abstract void paint (Graphics g)	Renders the Canvas. You must implement this method when you specialize the Canvas class to create concrete instances of it.
protected void pointerDragged (int x, int y)	Applies to a pointer applied to the screen. Processes such events when the pointer is dragged across the screen.

(Continued)

Table 13.1 Continued

Method	Description
`protected void pointerPressed (int x, int y)`	Invoked when the pointer is pressed.
`protected void pointerReleased (int x, int y)`	Invoked when the pointer is released.
`void repaint()`	A centrally important method of the `Canvas` class. It works in conjunction with the `paint()` method. This method calls the `paint()` method, giving you a way to animate or in other ways change the appearance of the objects in the display. The method causes the entire canvas to be repainted.
`void repaint(int x, int y, int, int)`	A centrally important method of the `Canvas` class. It calls the `paint()` method. Its argument allows you to designate the area of the `Canvas` object you want to repaint. The first two arguments designate the coordinate position in the canvas of the upper left corner of the area to be repainted. The third argument establishes the distance extending from the corner coordinate to the right border of the area to be repainted. The final argument designates the distance downward from the corner coordinate to the bottom border of the area to be repainted.
`void serviceRepaints()`	When you call the `repaint()` method, your request is placed in a queue. This method provides a way to force the `repaint()` action to be performed immediately.
`void setFullScreenMode(boolean)`	A `Canvas` can be set to completely fill the display area or to display in a normal mode. The normal mode features a title and a bottom tray. Full-screen mode does not. It takes an argument of the `boolean` type. If set to `true`, then your display mode is full screen.
`protected void showNotify()`	The method allows you to issue a message just prior to the display of a `Canvas` object. It allows you to invoke actions that you wish to take to prepare for the display of the new `Canvas` object.
`protected void sizeChanged (int w, int h)`	Allows you to issue a message if the size of the area of the `Canvas` object on display is changed.
`Graphics`	An essential complementary class to the `Canvas` class. This class provides the data type for the argument of the `paint()` method, which is the primary vehicle you use to render images to the `Canvas` object.

method is implemented so that it renders an `Image` object visible and then supplements it with a few `Graphics` items. The `CGExplorer` class is located in the `Chapter13MIDlets` project in the Chapter 13 source folder. It is also available in a standalone version.

```
/*
 * Chapter 13 \ CGExplorer.java
 *
 */
import javax.microedition.midlet.*;
import javax.microedition.lcdui.*;
import java.util.*;
import java.io.*;

// #1
public class CGExplorer extends MIDlet{
  Canvas canvas;
  Display display;
   public CGExplorer(){
      canvas = new SimpleCanvas();
      display = Display.getDisplay(this);
   }
   // #1.1
   public void startApp(){
      display.setCurrent(canvas);
   }

   public void pauseApp(){
   }

   public void destroyApp(boolean unconditional){
   }
   //=======Inner Canvas Class =================================
   // #2
   public class SimpleCanvas extends Canvas{
       Image image;
       public void paint(Graphics g){
          // #2.1
          g.setColor(176, 224, 230);
          g.fillRect(0, 0, getWidth(), getHeight(  ));

          //Upper left
          g.setColor(250, 250, 210);
          g.fillRect(getWidth()/2, 0, getWidth(), getHeight()/2);

          //Lower right

          g.fillRect(0, getHeight()/2, getWidth()/2, getHeight() );
```

```
        g.setColor(0, 0, 0);
        // #2.2
        g.setColor(18, 18, 18);
        g.drawString("Peace of mind.",
                    getWidth()/8,
                    getHeight()/4,
                    g.TOP | g.LEFT);

        g.drawString("Mind the peace.",
                    5 * getWidth()/8,
                    3 * getHeight()/4,
                    g.TOP | g.LEFT);

        // #2.3
        g.setColor(255,0,0);
        g.drawLine(0, this.getHeight()/2, this.getWidth(),
                                        this.getHeight()/2);
        g.drawLine(this.getWidth()/2, 0,  this.getWidth()/2,
                                        this.getHeight());
        g.setColor(225, 25, 112);
        // #2.4
        try{
            image = Image.createImage("/Paca.gif");
        }catch( IOException ioe ){
                System.out.println(ioe.toString());
        }

        // #2.5
        int xPos = this.getWidth()/2 - image.getWidth()/2;
        int yPos = this.getHeight()/2 - image.getHeight()/2;
        //In a rectangle that overlays the area of the image
        g.setStrokeStyle(Graphics.SOLID);
        g.drawArc(xPos,
                yPos,
                image.getWidth(),
                image.getHeight(), 0, 360);

        g.drawImage(image, this.getWidth()/2-image.getWidth()/2,
                    this.getHeight()/2-image.getHeight()/2,
                    0);

    // #2.7
    g.translate(0, 0);
```

```
        g.drawRect(0, 0, 10, 10 );
        //Translate the intial (0,0) coordinate
        g.translate( this.getWidth()/10, this.getHeight()/5);
        g.drawRect(0, 0, 10, 10 );

        //Origin moved to the right, no further down
        g.translate(2 * this.getWidth()/3, 0);
        g.drawRect(0, 0, 10, 10 );
     }
   }// end SimpleCanvas
   //=========================================================
}// end outer class
```

Definition and Construction

In the lines following comment #1 in the CGExplorer class, you declare Canvas and display attributes and then move on to define the constructor for the class. The primary purpose of the constructor is to create an instance of the Canvas class. In this case, you use the constructor for the SimpleCanvas class, which is an inner class that extends the Canvas class. Since the SimpleCanvas class is a specialized version of the Canvas class, assigning an instance of it to the Canvas attribute (canvas) creates no problem. Having created an instance of the Simple-Canvas class, you then call the Display::getDisplay() method to obtain an instance of the Display class to assign to the display attribute.

Following definition of the constructor for the CGExplorer class, you call the startApp() method, as is shown in the lines following comment #1.1. To define this method, you use the display attribute to call the setCurrent() method. As an argument to the setCurrent() method, you furnish a reference to a Canvas object. The setCurrent() method accepts an argument of the Displayable type, which is a super class of the Canvas class. The Canvas object (canvas) at this point becomes the primary medium of display for the MIDlet.

Specializing the Canvas Class

To use the Canvas class, it is necessary to specialize it. Specialization of the Canvas class primarily involves overriding the paint() method. As is evident in the lines following comment #2 of the CGExplorer class, to specialize the Canvas class in this context, you create an inner class. As mentioned previously, the name of the inner class is SimpleCanvas, and its definition includes one attribute, image, of the Image type, and one method, paint().

The data type of the one argument taken by the paint() method is Graphics. This argument represents the Canvas object and allows you to use the fairly extensive list of methods provided by the Graphics interface to render text, geometrical forms, and pictures for display. As Table 13.2 makes clear, these three activities, complemented by clipping and translating, constitute the primary services offered by the interface of the Graphics class.

Color

As a demonstration of some of the interface features offered by the Graphics class, consider that in the lines following comment #2.1, you call the Graphics::setColor() method. As Table 13.2 discusses, there are two overloaded versions of this method. One accepts a trio of integer values to create an RGB value. For example, the set consisting of 176, 224, 230 is used to set the background color for the Graphics display area. This is a light blue color.

Note

A useful Internet site to keep open or bookmarked when you are working with either hexadecimal or 3-integer RBG values is as follows:

http://www.pitt.edu/~nisg/cis/web/cgi/rgb.html.

This site provides an extensive table, along with the names and samples of colors generated, and you can easily copy and paste the information you require to your programs.

As Figure 13.2 illustrates, the color you apply to the Graphics object affects objects in the flow of the program that follows, until you apply another color. The pattern established is fairly straightforward. Apply a color, then call one or another of the methods used to create textual or geometrical forms. They adopt the applied color.

In the lines trailing comment #2.1, the first geometrical form to which color is applied is a filled rectangle. The method that generates the rectangle is fillRect(). Almost all of the Graphics methods work with the same basic set of parameters that you use with the fillRect() method. With respect to position, Figure 13.3 shows how geometrical and text forms generated by the Graphics class are usually positioned relative to x and y-coordinates that establish the upper left corner of the object to be displayed. The starting coordinate pair for the display area is by default (0,0). This is the upper left position in the display area. The values along the x- and y-axes then both increase one pixel at a time as you move to the right or downward.

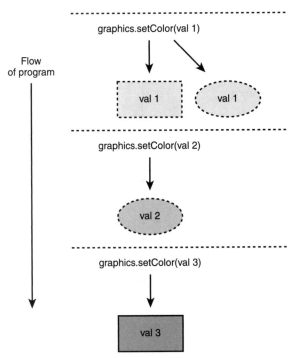

Figure 13.2
The flow of the program carries forward the color definitions you apply.

It is almost always the case that a coordinate pair (x, y) establishes the location of the upper left corner of a bounding box in which the form is drawn. The bounding box extends to the right along the x dimension to the width you define. It likewise extends downward along the y dimension to the height (or distance) you define. The area of the bounding box extends downward from the starting coordinates, not upward. One exception to the use of width and height dimensions is the line. The coordinates used to generate a line do not define a bounding box. Instead they establish only the beginning and end coordinate pairs of the line.

Figure 13.3 also reviews the notion of an *anchor*. Generally, whether you render text or a geometrical form, the item you render is positioned within a bounding box. An anchor is a distinct argument (of the int type) that allows you to adjust the location of the item you are rendering with relation to its position within the bounding box. In Figure 13.3, for example, the item in the bounding box is pulled down and to the right. The values you use to create anchors are defined by the Graphics class. An example of a value that might be used is Graphics.BOTTOM | Graphics.RIGHT. In this expression, two defined values are joined by a bit OR (|)

Canvas or Graphics Origin

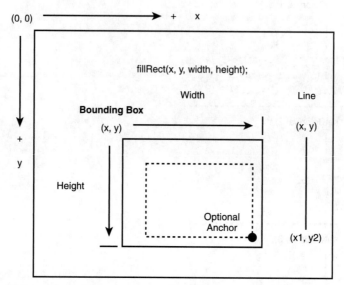

Figure 13.3
Geometrical forms use similar parameters.

operator to create an anchor value that pushes the item to which it is applied into the lower right corner of the bounding box.

Rectangles

The lines trailing comment #2.1 involve three calls to the drawRect() method. The drawRect() method takes four arguments. The first two set the coordinate of the upper left corner of the rectangle. The third sets the width of the rectangle. The final argument establishes the height of the rectangle. The first call to the drawRect() method creates a rectangle that is the same height and width as the display area. The next two calls create rectangles that are positioned in the upper left and lower right of the display area, as shown in Figure 13.4. Creation of the upper left rectangle involves obtaining the value returned by the getWidth() method and dividing it by 2. This value is assigned to the x-coordinate that sets the position of the upper left corner of the rectangle in the middle of the display at the top. The value of 0 is then assigned to the y-coordinate. The distance given by getWidth() is used to establish the left border. The distance given by getHeight()/ 2 is used to establish the height. The approach used to create the rectangle in the lower left follows the same logic:

```
0, getHeight()/2, getWidth()/2, getHeight()
```

drawRect(getWidth( )/2,0, getWidth( ), getHeight( )/2)

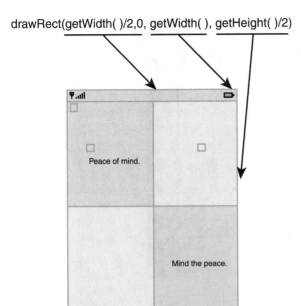

Figure 13.4
The methods of the Display class provide a way to define the rectangles for the background.

Strings

Trailing comment #2.2 in the CGExplorer class, a call is made to the drawString() method of the Graphics class. As mentioned in the last section, the arguments to the method are in many ways predictable. The first argument provides either a reference to a String object or, in this case, a string constant. The second and third arguments provide the coordinate pair used to position the upper left corner of the bounding box that contains the text. The final argument is the anchor, which in this case consists of a value created by joining Graphics:TOP and Graphics:LEFT using an OR operator. This anchor argument pulls the text to the upper left of the bounding box.

In the definition of the call to the drawString() and drawLine() methods (see comment #2.3), calls are made to the getWidth() and getHeight() methods of the Display class. For the first call to the drawString() method, the value returned by the getWidth() method is divided by 8, rendering a value that represents an eighth of the width of the display area. A similar approach is used to position the text with relation to the height of the display. The value returned by getHeight() is divided by 4. As is shown in Figure 13.5, the "P" in the string "Peace of mind" begins at a position that is roughly one eighth of the way across from the left edge of the

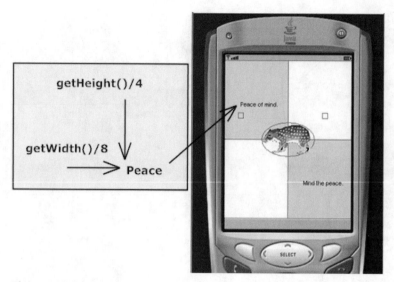

Figure 13.5
Using values retrieved from the `Display` eliminates the use of embedded constants.

display area. Likewise, the top of the "P" is roughly a fourth of the distance down from the top edge of the display area.

The technique used to position the two strings of text is also employed to draw two lines that divide the display area into quadrants. Drawing a line requires two coordinate pairs, and to calculate the value of x for one of the coordinate pairs, for the vertical line, you divide the value furnished by `getWidth()` by 2. You then set value of y to 0 to form the first coordinate pair (`getWidth()/2, 0`). The second coordinate pair used to define the vertical line uses a similar approach (`getWidth()/2, getHeight()`).

Rendering the Image and Drawing an Arc

The lines following comment #2.4 in the `CGExplorer` class trace activities that have been reviewed in previous chapters, but it proves helpful to examine them once again in the context provided by the `Canvas` (or `SimpleCanvas`) class. When you call the `Image::createImage()` method, you load the contents of a GIF file into the `image` attribute. To perform this action, you must wrap the create-Image() method in a `try` block, because it is defined to throw an exception under several conditions. In this instance, the general `IOException` type is used as the argument to the `catch` block to handle the exceptions.

The image loaded depicts a paca, a rodent that is common in countries like Paraguay. Prior to rendering the picture of the paca visible, you first calculate the values needed to position the picture in the center of the display. The two values required for this are those assigned to the local identifiers, xPos and yPos.

As is evident in the lines following comment #2.5, to calculate values to assign to the xPos and yPos identifiers, the getWidth() and getHeight() methods of the Image class are used along with the methods of the same name from the Display class. You divide the values the methods return by 2. You then subtract the Image values from the Display values. The result is a coordinate pair (xPos, yPos) that positions the upper left corner of the bounding box for the Image object so that the picture appears roughly in the center of the display (refer back to Figure 13.5).

In a similar fashion, as the lines associated with comment #2.6 reveal, you draw an oval around the picture of the paca by calling the drawArc() method of the Graphics class. The first two arguments to the drawArc() method provide the x and y values that designate the upper left corner of the bounding box for the arc. These are supplied by the xPos and yPos values calculated previously to position the picture of the paca. The next two arguments provide the width and height of the picture of the paca, and to provide these, once again, you call the getWidth() and getHeight() methods of the Image class.

The final two arguments of the drawArc() method designate the starting and end degree values used to define the arc. An arc is a curved line that runs along the circumference of a circle. The arc begins at any point on the circle, and as it progresses around the circle, you can measure it in degrees. As Figure 13.6 illustrates, if you set the values of the drawArc() method at 0 and 90, the resulting

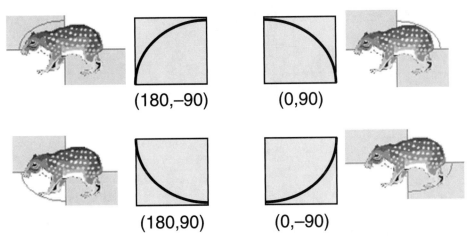

Figure 13.6
The drawArc() method uses arguments that designate degree values.

curve projects upward and to the left. If you set the values at 180 and −90, the line curves over to the right. The values you use to generate a given arc can be positive or negative and of almost any integer magnitude. The values 0 and 720 in effect draw a complete circle twice over.

Translation

In the lines following comment #2.7 in the CGExplorer class, three calls to the translate() method are made. Generally, translation involves relocating the origin of the Canvas object with respect to the display area. As is shown in the lines immediately following comment #2.7, although you make three calls to the drawRect() method using exactly the same arguments each time, the rectangles rendered appear in different locations. The changes of location are the work of the translate() method.

As Figure 13.7 shows, the first translation effects no change at all, for the arguments to the translate() method are both zeros. The origin is originally set at

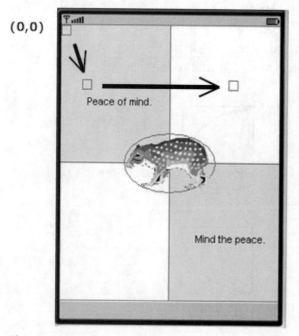

Figure 13.7
Translation allows you to change the coordinate values associated with the origin of the Canvas.

Table 13.2 Graphics Class Methods

Method	Description
Methods That Process Color	
`int getColor()`	Gets the currently set color.
`void setColor(int)`	Changes the current drawing color. This method is overridden to allow you to use a single value for the color.
`void setColor(int, int, int)`	Changes the current drawing color. All three arguments are of the `int` type. The three together provide the RGB (red, green, blue) values used to define a color.
`int getRedComponent()`	Gets the red component (0–255) of the current drawing color.
`int getGreenComponent()`	Gets the green component (0–255) of the current drawing color.
`int getBlueComponent()`	Gets the blue component (0–255) of the current drawing color.
`void setGrayScale(int)`	Sets the current grayscale drawing color.
`int getGrayScale()`	Gets the current grayscale drawing color.
Methods That Retrieve Coordinate Values of the Graphics Object	
`int getTranslateX()`	Returns the current translated x origin.
`int getTranslateY()`	Returns the current translated y origin.
`void translate (int x, int y)`	Translates the origin in the current graphics context.
Methods That Accommodate Clipping	
`void clipRect (int, int, int, int)`	Sets the current clipping rectangle. The first two arguments determine the position of the upper left corner of the clipping. The third argument is the distance to the right of the corner coordinate of the right border of the clipping area. The last argument is the distance from the corner coordinate to the bottom of the clipping area.
`int getClipHeight()`	Returns the height defined for the current clipping rectangle.
`int getClipWidth()`	Returns the width of the current clipping rectangle.
`int getClipX()`	Returns the offset that has been assigned to the x-coordinate of the clipping rectangle.
`int getClipY()`	Returns the offset that has been assigned to the y-coordinate of the clipping rectangle.
`void setClip(int x, int y, int, int)`	Intersects the current clipping rectangle with the one passed to the method. The first two arguments determine the position of the upper left corner of the clipping. The third argument is the distance to the right of the corner coordinate of the right border of the clipping area. The last argument is the distance from the corner coordinate to the bottom of the clipping area.
Methods for Drawing Geometrical Forms	
`void drawArc(int x, int y, int, int, int, int)`	Draws an arc, which can be any outline of a figure with curved or rounded sides. The first two arguments establish the coordinates of the upper left corner. The next two set the height and width of the figure relative to these corner coordinates. The final two arguments

(Continued)

Table 13.2 Continued

Method	Description
	establish the starting and ending angles of the arc to be drawn. For example, if you use the successive values 180 and 360, you get the bottom half of a circle. If you use 0 and 180, you get the top half of a circle.
void drawLine (int, int, int, int)	Draws a line. The first two values set the coordinate position of one end of the line. The second two values set the coordinate position of the other end of the line.
void drawRect (int, int, int, int)	Draws the outline of a rectangle. The first two arguments establish the coordinates of the upper left corner of the rectangle. The third argument is the width of the rectangle relative to the corner coordinates. The fourth argument is distance to the bottom relative to the corner coordinates.
void drawRoundRect(int, int, int, int, int, int)	Draws the outline of a rectangle with rounded corners. The first two arguments establish the coordinates of the upper left corner of the rectangle. The third argument is the width of the rectangle relative to the corner coordinates. The fourth argument is distance to the bottom relative to the corner coordinates. The last two arguments gauge the amount of curvature you want to apply to the arcs that characterize the corners. The larger the numbers, the more the curvature.
void fillArc(int x, int y, int, int, int, int)	Draws a filled arc. The first two arguments establish the coordinates of the upper left corner. The next two set the height and width of the figure relative to these corner coordinates. The final two arguments establish the starting and ending angles of the arc to be drawn. If you use the successive values 180 and 360, you get the filled bottom half of a circle. If you use 0 and 180, you get the filled top half of a circle. The values 0 and 360 draw a complete circle.
void fillRect(int x, int y, int, int)	Draws a filled rectangle. The first two arguments establish the coordinates of the upper left corner of the rectangle. The third argument is the width of the rectangle relative to the corner coordinates. The fourth argument is distance to the bottom relative to the corner coordinates.
void fillRoundRect(int int, int, int, int, int)	Draws a filled rectangle with rounded corners. The first two arguments establish the coordinates of the upper left corner of the rectangle. The third argument is the width of the rectangle relative to the corner coordinates. The fourth argument is distance to the bottom relative to the corner coordinates. The last two arguments gauge the amount of curvature you want to apply to the arcs that characterize the corners. The larger the numbers, the more the curvature.
int getStrokeStyle()	Gets the current stroke style.
void setStrokeStyle(int style)	Sets the current stroke style.

Table 13.2 Continued

Method	Description
Methods for Working with String, Char, and Font Objects	
void drawString(String, int, int, int)	The first argument is of the String type and provides the text you want to display. The second and third arguments set the upper left corner of the rectangle that contains the text. The final argument is the anchor. It shifts the relative position of the text within the rectangle according to defined values provided by the Graphics class. For example, the values Graphics.BOTTOM | Graphics.RIGHT force the text to the bottom right of the rectangle in which it is located.
void drawSubstring (String, int, int, int, int, int)	The first argument is of the String type and provides the text you want to display. The second argument is the starting index (or offset) within the String object you have provided. The third argument determines how many characters you want to display starting at the starting index. The fourth and fifth arguments set the upper left corner of the rectangle that contains the text. The final argument is the anchor. It shifts the relative position of the text within the rectangle according to defined values provided by the Graphics class. For example, the values Graphics.BOTTOM | Graphics.RIGHT force the text to the bottom right of the rectangle in which it is located.
void drawChar(char, int, int, int)	The first argument is of the char type and provides the character you want to display. The second and third arguments set the upper left corner of the rectangle that contains the text. The final argument is the anchor. It shifts the relative position of the text within the rectangle according to defined values provided by the Graphics class. For example, the values Graphics.BOTTOM | Graphics.RIGHT force the text to the bottom right of the rectangle that contains the text.
void drawChars(char[], int, int, int, int, int)	The first argument is an array of the char type and provides the text you want to display. The second argument is the starting index (or offset) within the array you have provided. The third argument determines how many characters you want to display starting at the starting index. The fourth and fifth arguments set the upper left corner of the rectangle that contains the text. The final argument is the anchor. It shifts the relative position of the text within the rectangle according to defined values provided by the Graphics class. For example, the values Graphics.BOTTOM | Graphics.RIGHT force the text to the bottom right of the rectangle that contains the text.
Font getFont()	Returns a reference to the font that has been assigned to the Graphics object.
void setFont(Font)	Allows you to set the current drawing font.

(Continued)

Table 13.2 Concluded

Method	Description
Methods for Working with the Canvas Area and Images	
void drawImage(Image, int, int, int)	Draws an image. The first argument is of the Image type. The second and third arguments determine the upper left corner of the image as it is drawn on the canvas. The last argument can be used to align the image within the area set for drawing. This is the anchor. The anchor Graphics.BOTTOM | Graphics.RIGHT forces the image to the bottom right of the area set for the display of the image.
void copyArea(int, int, int, int, int, int, int)	Copies the contents of a rectangular area. The first four arguments set the upper left corner of the area to be copied, along with its width and height. The next two arguments establish the coordinates to which the area is to be copied. This is upper left of the area. The final argument is the anchor. An example of an anchor that forces the image to the bottom right of the area set for the display of the image is Graphics.BOTTOM | Graphics.RIGHT.

coordinate (0,0), so translating it to (0,0) brings no change. The second call to the translate() method does effect a change, because in this case, you move the y-coordinate origin down by a fifth of the height of the display area while moving the x-coordinate over by a tenth of the width of the display area. As a result, although you do not change the values assigned to the drawRect() method (0, 0, 10, 10), the rectangle you render is roughly a third of the way down in the display area. It is also moved a bit further to the right.

A third call the to translate() method moves the origin once again, this time so that the drawRect() method—again set with the same values as before—renders a rectangle in the upper right quadrant of the display. Note that since the translate() method is called last in the paint() method, the previously drawn graphical items (the paca, the crossed lines, the colored quadrants, and the text) remain unaffected.

Extended Canvas Work

The GameStart and GSCanvas classes combine to form the rudimentary framework of a game based on the standard MIDP classes alone. Prior to the introduction of the MIDP Game API, this type of MIDlet characterized device games. The picture has now changed, however. When developing an action-oriented game, the best approach is to use the Game API, which receives extended treatment in Chapters 14 and 15.

Table 13.3 GSCanvas Actions

Key to Press	Action
Keyboard 1	Changes the color in the arc (oval) behind the drawing of the animal that appears in the middle of the display.
Keyboard 3	Toggles the action mode. When this is toggled on, clicking a direction key using the SELECT button causes the image to move continuously in that direction until it comes to the edge of the display area or you press another direction key.
Keyboard 5	Changes the background color of the display using a random color value.
Keyboard 7	Toggles through a set of four drawings of animals.
Keyboard 9	Restores the background color to the starting color.
Arrows on the SELECT button	The Up, Down, Right, and Left arrow keys cause the drawing of the animal to move. They correspond to the Up, Down, Right, and Left arrows on the SELECT button.
Upper left collision	If you move the picture of the animal to the upper left of the display, a collision event causes a message to be displayed.
Upper right collision	If you move the picture of the animal to the upper right of the display, a collision event causes a message to be displayed.
Center collision	At the start of the application and whenever you move the drawing of the animal to the center of the display, a message is displayed.
Lower border	If you move the picture to the bottom of the display, although no message is shown, your motion is stopped.

In the current setting, use of the standard GUI components of the MIDP remains an effective way to learn the basics. The current set of classes allows you to explore event handling with respect to the Canvas class and thread implementation. In addition, you explore a few applications of collision detection. These and other features of the MIDlet are brought into focus through events generated by the keypad. Table 13.3 provides summary of the key actions the MIDlet supports.

Figure 13.8 illustrates the GameStart MIDlet after you have invoked the 7 key to change the drawing of the animal to that of an addax. The message to the left of the addax is displayed as the result of a collision event. At the top of the display area, note that the coordinate position of the drawing is shown on the left. On the right, you see whether the animation key has been pressed. When the key has been pressed to set animation on, the drawing of the animal moves automatically. When it is off, it moves in small increments, and only with repeated presses of the arrow keys.

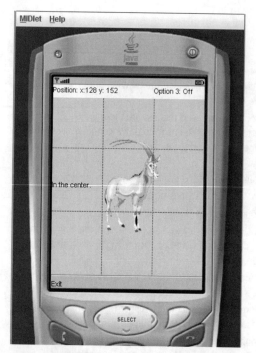

Figure 13.8
Key presses invoke some of the events supported by the GameStart MIDlet, while other actions result from internally generated events.

GameStart

The GameStart class provides a way to control how the user enters into the event context that the GSCanvas class provides. It furnishes a splash screen, a game-over screen, and commands for starting and stopping the application. When the user presses the Start key, the GameStart class constructs an instance of the GSCanvas class and moves the context of interaction into the event arena defined by Canvas class methods. You can find the code for the GameStart and GSCanvas classes in the Chapter 13 source folder. The classes are included in the NetBeans Chapter13MIDlets project and also in the standalone folder. Here is the code for the GameStart class. The GSCanvas class is presented further along in this chapter.

```
/*
 * Chapter 13 \ GameStart.java
 *
 */
import javax.microedition.midlet.*;
import javax.microedition.lcdui.*;
import java.io.IOException;
```

```java
import java.util.*;
// #1
public class GameStart extends MIDlet implements CommandListener{
        Form form;
        Command exitCmd;
        Command startCmd;
        GSCanvas canvas;
        Display display;
        ImageItem splash;

        public GameStart(){
              form = new Form("Starter Canvas");
              display = Display.getDisplay( this );
         // #1.1
              canvas = new GSCanvas(display, form);
              exitCmd = new Command("Exit", Command.EXIT, 1);
              startCmd = new Command("Start", Command.OK, 1);
              form.append(new Spacer(50,100));
          // #1.2
              splash = new ImageItem("Canvas Explorations", null,
                                  ImageItem.LAYOUT_CENTER,null);

              try{
                  Image image = Image.createImage("/Alien-bird.gif");
                  splash.setImage(image);

              }catch( IOException ioe ){
                  System.out.println(ioe.toString());
              }
              form.append(splash);

              form.addCommand(startCmd);
              form.addCommand(exitCmd);
              form.setCommandListener(this);
         }
        // #2
        protected void startApp()
               throws MIDletStateChangeException{
                  display.setCurrent(form);
          }

        protected void destroyApp( boolean unconditional )
                               throws MIDletStateChangeException{

          }
```

```
// #3
public void commandAction(Command cmd, Displayable dsp){
    if(cmd == startCmd){
        form.deleteAll();
        canvas = new GSCanvas(display, form);
        display.setCurrent( canvas);
        System.out.println("startCmd");
    }
    if (cmd == exitCmd){
        try{
            destroyApp(true);
            notifyDestroyed();
        }catch(Exception e){
            e.toString();
        }
    }
}
protected void pauseApp(){
}
}
```

Definition and Construction

In the lines associated with comment #1, you define a series of class attributes that involve identifiers of the Form, Display, and Command types. You also declare an attribute of the ImageItem type (splash) to accommodate a drawing used for the splash screen. In addition, you declare an attribute of the GSCanvas type (canvas). This attribute becomes a major feature in the life of the application.

In the lines immediately preceding comment #1.1, you create instances of the Form and Display classes and then assign them to the appropriate class attributes. In the lines following comment #1.1, you create an instance of the GSCanvas class. The constructor for the GSCanvas requires two arguments, the first of the Display type, and the second of the Form type. As the discussion of the GSCanvas reveals, references to these two objects are needed to process the messages that allow the user to exit the event context sustained by the GSCanvas class and re-enter the event context sustained in the Form class.

After creating the Command objects needed to control entry to and exit from the application, in the lines associated with comment #1.2 you create an instance of the ImageItem class and assign it to the splash attribute. The file that provides the

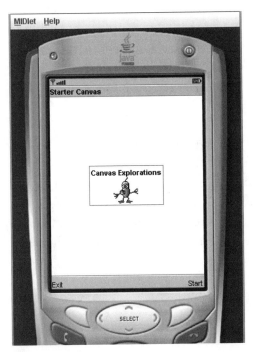

Figure 13.9
The Alien-bird.gif file provides a drawing for the splash screen.

drawing for the splash object is called Alien-bird.gif. The createImage() method of the Image class is able to use such formats as GIF and PNG to generate an image, and the result is assigned to the image attribute. Having created the Image object, you then assign it to the splash attribute for display by calling the set-Image() method. After you call the Form::append() method and use the splash attribute as its argument, the splash screen can be brought to life.

The actual moment of appearance for the splash screen is occasioned by the lines accompanying comment #2, where the startApp() method is defined. The one active line of code in the method is a call to the Form::setCurrent() method, which calls the Form object defined into the constructor into view. Figure 13.9 illustrates the result.

The Splash Screen

The splash screen provides only a momentary pausing place. In the lines following comment #3 of the GameStart class, you process the startCmd and exitCmd messages. The startCmd message calls the deleteAll() method of the Form class, which clears command definitions made so far. On the next line, the constructor of the GSCanvas class is called. Provided with arguments of the Display and Form types, it serves to create a GSCanvas reference that is assigned to the canvas attribute.

GSCanvas

The GSCanvas class provides a large variety of event-processing capabilities, in addition to other features, such as a Thread object and double buffering of images. To use the GSCanvas class, you require an entrance point; this is provided by the GameStart class, which has been discussed already. The code for the GSCanvas class is located in the Chapter 13 source folder, in the NetBeans Chapter13MIDlets project. It is also available in the standalone folder. Here is the code for the class.

```
/*
* Chapter 13 \ GSCanvas.java
*
*/


import javax.microedition.midlet.*;
import javax.microedition.lcdui.*;
import java.util.*;

// #1
public class GSCanvas extends Canvas implements Runnable, CommandListener{
    // #1.1
    private Random random;
    private Graphics buffer;
    private Image movingImage;
    private Image bufferImage;
    private int imageID;
    private String imageNames[] = new String[4];
    private final int SPEED = 4;
    private int imageXPos;
    private int imageYPos;
    private int positionChange;
    private int speedOfMove;
    private int color;
    private int imageColor;
    private boolean moveFlag;
    private String option3;
    private Command exitCmd;
    private Display display;
```

```
private Thread thread;
private Form form;
private final int CDIV=3;

public GSCanvas(Display start, Form stform){
    // #2
        form = stform;
        display = start;
        imageXPos = getWidth()/2;
        imageYPos = getHeight()/2;
        random = new Random( System.currentTimeMillis() );
        speedOfMove = SPEED;
        imageID = 0;
        moveFlag = false;
        option3 = new String("Off");
        // #2.1 Load the images
        setImages();
        // #2.2
        color = makeColor(0);
        imageColor = makeColor(1);


        makeImage(getImage(0));

        // #2.3
        exitCmd = new Command("Exit", Command.EXIT, 1);
        this.addCommand(exitCmd);
        this.setCommandListener(this);

        // #2.4
        thread = new Thread(this, "Game Thread");
        thread.start();

}

// #3
private void setImages(){
    imageNames[0]= "/Paca.gif";
    imageNames[1]= "/WhiteRhino.gif";
    imageNames[2]= "/Zebra.gif";
    imageNames[3]= "/Addax.gif";
}
```

```
// #3.1
private String getImage(int iNum){
    String gImage;
    if(iNum < imageNames.length){
        gImage = imageNames[iNum];
    }else{
        gImage = imageNames[0];
    }
    return gImage;
}


// #4
public void makeImage(String imageName){
    bufferImage = null;
    movingImage = null;
    try{
        if( isDoubleBuffered() == false ){
            bufferImage = Image.createImage( getWidth(),
                                              getHeight() );
            buffer = bufferImage.getGraphics();
        }
        movingImage = Image.createImage(imageName);
    }catch( Exception e ){
    }
}//end makeImage()

// #5
public void run(){
    while( true ){
        int delayOfLoop = 1000 / 20;
        long loopStartTime = System.currentTimeMillis();
        runGame();
        long loopEndTime   = System.currentTimeMillis();
        int loopTime = (int)(loopEndTime - loopStartTime);
        if( loopTime < delayOfLoop ){
            try{
                thread.sleep( delayOfLoop - loopTime );
            }catch( Exception e ){
                e.toString();
            }
        }
    }
}// end run()
```

```
// #6
public void runGame(){
      checkBoundries();
      switch( positionChange ){
            case LEFT:
                imageXPos -= speedOfMove;
            break;
            case RIGHT:
                imageXPos += speedOfMove;
            break;
            case UP:
                 imageYPos -= speedOfMove;
            break;
            case DOWN:
                 imageYPos += speedOfMove;
            break;
      }
      repaint();
      serviceRepaints();
}// end tick()

// #6.1
void checkBoundries(){
      if(imageXPos < 20 ){
         imageXPos = 21;
       }
       if(imageXPos > this.getWidth()){
          imageXPos  = this.getWidth()-1;
       }
        if(imageYPos < 40 ){
          imageYPos = 41;
       }
       if(imageYPos > this.getHeight()){
          imageYPos  = this.getHeight() -1;
       }
   }

// #7 Repaint the Canvas object
 protected void paint( Graphics g ){
      Graphics buffContext = g;
      if( !isDoubleBuffered() )
      {
          g = buffer;
```

```
        }
        g.setColor( color );

        g.fillRect( 0, 0, this.getWidth(), this.getHeight() );

        g.setColor(imageColor);
        // #7.1
        g.drawArc(imageXPos - movingImage.getWidth()/2,
                imageYPos - movingImage.getHeight()/2,
                movingImage.getWidth(),
                movingImage.getHeight(),180, 360);

        g.fillArc(imageXPos - movingImage.getWidth()/2,
                imageYPos - movingImage.getHeight()/2,
                movingImage.getWidth(),
                movingImage.getHeight(),180, 360);
        // #7.2
        g.drawImage( movingImage, imageXPos, imageYPos,
                Graphics.VCENTER | Graphics.HCENTER );

        if( !isDoubleBuffered() ) {
            buffContext.drawImage( bufferImage, 0, 0,
                                Graphics.TOP | Graphics.LEFT );
        }

        // #7.3   Draw Divisions
        drawDivisons(g);

        // #7.4
        showPosition(g);


        // #7.5
        detectCollision(g);
    }// end paint()

// 7.6
void drawDivisons(Graphics g){
        g.setColor(   0, 0, 255);
        g.setStrokeStyle(Graphics.DOTTED);
        g.drawLine(0, this.getHeight()/CDIV, this.getWidth(),
                this.getHeight()/CDIV);
```

```
        g.drawLine(0, 2 * this.getHeight()/CDIV, 2 * this.getWidth(),
                   2 * this.getHeight()/CDIV);

        g.drawLine(this.getWidth()/CDIV, 0,   this.getWidth()/CDIV,
                   this.getHeight());

        g.drawLine(2 * this.getWidth()/CDIV, 0,
                   2 * this.getWidth()/CDIV,
                   2 * this.getHeight());
      }

// #7.7
void showPosition(Graphics g){
        g.setColor(0xf0fff0) ;
        String xCoord = String.valueOf(imageXPos);
        String yCoord = String.valueOf(imageYPos);
        g.setColor(0xf8f8ff) ;
        g.fillRect( 0, 0, this.getWidth(), 20 );
        g.setColor(0x0f0f0f) ;
        g.drawString("Position: x:" + xCoord + "\t y: "
                                    + yCoord , 0, 0, 0);
        g.drawString("Option 3: " +
                     option3, 2 * this.getWidth()/CDIV, 0, 0);
}// end showPosition()

// #7.8
void detectCollision(Graphics g){
         String message = new String();
         if(imageXPos < this.getWidth()/CDIV &&
            imageYPos < this.getHeight()/CDIV){
            message = "Top Left.";
         }
         if(imageXPos > 2 * this.getWidth()/CDIV &&
            imageYPos < this.getHeight()/CDIV){
            message = "Top Right.";
         }
         if(imageXPos < this.getWidth()/CDIV &&
            imageYPos > 2 * this.getHeight()/CDIV){
            message = "Lower Left.";
         }
         if(imageXPos > 2 * this.getWidth()/CDIV &&
            imageYPos > 2 * this.getHeight()/CDIV){
            message = "Lower Right.";
```

```
        }
        if(   ( imageXPos  > this.getWidth()/CDIV &&
               imageXPos < 2 * this.getWidth()/CDIV )
            &&
            ( imageYPos  > this.getHeight()/CDIV &&
               imageYPos < 2 * this.getHeight()/CDIV )
          ){
            message = "In the center.";
        }
        g.drawString(message, 0, this.getHeight()/2, 0);
    }//


    // #8
    protected void keyPressed(int keyCode) {
        if (keyCode > 0 && keyCode != 5) {
            System.out.println("keyPressed "
            + ((char)keyCode));
        // #8.1 ======================================
            switch((char)keyCode){

                case '1':
                    imageColor = makeColor(1);
                break;
                case '3':
                    if(moveFlag == false){
                        moveFlag = true;
                        option3 = "On";
                    }else{
                        moveFlag = false;
                        option3 = "Off";
                    }
                break;
                case '5':
                    color = makeColor(1);
                break;
                case '7':
                    //Change image
                    imageID++;
                    if(imageID > 3 ){
                        imageID = 0;
                    }
                    System.out.println("Inside 7"
                                    + ((char)keyCode));
```

```java
                makeImage(getImage(imageID));
            break;
            case '9':
                //Reset background
                color = makeColor(0);
            break;

        }// end switch
    //============================================
    }else{
        System.out.println("keyPressed action "
                            + getGameAction(keyCode));
    // #8.2 ===================================
      int gameAction = getGameAction( keyCode );
        switch( gameAction ){
            case LEFT:
                positionChange = LEFT;
            break;
            case RIGHT:
                positionChange = RIGHT;
            break;
            case UP:
                positionChange = UP;
            break;
                case DOWN:
                positionChange = DOWN;
            break;
    }//end switch
    //============================================
  }
}//end keyPressed

// #9
protected void keyReleased( int keyCode )
 {
        //Continuous movement
        if(moveFlag == false){
            positionChange = 0;
        }
 }// end keyReleased

// #10
private int makeColor(int clr ){
```

```
        int colorVal = 0;
        if (clr == 0){
            colorVal =  0xf0fff0 ;
        }
        if(clr == 1){
            colorVal = random.nextInt()&0xFFFFFF;
        }
        return colorVal;
    }// end makeColor()

    // #11
    public void commandAction(Command c, Displayable s){
        display.setCurrent(form);
        form.append("Game over.");
    }
}// end class
```

GSCanvas Definition and Construction

When the user presses the button corresponding to the Start command in the Form object the GameStart MIDlet provides, an instance of the GSCanvas class is created and the user enters into the event context sustained by the GSCanvas event handlers. To make this possible, immediately following comment #1 in the signature line of the GSCanvas class, you extend the Canvas class and implement the Runnable and CommandListener interfaces. The Runnable interface makes it necessary to implement the run() method. The GSCanvas class supports an instance of the Thread class, and when the Thread object is used to call the start() method, the run() method is also called. In addition to the use of a Thread, this implementation of the Canvas class requires you to implement the paint() method, and the Command-Listener interface requires to you implement the commandAction() method.

A fairly extensive list of attributes is defined in the lines associated with comment #1.1 in the GSCanvas class. The types of the attributes include Random, Graphics, Display, Form, and Image, among others. The Form and Image attributes accommodate references passed from the GameStart class through the GSCanvas constructor. The Random attribute allows you to generate colors for the background and the oval area that appears behind the drawings of the animals. You also create an array of the String type, which is used to store the names of files that provide drawings of animals. A number of attributes of the int type are used to process coordinate values and key events. One attribute of the int type is qualified with the final keyword, making it a constant. It is assigned a value of 4, which governs the speed of animation.

The constructor for the GSCanvas class is defined in the lines following comment #2. First the values obtained from the argument list of the constructor are assigned to the form and display attributes. The references to the Form and Display attributes of the GameStart class make it possible to return to the starter Form object and exit the MIDlet from there.

After attending to the Form and Display objects, you call the getWidth() and getHeight() methods of the Display class to capture the dimensions of the display. You divide the returned values of the methods by 2 and assign the results to the imageXPos and imageYPos attributes. Together, these allow you to position graphical objects in the center of the display.

You then create an instance of the Random class. As a seed time to the Random constructor, you make use of the System::currentTimeMillis() method, which returns a fairly substantial number representing the millisecond value of the current date. You then initialize a few of the attributes that process the events of the GSCanvas class and call a number of GSCanvas methods that are discussed in subsequent sections of this chapter.

Beyond the calls to the methods defined in the GSCanvas class, you close out the work in the constructor by creating an instance of the Command class and assigning it to the exitCmd attribute. This is the Exit command. You call the addCommand() and setCommandListener() methods to initiate event handling for the GSCanvas class. Note that the commandAction() method, which handles the message issued by the Exit command, is implemented in the lines trailing comment #11. There, you use the reference to the Display object passed to the constructor of the GSCanvas class to invoke the setCurrent() method. This method takes as its argument the Form reference passed to the constructor of the GSCanvas. Having exited the GSCanvas context, you are in effect back where you started and call the append() method to display the message "Game over."

Files, Images, and Colors

Four methods called in the context of the GSCanvas constructor are setImages(), makeImage(), getImage(), and makeColor(). The setImages() method is defined in the lines associated with comment #3, where the imageNames array is assigned the names of four GIF files that provide illustrations of animals. Use of the GIF file type provides a contrast to approaches shown in this book involving PNG files. When the files you use are to be displayed without being changed, then the GIF format presents no difficulties. Where rendering of the graphics requires clipping or transformation, it is in some respects preferable to use the PNG file type.

The getImage() method is defined in the lines following comment #3.1. The primary responsibility of this method is to extract file names from the imageNames array. This method takes one argument of the int type. It checks to ensure that the value of the argument is less than the length of the imageNames array. If this proves true, it returns a file name corresponding to the index identified. If the number is outside the range, then it always returns the file name that corresponds to index 0, in this case paca.gif.

Called in the constructor in the line following comment #2.2, the makeColor() method is defined in the lines trailing comment #10. This method is responsible for generating either a fixed or a random color value. It takes an argument of the int type and also returns a value of the int type. The argument directs the method to perform one of two actions. If the argument submitted to the method is 0, then the method assigns the hexadecimal value 0xF0FFF0 to the colorVal attribute. This color is used for the background when the GSCanvas object is first constructed. If the value submitted as an argument to the method is 1, then the random attribute is used to call the nextInt() method to generate a random integer value. The value returned is joined using the AND bit operator with the value of 0xffffffff, which results in a background color.

Perhaps the most complex method of those initially called in the GSCanvas constructor is the makeImages() method. This method takes an argument of the String type. The argument names a file suitable for creating an Image object. As the line associated with comment #2.2 shows, the getImage() method furnishes the value required as an argument by the makeImages() method.

The makeImage() method is defined in the lines following comment #4. Its primary responsibility is to create a double buffer if one is needed or can be used. To implement the method, you first assign null values to the bufferImage and movingImage attributes. You then set up a selection statement to determine whether the device works with double buffers. To accomplish this, you call the isDouble-Buffered() method. If the device does not provide double buffering, then it is necessary to create a buffer for the image. If this is not needed, then the Image object (movingImage) is created without a buffer using the createImage() method, and nothing more is needed. As has been noted elsewhere, a try block must wrap the call to the createImage() method.

The Runnable Interface and the Thread

Implementation of the Runnable interface requires that you define the run() method. This method is invoked when the Thread::start() method is called. In the GSCanvas constructor, a new Thread object is created in the lines immediately following comment #2.4. As Table 13.4 indicates, the constructor allows you to name the thread ("Game Thread" in this case) and to associate the Thread object with the GSCanvas object using the this keyword. Since the GSCanvas class implements the Runnable interface, you implement the run() method when you define it. The this keyword links the Thread object to the run() method of a Runnable class.

As Figure 13.10 illustrates, when you call the start() method of the Thread class within the scope of a class that implements the Runnable interface, the run() method is invoked. In a situation in which you implement a game loop, you can do so in the scope of the run() method. As the lines following comment #5 show, the run() method contains a while block set to run infinitely.

The while block is more than an infinite loop, however. Within it is embedded a selection statement that uses two measures of the system time to determine whether to call the Thread::sleep() method. The decision of whether to delay or force the action of the while loop to sleep is based on the value of a local

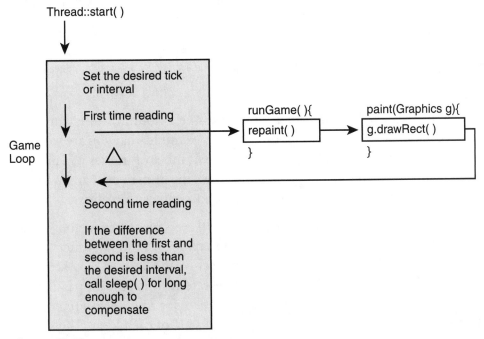

Figure 13.10
The run() method allows you to implement the game loop.

Table 13.4 Thread Methods and Values

Method/Value	Discussion
Thread()	The default Thread constructor.
Thread(Runnable)	Creates a thread that is associated with a specific object.
Thread(Runnable, String)	This constructor takes two arguments. The first is an object that implements the Runnable interface. The second is a String reference that names the thread.
Thread(String)	Creates a thread with a designated name.
void interrupt()	Interrupts the thread.
boolean isAlive()	Returns a value of the boolean type that indicates whether the thread is alive.
void run()	If the class you are working with implements the Runnable interface, then you must implement this method. It is called automatically when the Thread object calls the start() method.
static void sleep(long)	This argument takes an argument of the long type that designates how long you want the thread to pause. When sleeping, the thread ceases to be active.
void start()	Activates a thread and, in turn, calls the run() method associated with a class in which you have implemented the Runnable interface.
String toString()	Retrieves the name of a thread, if you have assigned one.
static void yield()	Temporarily pauses the thread that calls it and allows other threads to execute.
setPriority(int)	Allows you to set a priority for a thread. See the following defined values.
MAX_PRIORITY	A value of the int type. The maximum priority you can assign to a thread.
MIN_PRIORITY	A value of the int type. The minimum priority you can assign to a thread.
NORM_PRIORITY	A value of the int type. The default priority assigned to a thread.

identifier, delayOfLoop. This identifier establishes the amount of time you want to allow for each iteration of the loop. Imagine, for example, that you are working with a film projector. Such a value determines the number of frames you are able to see each second. At around 15 frames per second, the human eye can no longer detect individual frames, so the world of animation comes to reality.

Still, it is important to recognize that the delayOfLoop identifier establishes an amount of time that is a *minimum* value, not a maximum value. In other words, the loop must run at least as slowly as the time set by the delayOfLoop identifier (1000/15—15 times each second). To regulate the rate at which the loop is allowed to repeat, you create two local identifiers, loopStartTime and loopEndTime. The first of these allows you to capture the time at the start of each loop. The second allows you to capture the time at the end of each loop. To capture the time, you use calls to the `System::currentTimeMillis()` method to set the values of the two identifiers.

After you assign a time value to `loopStartTime`, you invoke all the action the game needs to perform during the iteration of the loop. This is accomplished with a call to a single method, `runGame()`. The `runGame()` method in turn calls the `repaint()` method, and the `repaint()` method calls the `paint()` method, which renders visible the graphical features of the game. The calls to the `runGame()`, `repaint()`, and `paint()` methods (in addition to several others used for processing events) require a certain amount of time. By subtracting the value assigned to the `loopStartTime` identifier from the value assigned to the `loopEndTime` identifier, you arrive at a suitable value to assign to `loopTime`. This identifier is then evaluated to determine whether enough time has elapsed to justify allowing the next cycle of the game to execute.

If more time is needed, you use the `Thread` object to call the `sleep()` method. To the `sleep()` method you supply a value that delays the loop long enough to make it preserve the minimum rate of change (or frame rate) established by the value assigned to the `delayOfLoop` identifier.

Key Values and Events

As a part of the `run()` method, you make a call to the `runGame()` method. Implemented in the lines following comment #6, this method performs two basic actions. As Figure 13.11 illustrates, since the `Image` object can be moved around the display area, the first action is to call the `checkBoundries()` method, which audits the position of the `Image` object to determine when it has reached the boundary of the display area. (The `checkBoundries()` method is defined in the lines associated with comment #6.1.) The second action of the `runGame()` method is to audit the current value assigned to the `positionChange` attribute to determine which event has been issued by the SELECT button. The value of the `positionChange` attribute is set in two or three places in the lines of the class. The values assigned to it can be either 0 or one of the four defined values for direction provided by the `Canvas` class: `UP`, `DOWN`, `LEFT`, and `RIGHT`. (See the sidebar "Using Key Codes" for more information on key codes.)

A value is assigned to the `positionChange` attribute when you press one of the direction arrows on the SELECT button. As is explained later, having pressed the button, the direction value is stored in the `positionChange` attribute. One of two actions can then occur, depending on the value assigned to the `positionChange`

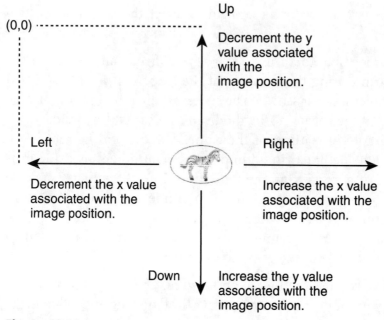

Figure 13.11
The x and y values that determine the position of the Image object are changed with each click of the
SELECT-button arrow keys.

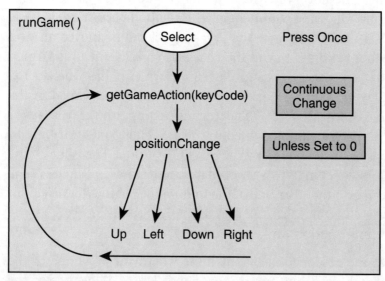

Figure 13.12
Motion can be set to be continuous.

attribute by the key actions. If it is allowed to retain the value of the direction pressed (one of the SELECT arrows, for example), then the affected object moves continuously. If the value of `positionChanged` is cancelled out (by the release of the key, for example), then the object does not move continuously. Figure 13.12 illustrates this activity.

Using Key Codes

In the `GSCanvas` class, event processing from keys is managed using character values. The standard approach is to use the constant values provided by the key codes. These values are defined in the `Canvas` class. Table 13.5 provides a selection of these defined values. To process the game action key codes, you call the `getGameAction()` method. To process the default keys, you can, among other things, call the `keyPressed()` or `keyReleased()` methods. In the `GSCanvas` class, having been retrieved by the `keyPressed()` method, the key values are cast to the `char` type before being processed. You can also simply process the integer value.

Table 13.5 Key Event Codes

Key Event	Description
Default Keys	
KEY_NUM0	Numerical keypad 0
KEY_NUM1	Numerical keypad 1
KEY_NUM2	Numerical keypad 2
KEY_NUM3	Numerical keypad 3
KEY_NUM4	Numerical keypad 4
KEY_NUM5	Numerical keypad 5
KEY_NUM6	Numerical keypad 6
KEY_NUM7	Numerical keypad 7
KEY_NUM8	Numerical keypad 8
KEY_NUM9	Numerical keypad 9
KEY_POUND	#
KEY_STAR	*
Keys Associated with Game Actions	
UP	Up arrow
DOWN	Down arrow
LEFT	Left arrow
RIGHT	Right arrow
FIRE	A fire button
GAME_A	Game function A
GAME_B	Game function B
GAME_C	Game function C
GAME_D	Game function D

Different Messages and Keys

In the lines associated with comment #8, the keyPressed() method of the Canvas class is implemented. The implementation of this method in this context involves processing two types of values. One type relates to the SELECT key. The other type relates to the keypad numbers. To process the values, you set up an if selection statement that tests the raw integer values passed through the keyCode identifier to determine which type they correspond to. If the message is from the keyboard, then you cast it to a char value and test it against a char constant (such as "1"). The specific char values you test are 1, 3, 5, 7, and 9. Table 13.5 provides a summary of the actions associated with each selection.

On the other hand, if the value the keyPressed() method tests is issued by the SELECT button, then as the lines following comment #8.2 reveal, you call the getGameAction() method to filter the message so that it can be recognized as a game action message. Such actions can be tested against the defined game action values of LEFT, RIGHT, UP, and DOWN. If any one of these values is generated, then its value is assigned to the positionChange attribute, which, as noted before, is used in the runGame() method to determine the direction in which the central picture (or sprite) in the game moves.

The work of determining how to handle specific events generated by keys begins at comment #8.1 with the processing of the case for 1. Here, you call the makeColor() method and provide it with an argument of 1. This argument causes the method to generate random color values that are assigned to the imageColor attribute. This attribute controls the color of the arc (oval) that lies behind the picture of the animal. Processing of the case for 3 is along the same lines as the case for 1 and resembles processing for the case for 5, with the exception that when the randomly generated color attribute is applied, the general background of the display area is affected.

One other call is made to the makeColor() method, in association with the case for 9. In this instance, the argument furnished to the method is 0. As mentioned previously, an argument of 0 to the makeColor() method causes the method to return a default color value. Assigned to the color attribute, this allows the user to reset the background to a color that makes the picture in the center to stand out readily.

The case for 7 makes use of the imageID attribute, incrementing it with each press of the 7 key through a range extending from 0 to 3. When the maximum is reached, the value of imageID is reset to 0. As the range is traversed, the values are fed to the getImage() method, and the returned value of the getImage() method is then used as an argument to the makeImage() method. The result is that with each press of the 7 key, a different picture of an animal is displayed.

Processing the event generated by the 3 key involves turning on and off a switch that allows the picture to continue moving after the user presses the SWITCH button. The flow of this activity is illustrated by Figure 13.12. In effect, if the user presses the 3 key the value of the moveFlag attribute is changed. When this flag is set to false (off), then as is evident in the lines associated with comment #9, the positionChange attribute is set to 0 with each release of a key.

When the positionChange attribute is set to 0, as the lines associated with comment #6 show, the picture can be moved only with successive presses of the SELECT button. When it is not set to 0, this is not the case. The loop continues to increment the value associated with the last SELECT event. (Again, see Figure 13.12.)

Painting and Repainting

In addition to allowing the user to change the position of the Image object in the display, the runGame() method calls two central methods of the Graphics class. The first is the repaint() method. The repaint() method calls the paint() method. The paint() method causes the Canvas area to be refreshed, erasing—unless told otherwise—all that has been painted previously. It is the action of the paint() method that allows you to change the appearance of the Canvas and create animated applications. In most cases, such changes involve things like pictures (images) selected for display, painting the text, or painting the geometrical forms.

Recall that since the GSCanvas class extends the Canvas class, it must implement the paint() method. Calling the repaint() method has the effect of requesting the Graphics object to schedule invocation of the paint() method. In other words, not every call of the repaint() method is necessarily immediately processed. To force the paint() method to execute, you also call the service-Repaints() method, which clears the queue of requested paint events.

As Figure 13.13 illustrates, the run(), repaint(), and paint() methods (with some help from the serviceRepaints() method) constitute the central set of methods used for rendering the visual effects you see displayed on the Canvas object. The Thread and Runnable classes support the run() method, and the Canvas class provides the paint(), repaint(), and serviceRepaints() methods. You associate the Thread object with the Canvas class by using the this keyword in the constructor for the Thread object (as mentioned previously). You can use

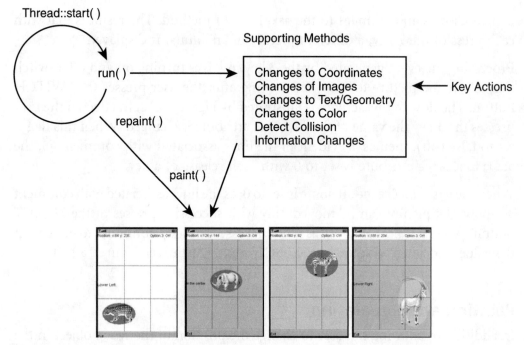

Figure 13.13
You can call the paint() method from the run() method to constantly refresh the Canvas display area.

an intermediary method within the run() method, such as runGame(), to remove clutter from the run() method.

The paint() method of the GSCanvas class is implemented in the lines associated with comment #7. As is evident in the lines associated with comments #7.1 and #7.2, most of the calls to methods made in the scope of the paint() method involve the use of the Graphics object or values that are defined through either keyboard actions or as default settings. The work of the methods associated with the Graphics class has been covered earlier in this chapter. The only exception to what has been discussed previously is the use of the selection statements to confirm the buffer status of the display area. If the display area is not double buffered, then a buffer is provided.

Boundaries, Coordinates, and Collisions

In the lines trailing comment #7.3 you call the drawDivisons() method, which is implemented in the lines associated with comment #7.6. The definition of this method begins with a call to the setColor() method, which provides the color used for the division lines. To accommodate the setColor() and other Graphics methods, the `drawDivisons()` method must accept an argument of the `Graphics` type. (This approach to refactoring the activities associated with the `paint()` method is also used with the other two methods discussed in the current section.)

After setting the color, you then call the `setStrokeStyle()` method to designate, using the `Graphics.DOTTED` value, that the lines drawn are to be dotted. After that, with four calls to the `drawLine()` method of the `Graphics` class, you draw the lines that divide the display area into six rectangles. To draw the lines, the `CDIV` attribute is used to set the distances between and lengths of the lines. This value has been set to 3. The `getWidth()` and `getHeight()` methods of the `Display` class are used to obtain the information about the display needed to position the lines.

In the lines associated with comment #7.4 in the `GSCanvas` class, you call the `showPosition()` method. This method is implemented in the lines associated with comment #7.7. It provides the coordinate position associated with the drawing of the animal that is painted to the display area. It also furnishes information on the drawing status. To implement the method, you first set the background color using the `setColor()` method. You then obtain the coordinate values. The coordinate values are provided by the `imageXPos` and `imageYPos` attributes. Calls to the `String::valueOf()` method are needed to convert the `int` values obtained from these attributes into `String` references that can be used as arguments to the `drawString()` method. You call the `drawString()` method twice, first to show the positions of the two coordinates, then to show whether the option toggled by the 3 key is on or off.

At comment #7.5 within the `paint()` method, you call the `detectCollision()` method. This method is defined in the lines that follow comment #7.8. The work of this method involves using five selection statements to evaluate whether the coordinate values supplied by the `imageXPos` and `imageYPos` attributes fall into certain regions of the display. To understand how the regions are defined, as shown in Figure 13.14, it can be helpful to picture the area of the display in terms given by the values retuned by the `getWidth()` and `getHeight()` methods and the value assigned to the `CDIV` attribute.

To set the detection values that define the upper left area, for example, it is necessary to create a compounded `AND` statement that takes the following form:

```
if(imageXPos < this.getWidth()/CDIV &&
             imageYPos < this.getHeight()/CDIV){
             message = "Top Left.";
}
```

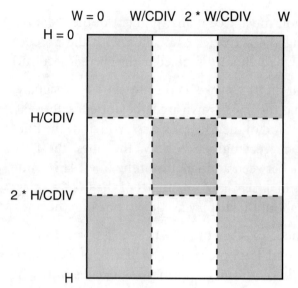

Figure 13.14
The active areas mapped for collision detection are identified using standard divisions.

The position defined is less than one third (CDIV is defined as 3) from the left edge and less than one third from the top. Other areas of detection require more extensive definitions to account for multiple division, but the strategy is the same.

Conclusion

In this chapter, you have explored the Canvas and Graphics classes, along with the Thread class, and implemented some of the functionality that often is found in games. The explorations in this chapter involve only the standard GUI classes, not those in the Game API. While implementing the game using the standard GUI classes tends to be cumbersome, it remains that working with them prepares you to more fully explore the features of the Game API. In many respects, this is the best approach because the features the Game API classes inherit are often those that have been initially provided in the interface of such classes as Canvas. Given the explorations offered in this chapter, you can proceed with confidence into work with the Game API.

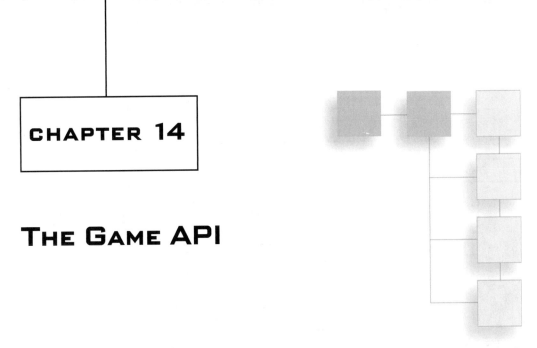

CHAPTER 14

THE GAME API

In this chapter you explore a few of the features of the MIDP Game API, which provides a number of components that allow you to readily implement games with relatively few lines of code. The Game API provides you with the Layer, LayerManager, GameCanvas, TiledLayer, and Sprite classes. The FacePlay class allows you to explore a few features of the GameCanvas, Sprite, and TiledLayer classes. The features you consider include messaging capabilities, frame sequences, transformation, layering, and painting, among others. Additional services extend to collision detection among Sprites and the ability to flush or clear specific regions of the GameCanvas object. Generally, the Game API offers an excellent set of tools for crafting games in a straightforward, convenient way. While the standard GUI classes remain an essential part of the work, you soon see that use of the Game API offers many useful extensions that tremendously augment your game efforts to develop games involving graphically oriented, rather than textually oriented, activities.

The Game API

Figure 14.1 provides a review of the class diagram for the classes that constitute the Game API and a few of the classes in the LCDUI package. The most important relationship between the two groups is that between the Canvas and GameCanvas classes. The GameCanvas class, like the Canvas and Form classes, provides

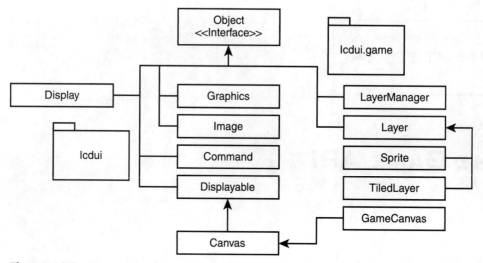

Figure 14.1
The specialized version of the Canvas class that the Game API provides allows you to work readily with a number of game features.

a convenient context in which to implement the display features of a game. Among other things, it readily accommodates objects of the Sprite and Tiled-Layer classes, both of which are derived from the Layer class. While both of the classes have similar uses, the TiledLayer class proves more suitable for managing background features, while the Sprite class offers an interface that readily accommodates such foreground activities as collision detection.

GameCanvas

The primary responsibility of the GameCanvas class is to allow you to manage the objects you display during the life of a game and the key events that you use to change those objects. While it offers only five new methods beyond those provided by the Canvas class, these methods are all extraordinarily helpful. For example, the getGraphics() method enables you to implement calls to Graphics methods without also having to center your activities using the paint() method. The getKeyStates() method provides a refined approach to processing messages. The flushGraphics() method is overloaded to enable you to render the contents of a selected region. With respect to message processing, as the discussion in Table 14.1 reveals, the GameCanvas class also furnishes a set of defined values that can be handled by the getKeyStates() method.

Table 14.1 Selected GameCanvas Class Features

Feature	Description
protected GameCanvas(boolean)	Creates a new instance of the GameCanvas class. The argument is of the boolean type and designates whether the GameCanvas object is to process key events. If set to false, it processes no events.
void flushGraphics()	Renders the entire area associated with the GameCanvas object.
void flushGraphics (x, y, int, int)	Renders the area designated to the display. The first two arguments are the coordinates of the upper left corner of the rectangular areas to be cleared. The third argument is the width of the area. The final argument is the height.
protected Graphics getGraphics()	Returns a Graphics object suitable for rendering graphics for a GameCanvas.
int getKeyStates()	Processes events generated by the keys named for game events. See the list below.
void paint(Graphics)	Serves the same role as the method of the same name in the Canvas class. This method paints GameCanvas.
static int DOWN_PRESSED	Associated with the DOWN key.
static int FIRE_PRESSED	Associated with the FIRE key.
static int GAME_A_PRESSED	Associated with the GAME_A key.
static int LEFT_PRESSED	Associated with the LEFT key.
static int RIGHT_PRESSED	Associated with the RIGHT key.
static int UP_PRESSED	Associated with the UP key.

The Sprite Class and Frame Sequences

The Sprite class allows you to manage Image objects. The constructors for the Sprite class allow you to create a Sprite object by using either an Image object or a Sprite object. If you create a Sprite object with an Image object, one of the constructors allows you to define the frame sequence of the object as you define it. In addition, the Sprite class provides the setTransform() and collidesWith() methods. The setTransform() method uses a number of defined values from the Sprite class to allow you to rotate and flip the Image object the Sprite embodies. The collidesWith() method allows you to detect whether one Sprite object is colliding with another.

While accommodating and managing Image objects in situations involving rotation, flipping, and collision, the Sprite class also enables you to work with *frames*. A frame is analogous to a cell in a table. As Figure 14.2 illustrates, a given picture or drawing (an Image object) can be divided into a set of frames, all the same size. Each frame in the set of frames is identified by frameWidth and frameHeight properties. One way to create such a set of frames is to use one of the

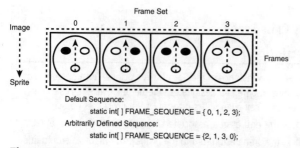

Figure 14.2
The frames of a given image are analogous to cells in a table or indexed elements in an array.

overloaded Sprite constructors, which allows you to furnish an Image and then the height and width dimensions you want to apply to it.

When you use a set of frames, you identify them with indexes. Each frame is associated with a unique index. In this way, a set of frames has a *sequence*. For example, in Figure 14.2, you see a sequence of four frames, each containing one face, and the *default frame sequence* begins at frame 0 and extends to frame 3. If the total size of the image of the four faces is 200 by 55 pixels, then each frame in the frame set is identified by a dimension of 50 (frameWidth) by 55 (frameHeight). If you use the default sequence of frames, then the face on the left is associated with index 0. As you move through the frame sequence, you move through its "horizontal" dimension, from one face frame to the next, until you reach frame 3.

The default sequence is not the only sequence. In fact, you can set any sequence you want by using a unique frame sequence array. As Figure 14.2 illustrates, you tell the Sprite object how to define the sequence by defining an array of the int type and populating it with a set of values that establishes the sequence in which you want the frames in the frame set to be accessed for display. The sequence you associate with a Sprite replaces the default sequence.

To associate a frame sequence with a Sprite, you call the Sprite::setFrame-Sequence() method. This method takes one argument, a reference to the sequence array. Then, to access the frames as defined by the frame sequence, you call one of three basic methods provided by the Sprite class. As Table 14.2 reveals, these are the setFrame(), prevFrame(), and nextFrame() methods. The first two of these methods take no arguments and each time they are called they move what might be viewed as a *frame pointer*. The pointer moves through the sequence to the next or previous frame with each new method call. In this respect, the prevFrame() and nextFrame() methods pose the danger of memory access violation. For this reason, the setFrame() method is useful.

Table 14.2 Sprite Methods and Properties

Method	Description
Sprite(Image)	Creates a new instance of the Sprite class. It takes an argument of the Image type. The Image object you use as an argument determines the size.
Sprite(Image, int, int)	Creates an instance of the Sprite class and defines the dimensions of the frame of the Sprite. Its first is argument is of the Image type. The Image object you use as an argument is sized according to the dimensions given by the second and third arguments. The second argument sets the width. The third argument sets the height.
Sprite(Sprite)	Takes another Sprite object as an argument. This allows you to easily duplicate Sprite objects. It produces an exact copy.
boolean collidesWith (Image, int, int, boolean)	Allows you to detect collision with a given Image object. The first argument is of the Image type and identifies the Image object with which collisions can occur. The second and third arguments identify the Sprite object to be detected. The final argument is the pixel level of the target object. If set to false, the detection takes place through evaluation of pixel values.
boolean collidesWith (Sprite, boolean)	Allows you to detect collision with a given Sprite object. The first argument is of the Sprite type and identifies the Sprite object with which collisions can occur. The second argument is the pixel level of the target object.
boolean collidesWith (TiledLayer, boolean)	Allows you to detect collision with a given Sprite object. The first argument is of the TiledLayer type and identifies the Sprite object with which collisions can occur. The second argument is the pixel level of the target object.
void defineCollisionRectangle (int, int, int, int)	Allows you to detect collision with the bounding box of a Sprite object. The first two arguments set the upper left corner of the bounding box. The third argument sets the width. The final argument sets the height.
void defineReferencePixel (int x, int y)	Designates a pixel within a Sprite object that you can use to define the position of the Sprite object. This provides you with an alternative to using the coordinates of the upper left corner. For this method, the two arguments designate the x- and y-coordinates to use to define the position of the Sprite object.
int getFrame()	Retrieves the current index in the frame sequence.
int getFrameSequenceLength()	Retrieves the number of elements in the frame sequence.
int getRawFrameCount()	Retrieves the number of raw frames for this Sprite.
int getRefPixelX()	Returns the horizontal position of the reference pixel of the Sprite object in the coordinate system of the painter.
int getRefPixelY()	Gets the vertical position of this Sprite's reference pixel in the painter's coordinate system.
void nextFrame()	Moves the frame pointer forward one position in the frame sequence that applies to the Sprite object.

(Continued)

Table 14.2 Continued

Method	Description
void paint(Graphics)	Draws the Sprite object. Note that you call this method using a reference to a Graphics object that you can retrieve with a call to the getGraphics() method of GameCanvas class. Painting of Sprites (and the Image objects they contain) does not require the implementation of a paint() method—as is the case with the Canvas class.
void prevFrame()	Moves the frame pointer backward one position in the frame sequence that applies to the Sprite object.
void setFrame(int)	Allows you to arbitrarily designate the position of the frame pointer in the frame sequence. The argument you supply designates which frame is to be accessed for display.
void setFrameSequence(int[])	The argument for this method is an array that you define. The array consists of integer values that define the sequence in which you want the frames in a frame set to be accessed.
void setImage(Image, int, int)	Allows you to initialize or replace the Image object associated with a Sprite. The first argument is a reference to the Image object you want to assign to the Sprite object. The last two arguments are the width and the height of the source image.
void setRefPixelPosition (int x, int y)	Sets the position of the Sprite object so that the coordinate pair used to position or detect the Sprite is set to an arbitrary position in the area defined for the Sprite.
void setTransform(int)	Allows you to transform the Sprite object using one of the defined values provided by the Sprite class definition. The defined values are all static int values. To find values that are not defined, divide the given value by integers. For example, TRANS_ROT90/2 transforms the Sprite object by 45 degrees.
TRANS_MIRROR	Reflects the Sprite image about its vertical center.
TRANS_MIRROR_ROT90	Reflects the Sprite image about its vertical center and rotates it clockwise 90 degrees.
TRANS_MIRROR_ROT180	Reflects the Sprite image about its vertical center and rotates it 180 degrees clockwise.
TRANS_MIRROR_ROT270	Reflects the Sprite image about its vertical center and rotates it 270 degrees clockwise.
TRANS_NONE	Makes the Sprite image appear as loaded.
TRANS_ROT90	Rotates the Sprite image clockwise 90 degrees.
TRANS_ROT180	Rotates the Sprite image 180 degrees clockwise.
TRANS_ROT270	Rotates the Sprite image 270 degrees clockwise.

The setFrame() method takes one argument, of the int type, and allows you to locate the pointer in the frame set without regard to sequence. That way, if you progress through the default sequence shown in Figure 14.2, then when you reach frame 3, you can call the setFrame() method to move back to frame 0. With the arbitrarily defined sequence, four calls in a series to the nextFrame() method move the pointer through the sequence established by 2, 1, 3, and 0, so when the pointer reaches 3, the setFrame() method can be called to reposition it to 0. As mentioned previously, Table 14.2 provides a summary of this method and other features of the Sprite class.

SpriteStart

The SpriteStart class furnishes a MIDlet entrance point for the SpritePlay class, which extends the GameCanvas class and implements the Runnable interface. The code for the SpriteStart class is located in the Chapter 14 source folder, it appears in the source folder for the NetBeans Chapter14MIDlets project and also in a standalone version in the Isolated Java Files folder. Here is the code for the SpriteStart class.

```
/*
 * Chapter 14 \ SpriteStart.java
 *
 */

import java.util.*;
import javax.microedition.lcdui.game.*;
import javax.microedition.midlet.*;
import javax.microedition.lcdui.*;

public class SpriteStart extends MIDlet{
        public void startApp(){
                SpritePlay game = new SpritePlay();
                Display.getDisplay(this).setCurrent(game);
                new Thread(game).start();
        }

        public void pauseApp(){
        }

        public void destroyApp(boolean uncon){
        }
}
```

Trimmed to the bare essentials, the SpriteStart class has two responsibilities. One is to create an instance of the SpritePlay class and assign it to the MIDlet Display object. The other is to create a thread and call the start() method of the

`Thread` object. The `start()` method calls the `run()` method in the `SpriteStart` object, which is overridden as part of the definition of the `SpriteStart` class. You can invoke the `start()` method because you use the version of the constructor for the `Thread` class that takes as an argument a reference to an object of the `Runnable` type. Since the `SpritePlay` class implements the `Runnable` interface, it is suitable as an argument to the `Thread` constructor.

SpritePlay

The `SpritePlay` class allows you to explore several features of the interfaces of the `Sprite` and `GameCanvas` classes. It also offers a few lines to illustrate the use of the `TiledLayer` class. The features of the `SpritePlay` class definition are kept to a minimum so that it is easy to explore such activities as using frame sets and working with collision detection and transformation. Figure 14.3 provides a view of a session with the `SpritePlay` class.

The faces you see in Figure 14.3 represent the implementation of the faces shown in shown in Figure 14.2, but only the image on the left is generated using a

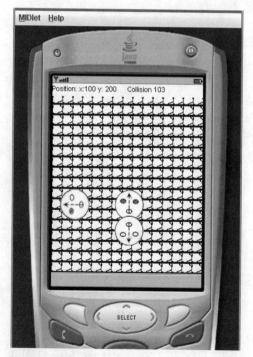

Figure 14.3
A collision event retrieves a frame from a sequence of frames and rotates the result by 45 degrees.

frame set. The other two are created by using Sprite objects that contain single images that feature one face only. This approach makes it easier for you to explore how to replace one Image or Sprite object with another.

In Figure 14.3, the face on the bottom is inverted because it is associated with key events that rotate it according to the direction of the SELECT button you have clicked. The face above it, in the center, displays dark eyes because its eyes begin to open and close whenever the object face on the bottom collides with it. To the left, you see a third face, this one rotated 45 degrees to the right. One of its eyes is closed. This face is taken from the frame sequence of four faces shown in Figure 14.2. It is also transformed (rotated) by using a simple calculation to customize the value provided by one of the default transformation properties the Sprite class furnishes.

In the background of the display shown in Figure 14.3, you see the work of a TiledLayer object. The abstract nature of the background allows you to see that a single tile within a TiledLayer array has been arbitrarily replicated across and downward over the display. To accomplish this, a for repetition statement is implemented that reads the contents of the TiledLayer in much the same way as you might read the contents of any two-dimensional array.

The SpritePlay class is included in the NetBeans Chapter14MIDlets project, which is included in the Chapter 14 code folder. You use it in conjunction with the SpriteStart class. Like the SpriteStart class, you can also find it in a standalone version in the Chapter 14 code folder. Here is the code for the SpritePlay class.

```
/*
 * Chapter 14 \ SpritePlay.java
 *
 */

import java.util.*;
import javax.microedition.lcdui.game.*;
import javax.microedition.midlet.*;
import javax.microedition.lcdui.*;

class SpritePlay extends GameCanvas implements Runnable{
        // #1
        private TiledLayer tlBackground = null;
        private int cols;
        private int rows;
        private int xPos;
```

```
        private int yPos;
        private Graphics graphics;
        private Image image;
        private Image otherImage;
        private Sprite spriteA;
        private Sprite spriteB;
        static int SPRITE_H_W = 48;
        static int GAME_TIME = 30;
        private boolean eventFlag;
        static int TILE_H_W = 16;
        static int WIDTH = 50;
        static int HEIGHT = 55;
        static int[] FRAME_SEQUENCE = { 1, 2, 3, 0};
        private Image facesImage;
        private Sprite facesSprite;

        private Random rNum;

    // #2
    public SpritePlay(){
        super(false);
        xPos = this.getWidth()/2;
        yPos = this.getHeight()/3;
        image = null;
        otherImage = null;
        eventFlag = true;
        rNum = new Random();

        // #2.1
        try{
            facesImage = Image.createImage("/FaceSet.png");
            facesSprite = new Sprite(facesImage, WIDTH, HEIGHT);
            facesSprite.setFrameSequence(FRAME_SEQUENCE);
        }catch (Exception ex){
            ex.toString();
        }

        // #2.2
        try{
            Image background = Image.createImage("/background.PNG");
            cols =  getWidth()/TILE_H_W;
            rows = getHeight()/TILE_H_W;
            /*
```

```
            System.out.println("Value of TILE_H_W: " + TILE_H_W);
            System.out.println("Pixel witdth of display: " + getWidth());
            System.out.println("Number of columns: " + getWidth()/TILE_H_W);
            System.out.println("Pixel height of display: " + getHeight());
            System.out.println("Number of rows: " + getHeight()/TILE_H_W);
        */
        tlBackground = new TiledLayer(cols, rows,
                                    background, TILE_H_W, TILE_H_W);


          //System.out.println("Number of rows: " +
        int tileCount = background.getWidth()/TILE_H_W;

        //System.out.println("Tile count " + tileCount);

        // #2.3
        drawSelectedTiles(tlBackground, false, tileCount);
        //drawSelectedTiles(tlBackground, true, tileCount);

        // #2.4
        //paintWallTilesOnly();

    }catch (Exception ex){
        ex.toString();
    }
}


// #3
public void run(){
    Graphics g = getGraphics();
    spriteA = createSprite("/Face.png", SPRITE_H_W, SPRITE_H_W);
    spriteB = createSprite("/OtherFace.png", SPRITE_H_W, SPRITE_H_W);
    spriteA.defineReferencePixel(3,3);
    spriteB.defineReferencePixel(0,0);

    // #3.1
    while (true){
            int keyState = getKeyStates();
            if ((keyState & UP_PRESSED) != 0) {
                yPos--;
                spriteA.setTransform(Sprite.TRANS_NONE);
            }else if ((keyState & RIGHT_PRESSED) != 0){
                xPos++;
                spriteA.setTransform(Sprite.TRANS_ROT90);
```

```
    }else if ((keyState & LEFT_PRESSED) != 0){
        xPos--;
        spriteA.setTransform(Sprite.TRANS_ROT270 );
    }else if ((keyState & DOWN_PRESSED) != 0){
        yPos++;
        spriteA.setTransform(spriteA.TRANS_MIRROR_ROT180);
    }

    // #3.2
    xPos = checkArea(xPos, true);
    yPos = checkArea(yPos, false);

    // #3.3
    spriteA.setPosition(xPos, yPos);

    spriteB.setPosition(this.getWidth()/2,
                        2 * this.getWidth()/3);

    /*
     System.out.println("facesSprite getX() (before set)" +
                         facesSprite.getX() );

     System.out.println("facesSprite getRefPixelX()" +
                         " (before set):" +
                         facesSprite.getRefPixelX() );
    facesSprite.setRefPixelPosition(facesSprite.getWidth()/2,
                                    facesSprite.getWidth()/2);
     System.out.println("facesSprite getRefPixelX() " +
                         " (after set):" +
                         facesSprite.getRefPixelX() );
     */
    facesSprite.setPosition(getWidth()/16,
                            2 * getWidth()/3);

    //   System.out.println("facesSprite getX() " +
    //                       "(after after ref pixel set)" +
    //                       facesSprite.getX() );

    clearScreen(g);
    // #3.4
    tlBackground.paint(g);
    spriteB.paint(g);
    spriteA.paint(g);
```

```
                  //facesSprite.setFrame(0);
                  //facesSprite.setFrame(1);
                  //facesSprite.setFrame(2);
                  facesSprite.setFrame(3);
                  facesSprite.paint(g);

                  // #3.5
                  showPosition();

                  // #3.6
                  changeSprites();

                  // #3.7
                  //detectWallTileCollision();

                  // #3.8
                  flushGraphics();

              try{
                Thread.currentThread().sleep(GAME_TIME);
              } catch (InterruptedException x){
              }
        }
  }


// #4
private void changeSprites(){

    if( spriteA.collidesWith(spriteB, true) ){
        this.reportEvent("Collision " + spriteA.getRefPixelX() );
        int num = rNum.nextInt(5);
        if(eventFlag == true){
            spriteB.setImage(createImage("/StrangeFace.png"),
                                        SPRITE_H_W, SPRITE_H_W );

            // #4.1
            if(num == 3){
                facesSprite.setTransform(Sprite.TRANS_ROT90/2);
            }
            facesSprite.nextFrame();
            eventFlag = false;
        }else{
            spriteB.setImage(createImage("/Face.png"),
                                        SPRITE_H_W, SPRITE_H_W );
```

```
                    eventFlag = true;
                    facesSprite.setFrame(2);
                    if(num == 2){
                        facesSprite.setTransform(Sprite.TRANS_ROT180/3);
                        facesSprite.setTransform(Sprite.TRANS_ROT270);
                    }
                }
            }
        }

    // #5
    public Graphics getGraphics(){
        return super.getGraphics();
    }


    // #6
    private Sprite createSprite(String fileName, int width, int height){
        Image tempImage = null;
        try{
            tempImage = Image.createImage(fileName);
        }catch (Exception ex){
            return null;
        }
        return new Sprite(tempImage, width, height);
    }


    // #7
    private Image createImage(String fileName) {
        Image tempImage = null;
        try{
            tempImage = Image.createImage(fileName);
        }catch (Exception ex){
            return null;
        }
        return tempImage;
    }


    // #8
    private void clearScreen(Graphics g){
        g.setColor(0xFFFFFF);
        g.fillRect(0, 0, getWidth(), getHeight());
    }
```

```
// #9
protected void showPosition(){
    Graphics g = getGraphics();
    g.setColor(0xf0fff0) ;
    String xCoord = String.valueOf(xPos);
    String yCoord = String.valueOf(yPos);
    g.setColor(0xf8f8ff) ;
    g.fillRect( 0, 0, this.getWidth(), 20 );
    g.setColor(0x0f0f0f) ;
    g.drawString("Position: x:" + xCoord + "\t y: "
                            + yCoord , 0, 0, 0);

}


// #10
protected void reportEvent(String event){
    Graphics g = getGraphics();
    g.setColor(0x0f0f0f) ;
    g.drawString(event, this.getWidth()/2, 0, 0);
}




// #11
private void drawSelectedTiles(TiledLayer tLayer,
                            boolean seeAll, int maxScrTiles){
    int srcTileNum = 1;
    for(int colcnt = 0; colcnt < tLayer.getColumns(); colcnt++){
        for(int rowcnt = 0; rowcnt < tLayer.getRows(); rowcnt++)
        {
            if(seeAll == true){
                srcTileNum++;
            }
            if( srcTileNum > maxScrTiles){
                srcTileNum = 0;
            }
            tlBackground.setCell(colcnt, rowcnt, srcTileNum);
        }
    }
}


// #12
private int checkArea(int crd, boolean isWidth){
```

```
            if (crd < 0){
                return 0;
            }
            if (isWidth && crd > getWidth()){
                return getWidth();
            }
            if (crd > getHeight()){
                return getHeight();
            }
            return crd;
        }

    // #13
    private void paintWallTilesOnly(){
            tlBackground.setCell(0, 0, 1);
            tlBackground.setCell(1, 1, 1);
            tlBackground.setCell(2, 2, 2);
            tlBackground.setCell(3, 3, 3);
            tlBackground.setCell(4, 4, 4);
            tlBackground.setCell(5, 5, 0);
            tlBackground.setCell(5, 5, 1);
            tlBackground.setCell(5, 6, 2);
            tlBackground.setCell(5, 7, 3);
            tlBackground.setCell(5, 8, 4);
            tlBackground.setCell(6, 5, 1);
            tlBackground.setCell(7, 5, 2);
            tlBackground.setCell(8, 5, 3);
            tlBackground.setCell(9, 5, 4);
    }


    // #14
    private void detectWallTileCollision(){
        if ( spriteA.collidesWith(tlBackground,true) ){
            reportEvent("Ran into a wall");
        }
    }
}//end class
```

Definition and Construction

As is evident from the signature line that precedes comment #1, the definition of the SpritePlay class extends the GameCanvas class and implements the Runnable interface. By extending the GameCanvas class, the SpritePlay class acquires the event handling capabilities furnished by the getKeyStates() method, which is discussed further along in the current chapter. By implementing the Runnable interface, the class gains access to the run() method, which houses the main animation (or game) loop. This activity is also discussed further along in this chapter.

In the lines following comment #1, a number of class attributes are defined. These include an attribute of the TiledLayer type (tlBackround) and a set of attributes of the int type that accommodate processing of the cells of the TiledLayer object. Next in the list are attributes of the Graphics and Image type, which allow you to explore how to replace one Image object with another.

In a further step, two constant values, WIDTH and HEIGHT, are defined. These two attributes provide the frame dimensions for the sequence of frames shown in Figure 14.2. Following the definition of the frame dimension values, you define an array of the int type that establishes the sequence that applies to the frames. Along with the definition of the frame sequence come the Image and Sprite attributes used to define and manage the sequence of frames.

In the lines trailing comment #2, the constructor for the SpritePlay class initializes the constructor for the parent GameCanvas class. This is accomplished by using the super keyword and supplying an argument of false. The constructor takes a single argument that allows you to designate whether you want your specialized definition of the GameCanvas class to exclude processing of key events. Since the GameCanvas class has only one constructor, you must provide a call to it as the first statement in the definition of your derived class. The argument of false indicates that you want to define the getKeyStates() method so that SpritePlay can process events initiated by keys. An argument of true results in a specialized version of the GameCanvas class that cannot process key events using the getKeyStates() method.

In addition to initialization of the parent class, you also attend to assigning values to the xPos and yPos attributes. To accomplish this, you can draw on the getWidth() and getHeight() methods of the GameCanvas class. You then initialize the various Image attributes to null, set the imageFlag attribute to true, and initialize the rNum attribute with an instance of the Random class.

The Frame Sequence

In the lines associated with comment #2.1, you carry forward the activities begun in the declaration section of the SpritePlay class and fully define the frame set used to generate the changing image features on the left side of the display illustrated in Figure 14.3. To review, to create the frame set, you require an Image object that contains a set of frames of the same size (facesImage). You also require a Sprite object to contain the Image object (facesSprite). Further, you require int values that you can use to set the width and height of each frame in the frame set (WIDTH and HEIGHT). Finally, you require an array of the int type that defines the frame sequence (FRAME_SEQUENCE).

Once you have established this set of six attributes, you can proceed to set up the frame set. As is evident in the lines following comment #2.1, you must perform this work in the context provided by a try block, and your first task involves creating an instance of the Image class. As an argument to the Image constructor, you employ a string constant naming the source file that contains the drawings or photographs to be used. In this case, you use FrameSet.png, and you assign the instance of the Image class to the facesImage attribute.

Next, you call the Sprite constructor to create a Sprite object that is characterized by a frame set. To accomplish this, you use the overloaded version of the Sprite constructor that allows you to provide two arguments. The first argument is of the Image type and provides the Image object the Sprite object is to contain. The second argument is of the int type and calls for an array. This argument furnishes the sequence of frames you want to apply to the Sprite object. For the first argument you use the facesImage attribute. For the second you use a reference FRAME_SEQUENCE array.

Use of the Sprite you have defined in association with the frame set is then pursued in the lines associated with comment #3.4, which occurs in the context provided by the run() method. Here you render the Sprite object visible, but prior to that, you call the setRefPixelPosition(), which adjusts the position of the reference pixel for each frame so that it is in the center of the image area. Immediately after setting the reference pixel, you set the position of the faces-Sprite object. In conjunction with these activities, you call the getRefPixelX() and getX() methods of the Sprite class to show the results. The output of these calls reveals that after setting the reference pixel, you do not change the coordinate value used to position the Sprite object. You change only the reference value, which can be used, among other things, to detect collisions. Figure 14.4 shows a sample of the output.

Rendering the Sprite object you have defined using a frame sequence can be accomplished most readily in the context of the run() method by calling the

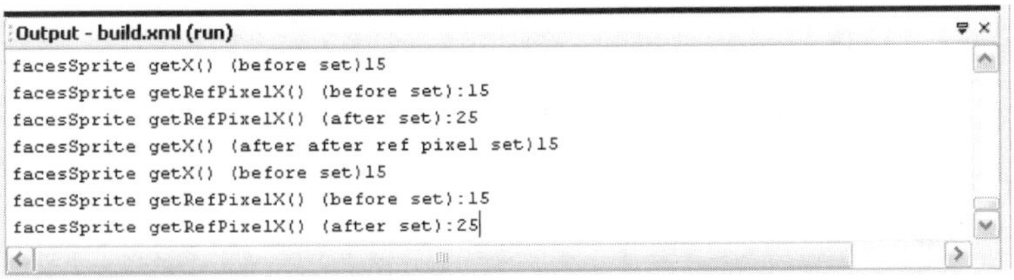

```
Output - build.xml (run)                                    ⬜ ✕
facesSprite getX() (before set)15                               ▲
facesSprite getRefPixelX() (before set):15
facesSprite getRefPixelX() (after set):25
facesSprite getX() (after after ref pixel set)15
facesSprite getX() (before set)15
facesSprite getRefPixelX() (before set):15
facesSprite getRefPixelX() (after set):25                       ▼
◄                               ▥                       ►
```

Figure 14.4
Setting the reference pixel has no effect on the position of the object, only on how the object is detected.

Sprite::paint() method, as is accomplished in the lines immediately following comment #3.4. Such a call paints the first frame in the sequence unless you have set an alternative frame. Comment out different lines to see the full range of face images the frame set provides. Test code is left in the class to allow you to experiment in this way.

```
//facesSprite.setFrame(0);
facesSprite.setFrame(1);
//facesSprite.setFrame(2);
//facesSprite.setFrame(3);
facesSprite.paint(g);
//changeSprites();
```

Figure 14.5 shows how the mapping of the frames using an arbitrary frame set effects the results of the arguments to the setFrame() method. When you supply the setFrame() method with an argument of 3, for example, it maps to the third index value in the FRAME_SEQUENCE array, which is 0. The face you see in the display, then, is the one with its left eye darkened.

Note

If you define several arrays containing different sequences of values, then you can use the same frame set to address a large number of scenarios. For example, a frame set might contain dozens of drawings or pictures of a character in different poses. You select from among this set of poses to address different scenarios: stand–run–stand; stand–walk–stand; stand–jump–fall. Reusing frame elements in this way, all drawn from a single Image object using a single Sprite object, reduces the number of assets you employ and allows you to concentrate on defining the sequences used to realize the scenarios.

Sprite and Image Creation

In the lines associated with comment #6, you define the createSprite() method, which can be used in any context in which you want to create a reference to a Sprite object. The method takes three arguments. The first is the name of the

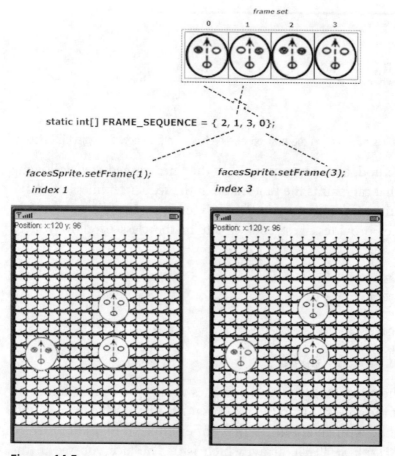

Figure 14.5
The setFrame() method allows you to explore the effects of the application of an arbitrarily defined frame sequence.

source file to use for the Image object. The second and third arguments provide integer values to establish the width and height values of the source image. Implementation of the method requires that you use a try block to load the file information into the Image object. To effect the creation of the Image object, you call the createImage() method in the context of the try block.

Once the file information is successfully loaded into the Image object, you can then make use of the Sprite constructor to create a new Sprite object. The Sprite constructor takes three arguments. The first is a reference to an Image object. The second and third are integer values that define the width and height of the Sprite object. Several instances in which this method is called are discussed in subsequent sections.

Wrapping the construction activity in the createSprite() method removes the necessity of repeatedly defining try blocks. It also makes it easier to move from the name of a source file to the creation of an instance of a Sprite object.

The createImage() method works much like the createSprite method. Create-Image wraps the Image::createImage() method so that it can be called locally without the need to repeatedly use static calls from the Image class. Like the overloaded version of the Image method that it wraps, it takes one argument, the name of the file used as the source of the Image object. To create the Image object, a call is made to the Image::createImage() method. Wrapping the creation activity in the Image::createImage() method removes the need to work with try. Uses of the createImage() method are discussed in subsequent sections.

TiledLayer

In the lines associated with comment #2.2, a try block is implemented to contain the definition of an object of the TiledLayer type. Definition of this object proceeds along lines similar to those used to define a Sprite object. You begin by calling the createImage() method to load the source file data into the Image object (background). Figure 14.6 shows a vastly enlarged view of the graphical file used for this purpose. The size of the image is 16 pixels high and 64 pixels long.

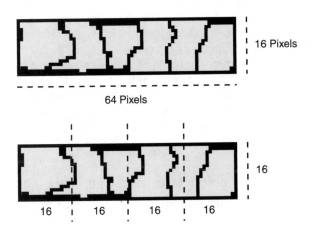

Figure 14.6
You create an image file that you can use to create cells for a TiledLayer object.

Table 14.3 TiledLayer Class Methods

Method	Description
TiledLayer(int, int, int, Image, int, int)	Creates a new TiledLayer object. The first two arguments designate the number of columns and rows you want the TiledLayer object to provide. The third argument is the Image object you want to use as a source for the TiledLayer object. The last two arguments provide the width and height of the tiles in the Image object. Note that the index values of tiles in the Image object begin at 1. The column and row values of the TiledLayer object begin at 0.
Int createAnimatedTile (int)	Creates a new animated tile and returns the index that refers to the new animated tile.
void fillCells(int, int, int, int, int)	Fills a region of cells in a TiledLayer object with the specified tile. The first two arguments designate the column and row of cell that is at the upper left corner of the area you want to fill. The third and fourth arguments designate the number of columns and rows extending to the left and downward from the cell defined by the first two arguments that you want to fill. The last argument is the index of the tile that you want to use to fill the cells.
int getAnimatedTile(int)	Retrieves the tile referenced by an animated tile.
int getCell(int, int)	Retrieves the contents of a cell. The first argument is the number of the column. The second argument is the number of the row.
int getCellHeight()	Returns the height of a single cell, in pixels.
int getCellWidth()	Returns width of a single cell, in pixels.
int getColumns()	Retrieves the number of columns in the TiledLayer grid.
int getRows()	Provides the number of rows in the TiledLayer grid.
void paint(Graphics g)	Draws the TiledLayer.
void setAnimatedTile (int, int)	Associates an animated tile with the specified static tile. The first argument identifies the animated index. The second argument identifies the static index.
void setCell(int, int, int)	The primary method of identifying the cells you want to display. The first argument identifies the column. The second argument identifies the row. The last argument designates the index of the tile to be set. The index value designates the position of the tile in the source Image object.
void setStaticTileSet (Image, int, int)	Allows you to set the static tile set. The second and third arguments designate the width and height of the Image object named by the first argument.

As mentioned in Table 14.3, the TiledLayer object takes five arguments. For convenience, here is the basic form of the constructor shown in Table 14.3:

```
TiledLayer(int, int, Image, int, int);
```

The first two arguments of the TiledLayer constructor define the TiledLayer object you are creating. This object consists of rows and columns of cells. The first argument designates the number of rows. The second argument designates the number of columns. The third argument applies to the Image object you use for source material for the TiledLayer object. In this case, you use the background attribute, as shown in Figure 14.6. The final two arguments define the dimensions of the tiles within the TileLayer object.

In the lines associated with comment #1, the TILE_H_W attribute is assigned a constant value of 16. This value is used in part because, as Figure 14.6 shows, the source file's contents can be divided evenly by 4, creating four uniform source tiles.

Using the TILE_H_W class attribute, you are in a position to create four 16-by-16 pixel tiles. To determine how many such cells are needed to fill the area provided by the display area, you call the getWidth() and getHeight() methods of the GameCanvas class and divide the returned values by the value assigned to TILE_H_W (16). Here is a refrain of test code you can use to obtain the values needed to determine the number of rows and columns the display area accommodates:

```
System.out.println("Value of TILE_H_W: " + TILE_H_W);
System.out.println("Pixel witdth of display: " + getWidth());
System.out.println("Number of columns: " + getWidth()/TILE_H_W);
System.out.println("Pixel height of display: " + getHeight());
System.out.println("Number of rows: " + getHeight()/TILE_H_W);
```

Running this refrain, the output to NetBeans appears as shown in Figure 14.7.

Suitable values to fill the display are, then, 15 columns and 18 rows. The TiledLayer object is constructed to consist of 15 columns and 18 rows, and this is what appears when the drawTiles() method is called. Defined in the lines associated with comment #11, the drawTiles() method takes three arguments. The first argument is of the TiledLayer type and furnishes a reference to the TiledLayer object whose contents you want to display. The second argument is of the boolean type and indicates whether you want to see all the tiles in the TiledLayer or just the one associated with index 1. Setting this value to true allows you to view all the tiles.

Figure 14.7
The output to NetBeans that is created by running the refrain.

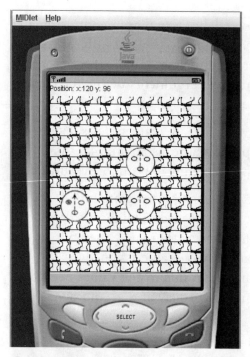

Figure 14.8
Set the second argument of the `drawSelectedTiles()` method to `true` to see all the source tiles provided by the `Image` object (comment #2.3).

The last argument is the maximum tile count as obtained from the source file. When you invoke the method with an argument of `true` to show all tiles, you see the background displayed by Figure 14.8.

Setting Cells

As mentioned previously, the `drawSelectedTiles()` method is called just following comment #2.3. This method is defined in association with the lines following comment #11. In its definition, a call is made to the `TiledLayer::setCell()` method. This method takes three arguments. The first argument is the column number of a cell in the `TiledLayer` object. The second argument is the row number of a cell in the `TiledLayer` object. Column and row values in a `TiledLayer` object begin at (0, 0).

The third argument of the `setCell()` method relates not to the `TiledLayer` object specifically but to the source tiles used to create it. To review a bit, in the `SpritePlay` class you create a `TiledLayer` object called `tlBackground`. To create

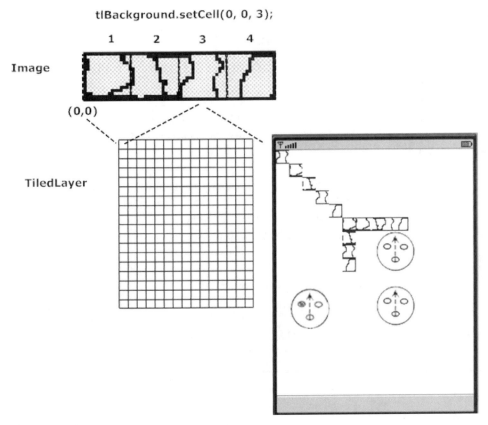

Figure 14.9
The upper left of the display area shows that you have used the setCell() method to set tile 3 from the source Image object in the TiledLayer cell identified by column 0, row 0.

this object, you use an Image object, background. The Image object offers four cells, as illustrated in Figure 14.9. The cells in the Image object are identified with index values that extend from 1 to 4. The third argument of the setCell() method, then, refers to the index value of the Image object. Consider, for example, this call to the setCell() method:

```
tlBackground.setCell(0, 0, 3);
```

This call to the setCell() method assigns a tile from the source Image object to a cell in the TiledLayer object. The cell to which the tile is assigned is located in column 0, row 0. The third argument identifies the third tile from the source Image file. As the display on the lower right shows, you see tile 3 from the source Image object displayed in the upper left corner of the display area. To see how this works for yourself, refer at this point to the sidebar "Selecting Specific Cells."

Selecting Specific Cells

To create the effects shown in Figure 14.9, use the following procedure.

1. In the SpritePlay class definition, locate comment #2.3. Comment out the line that reads as follows:

   `//drawSelectedTiles(t1Background, true, tileCount);`

2. In the SpritePlay class definition, locate the line associated with comment #2.4. Remove the comment so that the call to the method becomes active. Here is how your code appears when you finish this step:

   `paintWallTilesOnly();`

3. Now scroll through the source SpritePlay source code until you come to comment #13, which is associated with the definition of the paintWallTilesOnly() method. Notice that it is defined so that it sets the tiles you see painted in Figure 14.9.

4. Comment out the showPosition() method on the line following comment #3.5. This makes it so that row 0 of the TiledLayer object is visible.

   `// showPosition();`

5. Now recompile the program and view the results.

6. When you finish with this experiment, restore the code to its previous state. Remove the comment from the drawSelectedTiles() method (comment #2.3). Again comment out the call to the paintWallTilesOnly() method (comment #2.4). Also, remove the comments from the showPosition() method call (#3.5).

Sprite Collisions and Setting and Transforming Images

Having worked with Sprite and TiledLayer objects in the SpritePlay class definition, you are now in a good position to investigate a few basic operations involving collision detection. In this respect, in the line associated with comment #2.6, you see a call to the changeSprites() method. This method is defined in the lines associated with comment #4.

In the definition of the changeSprites() method, you begin by using the spriteA attribute to call the collidesWith() method. The Sprite class provides three overloaded versions of the collidesWith() method. This one takes as its first argument the name of the Sprite object with which collisions are to be detected. In this instance, you provide the spriteB identifier. The second argument of the method indicates whether you want to detect collisions using pixel values. Defined in this way, the method returns true if the spriteA object begins to overlap the spriteB object.

In the lines that follow, you call the nextInt() method of the Random class to retrieve a random value in the range from 0 to 4. You also check to see whether the attribute set up as a toggle (eventFlag) is true. If the eventFlag attribute is true, then you use the spriteB object to call the setImage() method of the Sprite class to acquire a new Image object for itself.

The setImage() method takes three arguments. The first is a reference to an Image object. This is provided by the SpritePlay::createImage() method, which returns an Image object if you provide it with the name of a file to use as a source file for the Image object. The second and third arguments to the setImage() methods are the width and height dimensions you want to assign to the newly assigned Image object. To provide these values, you use the SPRITE_W_H attribute, defined in the first few lines of the class definition, where it is set to a value of 48. The new Image object has two darkened eyes, so that the eyes of spriteB, the stationary sprite in center of the display area, begin to wink when a collision occurs.

In the lines trailing comment #4.1, a selection statement is implemented that tests for the value of 3. If the block of this selection statement is entered, then you call the setTransform() method of the Sprite class. This method takes as its argument a defined value obtained from the Sprite class (TRANS_ROT90). Dividing this value by 2 makes the Sprite object on the right of the display pivot 45 degrees.

Exiting the selection statement that evaluates num against 3, you call the nextFrame() method of the Sprite class. This has the effect of forcing the Sprite to augment its frame by one index. At this point, the eventFlag attribute is reset to false.

As an alternate cycle of activity, you again alter both the spriteB and the facesSprite objects. Begin by calling the setImage() method to restore the image of the face so that its eyes are once again clear. After setting eventFlag to true, you then call the setFrame() method to assign the face associated with index 2 of the facesSprite object. Given this new face for the object, you then set up another selection statement, this one calling the setTransform() method twice to once again pivot the sprite on the left of the display area.

TiledLayer Collisions

To review the activities presented in this section, perform the actions described in the sidebar entitled "Collision Detection with Specific Cells." When you have completed the instructions given there, return to this section. After you have changed the code, you see the display shown in Figure 14.10. When you click the

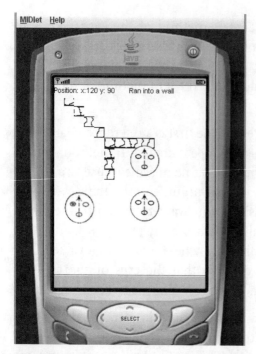

Figure 14.10
Collision between a TiledLayer object and a Sprite object creates an event.

Up arrow of the SELECT button (or use the Up arrow key on your keyboard), the active Sprite object moves upward and comes into contact with the broken images generated by the TiledLayer object. As soon as it makes contact with the tiled layer, you see a message at the top of the display: "Ran into a wall".

The detectWallTileCollision() method detects the collision between the active Sprite object and the TiledLayer object. The detectWallTileCollision() method is defined in the lines associated with comment #14. The code used to implement the collision detection capabilities involves a selection statement and a call to the collidesWith() method of the Sprite class. The spriteA object is used call the method, and as an argument to the method you provide the name of the TiledLayer object to be tested for collision. You also supply a boolean value to indicate that you want to use pixel values to test for the collision. This way, when the area of the Sprite object impinges on any cell of the TiledLayer object, an event is generated.

To report the event, the reportEvent() method is called. This method is defined in the lines associated with comment #10. The reportEvent() method takes as its argument a value of the String type. It writes the message it is given to the upper right of the console, as shown in Figure 14.10. To define this method, you use the getGraphics() method, which is supplied by the GameCanvas class. In this context, as is evident in the lines associated with comment #5, you wrap a call to the method as supplied by the parent class to return a reference to a Graphics object.

Collision Detection with Specific Cells

To work with collisions between a Sprite object and a TiledLayer object, make the following changes in the SpritePlay class.

1. In the SpritePlay class definition, locate comment #2.3. Comment out the line that reads as follows:

   ```
   // #2.3
   //drawSelectedTiles(tlBackground, true, tileCount);
   ```

2. In the SpritePlay class definition, locate the line associated with comment #2.4. Remove the comments from the line with the call to the paintWallTilesOnly() method:

   ```
   // #2.4
   paintWallTilesOnly();
   ```

3. Now locate the line associated with comment #3.7. Remove the comments from the call to the detectWallTileCollision() method:

   ```
   // #3.7
   detectWallTileCollision();
   ```

4. Compile and run the MIDlet.

5. When you now move the Sprite so that it makes contact with the jagged wall (TiledLayer) object, you see a new message, "Ran into a Wall".

6. When you finish with this experiment, restore the class to its previous state. Remove the comment from the drawSelectedTiles() method (comment #2.3). Again comment out the call to the paintWallTilesOnly() method (comment #2.4). Again comment out the call to the detectWallTileCollision() method (comment #3.7).

Key Events

To process key events, you use the getKeyStates() method. This method is called in the lines immediately following comment #3.1 within the scope of the run() method. The run() method, as has been mentioned previously, is supplied by the Runnable interface and allows you to use a Thread object to control the actions of the game loop. Accordingly, in the lines following comment #3, you create instances of a Graphics object to use for rendering by calling the getGraphics() method and then create instances of the Sprite class to assign to the spriteA and spriteB objects. After that, you call the defineReferencePixel() method to place in the two Sprite object reference pixels that might be used for any number of purposes. This sets up the first two actors or characters of the game.

The next step is to implement an infinite loop that is capable of processing events. The first call in this context, immediately following comment #3.1, is a call to the getKeyStates() method, which returns a value of the int type that can be used in a set of selection statements to manipulate the values of xPos and yPos. These values are associated with the spriteA object, so as you use them, you can constantly repost the spriteA object, which is the main "avatar" of the SpritePlay class.

The defined values supplied by the GameCanvas class are joined with the keyState value to make the selections possible. In this way, for example, the UP_PRESSED value serves to guide the flow of events into a selection block that allows you to decrement the value of yPos, which ultimately moves the spriteA object toward the top of the display area.

Showing the Position of the Avatar Sprite

As Figure 14.11 illustrates, at the top of the display, the coordinate values of the moving Sprite object are continuously shown. To provide this information to the display area, you call the showPosition() method in the line associated with comment #3.7. This method, which resides in the main game loop, is updated with each cycle of the animation or rendering loop of the application, and as it is called, if the position of the main Sprite object has changed, then you see a change in the values displayed.

The showPosition() method is defined in the lines trailing comment #9. The method takes no arguments and returns no values. To implement the method, you call the getGraphics() method. The Graphics reference, assigned to the g identifier, is then used to make a number of calls to methods of the Graphics class, including setColor(), fillRect(), and drawsString(). The getGraphics() method provides a convenient vehicle for obtaining a reference to the Graphics of the GameCanvas class to be used for specific purposes.

To obtain the coordinate values associated with the primary Sprite object (spriteA), you make use of the String::valueOf() method to convert the integer values into String objects. This measure is not absolutely necessary, but it makes it easier to use the values in display contexts if you want to expand the capabilities of the showPosition() method.

Clearing, Flushing, and Timing

With each cycle of the main animation loop, you have a number of options available to you as you deal with what is displayed. One of the most straightforward

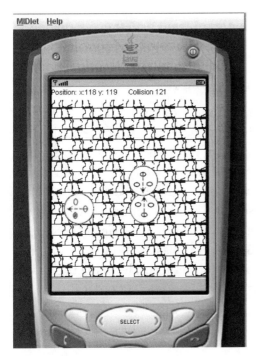

Figure 14.11
Coordinate positions are continuously updated.

options is to erase everything and render it again. To ensure that this can happen, you implement the clearScreen() method, which is called just prior to comment #3.4. Immediately after you call this method, you can invoke the Sprite::paint() method for the TiledLayer and Sprite objects that provide the foreground and background features of the display. For each of these calls, you make use of the Graphics object that has been instantiated in the run() method.

The definition of the clearScreen() method is in the lines following comment #8. The method takes a reference to a Graphics object as its sole argument. It then uses this argument to call the setColor() and fillRect() methods of the Graphics class. The fillRect() method requires several arguments. The first is to establish the position of the upper left corner of the rectangle. The last two arguments designate the width and height of the rectangle. To supply the last two arguments to the fillRect() method, the getWidth() and getHeight() methods of the GameCanvas class are called. The effect of the clearScreen() method is, then, to paint over the display area with a white rectangle.

A method at least conceptually akin to the clearSceen() method is the flush-Graphics() method, which is called in the lines following comment #3.8. This method is supplied by the GameCanvas class and allows you to clear the Graphics buffer to make it ready for a new round of rendering.

As has been discussed already, the implementation of the Runnable interface allows you to make use of the run() method as the location of the main animation loop of the MIDlet. To control the speed of the main loop, it is possible to implement controls of greater or lesser complexity. In Chapter 13, you saw a more typical example of a game loop control. In this context, no such approach is used. Instead, as is evident in the lines associated with comment #3.8, you see only the use of a call to the currentThread() method to retrieve the thread associated with the current instance of the SpritePlay class. The current instance of the Thread object is then used to call the sleep() method. The value used as an argument to the sleep() method is a constant value, GAME_TIME, defined in the attribute list for the class.

Parent Classes

In the context of the current discussion, few references have been made to the Layer class, which is the abstract class from which the TiledLayer and Sprite classes are derived. Table 14.4 provides a summary view of the Layer class. As is evident from a cursory inspection, such methods as getHeight(), getWidth(), and paint() are frequently used by the classes derived from the Layer class.

The LayerManager class is slightly beyond the scope of the discussion presented in this chapter, but it proves useful in the game developed in Chapter 15. In Chapter 15, you can find an example of how an instance of the class can be used to control the visibility of Sprite and TiledLayer objects. For present purposes, Table 14.5 furnishes a brief review of some of the methods.

Conclusion

This chapter has provided a preliminary examination of the Layer, LayerManager, GameCanvas, TiledLayer, and Sprite classes. The FacePlay class has provided opportunities to work with a number of the methods provided by the Game-Canvas, Sprite, and TiledLayer classes as related to the use of Image objects and collision detection. Such explorations provide the groundwork for Chapter 15, which extends the topics introduced in this chapter and involves you in the

Table 14.4 Layer Methods

Feature	Description
int getHeight()	Gets the current height of this layer, in pixels.
int getWidth()	Gets the current width of this layer, in pixels.
int getX()	Gets the horizontal position of this layer's upper left corner in the painter's coordinate system.
int getY()	Gets the vertical position of this layer's upper left corner in the painter's coordinate system.
boolean isVisible()	Gets the visibility of this Layer.
void move(int, int)	Moves this Layer by the specified horizontal and vertical distances. The first argument is the horizontal distance. The second is the vertical distance.
abstract void paint (Graphics g)	Paints this Layer if it is visible.
void setPosition (int x, int y)	Sets this layer's position such that its upper left corner is located at (x, y) in the painter's coordinate system.
void setVisible (boolean visible)	Sets the visibility of this Layer.

Table 14.5 LayerManager Methods

Feature	Description
LayerManager()	Creates a new LayerManager.
void append(Layer)	Appends a Layer to the LayerManager.
Layer getLayerAt(int)	Gets the Layer with the specified index.
int getSize()	Gets the number of Layers in the LayerManager.
void insert(Layer, int)	Inserts a new Layer in the LayerManager at the specified index.
void paint(Graphics g, int, int)	Renders the current view window of the LayerManager at the specified location.
void remove(Layer)	Removes the specified Layer from this LayerManager.
void setViewWindow (int, int, int, int)	The first and second arguments establish the upper left corner of the view window. The last two arguments set the width and height.

development of a game. As you refine your understanding of the Game API, you can find a multitude of ways that the knowledge you have acquired while working with the standard classes of the MIDP can be extended, in the end allowing you to create complex games.

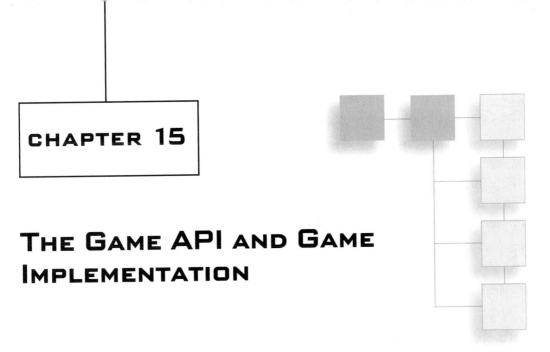

CHAPTER 15

THE GAME API AND GAME IMPLEMENTATION

This chapter uses a number of the Game API classes and provides a rudimentary but fairly complete game called Diamond Dasher. This is also the final chapter of this book, so it represents the culmination of the lessons this volume has to offer. Diamond Dasher incorporates relatively few of the classes explored during the course of this book, but it leaves open a number of opportunities for enhancement. By examining the way the class is implemented, you can put yourself in an excellent position for creating any number of modifications. This can be done fairly readily by, for example, changing the background or using different resource files to create the background. You can also add extra key options so that the player can control the avatar more directly. The lessons provided in previous chapters can be of great value in these and other respects.

Diamond Dasher

Diamond Dasher is a game that incorporates a number of the MIDP classes you have examined in previous chapters, pulling them together to create a game that involves guiding a seeking sprite as it explores a mine in search of diamonds. The diamonds are generated randomly, and to win the game, the seeker must find a given number of them before the allotted time expires. The number of diamonds set as the goal varies with each instance of the game. When you work with the game, you can increase the range of possible goals to make the game more difficult. The default settings are low largely to make the features of the game easier to test.

Diamond Dasher uses three primary classes, DasherStart, DasherCanvas, and DasherSprite. A fourth class, DTimerTask, is an inner class of DasherCanvas. Use of an inner class for the timer cuts down on the number of files, but since the game timer is closely coupled with the DasherCanvas class, it makes sense to implement the two classes as a single working unit.

Figure 15.1 provides a rough class diagram of the components of Diamond Dasher. For example, the DasherCanvas class is composed of an instance of the Layer-Manager class, as is the DasherSprite class.

The arrow pointing to the GameCanvas box from the DasherCanvas box indicates that the DasherCanvas class extends the GameCanvas class. The lines tipped by open circles indicate implementation of an interface, and in this case the DasherCanvas and DasherSprite classes implement the Runnable interface.

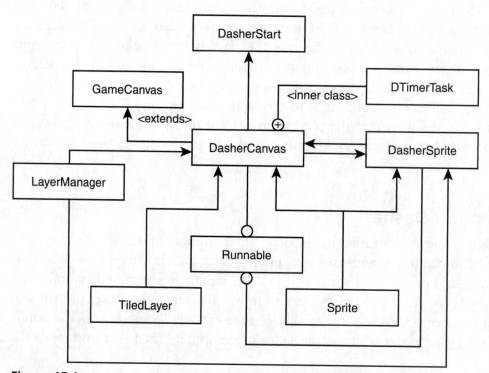

Figure 15.1
Diamond Dasher allows you to use three primary classes, along with one inner class, to explore the capabilities offered by four of the Game API classes.

The line tipped by the circle that contains a plus sign indicates that DTimerTask is an inner class of the DasherCanvas class.

The structure of the game is not as compact as it might be, but spreading it out makes it easier to examine for learning purposes. For example, duplicate use of the Runnable interface and the LayerManager class makes it possible to set up threads to support different animated Sprite objects and to create fairly involved collision effects. Together, the work of four of the Game API classes, Sprite, GameCanvas, TiledLayer, and LayerManager, allows you to gain a sense of the ways that you can use the Game API. Only the Layer class of the Game API is not used.

DasherStart

The DasherStart class provides the entry point of the game. Its primary functions are to create instances of the Display and DasherCanvas classes and to invoke the start() method of the DasherCanvas object. You can find the code for the DasherStart class in the Chapter 15 code folder. There are two copies, one in the NetBeans Chapter15MIDlets project, the other in a folder for standalone files. Here is the code for the class.

```
/*
 * Chapter 15 \ DasherStart.java
 *
 */
import javax.microedition.midlet.*;
import javax.microedition.lcdui.*;
public class DasherStart extends MIDlet{

    private DasherCanvas dashCanvas;
        private Display display;
// #1
      public DasherStart(){
        dashCanvas = new DasherCanvas("Diamond Dasher");
}
        // #2
    public void startApp(){
        display = Display.getDisplay(this);
        dashCanvas.start();
        display.setCurrent(dashCanvas);
    }
    public void pauseApp(){
    }
```

```
    public void destroyApp(boolean unconditional){
    }
}
```

The `DasherStart` class provides the entry point of the game, and its implementation involves routines you have dealt with in previous chapters. In the line of code preceding comment #1 of the `DasherStart` class, you declare class attributes of the `DasherCanvas` (dashCanvas) and `Display` types (display). The dashCanvas attribute becomes the focus of the implementation of the constructor of the `DasherStart` class, which follows comment #1. The `DasherCanvas` constructor takes one argument, the name of the game. You assign the new instance of DasherCanvas to the dashCanvas attribute and then proceed, in the scope of the startApp() method following comment #2, to call the `Display::getDisplay()` method, which returns a reference to the current `Display` object.

You are then in a position to call the `start()` method of the `DasherCanvas` class. This method is available to you because the `DasherCanvas` class implements the `Runnable` interface. Having initiated the thread, you call the setCurrent() method of the `Display` class to make the `DasherCanvas` object visible. When you do so, `Sprite` objects are already in motion, and the seeker can begin acquiring points, as Figure 15.2 shows.

DasherSprite

The `DasherSprite` class provides diamonds for Diamond Dasher. The diamonds are randomly generated `Sprite` objects with lifetimes limited to a few seconds. Manipulating the avatar to make contact with a diamond before it vanishes allows the player of the game to earn points. Diamonds are found using collision detection methods provided by the `Sprite` class. The code for the `DasherCanvas` class can be found in the `Chapter15MIDlets` folder, in standalone and NetBeans versions. The source files for the diamond (diamond.png) are also found in these folders. Here is the code.

```
/*
 * Chapter 15 \ DasherSprite.java
 *
 */

import java.util.*;
import javax.microedition.lcdui.*;
import javax.microedition.lcdui.game.*;
```

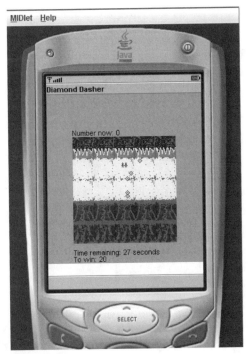

Figure 15.2
With the first view of the game, the Sprite objects are already in action.

```java
public class DasherSprite implements Runnable{
    // #1
    private Sprite diamondSprite;
    private Image diamondImage;
    private DasherCanvas gameCanvas;
    private LayerManager manager;
    private Thread thread;
    // #1.1
    private int currentDiamonds;
    private int diamondsFound;
    // #1.2
    private static final int MAX_DIAMONDS = 20;
    private static final int SLEEP = 500;
    private static final int SWTH = 10;
    private static final int SHTH = 10;

    // #2
    public DasherSprite(DasherCanvas canvasUsed){
        gameCanvas = canvasUsed;
        manager = gameCanvas.getManager();
    }
```

```
// #3
public void start() {
    diamondImage = createImage("/diamond.png");
    thread = new Thread(this);
    thread.start();
}
// #4
public void run(){
    try{
        while(true){
            randomDiamond();
            thread.sleep(SLEEP);
        }
    }catch(Exception e){
            System.out.println(e.toString()); }
}


// #5
 private void randomDiamond(){
     // #5.1
     if(currentDiamonds == MAX_DIAMONDS){
          return;
     }
     diamondSprite = new Sprite(diamondImage, SWTH, SHTH);
     // #5.2
     int randomDiamondX = gameCanvas.getRandom().nextInt(
                          gameCanvas.AREA_WIDTH);
     int randomDiamondY =
         (gameCanvas.FLOOR -
         gameCanvas.getRandom().nextInt(
                             gameCanvas.MAX_HEIGHT)
                           - diamondSprite.getHeight());

     // #5.3
     if(randomDiamondX < gameCanvas.AREA_ORIGIN_X){
         randomDiamondX = gameCanvas.CENTER_X;
     }
     if(randomDiamondY < (gameCanvas.FLOOR - gameCanvas.MAX_HEIGHT)){
         randomDiamondY = gameCanvas.CENTER_Y;
     }

     // #5.4
     diamondSprite.setPosition(randomDiamondX, randomDiamondY);
```

```
        manager.insert(diamondSprite, 0);
        currentDiamonds++;
    }
    // #6
    public void checkForCollision(){
        if(manager.getSize() == 2){
            return;
        }
        for(int itr = 0; itr < (manager.getSize() - 2); itr++) {
            if(gameCanvas.getSeekerSprite().collidesWith(
                        (Sprite)manager.getLayerAt(itr), true)){
                manager.remove(manager.getLayerAt(itr));
                currentDiamonds--;
                diamondsFound++;
            }
        }
    }


    // #7
    public Image createImage(String image){
        Image locImage = null;
        try{
            locImage = Image.createImage(image);
        }catch(Exception e){
            System.out.println(e);
        }
        return locImage;
    }


    // #8
    public int getDiamondsFound(){
        return diamondsFound;
    }
}// end of class
```

Definition and Construction

In the signature line of the DasherSprite class, you implement the Runnable interface. Use of the Runnable interface obligates you to implement the start() and run() methods, and these in turn enable to you to implement a Thread object to control the behavior of the class objects, which must be defined distinctly from the object that is composed of DasherSprite objects.

In the lines associated with comment #1 of the DasherSprite class, you declare 11 class attributes. The Sprite attribute (diamondImage) provides the container for the Image attribute (diamondImage), and the two together furnish you with the visual presence of diamonds. You also declare an attribute of the DasherCanvas type (gameCanvas). This is used largely to acquire services the DasherCanvas class provides, such as the dimensions of the display and random numbers. In addition to the DasherCanvas attribute, you make use of a LayerManager attribute, which allows you to control the appearance of the diamond, and the Thread attribute, mentioned previously, which enables you to separate the timing behavior of the DasherSprite canvas from that of its containing class.

After declaration of the first five attributes, you attend to the attributes that either track values as they change or establish constants. In the lines trailing comment #1.2, the currentDiamonds attribute allows you to tell how many instances of the Sprite object have been created, while the diamondsFound attribute enables you to identify the number of such objects that have been found. Both of these attributes are of the int type.

With respect to the constant values, you create attributes to control the maximum number of diamonds (MAX_DIAMONDS), the rate at which diamonds are created (SLEEP), and the width (SWTH) and height (SHTH) of the sprite that represents each diamond. The maximum number of diamonds is set at 20. The rate of diamond creation is set at half a second (500 milliseconds). The width and height of the Sprite object are both set at 10 pixels.

In the lines following comment #2, you define an overloaded version of the DasherSprite constructor. The constructor takes one argument, of the DasherCanvas type, which identifies the DasherCanvas object that contains the DasherSprite object. The DasherSprite class is dependent overall on the DasherCanvas class; this explicit show of dependency makes it clear that it is not possible to separate the two classes without creating problems. A reference to the containing class is assigned to the gameCanvas attribute, which is used repeatedly to provide information about the containing object.

In addition to identifying the containing class, the constructor calls the get-Manager() method of the DasherCanvas class. This is an accessor method that allows the DasherCanvas class to use the same LayerManager that the DasherCanvas class uses. The LayerManager object furnishes a number of services, one of the most important of which is making it possible to detect collisions between the diamond and the seeker entities. To generate the values discussed in this chapter, see the sidebar, "Printing Attribute Values."

Diamond Production

The activity of creating a diamond is governed primarily by the start() and run() methods. Defined in the lines associated with comment #2, the start() method is a feature of the Runnable interface and is invoked as soon as an instance of the DasherSprite class is instantiated. It performs two functions. The first is to call the DasherSprite::createImage() method, which creates an Image object from the information stored in the diamond.png file and assigns it to the diamond-Image interface. The second is to create an instance of the Thread class, assign this to the thread attribute, and then call the Thread::start() method to bring the thread to life.

With respect to calling the createImage() method, the approach to creating Image objects in this class definition resembles the approach you have seen in previous chapters. This becomes evident in the lines trailing comment #7. The createImage() method wraps the Image::createImage(), attending to the definition of the try block necessitated by the use of the method directly from the Image class.

After creating an instance of the Image class in the context provided by the start() method, in the lines associated with comment #4 you proceed to define the run() method, the primary purpose of which is to control the intervals at which instances of diamonds are created. This is accomplished using a call to the Thread::sleep() method. To make the call, you employ the thread attribute and supply the SLEEP constant as an argument to the sleep() method. A new diamond is created during each half-second cycle the sleep() method regulates.

To place the diamonds in the display area, within the scope of the run() method, you call the randomDiamond() method, which is defined in the lines trailing comment #5. The definition of this method involves four rudimentary activities. The first, attended to in the lines following comment #5.1, involves preventing diamonds from being created if the maximum number already exists. In other words, at no time can more diamonds appear in the display area than the number you designate by the value you assign to the MAX_DIAMONDS attribute (20). The number of existing diamonds is tracked using the currentDiamonds attribute. An if selection statement tests one value against the other, and if the two values are equal and the selection statement returns `true`, then the flow of the program does not proceed beyond this point, because the `return` keyword is called to exit the method.

If the selection statement does not return `true`, then the flow of the program proceeds to the following line, where an instance of a `Sprite` object is created and assigned to the `diamondSprite` attribute. The `Sprite` constructor takes three arguments. The first is a reference to an `Image` object, provided by the `diamondImage` attribute. The second and third are the width and height of the `Sprite` object, provided by the `SWTH` and `SHTH` constants.

Positioning Diamonds

Given the creation of the `Sprite` object, you then proceed to the second task of the `randomDiamond()` method, which unfolds in the lines following comment #5.2. Here you seek to create two random coordinate values, x and y, that can be used to place the diamond within the area of the display that represents the area of the cave. For the value of the x-coordinate, you call the `getRandom()` method of the `DasherCanvas` class, which returns a reference to a `Random` object. Using the `Random` object, you call the `nextInt()` method, and as an argument to the `nextInt()` method use the `AREA_WIDTH` attribute of the `DasherCanvas` class, which is set to a value of 160, as shown in Table 15.1. The value you obtain in this way lies in the range extending from 0 up to 160, and you assign it to the `randomDiamondX` identifier, which is locally defined.

Generating the value for the y-coordinate proves more complicated but involves incorporating the same strategy. As shown in Figure 15.3, the area defined for the height of the cave is given by the `MAX_HEIGHT` constant (64), and to make it so that the diamonds always appear in places in which the seeker (or miner) sprites can find them, they must be safely below the ceiling of the cave. To obtain this value, you subtract the height of the diamond, a value returned by the `getHeight()` method of the `Sprite` class, from the value provided by `MAX_HEIGHT`. The resulting value is then assigned to the `randomDiamondY` identifier, which is also locally defined.

Printing Attribute Values

To view the values of the various attributes of the `DasherCanvas` class, remove the comments from the `reportSettings()` method. The `reportSettings()` method is defined in association with comment #15 in the `DasherCanvas` class. Here is the code for the method:

```
private void reportSettings(){
    System.out.println("AREA_HEIGHT:\t\t" + AREA_HEIGHT);
    System.out.println("AREA_ORIGIN_X:\t\t" + AREA_ORIGIN_X);
```

```
        System.out.println("AREA_ORIGIN_Y:\t\t" + AREA_ORIGIN_Y);
        System.out.println("AREA_WIDTH:\t\t" + AREA_WIDTH);
        System.out.println("CAVE_HEIGHT:\t\t" + CAVE_HEIGHT);
        System.out.println("CENTER_X:\t\t" + CENTER_X);
        System.out.println("CENTER_Y:\t\t" + CENTER_Y);
        System.out.println("Dasher Canvas Height:\t" + getHeight() );
        System.out.println("Dasher Canvas Width:\t" + getWidth() );
        System.out.println("DMD_RANGE:\t\t" + DMD_RANGE);
        System.out.println("FLOOR:\t\t\t" + FLOOR);
        System.out.println("jumpHeight:\t\t" + jumpHeight);
        System.out.println("MAX_HEIGHT:\t\t" + MAX_HEIGHT);
        System.out.println("MIN_DIAMOND:\t\t" + MIN_DIAMONDS);
        System.out.println("SKR_HEIGHT :\t\t" + SKR_HEIGHT);
        System.out.println("SKR_WIDTH:\t\t" + SKR_WIDTH);
        System.out.println("TILE_HEIGHT:\t\t" + TILE_HEIGHT);
        System.out.println("TILE_WIDTH:\t\t" + TILE_WIDTH);
        System.out.println("TCOLS:\t\t\t" +   TCOLS);
        System.out.println("TROWS:\t\t\t" + TROWS);
    }
```

Representative values you see generated by this method appear in the Value column of Table 15.1. You can find this method at the end of the DasherCanvas class, covered in the next section.

To include this method in your program, remove the comments from the call to the reportSettings() method, which occurs at the last line of the DasherCanvas constructor. Discussion of the values the method prints is provided throughout the current chapter.

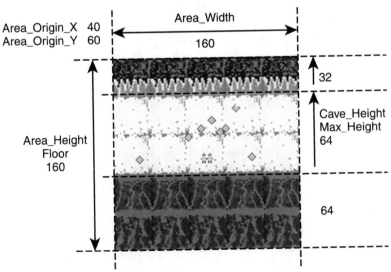

Figure 15.3
Positioning diamonds involves generating random values that place them in the area of the cave.

Table 15.1 DasherSprite and DasherCanvas Values

Attribute	Value	Description
AREA_HEIGHT	160	The height of the game rectangle.
AREA_ORIGIN_X	40	The x-coordinate position in the display that designates the upper left corner of the rectangle used for the active game.
AREA_ORIGIN_Y	64	The y-coordinate position in the display that designates the upper left corner of the rectangle used for the active game.
AREA_WIDTH	160	The width of the rectangle used for the active game. This distance leaves 40 pixels on the left and right sides of the rectangle.
CAVE_HEIGHT	64	The height of the area in which the seeker or dasher can find diamonds.
CENTER_X	120	The distance from the left margin of the display to the center of the game rectangle.
CENTER_Y	144	The distance from the top of the display to the approximate horizontal center of the game rectangle.
DasherCanvas Height	272	The height of the display area as obtained by the `Canvas::getHeight()` method.
DasherCanvas Width	240	The width of the display area as obtained by the `Canvas::getWidth()` method.
DMD_RANGE	30	The value used to set the range of random numbers that determines how many diamonds must be found for the game to be won.
FLOOR	160	The distance from the top to the bottom of the display.
jumpHeight	64	A varying value that is used to change the height to which the seeker moves as the game is played.
MAX_HEIGHT	64	The maximum height the seeker or dasher can climb when seeking diamonds.
MIN_DIAMONDS	20	The minimum number of diamonds to be generated during a play session.
SKR_HEIGHT	10	The height of the Sprite or Image that represents the seeker or dasher.
SKR_WIDTH	10	The width of the Sprite or Image that represents the seeker or dasher.
TILE_HEIGHT	32	The height of each tile in the `TiledLayer` object.
TILE_WIDTH	32	The width of each tile or cell in the `TiledLayer` object.
TCOLS	6	The number of columns in the `TiledLayer` object.
TROWS	6	The number of rows in the `TiledLayer` object.

See the sidebar "Printing Attribute Values" for a summary of the work of the `reportSettings()` method, which is a part of the interface of the `DasherCanvas` class.

As an extension of the activity involved in generating x- and y-coordinate values, you also make certain that the values you use do indeed place the diamonds in the area of the cave. To accomplish this, you employ two selection statements. Again referring to Table 15.1, the first selection statement, immediately following comment #5.3, assigns the value of CENTER_X (120) to the randomDiamondX identifier if the randomly generated value places the diamond outside and to the left of the cave area. On the other hand, the selection statement assigns the value CENTER_Y to randomDiamondY if the randomly generated value places the diamond above the top of the cave.

Having taken measures to ensure that the diamonds appear only in the area of the cave, in the lines associated with comment #5.4 you call the Layer::setPosition() method, which the Sprite class inherits from the Layer class. Using this method, you assign the values of randomDiamondX and randomDiamondY to the diamondSprite object. To make the diamond visible, you call the insert() method employing the LayerManager attribute that you have defined using the DasherCanvas object. The insert() method takes two arguments. The first is a reference to the Sprite to be made visible. The second is the index that designates the Layer object you want to associate with the Sprite. In this case, only one layer is used, so a value of 0 suffices.

The final action in the definition of the randomDiamond() method involves incrementing the count of the diamonds. To accomplish this, you increment the currentDiamonds attribute. As mentioned previously, with reference to comment #5.1, this attribute is continuously evaluated against the value of MAX_DIAMONDS to determine whether new diamonds are to be created.

Collisions

In the lines associated with comment #6, you define the checkForCollision() method. This method is called in the scope of the DasherCanvas class as part of the public interface of the DasherSprite class. It allows the DasherSprite object to determine when diamonds have been detected and remove them from the display. To define this method, you start by accessing the LayerManager attribute (manager) that represents the DasherCanvas LayerManager object. To identify the number of sprites, you call the LayerManager::getSize() method, which returns an integer value establishing the total number of sprites. The background and the seeker sprites must be excluded from collision detection actions involving deletion, so you begin by using a selection statement to ensure that no deletions occur when there are only two objects.

From there, you move on to iterate through the LayerManager object to discover the Sprites that the seeker collides with. This approach to collision detection involves visiting every Sprite contained by the DasherCanvas during each invocation of the checkForCollision() method. To make this possible, as part of an if selection statement, you call the getSeekerSpirte() method of the DasherCanvas class, which returns a reference to the diamond seeker avatar. You then use the returned reference to call the Sprite::collidesWith() method, which returns true if it detects a collision.

The collidesWith() method takes as an argument a reference to a Sprite object. To obtain references to a Sprite object, you use the manager attribute to call the getLaterAt() method, which returns each Layer in the LayerManager object. Since the Sprite class is a subclass of the Layer class, you find all the Sprite objects in the layer. At the same time, however, you must cast the Layer object as a Sprite object so that it is suitable as an argument to the collidesWith() method.

Given the detection of a Sprite object, you call the LayerManager::remove() method. As an argument to the method, you once again call the getLayerAt() method. The instance of the Sprite identified by the current value of itr is then deleted. Having deleted a sprite, you decrement the value of currentDiamonds while incrementing the value of diamondsFound. To make it possible for the value of diamondsFound to be retrieved by the DasherCanvas class to create a score, you create the getDiamondsFound() accessor method, which appears in the lines following comment #8.

DasherCanvas

The DasherCanvas class is the largest class in the set of classes that make up the Diamond Dasher game. This class allows you to create a Sprite object that dashes after diamonds (giving the game its name). A TiledLayer object furnishes the background, which consists of a set of tiles that provide a crude representation of a cave, along with a number of lines, created using the Graphics::drawString() method, that furnish the score of the game and reports about its progress. The DasherCanvas class contains one inner class, DTimerTask, which specializes the TimerTask class and serves to define a Timer object used to control the duration of the game. The class also provides a Thread object, which serves to govern the frame rate of the game. You can find the DasherCanvas class in the source code folder for Chapter 15. Two versions are provided, one in the Chapter15MIDlets NetBeans folder, the other in the standalone files folder. The two resource files the class requires, backtiles.png and dasher.png, reside in the folders along with the source code files. Here is the code for the DasherCanvas class; discussion of specifics follow.

```
/*
 *   Chapter 15 \ DasherCanvas
 *
 */

import javax.microedition.lcdui.*;
import javax.microedition.lcdui.game.*;
import java.util.*;
import java.io.*;

public class DasherCanvas extends GameCanvas
                          implements Runnable{
    // #1
    private Image seekerImg;
    private Image backgroundImg;
    private Sprite seekerSprite;
    private DasherSprite dasherSprite;
    private Graphics graphics;
    private TiledLayer background;
    private LayerManager manager;

    // #1.1
    private int seekerX;
    private int seekerY;
    private int moveX = 1;
    private int moveY = 1;
    private boolean up = true;

    // #1.2
    public final int CENTER_X = getWidth()/2;
    public final int CENTER_Y = getHeight()/2;
    public final int AREA_WIDTH = 160;
    public final int AREA_HEIGHT = 160;
    public final int AREA_ORIGIN_X = ( getWidth() - AREA_WIDTH )/2;
    public final int AREA_ORIGIN_Y = ( getHeight() - AREA_HEIGHT )/2;
    public final int CAVE_HEIGHT = 64;
    public final int FLOOR = AREA_ORIGIN_Y
                            + AREA_HEIGHT - CAVE_HEIGHT;
    public final int MAX_HEIGHT = 64;
```

```java
    // #1.3
    public final int TILE_HEIGHT = 32;
    public final int TILE_WIDTH = 32;
    public final int TCOLS = 5;
    public final int TROWS = 5;
    public final int SKR_WIDTH = 10;
    public final int SKR_HEIGHT   = 10;
    private int jumpHeight = MAX_HEIGHT;

    // #1.4
    public final int DMD_RANGE = 30;
    public final int MIN_DIAMONDS = 20;
    private int diamondsNeeded;
    private boolean winner;
    public Random random;
    private DTimerTask clock;
    private Timer gameTimer;
    private Thread runner;
    private boolean endSearch = false;
    public final int LTEXT = AREA_ORIGIN_X;

    public DasherCanvas(String title){
        super(true);
        setTitle(title);
        reportSettings();
    }

    // #2
    public void start(){
        seekerX = CENTER_X;
        seekerY = FLOOR;
        winner = false;
        random = new Random();
        diamondsNeeded = random.nextInt(DMD_RANGE);
        if(diamondsNeeded < MIN_DIAMONDS){
            diamondsNeeded = MIN_DIAMONDS;
        }

        // #2.1
        seekerImg = createImage("/dasher.png");
        seekerSprite = new Sprite(seekerImg, SKR_WIDTH, SKR_HEIGHT);
        seekerSprite.defineReferencePixel(SKR_WIDTH/2, SKR_HEIGHT);
```

```
        manager = new LayerManager();
        manager.append(seekerSprite);

        createBackground();
        // #2.2
        manager.append(background);
        dasherSprite = new DasherSprite(this);
        dasherSprite.start();

        runner = new Thread(this);
        runner.start();
}

// #3
public void run(){
        clock = new DTimerTask(30);
        gameTimer = new Timer();
        gameTimer.schedule(clock, 0, 1000);
        while(endSearch == false){ // loop
            confirmStatus();
            getUserActions();
            updateScreen();
            try {
                Thread.currentThread().sleep(30);
              } catch(Exception e) {}
        }
        showGameScore();
}

// #4
private void makeGameScreen(){
        graphics = getGraphics();
        graphics.setColor(100, 149, 237);
        graphics.fillRect(0, 0, getWidth(),
                                    getHeight());
        showStatus();
}

// #5
private void createBackground(){
        backgroundImg = createImage("/backtiles.png");
        background = new TiledLayer(TCOLS, TROWS, backgroundImg,
                                    TILE_WIDTH, TILE_HEIGHT);
        int[] tiles = makeTileCells();
```

```
        // #5.1
        int itr = 0;
        for(int row = 0; row < TROWS; row++){
            for(int col = 0; col < TCOLS; col++){
                background.setCell(col, row, tiles[itr++]);
            }
        }
        background.setPosition(AREA_ORIGIN_X, AREA_ORIGIN_Y);
    }


    // # 5.2
    private int[] makeTileCells(){
        int[] cells = {
                3, 3, 3, 3, 3, // top
                1, 1, 1, 1, 1, // cave
                1, 1, 1, 1, 1, // cave
                2, 2, 2, 2, 2, // floor layer
                4, 4, 4, 4, 4   // bottom layer
                };
        return cells;
    }


    // #5.3
    Image createImage(String fileName){
        Image tempImage = null;
        try{
         tempImage = Image.createImage(fileName);
        }catch(Exception ioe){
            System.out.println(ioe.toString());
        }
        return tempImage;
    }


    // #6
    private void confirmStatus(){
        if(clock.getTimeLeft() == 0) {

            endSearch = true;
            return;
        }
        dasherSprite.checkForCollision();
    }
```

```
// #7
private void getUserActions(){
    int keyState = getKeyStates();
    findXBoundry(keyState);
    findYBoundry(keyState);
}

// #8
private void updateScreen(){
    makeGameScreen();
    seekerSprite.nextFrame();
    seekerSprite.setRefPixelPosition(seekerX, seekerY);
    manager.paint(graphics, 0, 0);
    flushGraphics();
}

// #9
private void showStatus(){
    graphics = getGraphics();
    int timeLeft = clock.getTimeLeft();
    if(timeLeft < 6){
        if((timeLeft % 2) == 0){
            graphics.setColor(0xff0000);
        }else{
            graphics.setColor(0x000000);
        }
    }
    // #9.1
    graphics.drawString("Time remaining: " + timeLeft + " seconds",
                                        LTEXT, 225, 0);
    graphics.drawString("To win: " +  diamondsNeeded,
                                        LTEXT, 238, 0);
    graphics.drawString("Number now: "
                        + dasherSprite.getDiamondsFound(),
                                        LTEXT, 50, 0);
    // #9.2
    int goal = 0;
    if(dasherSprite.getDiamondsFound() >= diamondsNeeded){
        graphics.setColor(0xf5f5f5);
        graphics.drawString("You win!!!! ******",
                                        LTEXT, 40, 0);
    }
}
```

```
// #10
private void showGameScore(){
      graphics.setColor(0xf5f5f5);
      graphics.fillRect(0, CENTER_Y - 20, getWidth(), 40);
      graphics.setColor(0x000000);
      graphics.drawString("You have found " +
                          dasherSprite.getDiamondsFound()
                          + " diamonds.",
                          CENTER_X, CENTER_Y,
                          Graphics.HCENTER | Graphics.BASELINE);
      flushGraphics();
}


// #11
private void findXBoundry(int keyState){
    if((keyState & LEFT_PRESSED) != 0) {
        seekerX = Math.max(AREA_ORIGIN_X
                          + seekerSprite.getWidth()/2,
                           seekerX - moveX);
    }
    if((keyState & RIGHT_PRESSED) != 0) {
        seekerX =  Math.min(AREA_ORIGIN_X + AREA_WIDTH
                          - seekerSprite.getWidth()/2,
                             seekerX + moveX);;
    }
}


// #12
private void findYBoundry(int keyState){
    // #12.1
    if(up){//up
        if(seekerY > FLOOR - jumpHeight
                         + SKR_HEIGHT){
          seekerY -= moveY;
        }
        if(seekerY == FLOOR - jumpHeight
                         + SKR_HEIGHT){
          seekerY += moveY;
          up = false;
        }//end else if
    }else{
    // #12.2
        if(seekerY < FLOOR){
```

```
                  seekerY += moveY;
              }
          if(seekerY == FLOOR){
              int jumpTry = random.nextInt(MAX_HEIGHT + 1);
              if(jumpTry > SKR_HEIGHT){
                  jumpHeight = jumpTry;
              }//end if
                  seekerY -= moveY;
                  up = true;
          }
      }// end else
}//end calculateSeekerY



// #13
public Sprite getSeekerSprite(){
      return seekerSprite;
}
public LayerManager getManager(){
      return manager;
}
public Random getRandom(){
      return random;
}
// #14
//=============================================
//Inner class for the timer
public class DTimerTask extends TimerTask{
      int timeLeft;
      public DTimerTask(int maxTime){
          timeLeft = maxTime;
      }
      public void run(){
          timeLeft--;
      }
      public int getTimeLeft(){
          return timeLeft;
      }
   }// End inner class
    //=======================================



// #15
```

```
      // Generate values for testing and exploration
      private void reportSettings(){
          System.out.println("AREA_HEIGHT:\t\t" + AREA_HEIGHT);
          System.out.println("AREA_ORIGIN_X:\t\t" + AREA_ORIGIN_X);
          System.out.println("AREA_ORIGIN_Y:\t\t" + AREA_ORIGIN_Y);
          System.out.println("AREA_WIDTH:\t\t" + AREA_WIDTH);
          System.out.println("CAVE_HEIGHT:\t\t" + CAVE_HEIGHT);
          System.out.println("CENTER_X:\t\t" + CENTER_X);
          System.out.println("CENTER_Y:\t\t" + CENTER_Y);
          System.out.println("Dasher Canvas Height:\t" + getHeight() );
          System.out.println("Dasher Canvas Width:\t" + getWidth() );
          System.out.println("DMD_RANGE:\t\t" + DMD_RANGE);
          System.out.println("FLOOR:\t\t\t" + FLOOR);
          System.out.println("jumpHeight:\t\t" + jumpHeight);
          System.out.println("MIN_DIAMOND:\t\t" + MIN_DIAMONDS);
          System.out.println("MAX_HEIGHT:\t\t" + MAX_HEIGHT);
          System.out.println("SKR_WIDTH:\t\t" + SKR_WIDTH);
          System.out.println("SKR_HEIGHT :\t\t" + SKR_HEIGHT);
          System.out.println("TILE_HEIGHT:\t\t" + TILE_HEIGHT);
          System.out.println("TILE_WIDTH:\t\t" + TILE_WIDTH);
          System.out.println("TCOLS:\t\t\t" +   TCOLS);
          System.out.println("TROWS:\t\t\t" + TROWS);
      }
}// End class
```

Construction and Definition

In the signature line of the DasherCanvas class, you begin the definition of the class by extending the GameCanvas class and implementing the Runnable interface. Extension of the GameCanvas class provides you with a number of useful services that have been explored in previous chapters and continue to furnish topics for discussion in the current context. The Runnable interface allows you to implement start() and run() methods, and using Timer and Thread objects, you make use of these services to control the speed of the game and to define the challenge the player of the game encounters. In the lines immediately following comment #1, you attend to the declaration of attributes of the Image, Sprite, DasherSprite, Graphics, TiledLayer, and LayerManager types. The attribute of the Sprite type (DasherSprite) is the visible dasher (or seeker) image that moves around the cave seeking diamonds. The attribute of the DasherSprite type (dasherSprite) provides the diamonds. All of the functionality needed to generate, detect, and remove the diamonds is included in the `DasherSprite` class definition, so when you create an instance of the `DasherSprite` class, you need to do little more with it.

In the lines following comment #1.1, attributes of the `int` type are declared, and these help you track and move the `seekerSprite` object. To track this object, you audit the x- (`seekerX`) and y- (`seekerY`) coordinates associated with it. These coordinates are by default associated with the upper left corner of a `Sprite` object, but by using the `defineReferencePixel()` method, you can change this. To control the movement of the `seekerSprite` object, you define the `moveX` and `moveY` attributes, which allow the object to move one pixel at a time if you press the arrow keys.

The attributes defined in association with comment #1.2 are used to manage the objects within the display area and to translate the dimensions of the display into the local world coordinates of the central rectangle. The display measures 240 pixels wide by 272 pixels high, while the central rectangle measures 160 pixels by 160 pixels (see Figure 15.3 and Table 15.1, shown previously). To find the center of the display area, you use the `getWidth()` and `getHeight()` methods of the `DasherCanvas` class and divide each of the returned values by two. You assign the results to the `CENTER_X` and `CENTER_Y` attributes.

To find a coordinate value that can be used to establish the center of the game rectangle, you first define the `AREA_WIDTH` and `AREA_HEIGHT` using values of 160. After that, you subtract the width and height dimensions of the game area from the width and height of the display and each value by 2, assigning the results to `AREA_ORIGIN_X` and `AREA_ORIGIN_Y`. Following the definition of the two game origin values, you define the height of the play area (`CAVE_HEIGHT`) at 64. You can then set the lower boundary of the play area (`FLOOR`). This involves subtracting the height of the play area from the height of the game area. You also set the maximum height to which the seeker can jump (`MAX_HEIGHT`) at 64.

After establishing the dimensions of the play area, you then declare and initialize a number of attributes that enable you to define the `Image`, `TiledLayer`, and `Sprite` properties of the seeker sprite and the background. This activity begins in the lines following comment #1.3, where you first set the width and height of the tiles used for the background. Figure 15.4 illustrates the relationships between these values. Each of the tiles in the `Image` object used for the background has dimensions of 32 by 32 pixels. The `TILE_HEIGHT` and `TILE_WIDTH` attributes are used to set these values. There are four such tiles. In the `TiledLayer` object, you create a cell grid consisting of 5-by-5 squares. The `TCOLS` and `TROWS` attributes set these values. To set the size of

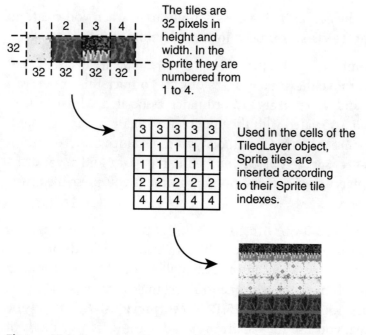

Figure 15.4
The Sprite tile and TiledLayer cell dimensions allow you to create the background of the game world.

the seekerSprite object, you use the SKR_WIDTH and SKR_HEIGHT attributes, both set to 10. To track the distance the seeker jumps, you create the jumpHeight attribute, which is set at the same value of MAX_HEIGHT.

The final set of attributes, following comment #1.4, allows you attend to Timer, Thread, and random number events. To set the range of diamonds the game can ask the player to find, you set the DMD_RANGE attribute. To set the minimum number of diamonds, you set the MIN_DIAMONDS attribute. The diamondsNeeded attribute allows you to determine when the player has collected enough diamonds to win. The winner attribute is used to indicate when the player has won. To generate a value to use to set the number of diamonds a player must collect to win the game, you declare the random attribute. The duration of the game is set using the clock attribute, which is of the DTimerTask type, which is defined in an inner class. To control the speed of the game, you declarer the runner attribute, which is of the Thread type. To determine whether the game is still in progress, you declare the endSearch attribute. As a final measure, the LTEXT attribute is declared. This is used to establish the left margin of the lines of text used to display the score and related information about the game.

Starting the Game

In the lines trailing comment #2, you define the start() method. The start() method is called by the DasherCanvas object as soon as it is initiated. You use the CENTER_X and FLOOR attributes to define the initial position associated with the seekerSprite object. You then set the initial objective of the game. To accomplish this, you use the random attribute to call the Random::nextInt() method, which takes the maximum range set by DMD_RANGE as an argument. You assign the returned random value to the diamondsNeeded attribute. In the lines immediately following, you create a selection statement which resets the value of diamonds-Needed if it has been set to less than the game minimum (MIN_DIAMONDS).

In the lines following comment #2.2, you call the createImage() method to provide the game with a seeker image (which is provided by the dasher.png file). The createImage() method takes one argument, which is of the String type. It is defined in the lines associated with comment #5.1. Its main characteristic is that it wraps the Image::createImage() method, making it unnecessary to repeatedly create a try block to handle the Exception message the method is defined to throw if it fails to find a valid file. Using the value returned by the createImage() method, you define the seekerImg attribute, which you employ as an argument to the constructor of the Sprite class.

The Sprite constructor takes three arguments. The first is the Image object used to define the visual representation of the Sprite object. The last two arguments provide the width and height of the Sprite objects, and for these values you employ the SKR_WIDTH and SKR_HEIGHT attributes. You assign the instance of the Sprite class to the seekerSprite attribute, and to finish off the definition of this attribute, you call the defineReferencePixel() method. This method resets values of the x-y coordinate pair so that they no longer identify the upper left corner of the Sprite object. Instead, the position is now set as the middle of the bottom border of the Sprite object.

Given the instance of a Sprite object, you then create an instance of a Layer-Manager object, which you assign to the manager attribute. The LayerManager class provides a container for Sprite objects. You use the append() method to store Sprite objects in a LayerManager object. Each Sprite object you store is identified using an index, so that with the first call of the append() method you store the seekerSprite object in the manager object and associate it with index 0.

You then call the createBackground() method, which is defined in the lines associated with comment #5. The createBackground() method first creates a background Image object, which is assigned to the backgroundImg attribute. This attribute is then used as an argument to the constructor of the TiledLayer class. The constructor takes five arguments. The first two are the number of rows and columns you want to define for the TiledLayer object. The second is the Image object that provides the tiles to the TiledLayer object. The final two objects establish the width and height of the cells in the in the TiledLayer object. Refer to Figure 15.4, shown previously, to review these values.

To create a configuration of cells to use for the TiledLayer object you call the makeTileCells() method, which is defined in the lines following comment #5.2. In this method, a one-dimensional array of integers is used to define five rows of values. On the first row, tile 3 of the image is to be used. On the next two rows, tile 1 is to be used. This is the tile that is lightest in color, as Figure 15.4 illustrates, so it makes the diamonds easiest to see. For the bottom two rows you use tiles 2 and 4, which provide increasingly darker background colors.

The makeTileCells() returns a reference to an array of the int type, which in the lines following comment #5.1 you assign to the tiles array and use in a for repletion block that iterates through all the cells in the TiledLayer object and assigns tiles to them. The approach used involves using the itr identifier to identify the successive tiles identified in the tiles array while employing the row and col identifiers in the for statements to identify the specific cells in the TiledLayer object. These range from 1 to 4, as Figure 15.4 illustrates. After placing the tiles in the TiledLayer object, you then call the setPosition() method to position the TiledLayer object using the AREA_ORIGIN_X and AREA_ORIGIN_Y values.

To return to the start() method, in the lines following comment #2.2, you again call the append method of the LayerManager object to assign the background object to the manager object. The index for the layer object is 1. You thus have a way of distinctly identifying the seeker and background Sprite objects. The first resides at layer 0. The second resides at layer 1.

Having appended the background Sprite object, you then create an instance of the DasherSprite class and assign it to the dasherSprite attribute. This single call initiates the creation and random distribution of diamonds. The diamonds you create in this way continue to appear in the active game area until they reach the maximum number you set for them. You also call the start() method associated with the DasherSprite class, which uses its own thread to regulate its behavior as it produces diamonds. Having started the DasherStart thread, you can then create an instance of the Thread class to assign to the runner attribute, which is used start and control the game.

Running the Game

In the lines following comment #3 of the DasherCanvas class, within the scope of the run() method, you create an instance of the DTimerTask class. This class is defined in the lines following comment #14 and provides a constructor that sets the maximum time allowed for the game. This value is assigned to the timeLeft attribute. It also defines a run() method so that with each call by the Ticker object to the DTimerTask object, the value of timeLeft is decremented by one. To supplement the work of the DTimerTask class, an accessor method, getTimeLeft(), returns the value of timeLeft.

Back in the scope of the run() method following comment #3, you create an instance of the Timer class and assign it to the gameTimer attribute, which you then use to call the schedule() method. This method takes as its first argument the instance of the DTimerTask class (clock). The second argument establishes that there is no delay in the action of the Timer object. The last argument sets the period of the Timer object at 1000 milliseconds (one second).

In the while loop inside the run() method, the confirmStatus(), getUserActions(), and updateScreen() methods are called. The confirmStatus() method is defined in the lines following comment #6. Its responsibilities are to check on the game ticker by using the clock attribute to call the getTimeLeft() method and to determine whether the time allotted for the game has been decremented to 0. If the time has reached 0, then the endSearch attribute is set to true, and the game is ended. If time remains, then the checkForCollision() method of the DasherSprite class is called. As was pointed out in the discussion of the DasherSprite class, this method detects collisions between the Sprite objects representing the seeker and the diamonds.

The definition of the getUserAction() method follows comment #7. This method calls the getKeyStates() method, which returns the unique identifier associated with the keys used to play the game (which include the SELECT button and the keyboard game keys). The key value is then processed by the findXBoundary() and findYBoundary() methods.

Boundaries and Random Jumps

The findYBoundary() method receives its definition in the lines trailing comment #11, where two if selection statements are used to process the value returned by the getKeyStates() method. Each of the selection statements first tests for the value of either the left arrow key or the right arrow key (LEFT_PRESSED or

RIGHT_PRESSED). It then uses the Math::max() and Math::min() methods to determine whether to move the seeker object to the right or left within the active game area. For the LEFT_PRESSED motion, the value used to set the position of the seeker object involves taking the maximum of the two values. The first is half the width of the Sprite object added to the value of the x-coordinate of the active game area. The second is the sum of the current x-coordinate assigned to the seeker and the distance defined by moveX attribute (1). The max() method returns the larger of these two values.

Movement to the right (RIGHT_PRESSED) takes the same approach, except that the Math::min() method is used. The first argument to the min() method is arrived at by taking the sum of the x-coordinate value of active game area and the width of the game area and subtracting half the width of the seeker object from it. The second argument to the min() method is the sum of the current seeker position and the value of moveX. The min() method returns the smaller of these two values.

The work of the findYBoundary() method is much more complex than that of the findXBoundary() method: rather than moving the seeker object in a determined, incremental fashion, it moves it in a random way. The definition of the findY-Boundary() method begins with comment #12.1, where an if selection statement checks whether the value of up is set to true. If so, then the flow of the program enters this block. Inside the block, an inner selection statement determines whether the position of the seeker object is greater than the value of the bottom of the active game area minus the sum of jumpHeight (set initially at 64, the value of MAX-HEIGHT, but then generated randomly) and the height of the seeker (10). If so, then it continues to move upward. On the other hand, a second inner selection statement audits whether the seeker object has reached the top. If so, it is sent on a downward path, and the value of up is set to false.

In the lines associated with comment #12.2, within an else block, the first if selection statement evaluates whether the seeker object has reached its maximum point of descent. If not, then it continues on its way downward. On the other hand, the second inner if selection statement evaluates to true if the seeker object has reached its maximum point of descent. If so, then a random number is generated for the jumpHeight attribute. To assign the random value to jumpHeight (which is initially set to MAX_HEIGHT), the random value is first assigned to the local jumpTry identifier. If the value of jumpTry is greater than the height of the seeker object, then it is assigned to jumpHeight attribute, replacing the previously assigned value. If not, then the previous value remains unchanged. After that, the flow of the program continues, and the movement of the seeker object is changed so that it begins to move upward. The up attribute is set to true. With the next cycle of the game, then, the up block is entered, and the value of jumpHeight regulates how far the seeker object can climb.

Updating

As mentioned previously, within the while loop of the DasherCanvas::run() method (comment #3), the updateScreen() method is called. This method is defined in the lines associated with comment #8. The updateScreen() method possesses four basic responsibilities. The first is to call the makeGameScreen() method, which is defined in the lines trailing comment #4. In the definition of this method, you begin by creating a colored rectangle to fill the display. The setColor() and fillRect() methods are used to accomplish this task. For the first two of the four arguments of the fillRect() method, you provide a coordinate pair (0,0) to set the origin of the background rectangle. The third and fourth of its arguments set the lower right corner of the rectangle using a coordinate pair defined by the width and height of the display area.

Having set the background color of the display area, you call the showStatus() method. To define this method, you first use the clock attribute to call the getTimeLeft() method. This method returns the amount of time left for the game, which you assign to a local identifier, timeLeft. You then assess the value assigned to the timeLeft identifier, making the message blink if the number of seconds is less than 6.

In the lines following comment #9.1, you call the drawString() method three times, first to display the time remaining, next to display the number of diamonds that must be found to win the game, and last to show the current number of diamonds found. Then, in the lines associated with comment #9.2, you use an if selection statement to determine whether the number of diamonds found equals or exceeds the number of diamonds needed to win the game. As illustrated by Figure 15.5, if the winning number has been reached, the game displays a message reading "You win!!!! ******". You call the setColor() method to set the color of this message so that it is lighter than the other messages.

Returning to the updateScreen() method (see comment #8), following the call to the makeGameScreen() method, you use the seekerSprite object to call the

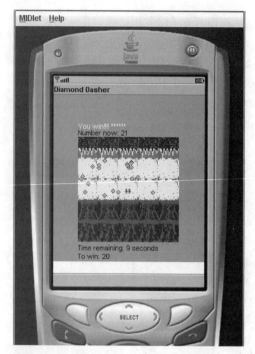

Figure 15.5
The color of the winner message is lighter than that of the other messages.

nextFrame() method. This method call has the effect of incrementing the tile of the seekerSprite object by one. This causes the seekerSprite object to blink, as Figure 15.6 illustrates.

In addition to calling the nextFrame() message, you also call the setRefPixel-Position() method in the scope of the updateScreen() method. The effect of this method is to position the coordinates of the seeker sprite used for collision detection in the middle of the top boundary of the seekerSprite object. You use the LayerManager object, manager, to call the LayerManager::paint() method. The paint() method takes three arguments. The first is the Graphics object to be painted. The second and third are the x- and y-coordinates that identify the origin to be assigned to the graphics object. In this case, the Graphics object affiliated with the current instance of the DasherCanvas class is used for the first argument, and the origin is set in the upper left corner of the display. In this way, the entire DasherCanvas area is painted. Following the call to the paint() method, the flushGraphics() method is called to bring the objects set for display into visibility.

The Sprite frames are 10 pixels in height and width. The Sprite is 20 pixels wide, providing two frames. The nextFrame( ) method repeatedly moves the display forward one frame, causing the Sprite object to flicker.

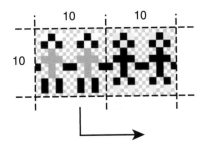

Figure 15.6
One frame advances to another, causing a flicker.

Showing the Final Score

In the lines trailing comment #10, you show the final game banner, which lists the total number of diamonds the player has discovered. As Figure 15.7 illustrates, the final banner displays whether or not the player wins. To create the banner, you first call the setColor() method to make the color of the banner off-white. Next, you call the fillRect() method to create the banner. You then call the setColor() method once again, setting the font color to black. All that remains after that is to call the drawString() method, providing for its first argument a message that incorporates the value returned by the getDiamonds() method of the DasherSprite class. For the second and third arguments, which position the message, you provide the CENTER_X and CENTER_Y values. For the final argument, you use the OR operator to create an anchor value by joining the HCENTER and BASELINE properties of the Graphics class. Finally, you call the flushGraphics() method to bring the banner and its message to visibility.

Conclusion

In this chapter you reach the end of this book's exploration of the MIDP classes as they might be applied in the context of game development. Clearly, there is much more to be said about the use of the MIDP classes. However, for introductory purposes, a discussion that keeps things simple is best. As pertains to any

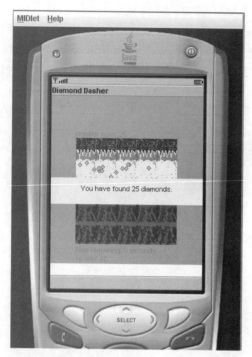

Figure 15.7
A banner is displayed to show the end of the game and provide summary information.

work with Java class libraries, the documentation available on the Internet remains your best resource with respect to fully exploring the capabilities the classes offer. The most a book can do is put starter and other information in a context that enables you to learn on your own. That has been the goal of this book.

Making use of the Java Wireless Toolkit or the NetBeans IDE tremendously augments your work with the MIDP, so I hope that in the course of reading this book, you have been persuaded to start developing with one or both of these tools. The hours you save by using such an IDE can be put toward extending your explorations of the intricacies of the Java MIDP classes.

Clearly, this book might have begun with a discussion of the Game API or, given an introduction of the fundamentals of the MIDP classes, made the Game API its primary topic. This is, indeed, the approach used in many books currently on the market. The approach here differs from those for a reason. Regardless of proliferation of graphically oriented games developed for mobile devices, opportunities still abound for developing text-based MIDlets that incorporate game elements. Familiarity with the full range of the MIDP classes is the best grounding for someone seeking to make the best use of the MIDP in all contexts in which games might be developed.

Whatever avenue you follow after beginning work with the MIDP through a book like this, the prospects are endless. Perhaps the most promising aspect of programming using the MIDP is that with relatively little effort it is possible for an isolated developer to create products that might be marketed on an entrepreneurial basis. This is hardly ever the case with games developed for console and PC games, where the efforts of many people are required. It is also the case that the MIDP classes provide an excellent way to learn how to program games in an educational context.

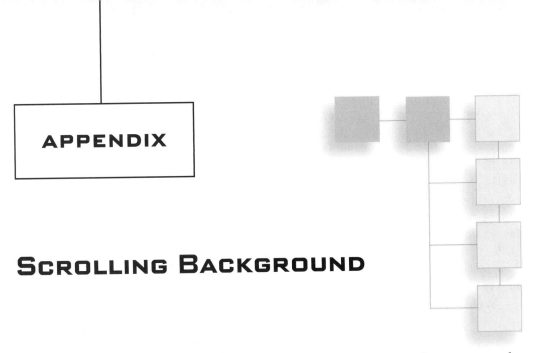

APPENDIX

SCROLLING BACKGROUND

The effort you have put into the classes in this book's 15 chapters may be continued by developing games that involve scrolling backgrounds. Such a game can be built using the framework established in Chapter 15, with the exception or addition of a background that is set up to scroll through a number of tiles.

ScrollStart

The ScrollStart class is the entry point of a MIDlet that demonstrates a scrolling background. Within the scope of the startApp() method, you create an instance of the ScrollCanvas class and assign it to the game identifier, which is of the ScrollCanvas type. You then use the getDisplay() method to invoke the current instance of the Display class, which you use to call the setCurrent() method. The setCurrent() method takes the game identifier as its sole argument. To initiate a thread for the MIDlet, you use the constructor of the thread class and again use the game identifier as an argument. The instance of the thread is returned anonymously; using it, you call the start() method. The effect is to invoke the run() method after the instance of the ScrollCanvas class is created. The code for the ScrollStart class is in the source code folder for the Appendix. You can find it in both the standalone and NetBeans project folders. Here is the code for the class.

```
/*
 * Appendix A \ ScrollStart.java
 *
 *
 */

import java.util.*;
import javax.microedition.lcdui.game.*;
import javax.microedition.midlet.*;
import javax.microedition.lcdui.*;

public class ScrollStart extends MIDlet{
    public void startApp(){
        ScrollCanvas game = new ScrollCanvas();
        Display.getDisplay(this).setCurrent(game);
         new Thread(game).start();
    }

    public void pauseApp(){
    }

    public void destroyApp(boolean unc){
    }
}
```

ScrollCanvas

The ScrollCanvas class creates a tiled layer and then allows you to use a sequence of index values to display its cells sequentially. In this way, a scrolling background is created. This approach to a scrolling background is a simplified one. There are more advanced techniques that produce a much more refined and smooth motion. The approach used here is intended to provide a suitable starting point for exploring how a background can be animated. Like the ScrollStart class, the ScrollCanvas class is included in the NetBeans and standalone folders for the Appendix. These folders also contain the backtiles.png file, which is the source of the background tiles. Here is the code for the ScrollCanvas class.

```
/*
 * Appendix  \ ScrollCanvas
 *
 *
 */
```

```java
import java.util.*;
import javax.microedition.lcdui.game.*;
import javax.microedition.midlet.*;
import javax.microedition.lcdui.*;

// #1
class ScrollCanvas extends GameCanvas implements Runnable{
        TiledLayer bkgnd = null;
         Image tempImage = null;
        int[] tileIndex = {1,2, 3, 4, 5, 6};
        int cols;
        int rows;

          // #1.1
          public void run(){
                scrollTiles();
          }

          // #2
          public ScrollCanvas(){
               super(false);
               System.out.println("width "+ getWidth() );
               Image bkgrndImage = createImage("/backtiles.png");
               rows = getHeight()/240;
              cols = getWidth()/120;    // s
              System.out.println("cols" + cols);
              // #2.1
              bkgnd = new TiledLayer(6, rows, bkgrndImage, 120, 240);
              System.out.println("cols" + bkgnd.getColumns());
              System.out.println("rows" + bkgnd.getRows());
          }

          // #3
        private void scrollTiles(){
           Graphics g = getGraphics();
            int itr = 0;
            while (true) {
                 bkgnd.setCell(0,0,tileIndex[itr++]);
                 bkgnd.setCell(1,0,tileIndex[itr++]);
               if(itr==6){
                    itr = 0;
                 }
                 bkgnd.paint(g);
```

```
            flushGraphics();
            try{
             Thread.currentThread().sleep(200);
          }catch (InterruptedException iex){
              System.out.println(iex.toString());
            }
          }
       }


    public Image createImage(String file){
        try{
           tempImage = Image.createImage(file);
        } catch (Exception exc){
          exc.printStackTrace();
          }
          return tempImage;
        }
}
```

Definition and Construction

In the lines associated with comment #1, you extend the GameCanvas class and the Runnable interface. The Runnable interface enables you to implement the run() and start() methods, which are necessary to support animated activities. Following the signature line, you declare attributes of the TiledLayer and Image types. The Image object is the source of the background tiles. The TiledLayer attribute allows you to manage the display of tiles. A third attribute is an array of the int type, which stores values that designate the sequence in which you what to display tiles (tileIndex).

How these three attributes work together becomes evident in the lines following comment #2, where you call the getWidth() method to learn the width of the ScrollCanvas area. The value returned reveals that the width of the ScrollCanvas object is 240 pixels. To create a set of tiles that can produce an animated background, it is necessary to have a source figure that is either 240 pixels wide or can be evenly divided so that the tiles that result from its division can produce an image that is not fragmented as it is displayed.

You then call the createImage() method to create an instance of the Image class that uses the range of hills illustrated in Figure A.1 as its source. You can resize the Image object in any number of ways, but since you know that the value

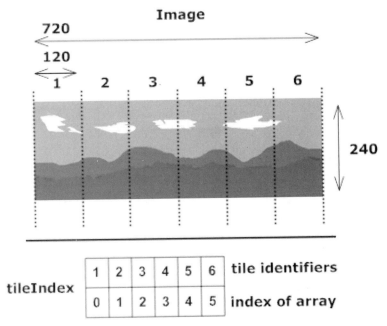

Figure A.1
Determine how you want to sequence the tiles.

returned from the getWidth() method reveals that the ScrollCanvas area is 240 pixels wide, you can use an application like Photoshop to resize the source figure to fit the dimensions of the display.

Accordingly, although the illustrated range of hills shown in Figure A.1 was drawn without considerations of the size of the ScrollCanvas display area, using Photoshop it proves fairly easy to modify it so that its width can be evenly divided by the width of the ScrollCanvas display area. The source image that results measures 720 by 240 pixels.

Precisely three times as long as it is high, the dimensions of the image depicting the range of hills now open up different possibilities for creating a scrolling background. One option is to segment the range into three tiles, each 240 pixels wide. Another is to segment it into six tiles, as shown in Figure A.1, each 120 pixels wide and 240 pixels high. Segmenting the image into six tiles allows you to define the index values of the tileIndex attribute.

In the lines following comment #2.1, you create a TiledLayer object and make use of the information developed so far regarding the use of the Image object. The TiledLayer object you create has six columns and one row. It uses the Image

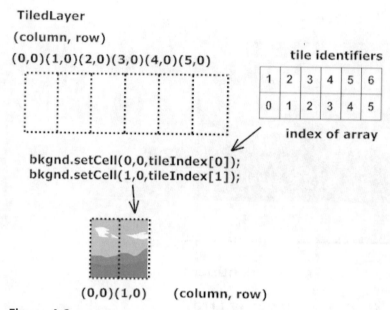

Figure A.2
Set two cells at a time in the TiledLayer object, creating an entity that is wide enough to cover the display.

object (bkgrndImage) object as its source. The dimensions of each cell in the TiledLayer object are 120 pixels wide and 240 pixels high. As Figure A.2 illustrates, you can make use of the tileIndex array to set the values in the TiledLayer object so that it displays tiles successively.

The specific activity of loading the tiles into the TiledLayer object is attended to in the lines following comment #3, where the scrollTiles() method is defined. This method is called from the run() method. The scrollTiles() method possesses only two responsibilities. The first is that of providing in infinite while block in which the setCell() method is called twice in succession, loading as it is called two successive tiles. The second responsibility is to create a Thread object that can regulate the number of times each second the display of tiles is refreshed.

Making it so that tiles are displayed involves calling the setCell() method. This method takes three arguments. The first two values define a cell within the TiledLayer object. As Figure A.2 illustrates, six cells are defined for the bkgnd TiledLayer object. Two successive cells, on the first row and in the first and second columns, are used to display the tiles.

Figure A.3
The successive display of tiles creates the illusion of movement.

To select the tiles that are displayed during each iteration of the while block, the itr identifier is defined with a value of 0. When the flow of the program enters the while block, the itr identifier is used as an argument to two successive calls to the setCell() method. During each call, the itr identifier is incremented. As it is incremented, it is used to retrieve tile identifiers from the tileIndex array. These identifiers, in turn, are used to locate two successive tiles from the set of tiles provided by the Image object.

The display that results during each iteration of the loop consists of two tiles and covers the ScrollCanvas area, providing the illusion of a rolling range of hills. When all size tiles have been displayed, the itr identifier is reset to 0, and the first pair of frames is again accessed for display.

To display the tiles, the paint() and flushGraphics() methods are called. With the call to these two methods, the entire area of the ScrollCanvas object is cleared and repainted. The rate of display is controlled by the Thread::sleep() method, which is set at 200, refreshing the display five times each second. The refresh rate is roughly only a third of what is needed to create a realistic animation, but for purposes of exploration, it provides a good beginning. Figure A.3 shows successive views of the scrolling range of hills as they scroll across the display.

INDEX